# Mathematical Economics and the Dynamics of Capitalism

I0867162

Richard Goodwin was a pioneer in the use of mathematical tools to understand the dynamics of capitalist economies. This book contains contributions which focus on the rigorous extension of Goodwin's modelling of macro-dynamics and the micro-structures underlying them, and also research with a wider perspective related to Goodwin's vision of an integrated Marx-Keynes-Schumpeter (M-K-S) system of the dynamics of capitalist economies.

The variety of approaches in this book range from detailed business cycle analyses to Schumpeterian processes of creative destruction. They include

- thorough theoretical analysis of delayed dynamical systems;
- empirical studies of Goodwin's classical growth cycle model and the integration of Keynesian aspects of effective demand and of financial mechanisms that impact the real macro-economy;
- micro-economic structural analysis;
- expectations driven aspects of micro-founded business cycle modelling.

Providing both theoretical analysis and empirical evidence for approaches in the tradition of Goodwin's M-K-S system, this book represents a significant step forward in this type of research agenda. The volume is useful for students and researchers in the areas of nonlinear macro and micro-economic modelling, in business cycle modelling and in frontier research regarding classical, Schumpeterian and Keynesian modelling of the dynamics of capitalist economies.

**Peter Flaschel** is Professor of Economics at the Department of Economics and Business Administration, Bielefeld University, Bielefeld, Germany

**Michael Landesmann** is Scientific Director of the Vienna Institute for International Economic Studies and Professor and Chair of the Department of Economics at the Johannes Kepler University in Linz, Austria.

# Routledge Frontiers of Political Economy

1 **Equilibrium Versus Understanding**
Towards the rehumanization of economics within social theory
*Mark Addleson*

2 **Evolution, Order and Complexity**
*Edited by Elias L. Khalil and Kenneth E. Boulding*

3 **Interactions in Political Economy**
Malvern after ten years
*Edited by Steven Pressman*

4 **The End of Economics**
*Michael Perelman*

5 **Probability in Economics**
*Omar F. Hamouda and Robin Rowley*

6 **Capital Controversy, Post Keynesian Economics and the History of Economics**
Essays in honour of Geoff Harcourt, Volume 1
*Edited by Philip Arestis, Gabriel Palma and Malcolm Sawyer*

7 **Markets, Unemployment and Economic Policy**
Essays in honour of Geoff Harcourt, Volume 2
*Edited by Philip Arestis, Gabriel Palma and Malcolm Sawyer*

8 **Social Economy**
The logic of capitalist development
*Clark Everling*

9 **New Keynesian Economics/Post Keynesian Alternatives**
*Edited by Roy J. Rotheim*

10 **The Representative Agent in Macroeconomics**
*James E. Hartley*

11 **Borderlands of Economics**
Essays in honour of Daniel R. Fusfeld
*Edited by Nahid Aslanbeigui and Young Back Choi*

12 **Value, Distribution and Capital**
Essays in honour of Pierangelo Garegnani
*Edited by Gary Mongiovi and Fabio Petri*

13 **The Economics of Science**
Methodology and epistemology as if economics really mattered
*James R. Wible*

14 **Competitiveness, Localised Learning and Regional Development**
Specialisation and prosperity in small open economies
*Peter Maskell, Heikki Eskelinen, Ingjaldur Hannibalsson, Anders Malmberg and Eirik Vatne*

15 **Labour Market Theory**
A constructive reassessment
*Ben J. Fine*

16 **Women and European Employment**
*Jill Rubery, Mark Smith, Colette Fagan, Damian Grimshaw*

17 **Explorations in Economic Methodology**
From Lakatos to empirical philosophy of science
*Roger Backhouse*

18 **Subjectivity in Political Economy**
Essays on wanting and choosing
*David P. Levine*

19 **The Political Economy of Middle East Peace**
The impact of competing trade agendas
*Edited by J.W. Wright, Jnr*

20 **The Active Consumer**
Novelty and surprise in consumer choice
*Edited by Marina Bianchi*

21 **Subjectivism and Economic Analysis**
Essays in memory of Ludwig Lachmann
*Edited by Roger Koppl and Gary Mongiovi*

22 **Themes in Post-Keynesian Economics**
Essays in honour of Geoff Harcourt, Volume 3
*Edited by Claudio Sardoni and Peter Kriesler*

23 **The Dynamics of Technological Knowledge**
*Cristiano Antonelli*

24 **The Political Economy of Diet, Health and Food Policy**
*Ben J. Fine*

25 **The End of Finance**
Capital market inflation, financial derivatives and pension fund capitalism
*Jan Toporowski*

26 **Political Economy and the New Capitalism**
*Edited by Jan Toporowski*

27 **Growth Theory**
A philosophical perspective
*Patricia Northover*

28 **The Political Economy of the Small Firm**
*Edited by Charlie Dannreuther*

29 **Hahn and Economic Methodology**
*Edited by Thomas Boylan and Paschal F O'Gorman*

30 **Gender, Growth and Trade**
The miracle economies of the postwar years
*David Kucera*

31 **Normative Political Economy**
Subjective freedom, the market and the state
*David Levine*

32 **Economist with a Public Purpose**
Essays in honour of John Kenneth Galbraith
*Edited by Michael Keaney*

33 **Involuntary Unemployment**
The elusive quest for a theory
*Michel De Vroey*

34 **The Fundamental Institutions of Capitalism**
*Ernesto Screpanti*

35 **Transcending Transaction**
The search for self-generating markets
*Alan Shipman*

36 **Power in Business and the State**
An historical analysis of its concentration
*Frank Bealey*

37 **Editing Economics**
Essays in honour of Mark Perlman
*Hank Lim, Ungsuh K. Park and Geoff Harcourt*

38 **Money, Macroeconomics and Keynes**
Essays in honour of Victoria Chick, Volume 1
*Philip Arestis, Meghnad Desai and Sheila Dow*

39 **Methodology, Microeconomics and Keynes**
Essays in honour of Victoria Chick, Volume 2
*Philip Arestis, Meghnad Desai and Sheila Dow*

40 **Market Drive and Governance**
Reexamining the rules for economic and commercial contest
*Ralf Boscheck*

41 **The Value of Marx**
Political economy for contemporary capitalism
*Alfredo Saad-Filho*

42 **Issues in Positive Political Economy**
*S Mansoob Murshed*

43 **The Enigma of Globalisation**
A journey to a new stage of capitalism
*Robert Went*

44 **The Market**
Equilibrium, stability, mythology
*S N Afriat*

45 **The Political Economy of Rule Evasion and Policy Reform**
*Jim Leitzel*

46 **Unpaid Work and the Economy**
*Edited by Antonella Picchio*

47 **Distributional Justice**
Theory and measurement
*Hilde Bojer*

48 **Cognitive Developments in Economics**
*Edited by Salvatore Rizzello*

49 **Social Foundations of Markets, Money and Credit**
*Costas Lapavitsas*

50 **Rethinking Capitalist Development**
Essays on the economics of Josef Steindl
*Edited by Tracy Mott and Nina Shapiro*

51 **An Evolutionary Approach to Social Welfare**
*Christian Sartorius*

52 **Kalecki's Economics Today**
*Edited by Zdzislaw L. Sadowski and Adam Szeworski*

53 **Fiscal Policy from Reagan to Blair**
The left veers right
*Ravi K. Roy and Arthur T. Denzau*

54 **The Cognitive Mechanics of Economic Development and Institutional Change**
*Bertin Martens*

55 **Individualism and the Social Order**
The social element in liberal thought
*Charles R. McCann Jnr.*

56 **Affirmative Action in the United States and India**
A comparative perspective
*Thomas E. Weisskopf*

57 **Global Political Economy and the Wealth of Nations**
Performance, institutions, problems and policies
*Edited by Phillip Anthony O'Hara*

58 **Structural Economics**
*Thijs ten Raa*

59 **Macroeconomic Theory and Economic Policy**
Essays in honour of Jean-Paul Fitoussi
*Edited by K. Vela Velupillai*

60 **The Struggle Over Work**
The 'end of work' and employment alternatives in post-industrial societies
*Shaun Wilson*

61 **The Political Economy of Global Sporting Organisations**
*John Forster and Nigel Pope*

62 **The Flawed Foundations of General Equilibrium Theory**
Critical essays on economic theory
*Frank Ackerman and Alejandro Nadal*

63 **Uncertainty in Economic Theory**
Essays in honor of David Schmeidler's 65th birthday
*Edited by Itzhak Gilboa*

64 **The New Institutional Economics of Corruption**
*Edited by Johann Graf Lambsdorff, Markus Taube and Matthias Schramm*

65 **The Price Index and its Extension**
A chapter in economic measurement
*S.N. Afriat*

66 **Reduction, Rationality and Game Theory in Marxian Economics**
*Bruce Philp*

67 **Culture and Politics in Economic Development**
*Volker Bornschier*

68 **Modern Applications of Austrian Thought**
*Edited by Jürgen G. Backhaus*

69 **Ordinary Choices**
Individuals, incommensurability, and democracy
*Robert Urquhart*

70 **Labour Theory of Value**
*Peter C. Dooley*

71 **Capitalism**
*Victor D. Lippit*

72 **Macroeconomic Foundations of Macroeconomics**
*Alvaro Cencini*

73 **Marx for the 21st Century**
*Edited by Hiroshi Uchida*

74 **Growth and Development in the Global Political Economy**
Social structures of accumulation and modes of regulation
*Phillip Anthony O'Hara*

75 **The New Economy and Macroeconomic Stability**
A neo-modern perspective drawing on the complexity approach and Keynesian economics
*Teodoro Dario Togati*

76 **The Future of Social Security Policy**
Women, work and a citizens basic income
*Ailsa McKay*

77 **Clinton and Blair**
The political economy of the third way
*Flavio Romano*

78 **Marxian Reproduction Schema**
Money and aggregate demand in a capitalist economy
*A.B. Trigg*

79 **The Core Theory in Economics**
Problems and solutions
*Lester G. Telser*

80 **Economics, Ethics and the Market**
Introduction and applications
*Johan J. Graafland*

81 **Social Costs and Public Action in Modern Capitalism**
Essays inspired by Karl William Kapp's theory of social costs
*Edited by Wolfram Elsner, Pietro Frigato and Paolo Ramazzotti*

82 **Globalization and the Myths of Free Trade**
History, theory and empirical evidence
*Edited by Anwar Shaikh*

83 **Equilibrium in Economics: Scope and Limits**
*Edited by Valeria Mosini*

84 **Globalization**
State of the art and perspectives
*Edited by Stefan A. Schirm*

85 **Neoliberalism**
National and regional experiments with global ideas
*Edited by Ravi K. Roy, Arthur T. Denzau and Thomas D. Willett*

86 **Post-Keynesian Macroeconomic Economics**
Essays in honour of Ingrid Rima
*Edited by Mathew Forstater, Gary Mongiovi and Steven Pressman*

87 **Consumer Capitalism**
*Anastasios S. Korkotsides*

88 **Remapping Gender in the New Global Order**
*Edited by Marjorie Griffin Cohen and Janine Brodie*

89 **Hayek and Natural Law**
*Eric Angner*

90 **Race and Economic Opportunity in the Twenty-First Century**
*Edited by Marlene Kim*

91 **Renaissance in Behavioural Economics**
Harvey Leibenstein's impact on contemporary economic analysis
*Edited by Roger Frantz*

92 **Human Ecology Economics**
A new framework for global sustainability
*Edited by Roy E. Allen*

93 **Imagining Economics Otherwise**
Encounters with identity/difference
*Nitasha Kaul*

94 **Reigniting the Labor Movement**
Restoring means to ends in a democratic labor movement
*Gerald Friedman*

95 **The Spatial Model of Politics**
*Norman Schofield*

96 **The Economics of American Judaism**
*Carmel Ullman Chiswick*

97 **Critical Political Economy**
*Christian Arnsperger*

98 **Culture and Economic Explanation**
Economics in the US and Japan
*Donald W. Katzner*

99 **Feminism, Economics and Utopia**
Time travelling through paradigms
*Karin Schönpflug*

100 **Risk in International Finance**
*Vikash Yadav*

101 **Economic Policy and Performance in Industrial Democracies**
Party governments, central banks and the fiscal-monetary policy mix
*Takayuki Sakamoto*

102 **Advances on Income Inequality and Concentration Measures**
*Edited by Gianni Betti and Achille Lemmi*

103 **Economic Representations**
Academic and everyday
*Edited by David F. Ruccio*

104 **Mathematical Economics and the Dynamics of Capitalism**
Goodwin's legacy continued
*Edited by Peter Flaschel and Michael Landesmann*

# Mathematical Economics and the Dynamics of Capitalism

## Goodwin's legacy continued

**Edited by Peter Flaschel and Michael Landesmann**

Routledge
Taylor & Francis Group
LONDON AND NEW YORK

First published 2008
by Routledge

Published 2014 by Routledge
2 Park Square, Milton Park, Abingdon, Oxfordshire OX14 4RN

Simultaneously published in the USA and Canada
by Routledge
711 Third Avenue, New York, NY 10017

First issued in paperback 2014
*Routledge is an imprint of the Taylor & Francis Group, an informa business*



Typeset in Times New Roman by
HWA Text and Data Management, London



*British Library Cataloguing in Publication Data*
A catalogue record for this book is available from the British Library

*Library of Congress Cataloging-in-Publication Data*
A catalog record for this book has been requested

ISBN 978–0–415–45145–1 (hbk)
ISBN 978–0–415–76201–4 **(pbk)**
ISBN 978–0–203–92664–2 (ebk)

# Contents

# Figures

# Tables

# Contributors

**Richard Day** Professor Emeritus, University of Southern California, USA.

**Peter Flaschel** Professor of Economics, Bielefeld University, Germany.

**Reiner Franke** Lecturer, Department of Economics, Kiel University, Germany.

**Nicolás Garrido** Associate Professor of Economics, Universidad Católica del Norte, Chile.

**Jörg Glombowski** Professor of Economics, Osnabrück University, Germany.

**Alfred Greiner** Professor of Economics, Bielefeld University, Germany.

**Gangolf Groh** One-Year-Subsitute (Chair Professor Peter Flaschel), Bielefeld University, Germany.

**Göran Kauermann** Professor Statistics, Bielefeld University, Germany.

**Michael Krüger** Professor of Economics and Finance, Touro College, Berlin.

**Michael Landesmann** Scientific Director, The Vienna Institute for International Economic Studies (wiiw) and Professor of Economics, Johannes Kepler University Linz, Austria.

**Sigrid Luchtenberg** Professor of Education, University of Duisburg–Essen, Germany.

**Christopher Malikane** Lecturer, Department of Economics, University of Witwatersrand, Johannesburg, South Africa.

**Akio Matsumoto** Professor for Economics, Chuo University, Japan.

**Simon Mohun** Professor of Political Economy, School of Business and Management, Queen Mary, University of London, UK.

**Edward Nell** Professor of Economics, New School for Social Research, New School University, USA.

**Christian R. Proaño** PhD Candidate, Bielefeld University and Associate Researcher, Macroeconomic Policy Institute (IMK), Germany.

**Codrina Rada von Arnim** Assistant Professor of Economics, University of Utah, USA.

**Srinivas Raghavendra** Lecturer, Department of Economics, National University of Ireland, Galway.

**Willi Semmler** Professor of Economics, New School for Social Research, New School University, USA.

**Robert Stehrer** Senior Researcher, The Vienna Institute for International Economic Studies (WIIW), Austria.

**Mami Suzuki** Department of Mathematics, Obirin University.

**Lance Taylor** Professor of Economics and Director of the Schwartz Center for Economic Policy Analysis, New School for Social Research, New School University, USA.

**Timo Teuber** PhD Candidate, Bielefeld University, Germany.

**Roberto Veneziani** Lecturer, Department of Economics, Queen Mary, University of London, UK.

**Chengyu Yang** Assistant Professor of Business Economics, Central Florida University, USA.

Richard Murphey Goodwin (1913–1996)
Photograph by Dorothy Hahn

# Introduction

## Mathematical economics and the dynamics of capitalism

*Peter Flaschel and Michael Landesmann*

> The capitalist system is of great interest and importance in view of its outstanding dynamism relative to that of other systems tried in the past century. Yet the established body of economic theory – intertemporal, information-theoretic and game-theoretic – does not incorporate key elements of the capitalist dynamic: business innovation as distinct from technological advance and the contributions of entrepreneurs and financiers to the innovation process. As a consequence, established theory cannot capture the core of the dynamism. In fact it contradicts the existence of such dynamism: Capitalism is an evolving, unruly, open-ended system while the theory implies a deterministic future however buffeted it is by stochastic shocks [1]

The editors of this book believe that – going back in history – an ideal candidate for supporting and for actively and significantly contributing to the objectives expressed in the above quotation would have been Richard Goodwin. He was a student of Josef Alois Schumpeter and a colleague of Paul Samuelson, and he experienced his formative period as a researcher at Harvard, Oxford and Cambridge at a time when many new ideas for understanding and modeling capitalism were born and tested. His vision of the workings of capitalism is exemplified and summarized in his article on 'The M-K-S system. Functioning and Evolution of Capitalism' (Goodwin, 1989). There he sketched an analytic system consisting of selected elements, suitably combined, of the concepts of three great economists, Marx, Keynes and Schumpeter. The dynamics of capitalism was surely at the center of Marx's as well as Schumpeter's theory, while Keynes' General Theory only sketches in a closing chapter the implications of his approach for economic dynamics. Of course, not all results in Marx's, Schumpeter's and Keynes's main oeuvre are consistent with each other, but suitably combined concepts from these three great economists can be viewed as providing a research agenda which not only guided Goodwin's research but will continue to provide an anchor to the understanding of the dynamics of capitalism.

Richard Murphey Goodwin (1913–1996) was a pioneer in the use of mathematical tools to understand the dynamics of capitalist economies (see the selected references below). Goodwin's first productive period was a period in which exciting new techniques of nonlinear dynamics were taken up both in neoclassical and in heterodox economics. From the early 1950s he developed and applied nonlinear dynamic modeling tools to understand problems of cyclical growth and distributional dynamics. At the same time, he was also interested in changes in the structure of economies, in the composition of activities and of techniques of production, following the traditions of von Neumann and Leontief. Investigating these two research lines led him to innovative formulations to combine decomposition techniques with tools which allow the tracking of macroeconomic dynamics. With respect to the latter, he not only applied interesting modeling techniques to represent (regular) cyclical patterns, but also explored in a number of ways how the irregularity inherent in economic fluctuations can be modeled.

After the Second World War, Richard Goodwin was in a very fertile phase of pursuing and synthesizing a range of contributions to the theory of economic fluctuations, distributional dynamics and economic growth. He also always worked on structural, disaggregated features of capitalist dynamics, thus attempting to bring Schumpeterian features into the analysis of macroeconomic dynamics of capitalist economies. His research program was influenced by economists as diverse as Marx and Schumpeter, Keynes, Hicks and Harrod, Leontief and Sraffa, as well as physicists and mathematicians such as Poincare, LeCorbeiller, Smale, Haken and Roessler. It was persistently shaped by Goodwin into a consistent and rich picture of the dynamics of capitalist economies. His ambitious oeuvre will remain a motivating point of departure for current and future generations of researchers. In particular, Goodwin's seminal contribution, his famous growth cycle model, Goodwin (1967), much admired by Nobel Laureate Robert Solow (1990), had a very strong impact on younger scholars in his fields of research.

Goodwin retired from the University of Cambridge in 1980 where he had been teaching since 1950 and took up a professorship at the University Siena. During the last two decades of his life, Richard Goodwin continued to do research both in Italy and in Cambridge, and he was a focal point for a sizable group of young economists who had taken up his ambitious research programme to advance the study of macroeconomic and structural dynamics.

Richard Goodwin died in 1996. His inspirations continue to exert a significant influence in many respects, as Richard Goodwin managed to inspire a succession of generations of young scholars to continue pursuing his innovative research agenda. In 2005, the editors of this book decided to organize a conference to honor Goodwin's work on the occasion of the tenth anniversary of his death. The conference aimed at bringing together senior as well as younger economists who were actively pursuing research in the areas pushed forward by Goodwin's life-long contributions. The conference was well attended with numerous contributions based on Goodwin's macroeconomic as well as his structural and microeconomic contributions. The contributions in this book, drawn from this conference,[2] as well as the recently published books by Chiarella *et al.* (2000, 2005) and Taylor (2004), see also Barbosa-Filho and Taylor (2006), testify to the continued influence of Goodwin's work. Goodwin's ambitious oeuvre will remain a motivating point of departure for current and future generations of researchers in mathematical economics and the dynamics of capitalism, a combination in which Richard Goodwin was truly a pioneer.

The introductory quotation points to research lines that are somewhat lacking in mainstream research programs. The quotation represents a vast and demanding research agenda to which the chapters in this book contribute in specific ways, concentrating on theories of fluctuating growth and its interaction with financial markets. Mostly this is put in the context of heterogeneity of economic agents at the micro-level. In contrast to most of the standard approaches to macroeconomic dynamics which are based on representative agents, market clearing and rational expectations, they aim to investigate rigorous, macro-dynamic theory which avoids these assumptions and relate the theory to quantitative and empirical insights and hence provide a foundation for economic and social policy analysis.

In brief, the edited book, which can be considered as a continuation of the research contributions contained in the collected contributions in Velupillai (1990) and Punzo (2001), consists of three parts which significantly extend work in the tradition of Goodwin's research program. Part I studies from various perspectives major, but also some more technical, components of the Marx-Keynes-Schumpeter vision of Richard Goodwin (including also a Kaleckian contribution). Part II provides empirical applications of Goodwin's original macro-dynamics, its extension with financial features as well as its application to monetary policy debates. Part III contains chapters which focus on structural and micro-questions of the research programme.

Starting from the well known fact that Goodwin's 1951 business cycle model gives rise to cyclical oscillations when its stationary point is unstable, Aoki Matsumoto and Mami Suzuki show in Chapter 1 the coexistence of multiple closed orbits; namely, besides a stable stationary point, an unstable limit cycle and a stable limit cycle in the case where the stationary point is locally stable. The authors demonstrate that the model is globally stable in the sense that the trajectories are bounded for any disturbances but its dynamics are different for different disturbances. From these findings the authors derive two properties for Goodwin's (1951) model: first, the existence of robust cyclical oscillations regardless of the local dynamic properties of the steady state and, second, the existence of corridor stability in the locally unstable case.

Richard Day and Chengyu Yang specify in Chapter 2 a Keynesian out–of–equilibrium model of aggregate demand and supply and derive the conditions under which it converges to a Solow growth model. By establishing the conditions for existence of and convergence to steady-state growth – which in turn implies the existence of a supporting social utility function – Day and Yang encompass the independently formulated major macroeconomic theories of Keynes, Solow, and the optimal growth school.

The main topic of Chapter 3 is the role of the welfare state in post-war industrialized economies. Using a Kaleckian framework, Peter Flaschel, Reiner Franke and Willi Semmler consider an economy where investment depends positively on the rate of return on capital and negatively on the rate of employment.

This simple assumption allows the authors to study Kalecki's (1943) analysis of the economic and political aspects of full employment.

Flaschel *et al.* show that even though there is a balanced growth path solution for the resulting model, it is likely to be locally unstable. The authors then show that, in contrast to the conflict-driven macroeconomy where profit-led goods demand in combination with declining real wages (enforced by mass unemployment and labor market reforms) may account for lower turning points during long-phased depressions, as Kalecki (1943) perceived it, the business leaders and policy makers could pursue a consensus driven macroeconomic strategy stressing a more collaborative and long-term approach which will take the economy on a stable growth path. Starting from the lack of micro-foundations in the original Goodwin (1951) business cycle model, Glombowski and Krüger propose in Chapter 4 a modified theoretical framework based on game theoretical considerations which allows labor unions and employers' organizations to behave more flexibly in the course of time. The authors establish a non-cooperative cyclical path of the economy á la Goodwin, and they allow for the possibility of cooperative behavior between workers and employers, which gives rise to higher employment rates resulting from wage restraints and high investment rates. These two 'regimes' may appear both in a more or less regular pattern, depending on a variety of social, political and institutional circumstances. Glombowski and Krüger do not work out deterministic patterns, but rather refer to stochastic mechanisms giving rise to different sequences of regimes and, therefore, different time paths of the variables under consideration. As the authors show, this procedure generates developments characterized by strong social partnership relations, and, likewise, situations in which workers and capitalists getting into conflict whenever the economic circumstances offer a chance in their favor.

In Chapter 5, Peter Flaschel, Alfred Greiner, Sigrid Luchtenberg and Edward Nell start from the finding that the main stabilizing device in Goodwin's (1967) growth cycle model, the Marxian reserve army mechanism, does not represent a process of social reproduction that can be considered an adequate socio-economic foundation for a democratic society in the long-run. They then derive a basic macro-dynamic framework where this distinct form of cyclical growth and social reproduction is overcome by an employer of 'first' resort, added to an economic reproduction process that is highly competitive and thus not of the type of the past Eastern socialism. There is high labor and capital mobility (concerning 'hiring' and 'firing' in particular) where fluctuations of employment in the private sector are made socially acceptable through a second labor market where all remaining workers get employment and income. The resulting socio-economic system is closely related to the flexicurity model developed and applied in Denmark in particular. The authors show that this economy exhibits a balanced growth path that is globally attracting. Moreover, pension-fund financed investment can be added to this model without disturbing the prevailing situation of stable full capacity growth. The closing section in this chapter shows that a paper credit formulation of this process can lead to Keynesian effective demand constraints and thus Keynesian business fluctuations.

Simon Mohun and Roberto Veneziani provide in Chapter 6 empirical support for an interpretation of the Goodwin growth cycle as identifying the main forces underlying distributive conflicts. However, this occurs in a fragile symbiotic manner as it generates endogenous forces that modify the balance of class power. Goodwin cycles can be seen as the shorter-run cycles that appear around a long-run motion which results from structural change. The authors describe long-run trends in the state variables of the Goodwin model for the US corporate economy from 1948 to 2004; these exhibit both a sharp break at the beginning of the 1980s, and no long-run cycles. Mohun and Veneziani also identify short-run de-trended Goodwin cycles which broadly coincide in period and timing with the NBER dating of (the troughs of) business cycles.

New empirical evidence for the existence of a long-phased cycle in the wage share and the employment rate as described by the Goodwin model and its successors is provided by Peter Flaschel, Gangolf Groh, Göran Kauermann and Timo Teuber in Chapter 7. Their investigation is based not only on new and recent data, now comprising a period of 50 years, but is also based on advanced econometric techniques aimed at a proper separation between trend and business cycles. Their results confirm not only the existence of a long-period clockwise loop with regard to the magnitudes mentioned, but also a similar result for the cyclical interaction between unemployment and inflation.

In Chapter 9, Christopher Malikane and Willi Semmmler formulate a Keynesian framework for practical policy analysis in small open economies. At the core of their model is a Goodwin growth cycle process which, when the model is subjected to shocks, produces instability in the macro aggregates. The model features two Phillips curves; one for prices and the other for nominal wages, an aggregate demand bloc with explicit consideration of income distribution effects, a dynamic multiplier output adjustment process, an investment-based version of Okun's law that links the goods market and the labor market, financial markets that exhibit Blanchard and Dornbusch type accelerators, and a Taylor type rule to describe the behavior of the central bank. The model is estimated using South African quarterly data from 1960:1–2006:4. The authors find macroeconomic stability when the central bank responds with sufficient strength to asset prices and when it targets a demand pressure term which is connected to the prevailing rigidities in the economy.

Peter Flaschel, Reiner Franke and Christian Proaño set up in Chapter 10 a Keynes-Goodwin framework to study the interaction between income distribution and the dynamics of wage and price inflation in a closed economy. The specification of labor productivity growth as an endogenous and not only a residual variable of the system allows the authors to specify a law of motion for the wage share which is determined by developments in both the labor and the goods markets. Together with an advanced specification of the inflationary expectations (the inflation climate in the economy) which accounts for central bank credibility and a simple Taylor rule, a semi-structural model is obtained which is rich in various macroeconomic channels that are of great importance in industrialized economies. Through eigen-value analysis of the resulting dynamical framework it is shown that both excessive wage and price flexibility might be destabilizing for the dynamic behavior of the economy.

Srinivas Raghavendra studies in Chapter 11 the world income distribution using a Richard Stone-Richard Goodwin type of decomposition method. The author's objective is to collate the social accounting matrices of a group of nations (with the Rest of the World treated exogenously) and to decompose the transactions matrix, expressed in a common unit of account, to delineate effects of intra- ('direct effects') country income disparity from inter- ('cross effects') group income disparities. As Raghavendra points out, this decomposition is pertinent from the point of view of understanding whether the inter-regional income disparities are mainly mediated through the intra-regional income disparities implied by their structure of production and thereby assessing the impact of various growth policies on the macro structure of the economies.

Following Goodwin (1947), in Chapter 12 Nicolás Garrido explores the effects of interdependencies between markets. First, Garrido analyzes a basic building block consisting of a Cobweb model with inventories and budget constraints. Second, these markets are interrelated vertically through their demands and supplies. Using simulation analysis, all types of vertical couplings that may exist among four markets are explored and, using the patterns produced by each topology, equivalence classes that generate a partition in the space of all possible topologies are created. Finally, the author analyzes the properties of five types of vertical couplings, identified in the Japanese industrial district of Ohta by Nakanao and White (2006).

In Chapter 13, Reiner Franke considers the formation of an average opinion index in a microfounded framework where the agents switch between two kinds of sentiments with certain transition probabilities. The index can thus represent a general business climate, or the famous animal spirits assumption of Keynes. Circumventing elaborated tools of statistical mechanics that are usually applied in this context, Franke puts forward a more elementary argument that allows one to derive a macroeconomic adjustment equation for the climate variable, which is also shown to contain a global self-stabilization mechanism. Combining this building block with a simple multiplier and a real wage Phillips curve, the author obtains a structurally stable model of Goodwinian growth cycles with a significant herding component.

Finally, in Chapter 14, Landesmann and Stehrer pursue work originally started with Richard Goodwin in the 1990s. In that phase, Goodwin attempted to synthesize, on the one hand, Schumpeterian and Keynesian elements of his various research lines and, on the other hand, to combine the analysis of macro-dynamics with disaggregated structural modeling. In this chapter, the authors introduce a complex model of interdependent economies and analyze the effects of catching-up processes of developing ('Southern') countries. In the first instance, the focus is the changing patterns of international trade specialization and, in the second place, the relative attractiveness of foreign direct investment (in 'Northern' and 'Southern' economies respectively). The authors show that periods in which there is a high level of structural change dynamic (such as that induced through catching-up of sizable 'Southern economies' such as China and India) are also periods which have a higher potential for effective demand failures. A particular issue which the authors highlight in their chapter, given many of the complex features of catching-up processes, are the additional effects which 'outsourcing' or a higher scope for global 'fragmentation' (of production processes) might induce in a global world of interdependencies.

Summing up, this book collects recent research papers in the tradition of Goodwin's work on Marx, Keynes and Schumpeter. It contains, on the one hand, contributions that focus on rigorous extensions of Goodwin's modeling of macro-dynamics and the structural features underlying them. On the other hand, and to a greater extent, it also provides research with a wider perspective, related to Goodwin's vision of an integrated Marx-Keynes-Schumpeter system. With its selection of theoretical macro and micro models and empirical investigations, this collection of papers therefore contributes to a deeper understanding and a continuation of the research agenda initiated by Richard Goodwin after the Second World, concerning cycles, growth and structural change.

Finally, we want to thank, in the first place, Wolfram Elsner and EAEPE for the possibility to organize the Goodwin conference within the larger framework of the annual conference of the European Association for Evolutionary Political Economy in 2005. We are also very grateful to Terry Clague and Sarah Hastings for all the editorial help we needed during the gestation period of this book. Finally, our thanks go to Christian Proaño for his invaluable assistance in the preparation of the final manuscript.

Peter Flaschel and Michael Landesmann
Bielefeld and Vienna, September 2007

## Notes

1 From *Capitalism and Society. A Journal of the Center on Capitalism and Society, Aims and Scope*. www.bepress.com/cas/aimsandscope.html

2 See the Special Issue 'Richard Murphey Goodwin (1913–1996): His Legacy Continued' of the journal *Structural Change and Economic Dynamics* (2006:4), edited by Peter Flaschel and Michael Landesmann, for further contributions from the Goodwin conference.

## References

### *Selected work by Richard Goodwin and co-authors*

Goodwin, R.M. (1946) Innovations and the irregularity of economic cycles. *Review of Economics and Statistics*, 28, 95–104.

Goodwin, R.M. (1947) Dynamical Coupling with Especial Reference to Markets Having Production Lags. *Econometrica*, 15, 181–204.

Goodwin, R.M. (1951) The nonlinear accelerator and the persistence of business cycles. *Econometrica*, 19, 1–17.

Goodwin, R.M. (1967) A Growth Cycle. In C.H. Feinstein, (ed.) *Socialism, Capitalism and Economic Growth*. Cambridge: Cambridge University Press. Also in Goodwin (1982)

Goodwin, R.M. (1982) *Essays in Economic Dynamics*. London: Macmillan.
Goodwin, R.M. (1983) *Essays in Linear Economic Structures*. London: Macmillan.
Goodwin, R., M. Krüger and A. Vercelli (eds) *Nonlinear Models of Fluctuating Growth*. Berlin: Springer.
Goodwin, R.M. (1989) The M-K-S system. Functioning and evolution of capitalisms. In R. Goodwin *Essays in Nonlinear Economic Dynamics*. Bern: Peter Lang, ch.6.
Goodwin, R.M. (1990) *Chaotic Economic Dynamics*. Oxford: Clarendon Press.
Goodwin, R.M. and L.F. Punzo (1987) *The Dynamics of a Capitalist Economy. A Multisectoral Approach*.Oxford and Boulder, CO: Polity Press and Westview.

## *Quoted work on Goodwin's approach to fluctuating growth and structural change*

Barbosa-Filho, N. and L. Taylor (2006) Distributive and demand cycles in the US economy: a structuralist Goodwin model. *Metroeconomica*, (57):3, 389–411.
Chiarella, C. and P. Flaschel (2000): *The Dynamics of Keynesian Monetary Growth. Macrofoundations*. Cambridge, UK: Cambridge University Press.
Chiarella, C., P. Flaschel and R. Franke (2005): *Foundations of a Disequilibrium Theory of the Business Cycle*. Cambridge: Cambridge University Press.
Kalecki, M. (1943) Political aspects of full employment. Reprinted in M. Kalecki (1971), *Selected Essays on the Dynamics of the Capitalist Economy*. Cambridge: Cambridge University Press,.
Nakano, T. and D.R. White (2006) *The Visible Hand in a Production-Chain Market: A Market Equilibrium from Network Analytical Perspective*. SFI Working Paper.
Punzo, L.F. (ed.) (2001) *Cycles, Growth and Structural Change*. London: Routledge.
Solow, R. (1990) Goodwin's growth cycle: reminiscence and rumination. In Velupillai, K. (ed.) *Nonlinear and Multisectoral Macrodynamics*. London: Macmillan.
Taylor, L. (2004) *Reconstructing Macroeconomics: Structuralists Proposals and Critiques of the Mainstream*. Cambridge, MA: Harvard University Press.
Velupillai, K., ed. (1990): *Nonlinear and Multisectoral Macrodynamics*. London: Macmillan.

# Part I
# Nonlinear macrodynamics: theory

# 1 Coexistence of multiple business cycles in Goodwin's 1951 model

*Akio Matsumoto and Mami Suzuki*

## Introduction

The contribution of Goodwin (1951) is reconsidered in this study. Goodwin developed a nonlinear accelerator business cycle model and showed that it could generate a stable limit cycle when a stationary point was locally unstable. Considerable effort has been devoted to investigate the dynamic structure of Goodwin's model since then. However, in the existing literature, not much has yet been revealed with respect to the circumstances under which the stationary point is locally stable. In particular, it is not yet known whether cyclical global dynamics may appear in the stable case. We draw attention to this unexplored case and exhibit the coexistence of multiple limit states, namely a stable stationary point, an unstable limit cycle and a stable limit cycle. Since very few explorations have been made in the global dynamics of the stable case, this study is intended as an investigation of an unexplored aspect of Goodwin's nonlinear business cycle model.

Goodwin proposed five different versions of his business cycle model. The first version assumes a piecewise linear function with three levels of investment, which can be thought as the crudest or simplest of the nonlinear accelerator. This is a textbook model that can give a simple exhibition of how nonlinearities give rise to endogenous cycles without relying on structurally unstable parameters, exogenous shocks, etc. The second version replaces the piecewise linear investment function with a smooth nonlinear investment function. Although persistent cyclical oscillations of output are shown to exist, the second version includes a unfavorable phenomenon, namely, discontinuous investment jumps, which is not observed in the real economic world. "In order to come close to reality" (Goodwin 1951: 11), a production lag is introduced in the third version. However, no dynamic considerations are given to this third version by Goodwin. The existence of a stable limit cycle is examined in the fourth version, which is a linear approximation of the third version with respect to the production lag. Goodwin's final modification makes the amount of autonomous expenditure alter over time. This fifth version is recently reconsidered by Lorenz (1987) as a forced oscillator system in which the emergence of chaotic motion is demonstrated. More recently Sasakura (1996) gave an elegant proof of the stability and uniqueness of Goodwin's cycle for the fourth version. Thus it has been confirmed that Goodwin's nonlinear accelerator model possesses a unique stable limit cycle. Since all these results are obtained when the stationary point is locally unstable, we can ask a basic question: *Is cyclical behavior robust under locally stable circumstances?*

The main result of this study is to provide a positive answer to this question. For this purpose, we augment Goodwin's fourth version by introducing a nonlinear investment function of arctangent type and demonstrate the coexistence of multiple cycles. We will combine the Poincaré-Bendixson theorem with the Hopf bifurcation theorem and characterize the global dynamics when the stationary state is locally stable. The coexistence of multiple cycles is also shown for Kaldor's business cycle model in Grasman and Wentzel (1994) and for a Metzlerian inventory cycle model in Matsumoto (1996) using an approach which we continue here.

We also examine the dynamics of the third version with an unstable stationary point. Only limited efforts has been devoted to this version in the past. Since it is a nonlinear differential equation, attempts at analytical solution seem fruitless. Hence, we perform numerical simulations to find what effects the production lag produces on the characteristics (i.e. length and amplitude) of cyclical oscillations of the output.

The following section "Goodwin business cycle model" overviews three versions (i.e. the second, third and fourth versions) of Goodwin's business cycle model and reveals the characteristics of Goodwin's cycle. The section "Coexistence of multiple cycles" presents the new results which shows that the linear approximated version exhibits corridor stability in which the solution is stable for small shocks but is unstable and generates multiple limit cycles for large shocks. Concluding remarks are made in the final section.

## Goodwin business cycle model

This section is divided into three parts. Each of three versions of Goodwin's model are reviewed in each subsection. In particular, we recapitulate the basic elements of the second version and numerically simulate the model to see what dynamics it can generate in "Basic model". We then introduce a production lag into the second version to get the third version and perform, again, numerical simulations to find out how the lag affects the characteristics (i.e. the length of a period and the amplitude) of endogenous cycles in "Delayed model". Finally, we derive the most popular version, the fourth version, by expanding the third version with respect to the lag and reveal its stability condition in "Approximated model".

### *Basic model*

The second model, which we call the *basic model*, is summarized as follows.

$$\begin{cases} \varepsilon\dot{y}(t) = \dot{k}(t) - (1-\alpha)y(t), \\ \dot{k}(t) = \varphi(\dot{y}(t)). \end{cases} \tag{1.1}$$

Here $k$ is the capital stock, $y$ the income, $\alpha$ the marginal propensity to consume which is positive and less than unity, and the reciprocal of $\varepsilon$ is the adjustment coefficient and positive. The first equation of (1.1) defines an adjustment process of national income in a such a way that national income rises or falls if investment is greater or less than savings. The second is an adjustment process of capital stock based on the acceleration principle, according to which investment depends on the rate of changes in national income. On the other hand, we depart from Goodwin's non-essential assumption of positive autonomous expenditure and will work with zero autonomous expenditure in the interest of simplicity. A direct consequence of this assumption is that an equilibrium solution or a stationary point of the basic model is $y(t) = \dot{y}(t) = 0$ for all $t$. Inserting the second equation of (1.1) into the first and arranging terms gives dynamics equation of the national income,

$$\varepsilon\dot{y}(t) - \varphi(\dot{y}(t)) + (1-\alpha)y(t) = 0. \tag{1.2}$$

This is a nonlinear differential equation. Although it may not be possible to derive an explicit form of the solution, it is possible to deduce qualitative properties of dynamics generated by (1.2). Once we specify an explicit from of the investment function and set an initial income, dynamics of $y$ is accordingly determined.

For the induced investment, $\varphi(\dot{y}(t))$, we adopt a *nonlinear* acceleration principle, by which we mean that the investment is proportional to the change in national income in the neighborhood of the equilibrium income but becomes inflexible (i.e. less elastic) for extremely large or small values of income. Goodwin assumed a piecewise linear investment function in his simulations. Following his spirit, but for the sake of analytical convenience, we assume a smooth nonlinear investment function summarized:

**Assumption 1** *The investment function takes the form of a hyperbolic tangent type,*

$$\varphi(\dot{y}(t)) = \delta\{\tanh(\dot{y}(t) - a) - \tanh(-a)\},\ \delta > 0 \text{ and } a > 0.$$

This function has endogenous "ceiling" and "floor" and is asymmetric when the parameter, $a$, is non-zero. We further assume, in this and the next subsection,

**Assumption 2** $\dfrac{d\varphi'(0)}{d\dot{y}}$ *is greater than* $\varepsilon$.

In what follows, we set $a = 1$ to shift the function upward by $\frac{\pi}{4}$ and rightward so as to make the function pass through the origin and $\delta = \frac{12}{\pi}$. Under these parameter specifications, the ceiling of the investment function is three times higher than the floor as in Goodwin's model.

To find out what dynamics the basic model can generate, we perform numerical simulations. The initial point is set at $y(0) = 10$, and in all numerical examples below, all the parameters are fixed at $\varepsilon = 0.5$ and $\alpha = 0.6$ as in Goodwin's model. The numerical results are given in Figure 1.1 in which an endogenous cycle is illustrated on the right and the corresponding time path of output on the left. Along the upside-down $N$-shaped locus on the right, the initial point denoted by $I_0$ is displaced slightly upward to point $A$, at which investment switches discontinuously from positive to negative. In consequence, the orbit jumps from point $A$ to point $B$. With negative $\dot{y}(t)$ at point $B$, the national income gradually declines from point $B$ to point $C$. Once point $C$ is reached, investment, again, switches discontinuously from negative to positive. In other words, the orbit jumps again to point $D$ from point $C$, from which the national income glides toward point $A$, and then the process repeats itself. Thus we have a closed orbit constituting a self-sustaining cycle. The points $A$ and $C$ are critical points at which one of the variables makes a discontinuous jump. The same dynamics are shown as a function of time $t$ on the left in Figure 1.1. There, the corresponding time path from $t = 0$ to $t = 20$ is illustrated. It can be seen that the time path has a kink at the turning point, which is an alternative expression of the discontinuous jump. Following Goodwin, if we interpret one time period to be one year, the five cycles are observed in 20 years on the left. The length of one business cycle in this simulation is approximately 4 years. The numerical simulations imply that the basic model can generate an endogenous cycle of output due to the nonlinearity involved in the investment accelerator, and investment suffers discontinuous jumps. We sum up these results in

**Result 1:** *Given Assumptions 1 and 2, a slow-rapid limit cycle is brought about in the basic model due to the nonlinear investment accelerator.*

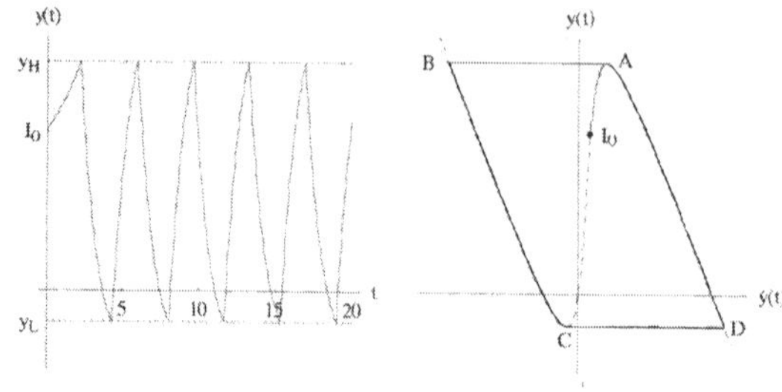


*Figure 1.1* Endogenous cycle with discontinuous jumps

*Table 1.1* Numerical results

| *Lag θ* | *Length of the cycle in years* | *Figure* |
|---|---|---|
| 0.125 | 5 years | 1.2a |
| 0.25 | 6 years | 1.2b |
| 0.5 | 7 years | 1.2c |
| 1.0 | 9 years | 1.2d |

## *Delayed Model*

In order to come closer to reality and to avoid discontinuous jumps, we introduce the production lag, $\theta$, between decisions to invest and the corresponding outlays. As a result, the third version can be expressed as:

$$\epsilon\dot{y}(t+\theta)+(1-\alpha)y(t+\theta)=\varphi(\dot{y}(t)). \tag{1.3}$$

This is a neutral delayed nonlinear differential equation, which we call the *delayed model*. Since a cycle has been shown to exist in the basic model, our next concern is on whether such a lag affects characteristics of the slow-rapid cycle. To put it more concretely, we will address the question: *What effects does the lag cause on the kink, length and amplitude of the cyclical oscillations generated in the basic model?*

Goodwin did not analyze the dynamics generated by the delayed model. Furthermore, to the best of our knowledge, no analytical solutions of the delayed model are available yet. However, it is possible to investigate dynamics of the model with the aid of numerical simulations. For this reason, we conduct simulations with various values of the production lag and then compare results. By doing so, we can deduce what effects the lag can produce.

In Figure 1.2 (a-d), we illustrate four simulation results in which time paths from $t=0$ to $t=20$ associated with different values of $\theta$ are depicted on the left and the corresponding limit cycles on the right.[1] In all these simulations, we choose the same initial condition and the same parameter values as in the previous simulations but use different values of the production lags. As can be observed on the left in each figure, the length of the period becomes longer as the production lag gets larger. In particular, we have the following numerical results shown in Table 1.1.

It is found from these simulation results that the length of the business cycles changes, roughly speaking, from four years to 10 years as the production lag increases from zero to one. In his simulations, Goodwin points out that the length of the whole cycle is 10.7 years, the upswing is prolonged to 6.5 years and the downswing shortened to 4.2 years. Although

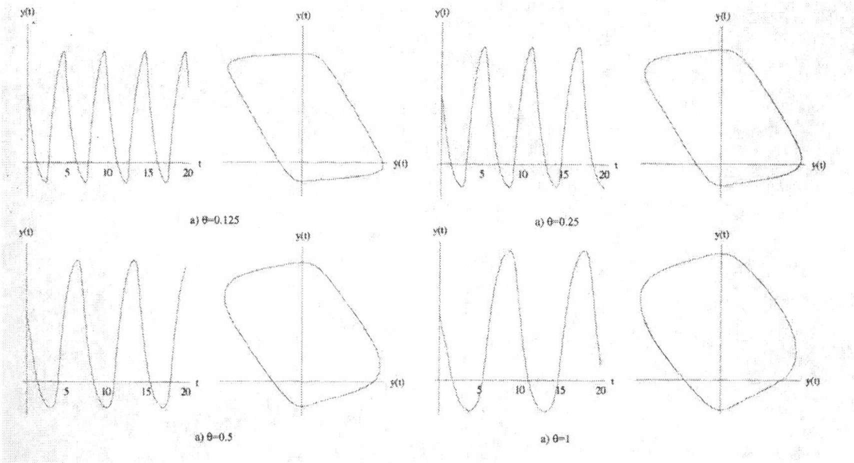

*Figure 1.2* Cyclical oscillations for different $\theta$ parameters

it is not clear from time paths in Figure 1.1, the asymmetry of the upswing and downswing is also observed in our simulations. When $\theta = 1$, careful observation reveals that the cycle has a nine-year period, its upswing is 4.8 years and its downswing is 4.2 years. Similar results are obtained in other simulations omitted here for brevity.[2]

On the right in each of Figure 1.2 (a-d), a limit cycle is illustrated in the phase plane in which we plot the national income on the vertical axis and its time derivative on the horizontal axis. In Figure 1.3 we superpose these limit cycles upon the one in Figure 1.2a. Comparing these limit cycles, we find that the limit cycle changes its shape from a parallelogram-type cycle to a vertically elongated parallelogram with rounded corners as the production lag increases; that is, the width of the cycle gets smaller and the height gets larger. Since the peak and bottom of the output-cycle are reached at the point where the time derivative is zero, the amplitude of the cycle is the distance between two points at which the limit cycle crosses the vertical axis. We also find that the amplitude of the cycles grows larger and the rate of output change becomes less as the production lag increases. These numerical results are summarized in

**Result 2:** *In the delayed model, increasing production lag makes the length of the business cycle longer and its amplitude larger.*

## *Approximated model*

To investigate the effect of the production lag on the emergence of cyclical development of output, Goodwin expands the delayed nonlinear differential equation with respect to $\theta$ and then gets the following second-order nonlinear differential equation as his fourth version,

$$\varepsilon\theta \ddot{y}(t) + [\varepsilon + (1-\alpha)\theta]\dot{y}(t) - \varphi(\dot{y}(t)) + (1-\alpha)y(t) = 0. \tag{1.4}$$

We call this the *approximated model*. One way to learn about the movement of output is to integrate equation (1.4) numerically for any given set of initial conditions on $y$ and $\dot{y}$. Our interest in this subsection is not on the specifics of how $y$ change in the short run but more in understanding whether the displaced output eventually returns to its stationary point. Thus,

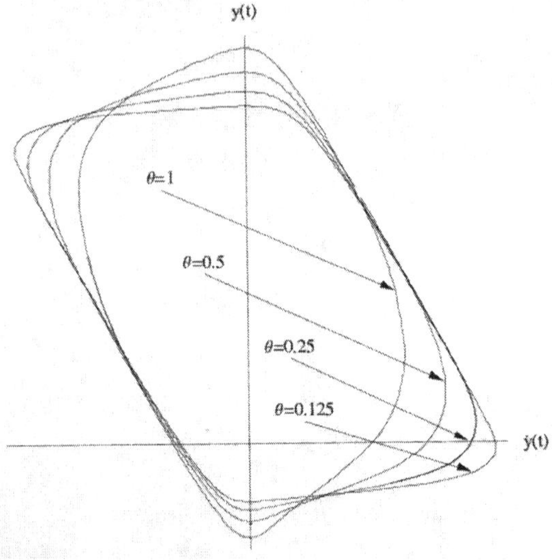


*Figure 1.3* Limit cycles with different lags

we raise the question of the stability, which can be resolved without solving the nonlinear differential equation (1.4).

To this end, we introduce a new variable, $x(t) = \dot{y}(t)$, and then transform the second-order nonlinear differential equation into a two-dimensional nonlinear system that can be put, after arranging terms, into the form,

$$\begin{cases} \dot{x}(t) = \dfrac{1}{\varepsilon\theta}\{\varphi(x(t)) - [\varepsilon + (1-\alpha)\theta]x(t) - (1-\alpha)y(t)\}, \\ \\ \dot{y}(t) = x(t). \end{cases} \tag{1.5}$$

On the $(x,y)$ plane, the $\dot{y}(t) = 0$ locus is identical with the vertical axis while the $\dot{x}(t) = 0$ locus becomes the upside-down $N$-shaped curve and passes through the origin. Thus the 2D-dynamical system possesses a unique stationary point, $(x,y) = (0,0)$, at which both loci cross each other.

We now proceed to stability analysis of the approximated model to gain insight into the qualitative behavior in a neighborhood of the stationary point. By developing a linearized version of the approximated model around the stationary point, we obtain the Jacobi matrix of the planar system,

$$J = \begin{bmatrix} \dfrac{1}{\varepsilon\theta}\{\varphi'(0) - [\varepsilon + (1-\alpha)\theta]\} & -\dfrac{1-\alpha}{\varepsilon\theta} \\ \\ 1 & 0 \end{bmatrix}.$$

The characteristic equation is:

$$\lambda^2 - \frac{k}{\varepsilon\theta}\lambda + \frac{1-\alpha}{\varepsilon\theta} = 0,$$

where we set $k = \varphi'(0) - [\varepsilon + (1-\alpha)\theta]$. The characteristic roots are:

$$\lambda_{1,2} = \frac{1}{2}\left\{\frac{k}{\varepsilon\theta} \pm \sqrt{\left(\frac{k}{\varepsilon\theta}\right)^2 - \frac{4(1-\alpha)}{\varepsilon\theta}}\right\}.$$

It follows that the product of the characteristic roots is positive due to the assumptions imposed on parameters, $0 < \alpha < 1$ and $\epsilon\theta > 0$,

$$\lambda_1\lambda_2 = \frac{1-\alpha}{\varepsilon\theta} > 0,$$

and thus this ensures that the stationary point is not a saddle point. It also follows that the sum of the characteristic root can be either positive or negative according to whether the slope of the investment function at the stationary point is larger or smaller than the sum of other parameter values,

$$\lambda_1 + \lambda_2 = \frac{1}{\varepsilon\theta}\{\varphi'(0) - [\varepsilon + (1-\alpha)\theta]\} \gtreqless 0.$$

The stationary point is locally stable or unstable according to whether the sum of terms in braces is negative or positive.

Putting this result in a different way, we can say that the parameter region is divided into two subregions, one stable and the other unstable, by the partition line satisfying:

$$v = [\varepsilon + (1-\alpha)\theta], \tag{1.6}$$

where $v = \varphi'(0)$. The value of the discriminant of the characteristic equation determines whether the local dynamics is oscillatory or monotonic. The locus along which the discriminant is zero is determined by:

$$v = [\varepsilon + (1-\alpha)\theta] \pm 2\sqrt{(1-\alpha)\varepsilon\theta}, \tag{1.7}$$

which distinguishes the parameter region for real roots from that for complex roots. These two loci (one straight line and one parabolic curve) divide the parameter region as shown in Figure 1.4 in which [MS] (in the bottom left and bottom right corners) and [MU] mean monotonic stable and unstable while [OS] and [OU] mean oscillatory stable and unstable.[3] In Figure 1.4, we plot $\theta$ on the horizontal axis and $v$ on the vertical axis. For certain combinations of parameters, $\theta$ and $v$, in either the light-gray region or the dark-gray region, the characteristic roots are complex and thus the system produces oscillations. Moreover, the fluctuations are explosive for the combinations in the light-gray region and damped for the those in the dark-gray region. On the other hand, for the combinations of $\theta$ and $v$ in the white regions, the characteristic roots are real and thus the system produces monotonic dynamics that is convergent or divergent according to whether the combination is in the lower-white region or the upper-white region. Figure 1.4 also implies that the approximated model may produce qualitatively the same dynamics as $v$ increases irrespective of the value of the production lag. Thus, for a given $\theta$, the linearized model generates monotonic stable dynamics, oscillatory stable dynamics, oscillatory unstable dynamics and then monotonic unstable dynamics as $v$ increases from zero.

Thus far, many studies have focused on cyclic dynamics of the approximated model when the stationary point is locally unstable; that is, the parameters are selected from the region above the partition line (1.6) in Figure 1.4. On the other hand, little attention has been paid to the case in which the stationary point is stable. In consequence, little is known about the dynamics for the parameter configurations selected from the region below the partition line. We move one step forward and address the following question: *What can be said about the global dynamics of the approximated model when the stationary point is locally stable?*

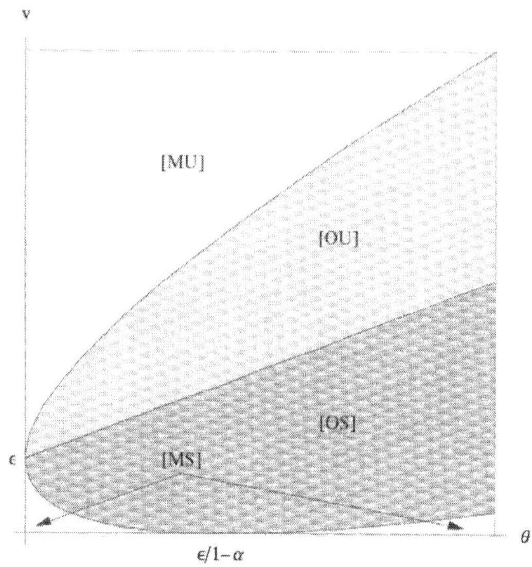


*Figure 1.4* Division of the parameter region

## Coexistence of multiple cycles

To answer the question raised above, we demonstrate multi-stability of the stable approximated model, that is, a coexistence of a stable stationary point, a unstable limit cycle and a stable limit cycle. We select the slope of the investment function evaluated at the stationary point as the bifurcation parameter and investigate the possibility of the supercritical bifurcation in the following section "Hopf cycle". After proving the existence of an unstable limit cycle, we construct an invariant set in the state space and apply the Poincaré-Bendixson theorem to find a stable limit cycle that encloses the unstable limit cycle in "Stable and unstable limit cycles".

### *Hopf Cycle*

We investigate, with the help of Hopf bifurcation theorem, whether there exists an unstable limit cycle in the approximated model. According to the theorem, the Hopf bifurcation occurs if the complex conjugate roots cross the imaginary axis. Obviously, the characteristic roots are complex conjugate with zero real part (i.e. purely imaginary) if $k = 0$. As there are no other roots in two-dimensional system, the consideration of the existence of closed orbits is complete if the eigenvalues cross the imaginary axis with non-zero speed at the bifurcation point. Though there may exist several possibilities to parameterize the approximated model, it seems interesting to choose the slope of the investment function evaluated at the stationary point as the bifurcation parameter.

Since we assume the local stability (i.e. $\varphi'(0) < \varepsilon + (1-\alpha)\theta$ where $\varphi'(0) = \frac{\delta}{2}$ and values of $\alpha$, $\varepsilon$ and $\theta$ are already given) in this section, it can be directly seen that there exists a value $v_0 = \varphi'(0)$ for which:

$$v_0 - [\varepsilon + (1-\alpha)\theta] = 0,$$

implying that the complex conjugate roots cross the imaginary axis. For $v > v_0$, respectively $v < v_0$, the real part becomes positive, respectively negative. Hence, $v_0$ is indeed a bifurcation value of the approximated model. According to the Hopf bifurcation theorem, this establishes the existence of closed orbits in a neighborhood of the stationary point $(0,0)$ at $v = v_0$.[4]

The Hopf theorem, however, is somewhat ambiguous about the nature of the closed orbit. There are two possibilities, one is that the orbits spiral outward from the stationary point toward a stable limit cycle, called the *supercritical bifurcation*, and the other is that all orbits starting inside the cycle spiral in toward the stationary point, called the *subcritical bifurcation*. To make the distinction between the sub- and super-critical Hopf bifurcation, we check the stability of the cycle by calculating the stability index.

The approximated model can be written as:

$$\begin{pmatrix} \dot{x} \\ \dot{y} \end{pmatrix} = J \begin{pmatrix} x \\ y \end{pmatrix} + \begin{pmatrix} f(x) \\ 0 \end{pmatrix}$$

where $J$ is the Jacobian defined above, and $f(x)$ is a nonlinear term that can be derived as:

$$f(x) = \frac{1}{\varepsilon\theta} \{\varphi(x) - \varphi'(0)x\}.$$

In order to transform the approximated model into the normal form, we make the coordinate transformation,

$$\begin{pmatrix} x \\ y \end{pmatrix} = D \begin{pmatrix} u \\ v \end{pmatrix} \quad \text{with} \quad D = \begin{pmatrix} 0 & 1 \\ -\sqrt{\dfrac{\varepsilon\theta}{1-\alpha}} & 0 \end{pmatrix}.$$

Since the matrix $D$ transforms the coordinate system $(x,y)$ into a new coordinate system $(u,v)$, the approximated model is put into the form

$$\begin{pmatrix} \dot{u} \\ \dot{v} \end{pmatrix} = \begin{pmatrix} 0 & -\sqrt{\dfrac{1-\alpha}{\varepsilon\theta}} \\ \sqrt{\dfrac{1-\alpha}{\varepsilon\theta}} & 0 \end{pmatrix} \begin{pmatrix} u \\ v \end{pmatrix} + \begin{pmatrix} 0 \\ f(v) \end{pmatrix}.$$

It is well-known that the stability of the emerging cycle depends on up to third-order derivatives of the nonlinear function, $f(v)$. In the approximated model, the stability index is calculated as:

$$I = \frac{1}{16\varepsilon\theta} \varphi'''(0) > 0.$$

The direction of the inequality indicates that the emerging cycle encloses the stable stationary point and is repelling (i.e. unstable). It follows that a subcritical Hopf bifurcation occurs for $v < v_0$ in the approximated model. We sum up the above result in

**Result 3:** *If the stationary point is stable, then, there exists an unstable limit cycle that encloses the stable equilibrium in the approximated model.*

### *Stable and unstable limit cycles*

Taking $v$ to be less than $v_0$ for which the stationary point is stable, we investigate a number of limit cycles in this subsection. As shown in Result 3, an unstable limit cycle exists for

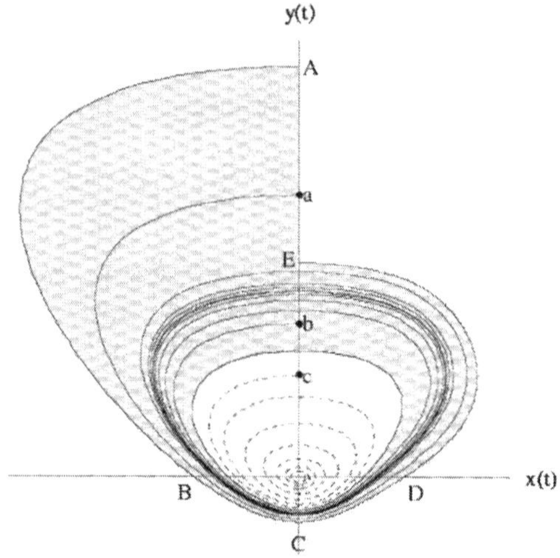


*Figure 1.5* Coexistence of limit cycles

$v < v_0$ due to the Hopf theorem. We proceed to show the existence of a stable limit cycle that encloses the unstable Hopf cycle when the stationary point is locally stable.

We construct an invariant set in such a way that once an orbit enters the set it cannot escape at some future time, and then apply the Poincaré-Bendixson theorem to examine whether a stable cycle can arise in the set. A typical application of this theorem is to the case in which there is a single unstable equilibrium in some invariant set. If we remove the neighborhood of the stationary point in which all orbits move away from it, then the theorem ensures that the remaining set must contain a limit cycle.[5] Since the stationary point is now assumed to be stable in the approximated model, we need another approach for searching for such an invariant set.

In Figure 1.5, we may find a point $A$ so high on the vertical axis that an orbit starting there comes back to meet the vertical axis at a lower point $E$ after crossing not only the horizontal axis at points $B$ and $D$ but also the vertical axis at point $C$. Consider the region bounded by $ABCDEA$ and an open region bounded by the unstable limit cycle that is shown to exist in "Hopf cycle". Then the invariant set to be considered can be constructed by deleting the latter region from the former region. The result is shown in Figure 1.5 in which the shaded region represents this invariant set. The boundary of the inner white region corresponds to the unstable limit cycle that surrounds the stable stationary point. The shaded region thus has no stationary point, and any orbit starting inside the region stays within this region. Two orbits, one starting at point $a$ and the other at point $b$, are examples that are shown to remain inside the invariant set and converge to the same limit cycle. On the other hand, it can be seen that a dotted orbit starting at point $c$ located inside of the white region spirals toward the stationary point. Formally, the Poincaré-Bendixson theorem guarantees the existence of one stable limit cycle in the shaded region. Combining up the discussion above with Result 3 yields the following.

**Result 4:** *If the stationary point is stable, then, a stable limit cycle coexists with an unstable limit cycle that encloses a stable equilibrium point in the approximated model.*

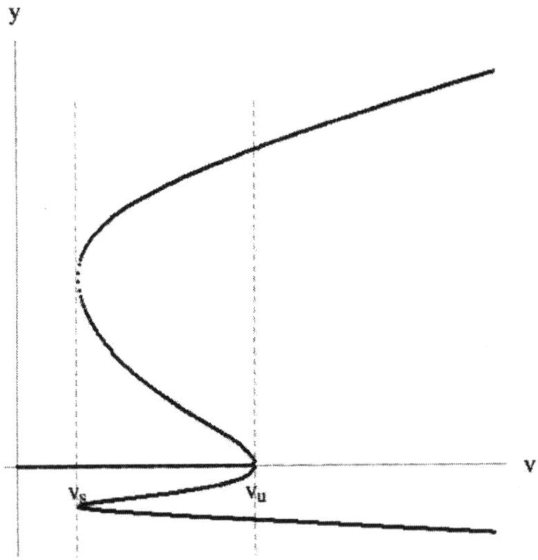


*Figure 1.6* Bifurcation diagram

In Figure 1.6, we present a bifurcation diagram in which the amplitude of the cycle is on the vertical axis and $v$, the bifurcation parameter, on the horizontal axis. $v_u$ is the critical value at which the approximated model loses its stability, and its stationary point is replaced by a limit cycle. For $v > v_u$, the model is destabilized for small perturbations so that any orbit moves away from the stationary point. Nonlinearity of the model prevents it from diverging globally but leads to a unique stable limit cycle. This is essentially the same cycle as the one that Goodwin demonstrates by applying the Lienard method. On the other hand, for $v < v_u$, it is locally stabilized but generates an unstable cycle as well as a stable cycle for $v$ in the interval $[v_s, v_u]$. It can be seen that as $v$ decreases from $v_u$, the amplitude of the inner unstable cycles increases and that of the outer stable cycle decreases. $v_s$ is the other critical value for which two cycles coincide each other. For a lower $v < v_s$, limit cycles no longer exit.

The coexistence of multiple cycles and a stable stationary point reminds us of "corridor stability," the notion which was introduced by Leijonhufvud (1973). It implies that a dynamic system is stable for small perturbations but unstable for large perturbations. The inside of the white curved triangular region in Figure 1.5 is the corridor in which the stationary point is stable. Thus, if perturbations around the stationary point are small enough not to take orbits out of the corridor, the restoring effect of the model works to return the trajectory to the stationary point. To the contrary, if perturbations are large enough to take orbits outside the corridor, the lasting effect of the model leads to persistent cyclical oscillations. The foregoing numerical analysis indicates that the nonlinearity of investment function can be a source of corridor stability in the approximated model.

## Concluding remarks

We investigate the characteristics and the robustness of Goodwin's business cycle in this study. It is confirmed numerically that the nonlinearity of the investment function generates cyclical oscillations of output as shown in Figure 1.1 and summarized in Result 1. It is also confirmed numerically that longer production lags make the amplitude of the cycle larger and the length of its period longer as shown in Figure 1.2. These results are summarized in Result 2. Further, it is seen in Figure 1.6 that the amplitude of the cycle is sensitive to the nonlinearity of investment function and becomes larger as the nonlinearity becomes stronger. It is demonstrated analytically that cyclical oscillations of output are brought about even when the stationary state is locally stable as summarized in Result 3. Finally, Result 4 shows the coexistence of multiple cycles, which then implies corridor stability of Goodwin's business cycle.

## Acknowledgements

The earlier version of the paper, entitled "Reconsiderations of Goodwin's Model", was presented at the Goodwin workshop in the EAEPE conference held in Bremen, Germany, on 10–12 November 2005, and Chuo Meeting for Economics of Time and Space (Chuo-Mets) held in Tokyo, Japan, on 30–31 August 2005. Both authors appreciate financial support from the Ministry of Education, Culture, Sports, Science and Technology (Grand-in-Aid for Scientific Research B, 15330037) and Chuo University (Joint Research Project 0382). This chapter benefited from comments by Serena Sordi, Peter Flaschel, Reiner Franke and Willi Semmler. The usual disclaimer applies.

## Notes

1 Since one unit of time is assumed to equal one year, "20 years" is long enough to see the lag-effects on business cycles.
2 We should note that for specified values of parameters (i.e. $\varphi'(0) = \frac{6}{\pi}$, $\alpha = 0.6$, $\epsilon = 0.5$ and $\theta \leq 1$), the stationary point is locally unstable in these simulations.
3 The partitioning, in equation (1.6), crosses the vertical axis for $v = \varepsilon$ and is upward sloping while the zero discriminant locus, equation (1.7), is tangent to the vertical line for $v = \varepsilon$ and to the horizontal line for $\theta = \frac{\varepsilon}{1-\alpha}$. Thus the similar divisions are obtained regardless of the specified values of parameters, although $\alpha = 0.6$ and $\varepsilon = 0.5$ in Figure 1.4.
4 See Lorenz (1993) for the Hopf bifurcation theorem, the stability index and the following coordinate transformations.
5 See Chapter 2.2 of Lorenz (1993) for an example.

## References

Goodwin, R. (1951) 'The Nonlinear Accelerator and the Persistence of Business Cycles', *Econometrica* 19, 1–17.

Grasman, J. and Wentzel, J. (1994)'Co-existence of a limit cycle and an equilibrium in Kaldor's Business Cycle Model and its Consequences', *Journal of Economic Behavior and Organization* 24, 369–77.

Leijonhufvud, A. (1973) 'Effective Demand Failures', *Swedish Journal of Economics* 75, 27–48.

Lorenz, H-W. (1993) *Nonlinear Dynamical Economics and Chaotic Motion*. Berlin: Springer-Verlag.

Lorenz, H-W. (1987) 'Goodwin's Nonlinear Accelerator and Chaotic Motion', *Journal of Economics* 47, 413–17.

Matsumoto, A. (1997) 'A Non-linear Macro Model of Endogenous Inventory Oscillations', *Research in Economics* 51, 101–29.

Puu, T. (2003) *Attractors, Bifurcations, and Chaos*, 2nd edn, Berlin Heidelberg New York: Springer-Verlag.

Sasakura, K. (1996) 'The Business Cycle Model with a Unique Stable Limit Cycle', *Journal of Economic Dynamics and Control* 20, 1763–73.

# 2 An encompassing theory of macroeconomic growth and fluctuation

*Richard Day and Chengyu Yang*

## Macroeconomics in equilibrium and out

A Dynamic Aggregate Demand and Supply (DADS) model of real economic growth is assembled from well-known Keynesian consumption, investment, monetary and government components together with a production function and equation of capital accumulation. Conditions for which model solutions grow and converge to or fluctuate about a steady state are derived. Further conditions – including a pay-as-you-go fiscal policy – imply convergence to a Solow model and hence to a competitive equilibrium. This, in turn, implies the existence of a supporting aggregate social utility function. The DADS model thus constitutes a framework that encompasses and effectively unifies the major, independently formulated macroeconomic theories of Keynes, Solow and the optimal growth school of Ramsey, Cass, Koopmans, Barro, Kydland, Prescott, Stokey, Lucas, Cooley-Prescott, et al.

A similar, yet quite different effort at synthesis, was achieved some four decades ago by Richard Goodwin whose aim was to capture in one or two dynamic equations the essence of growth and the business cycle, as described by Marx and Schumpeter, while incorporating Keynes' consumption function as a fundamental structural ingredient. He called his model the Marx–Keynes–Schumpeter (M–K–S) System. To accomplish this task, he drew upon the differential equations developed by mathematical physicists such as van der Pol and Rössler. I personally found discrete time dynamics more congenial and based my work on difference equations and their set valued analogs. What follows is an example in discrete time of a macroeconomic model intended to accomplish much the same synthesis that motivated Goodwin but based on discrete dynamics. Its objective is shared by the mathematical macroeconomists of the Bielefeld–New School of Chiarella, Flaschel, Franke, Groh, and Semmler who, like Goodwin, carry out much of their work in continuous time.

For a generation, macroeconomic theory has been couched in microeconomic, general, intertemporal equilibrium terms but with the assumptions that the component households and firms are identical. The existence of an interagent, intertemporal state of perfect coordination, given its definitive mathematical form in Arrow and Debreu (1954), boils down to the solution of an infinite horizon optimal control problem that satisfies Bellman's Principle of Optimality, as in, for example, Cooley and Prescott (1995). This elegant formalization characterizes the intertemporal coordination problem that plagues every society.

On the other hand, the microeconomic argument for its relevance is scarcely convincing from an empirical point of view. The real private ownership market economy is vastly more complicated microeconomically than assumed in the theory. Its components are quite heterogeneous: households vary in composition, wealth, and preferences; firms vary in their production technologies, the numbers and types of goods produced, and the managerial structures employed. These private sector components interact with various government agencies which thereby generate a significant fraction of total demand for and supply of goods and services. Moreover, the macroeconomic data show that equilibrium properties are not and never have been fulfilled: *always* some measured excess capacity and involuntary unemployment. Certainly, these phenomena are what invites government and monetary authorities to mitigate their effects by means of the policy instruments available to them. But the basic optimal growth models do not incorporate a monetary authority or a government sector.

In our approach equilibrium arises as the limit of out-of-equilibrium adjustments in a model that includes government and is based on emergent 'causal' regularities in the macroeconomic data. In this way an optimal growth model characterizes a market economy's long-run potential, a potential that "exists" but changes every period in reality due to changes in the exogenous variables on which it depends.

Further work should endogenize the general price level, employment, worker compensation, capital utilization, and the money supply while retaining a framework that places the desirable properties of equilibrium and long-run policy in an operational context. What we have accomplished here is a minimalist representation of the classic Keynesian approach that incorporates growth explicitly, that converges to or oscillates around a steady state, and that permits repercussion analyzes of both long-run as well as the usual short-run fiscal and monetary policies, a potential that we explore in a separate paper which also provides empirical estimates of parameters.[1]

## Demand generated output and capital accumulation

The components of per capita aggregate demand, $z_t$, are private consumption, $c_t^p$, private investment, $j_t^p$, government consumption, $c_t^g$, government investment, $j_t^g$, and net foreign trade, $x_t$. Gross real per capita output is $q_t$. Real income per capita is $y_t$. Adding the endogenous private demand with the exogenous public demand and net foreign trade, we have aggregate demand in per capita terms,

$$z_t = c_t^p + j_t^p + c_t^g + j_t^g + x_t. \tag{2.1}$$

Fundamental to the Keynesian approach is the working hypothesis that production in a given year, $q_t$, is determined by the level of demand in that year, $z_t$.[2] From this hypothesis follows the *aggregate balance equation*,

$$q_t = z_t. \tag{2.2}$$

As real output is equal to real income flows less net trade, and as the latter is a relatively small fraction of real income, real output serves as a reasonable proxy for that variable. Given this, the functional forms used in what follows are conventional. Private nondurable consumption demand is represented by a consumption function,

$$c_t^p = c' + \alpha q^d, \tag{2.3}$$

where disposable real income is $q_t^d = (1-\tau)q_t$, $\tau$ is the average net tax rate, $\alpha$ is the marginal propensity to consume (MPC) from disposable income, and and $c'$ is a positive constant parameter.[3]

Private investment includes business capital, new housing, and consumer durables. The private investment function is the product of projected income, $\hat{q}_{t+1} = (1+b)q_t$, and real interest effects,

$$j_{t+1}^p = j(\hat{q}_{t+1}, r_t) = \psi\Big((1+b)q_t - q'\Big) \cdot g(r_t),\ q_{t+1} \geq q' \tag{2.4}$$

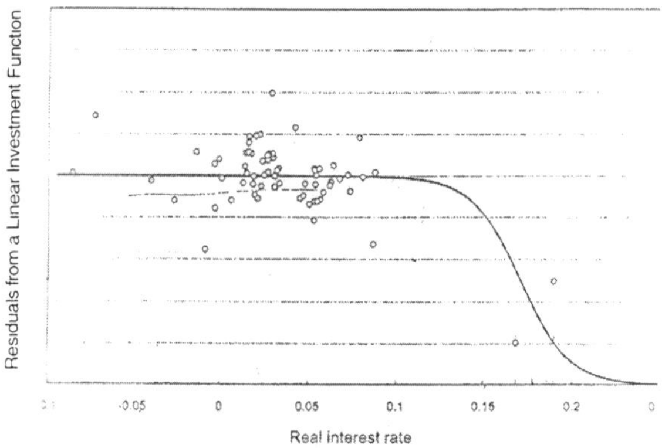


*Figure 2.1* The influence of real interest on investment

where $\psi$ is the private marginal propensity to invest (MPI), and where $r_t$ is the real monetary interest rate.[4] The parameter $q'$ is a positive income threshold below which no private investment would occur.

The real interest has virtually no observable influence on investment except within an intermediate range within which an increase reduces investment sharply until with further increases (not yet observed), investment would apparently dwindle to nothing. The inverse logistic,

$$g(r_t) := \left(1 + e^{\nu(r_t - r')}\right)^{-1}, \tag{2.5}$$

is used to represent this evidently nonlinear effect. Its properties play a crucial role in the subsequent analysis. The parameters $r'$ and $\nu$ are positive. The function is negatively sloping, its image ranging between 1 and 0, asymptotic to 1 when $r$ becomes negative and to 0 when $r$ becomes very positive. The parameter $r'$ is the value of the real rate which reduces the income effect on investment by half. (Thus, if $r_t = r'$, then $g(r') = 1/2$.) Routine calculations show that the slope of the function takes on its most negative value at that point with $g'(r') = -\nu/4$. Obviously, *the greater the parameter $\nu$, the more powerful the interest rate effect in the neighborhood of $r'$ but the closer the rate must be to $r'$ before that powerful effect is realized*. That is what is suggested by the data,[5] as shown in Figure 2.1.

The demand for money is represented in nominal terms by:

$$M_t^d = \mu P_t q_t (i_t - i')^{-\lambda} \tag{2.6}$$

where $M_t^d$ is nominal money demand per capita, $i'$ is a non-negative 'liquidity trap' parameter. The real LM function implied by the money demand equation is:

$$r_t = \ell^r(q_t, m_t, p_t) = \left[i' + (\mu q_t / m_t)^{1/\lambda} - p_t\right] / (1 + p_t) \tag{2.7}$$

where $m_t = M_t / P_t$ is the real money supply per capita.[6]

Substituting (2.7) into the interest effect function (2.5), we obtain a *monetary effect* function,

$$\begin{aligned} h(q_t,m_t,p_t) &= g\left(\ell^r(q_t,m_t,p_t)\right) \\ &= \left(1+e^{\nu\left([\imath'+(\mu q_t/m_t)^{1/\lambda}-p_t]/(1+p_t)-r'\right)}\right)^{-1}. \end{aligned} \tag{2.8}$$

Notice that the LM function is a monotonically increasing function of $q_t$. The real monetary effect function, therefore, has a qualitative profile similar to the real interest effect function except that as output increases the demand for money increases which strengthens the real monetary effect. The private investment function can now be represented by:

$$j^p_{t+1} = \psi\left((1+b)q_t - q'\right) \cdot h(q_t,m_t,p_t). \tag{2.9}$$

Putting together the separate components, we have the aggregate *demand equation*,

$$z_{t+1} = v_{t+1} + c' + \alpha\left((1-\tau)q_{t+1}\right) + \psi\left((1+b)q_t - q'\right) \cdot h(q_t,m_t,p_t), \tag{2.10}$$

where $v_{t+1} = j^g_{t+1} + c^g_{t+1} + x_{t+1}$.

For the production function we adopted the usual Cobb–Douglas form with constant returns to scale and labor augmenting productivity improvement,

$$q^u_t = (B_t)^{1-\beta}(k^u_t)^{\beta}, \tag{2.11}$$

where output per employed worker is $q^u_t := Q_t/E_t$ and utilized social capital per employed worker or *capital labor ratio* is $k^u_t := K^u_t/E_t$ which is treated here as an exogenous variable.[7]

The productivity index and population growth are assumed to be generated, respectively, by:

$$\begin{aligned} B_{t+1} &= (1+b)B_t = (1+b)^{t+1}B_0, & (a) \\ N_{t+1} &= (1+n)N_t = (1+n)^{t+1}N_0. & (b) \end{aligned} \tag{2.12}$$

Aggregate output, $Q_t = q^u_t E_t$, equals aggregate demand, $Z_t = z_t N_t$, where $E_t$ is employment and $N_t$ population. It follows that employment,

$$E_t = z_t N_t / q^u_t, \tag{2.13}$$

while aggregate *utilized* social capital,

$$K^u_t = k^u_t E_t. \tag{2.14}$$

To these equations is added the equation defining capital accumulation,

$$k_{t+1} = \left(\frac{1}{1+n}\right)\left((1-\delta)k_t + j^p_t + j^g_t\right) \tag{2.15}$$

where $k_t$ is social capital per capita. The population rate of growth, $n$, and the depreciation rate, $\delta$, as well as the average tax rate, $\tau$, are exogenous variables which for theoretical purposes are treated as parameters.

Taking advantage of the aggregate balance equation, we arrive at the *equation of demand generated output*,

$$q_{t+1} = \frac{1}{\sigma+\tau\alpha}\left(v_{t+1} - \alpha y' + \psi\left((1+b)q_t - q'\right) \cdot h(q_t,m_t,p_t)\right),\ q_t > q', \tag{2.16}$$

where $\sigma = 1 - \alpha$ is the private marginal propensity to save (MPS) and $v_{t+1} = c^g_{t+1} + j^g_{t+1} + x_{t+1}$. The equation of capital accumulation is

$$\begin{aligned} k_{t+1} = & \frac{1}{1+n}((1-\delta)k_t + \psi((1+b)q_{t-1} - q') \\ & \cdot h(q_{t-1}, m_{t-1}, p_{t-1}) + j^g_t), \\ & q_{t-1} > q'. \end{aligned} \tag{2.17}$$

## Existence and stability of steady states

To consider the existence of a steady state, imagine that each of the components of per capita exogenous demand grows at the rate of increase in productivity. Also, assume that the nominal money supply per capita grows at a constant rate of inflation, $p$. Then the *equation of demand generated output* becomes:

$$q_{t+1} = \frac{1}{\sigma + \tau\alpha}\left(B_{t+1}v + c' + \psi\left((1+b)q_t - q'\right) \cdot h(q_t, m, p)\right) \; \forall \, q_t > q' \tag{2.18}$$

where $m$ is the initial constant real money supply per capita, and $v$ is an initial level of exogenous demand, $v = c^g + j^g + x$.

Denote the real monetary effect in efficiency units by $h(q^e_t, m^e, p)$ where $q_t = B_t q^e_t$ and $m_t = B_t m^e_t$. Divide both sides of (2.18) by $B_{t+1}$ and observe that, as time passes, the phase equation for output generated demand in efficiency units converges to the process,[8]

$$q^e_{t+1} = \theta^e(q_t) := \frac{1}{\sigma + \tau\alpha}\left(v + \psi q^e_t \cdot h(q^e_t, m^e, p)\right), \; q^e_t > 0. \tag{2.19}$$

Evidently a unique positive steady state, $\tilde{q}^e$, exists satisfying the equation:

$$(\sigma + \tau\alpha)\tilde{q}^e = v + \psi h(\tilde{q}^e, m^e, p)\tilde{q}^e. \tag{2.20}$$

The capital accumulation equation in efficiency units converges to the process:

$$k^e_{t+1} = \frac{1}{(1+n)(1+b)}\left((1-\delta)k^e_t + j^g + \psi q^e_{t-1} \cdot h(q^e_{t-1}, m^e_{t-1}, p)\right), \tag{2.21}$$

so the steady state per capita capital stock in efficiency units is:

$$\tilde{k}^e = \frac{1}{n + nb + b + \delta}\left(\psi\tilde{q}^e \cdot h(\tilde{q}^e, m^e, p) + j^g\right). \tag{2.22}$$

The stability of demand generated output depends on whether or not:

$$-\frac{\sigma + \tau\alpha}{\psi} < \phi(\tilde{q}^e) < \frac{\sigma + \tau\alpha}{\psi} \tag{2.23}$$

where

$$\phi(q^e_t) := \left[h(q^e_t, m^e, p) + q^e_t h'(q^e_t, m^e, p)\right] \tag{2.24}$$

is the *marginal monetary effect function* and $\phi(\tilde{q}^e)$ is the *equilibrium marginal monetary effect* (EMME).

Notice that the first term in (2.24) lies in the interval $(0, 1)$ while the second term is negative. The function is positive at $q^e = 0$. It decreases with the steady state at an increasing

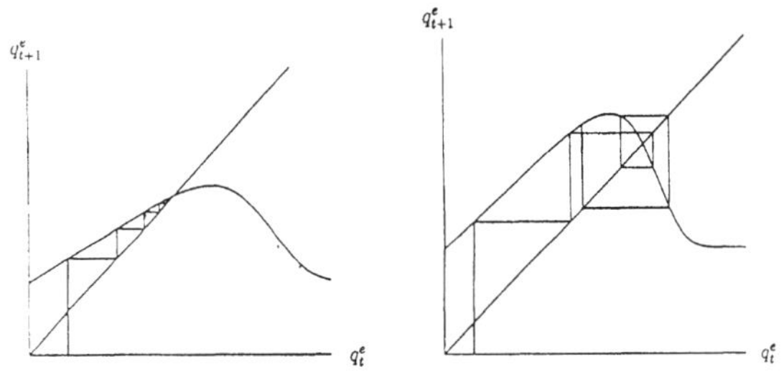


*Figure 2.2* Long-run demand-generated output in efficiency units: a) stable growth; b) fluctuating growth

rate, reaches a maximum, becomes negative, increasingly negative, then decreasingly negative and converges to zero. These properties imply that the supply of money can have either a positive or negative influence that is either negligible or substantial, *depending on where the steady state lies*. Notice that, *at a steady state*, a positive EMME implies that aggregate demand is upward sloping; whereas, a negative value implies it is downward sloping. Exploiting the explicit functional forms, you can show that the stability condition is:[9]

$$-1 < \frac{\psi g(\tilde{r})}{\sigma + \tau\alpha}\left[1 - \frac{\nu(1-g(\tilde{r})}{\lambda(1+p)}\left(\frac{\mu}{m^e}\tilde{q}^e\right)^{1/\lambda}\right] < 1. \tag{2.25}$$

**Proposition 2.1**

*Existence and Stability of Potential Steady State Growth. Assume that per capita exogenous demand and the real money supply grow at the same rate as productivity.*

(i) *There exists a unique positive steady state output per capita in efficiency units with employment and capital utilization growing at the same rate as output and income.*
(ii) *There exists an open set of parameter values for which the steady state in efficiency units is stable and a complementary set for which it is unstable. In the former case aggregate output converges to the exponential path $Q_t \to (1+b)^t(1+n)^t B_0 N_0 \tilde{q}^e$. In the latter case output grows but approaches and fluctuates around the steady state path.*

If $v > 0$, the phase diagram can have the appearances shown in Figure 2.2.

## A pay-as-you-go fiscal policy

In order to establish a budget balance suppose a 'pay-as-you-go' fiscal policy is adopted that limits government spending to estimated revenue, $\tau\hat{q}_{t+1}$, based on an extrapolation at the rate of productivity growth of actual income, $\hat{q}_{t+1} = (1+b)q_t$, so that public expenditure:

$$g_{t+1} = \tau(1+b)q_t.$$

Suppose further that the fractions of tax revenue allocated to public consumption and to public capital investment are $\alpha^g$ and $\psi^g$, respectively, so that the corresponding expenditure levels are:

$$c^g_{t+1} = \alpha^g g_{t+1} \quad \text{and} \quad j^g_{t+1} = \psi^g g_{t+1}$$

where $\alpha^g + \psi^g = 1$. Finally, suppose the trade deficit per capita can be held constant at a given level $x$ and that the population, depreciation, and inflation rates, $n, \delta$, and $p$ are all constant. Given these special conditions, the equation of demand generated output (2.16) becomes:

$$q_{t+1} = \frac{1}{\sigma+\tau\alpha}\left(xc' + +\tau(1+b)q_t + \psi\left((1+b)q_t - q'\right)\cdot h(q_t, m_t, p)\right)$$
$$q_t > q' \tag{2.26}$$

where, recall, $x$ is net exports.

If the real per capita money supply grows at the same rate as productivity and the inflation rate is constant, then, in terms of efficiency units, the demand generated output equation converges over time to:

$$q^e_{t+1} = \theta^b(q^e_t) := \frac{1}{\sigma+\tau\alpha}\left(\tau + \psi h(q^e_t, m^e, p)\right)q^e_t. \tag{2.27}$$

Investment in efficiency units converges to:

$$j^e_{t+1} = \psi^g \tau q^e_t + \psi h(q^e_{t-1}, m^e, p)q^e_t, \tag{2.28}$$

so capital accumulation in efficiency units converges to the process,

$$k^e_{t+1} = \frac{1}{(1+n)(1+b)}((1-\delta)k^e_t + \psi^g \tau q^e_{t-1} + \psi q^e_{t-1} \cdot h(q^e_{t-1}, m^e, p)). \tag{2.29}$$

Given the interest effect function, the existence of a steady state depends necessarily on whether or not the rate of change in $q^e_{t+1}$ in the neighborhood of $q^e = 0$ exceeds unity, that is, if:

$$\left.\frac{dq^e_{t+1}}{dq^e_t}\right|_{q^e=0} = \frac{1}{\sigma+\tau\alpha}\left(\tau + \psi h(0, m^e, p)\right) > 1, \tag{2.30}$$

or, equivalently, $h(0, m^e, p) > \frac{(1-\tau)\sigma}{\psi}$, such a state will exist because $\theta^b(q^e) \to \frac{\tau}{\sigma+\tau\alpha}q^e < q^e$ as $q^e$ becomes large.

From (2.27) steady state output (when it exists) satisfies the equation:

$$h(\tilde{q}^e, m^e, p) = \frac{(1-\tau)\sigma}{\psi}. \tag{2.31}$$

Its stability depends on the relationship

$$-1 < \frac{1}{\sigma+\tau\alpha}\left(\tau + \psi\tilde{\phi}\right) < 1 \tag{2.32}$$

where $\phi(\tilde{q}^e) = \tilde{\phi}$ is our familiar EMME (24). Using (2.24) and (2.31), we find that this condition is equivalent to:

$$\frac{-2(\sigma+\tau\alpha)}{\psi} < \tilde{q}^e h'(\tilde{q}^e, m, p) < 0. \tag{2.33}$$

The right side of this expression is always satisfied, so instability occurs only if (and only if):

$$\tilde{q}^e h'(\tilde{q}^e, m^e, p) < \frac{-2(\sigma+\tau\alpha)}{\psi}. \tag{2.34}$$

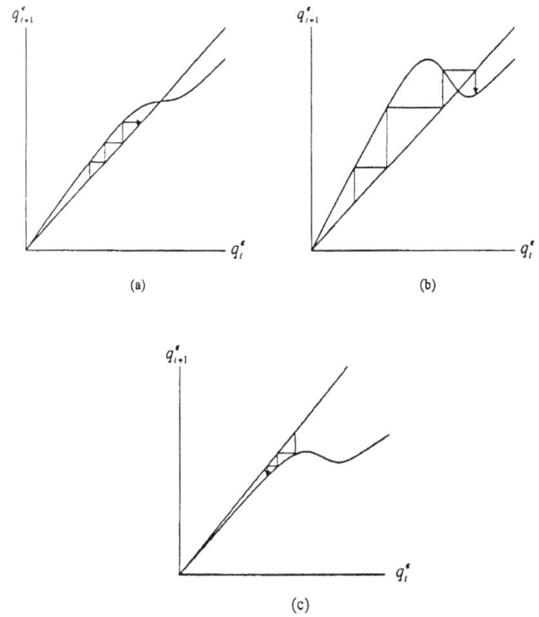

*Figure 2.3* The pay-as-you-go fiscal policy: a) convergent growth; b) fluctuating growth; c) long-run growth

From these relationships we infer:

**Proposition 2.2**
*Given the pay-as-you-go fiscal policy, if the real money supply grows at the rate of productivity growth and the inflation rate is constant, then:*

*(i) there exists an open set, $\mathcal{P}$, of parameter values for which there exists a unique positive equilibrium steady state in efficiency units and a complementary set, $Q$, of parameter values for which no positive steady state exists; and*
*(ii) there exists a subset, $\mathcal{P}^1$ in $\mathcal{P}$, for which the equilibrium steady state is stable and a set, $\mathcal{P}^2$, for which it is unstable. In the former case, the adjustment process converges to the equilibrium steady state; in the latter case, it fluctuates about it.*

The three qualitatively distinct cases are illustrated in Figure 2.3.

## Competitive macroeconomic equilibrium

Notice that in the convergent case aggregate investment approaches a constant fraction of output,

$$s = \psi^g \tau + (1-\tau)\sigma, \tag{2.35}$$

where the private investment rate equals the private savings rate,

$$\psi h(\tilde{q}^e, m^e, p) = (1-\tau)\sigma,$$

and government expenditure equals tax revenue (both in efficiency units),

$$\tilde{g}^e = (\psi^g + \alpha^g)\tau\tilde{q}^e = \tau\tilde{q}^e.$$

Defining $\sigma^g = 1 - \alpha^g$, government savings equals government investment,

$$\psi^g \tilde{g}^e = \sigma^g \tilde{g}^e.$$

Consequently, the conditions of Proposition 2.2 imply the following:

**Proposition 2.3**

*If the convergence criterion (2.32) is satisfied, the DADS model with a pay-as-you-go fiscal policy converges to the standard (Solow) growth model, that is, total investment converges to a constant fraction of output, so:*

$$k_{t+1}^e \longrightarrow \frac{1}{(1+n)(1+b)}\left((1-\delta)k_t^e + sk_t^{e\beta}\right)$$

*where both private and public sectors satisfy the aggregate equilibrium budget balance conditions,*

$$I = S \quad and \quad G = T$$

*at each period of time.*

## Revealed social preference

Among the results of general equilibrium theory is the existence of a well behaved utility function that 'supports' a competitive equilibrium for an economy of decentralized households and firms in the sense that the competitive equilibrium consumptions and productions maximize that utility function subject to the technology and resource constraints on production. An analogous idea was used by Cooley and Prescott who derive the parameter estimates for an aggregate utility function of an optimal growth model of the US economy, given the assumption that the latter has been evolving along an optimal balanced growth path. We use their method here to derive a supporting utility function in terms of the parameters of the DADS structural equations.

The Cooley–Prescott utility function is (with slight notational changes),

$$u(c_0, h_0, \ldots, c_t, h_t, \ldots) := \sum_{t=0}^{\infty} \rho^t \left[(1-\delta)\ln c_t + \gamma \ln(1-h_t)\right] \tag{2.36}$$

where $\rho$ is the time discount (or time preference) parameter and $\gamma$ the weight given the leisure component of utility. The conditions an optimal solution must satisfy include a requirement that the steady state rate of return on capital, $\beta\tilde{q}^e/\tilde{k}^e$, satisfies the equation,

$$\rho = \frac{(1+n)(1+b)}{\beta\tilde{q}^e/\tilde{k}^e + 1 - \delta}, \tag{2.37}$$

where

$$\beta\tilde{q}^e/\tilde{k}^e = \frac{\beta\left[(n+\delta)+(1+n)b\right]}{s},$$

and that investment as a fraction of output ($s = \tilde{j}/\tilde{q}$ in our terms) satisfies the equation,

$$\gamma = \frac{(1-\beta)(1-n)}{(1-s)h + (1-\beta)(1-h)}. \tag{2.38}$$

The optimal steady state employment fraction of the 'disposable time' is $h$.

**Proposition 2.4**

*Given the conditions of Proposition 2.2, the long-run steady state of the DADS model is optimal with respect to the revealed social utility function (2.36) with discount and preference parameters $\rho$ and $\gamma$ given by (2.37) and (2.38).*

## Conclusions

As argued in Day and Yang (2005a), we prefer to think of *revealed social utility* (2.36) as an aggregate economic *index* that reflects the outcome of the decisions made by the millions of heterogeneous agents in both private and public sectors. This interpretation does not imply that the economy's steady state is obtained by actually maximizing this function for no one can know what it is until it has been revealed, and it cannot be revealed out-of-equilibrium. Moreover, the economy is not – nor ever has been – in a competitive equilibrium – at least in terms of the National Economic Data (NIPA) for the exogenous data upon which equilibrium rests, keep changing. However, to the extent that those data do not change very much, the DADS model could be thought of *as a macroeconomic algorithm* based on an *emergent macroeconomic* order that, given special conditions, can seek out, converge to, or fluctuate about a competitive equilibrium path which would have a supporting rationale implicit in its macroeconomic parameters in the sense of revealed social preference. From this point of view the DADS model encompasses the major alternative ways of thinking about macroeconomic dynamics. However, we do not see the optimal control model as a micro foundation for macroeconomics, but rather as a normative characterization of an aggregate economy's long-run potential.

## Notes

1 Reference made to our working paper, "From Keynes to Solow to Optimal Growth: An Encompassing Model of Monetary and Fiscal Policy."

2 Income payments usually lag work but, as most labor and management income is received on a weekly or monthly basis, equation (2.2) is a close approximation on an annual basis.

3 The macroeconomic time series data suggest that the consumption and investment functions are nonlinear with respect to income. By breaking the past into three 'growth eras,' the income relationship is very closely approximated by assuming linearity. We refer the reader to a preliminary study, Day and Yang (2005b), for empirical estimates of the theoretical parameters and alternative policy repercussions.

4 The real interest rate is defined by:

$$r_t = (i_t - p_t)/(1 + p_t)$$

where $i_t$ is the nominal rate and the inflation rate is defined by $p_t := (P_t - P_{t-1})/P_{t-1}$, where $P_t$ is the general price level. The denominator in the definition of $r_t$ is sometimes omitted in text book treatments. Why it belongs can be seen by solving the identity:

$$S_t/P_t = (1 + r_t)S_{t-1}/P_{t-1} = (1 + i_t)S_{t-1}/P_t$$

for $r_t$ where $S_t$ is an asset yielding the nominal rate $i_t$. Then use the definition of $p_t$ to get the expression for $r_t$.

5 Standard texts usually portray the interest effects as linear, but this apparently grossly exaggerates the effects of low and high real rates. Linear econometric estimates would therefore overestimate the effects of interest considerably below or above and underestimate its effect in the intermediate range. See Day and Yang cited in note 1.

6 Note that the velocity of money is:

$$V_t := \frac{P_t q_t}{M_t} = \frac{q_t}{m_t} = (i_t - i')^{\lambda}/\mu.$$

7 Obviously, public and private capital can be complementary, for example, public highways and private trucks. But public and private ownership are matters of finance while complementarity and substitutability are matters of technology. It is obviously difficult to unscramble these aspects using aggregate indexes, a task for further research.

8 Notice that $h(0, m^e, p)$ is positive. As $\psi$ is positive near $q = 0$, the map $\theta(q)$ is greater than $v/(\sigma + \tau\alpha)$ and increasing. As $h(q^e, m^e, p)$ is monotonically decreasing and asymptotic to zero, $\theta(q) \to v/(\sigma + \tau\alpha)$ as $q$ increases. The existence of a unique positive steady state follows.

9 Note that:

$$h(\tilde{q}^e, m, p) = g\left[\ell^r(\tilde{q}^e, m, p)\right] = g(\tilde{r}),$$

and that $g'(\tilde{r}) = -\nu g(\tilde{r})\left(1 - g(\tilde{r})\right)$, so:

$$h'(\tilde{q}^e, m, p) = -\nu g(\tilde{r})\left(1 - g(\tilde{r})\right) \left.\frac{d\ell^r}{dq_t^e}\right|_{\tilde{q}^e}.$$

Using the fact that:

$$\left.\frac{d\ell^r}{dq_t^e}\right|_{\tilde{q}^e} = \frac{1}{\lambda(1+p)} \left(\frac{\mu}{m^e}\right)^{1/\lambda} \tilde{q}^{e 1/\lambda - 1} > 0,$$

The result is obtained.

## References

Arrow, K. and G. Debreu (1954) "Existence of an Equilibrium for a Competitive Economy." *Econometrica* 22: 265–290.

Chiarella, Carl, Peter Flaschel and Reiner Franke, 2005, *Foundations for a Disequilibrium Theory of the Business Cycle*, Cambridge: Cambridge University Press.

Cooley, Thomas F. and Edward C. Prescott, 1995, "Economic Growth and Business Cycles," Chapter 1 in Cooley (ed.), *Frontiers of Business Cycle Research*, Princeton: Princeton University Press.

Day, Richard H. and Chengyu Yang, 2005a, "Economic Growth and Revealed Social Preference," *Studies in Nonlinear Dynamics and Econometrics* 9(2): 1–18.

Day, Richard H. and Chengyu Yang, 2005b, "A Dynamic Analysis of the Bush Fiscal Policy," in *Difference Equations and Discrete Dynamical Systems*, edited by Linda J.S. Allen, Bernd Aulback, Saber Elaydi, and Robert Sacker, Hackensack, NJ: Word Scientific Publishing.

Fair, Ray C., 2004, *Estimating How the Macro Economy Works*, Cambridge, MA: Harvard University Press.

Flaschel, Peter, Reiner Franke and Willi Semmler, 1997, *Dynamic Macroeconomics*, Cambridge, MA: MIT Press.

Godley, Wynne, Alex Izurieta and Gennaro Zezza, 2004, "Prospects and Policies for the U.S. Economy," *Strategic Analysis*, August 2004. The Levy Institute of Bard College, Cambridge Endowment for Research in Finance, 1–12.

Stokey, N.L. and R.E. Lucas, Jr. with E.C. Prescott. 1989 *Recursive Methods in Economic Dynamics*. Cambridge, MA: Harvard University Press.

# 3 Kaleckian investment and employment cycles in post-war industrialized economies

*Peter Flaschel, Reiner Franke and Willi Semmler*

## Introduction

The issue whether the welfare state promotes or retards economic growth has become a major issue in recent macroeconomic studies. In this chapter we investigate some of the aspects of the welfare state in a macroeconomic model[1] with labor market adjustment process, wage-price spiral, and a Keynesian dynamic multiplier setup. The aggregate demand schedule underlying this dynamic multiplier is derived from Classical saving habits and an investment function which assumes that investment not only reacts to changing profitability in capitalist economies, but also to the conditions characterizing the capital-labor relationship, where persistently high employment rates may give rise to extensive welfare state measures. Those are usually labor market institutions in favor of labor, generous unemployment benefits, labor force participation in the firms' decision making (in the hiring and firing practices of firms) and a considerable reduction of the workday, not all liked by 'industrial leaders' as Kalecki (1943, Ch. 12) has characterized those achievements.

Our considered model has Kaleckian features with regard to investment and savings behavior and the multiplier approach to the market for goods. It is Goodwinian with respect to labor market dynamics and capital stock growth, though we will now find at least four possible regimes for real wage adjustment, see Rose (1967) in this regard, in place of the single one of the Goodwin (1967) growth cycle approach. There, only a profit-led coupled with a labor-market-led situation was considered, due to the supply side orientation of the Goodwin model, see the Table 3.1 for details.

In our model, we furthermore employ, in place of Goodwin's (1967) real wage Phillips curve, now a money-wage and a price-level Phillips curve, both of a fairly advanced type, where wage dynamics allows for insider-outsider considerations and Blanchard and Katz (1999) error correction. The price dynamics can be considered as a generalization of Kalecki's theory of markup pricing, with a markup that depends on the state of the business cycle and again a term that represents the Blanchard and Katz (1999) type error correction (a second positive – level – influence) of the real wage on the rate of price inflation. Due to the separate consideration of labor force and workforce utilization rates (the employment rate on the external labor market and the utilization ratio of the workforce within firms) we finally need a two stage Okun-type link between the goods and the labor market. The first stage leads from the utilization of the capital stock (as measured by the output-capital ratio) to the utilization ratio of the employed workforce (as a more or less technological relationship) and the second stage from there to the employment rate of the labor forces by way of the employment policy of firms. Here, firms' employment policies are viewed

*Table 3.1* Four types of real wage adjustment processes

| | *Wage-led goods demand* | *Profit-led goods-demand* |
|---|---|---|
| Labor-market-led real wage adjustment | Adverse = divergent | Normal = convergent |
| Goods-market-led real wage adjustment | Normal = convergent | Adverse = divergent |

as dependent on the utilization ratio of their workforce in comparison to a utilization ratio that is desired by them in view of the state of the external labor market.

We thus distinguish with respect to the labor market the rate of employment that is characterizing this market from the utilization ratio of the workforce of firms and thus pursue an insider-outsider approach as far as wage negotiations and the employment policy of firms are concerned. The utilization ratio of the workforce is always immediately adjusted to the utilization ratio of the capital stock and thus fluctuates as this ratio with the state of aggregate demand on the market for goods, though with a different amplitude (depending on the technology of the firm sector). The change in the external employment rate (on the labor market), by contrast, is determined by the employment policy of the firms which may be subject to many influences (economic and political ones) and thus represents the volatile element in this two stage formulation of Okun's (1970) law, leading from capacity utilization of firms to their labor force utilization and from there to the recruitment (or dismissal) of laborers into (from) the existing workforce of firms. As already stated firms in addition pay attention to the state of the labor market when deciding on their amount of their investment projects. We view the interaction of inside workforce utilization with outside employment rates as a capillary system where pressure as measured by rate of money wage growth is shifted from the inside component to the outside component and back in order to achieve – from the viewpoint of firms – as little combined pressure as possible.

As the model is formulated we can distinguish between wage-led and profit-led situations on the market for goods, depending on whether aggregate demand increases or decreases with increases in the real wage. In addition we can differentiate labor-market-led influences from goods-market-led influences of economic activity increases on the growth rate of real wages. The first situation is given when the growth rate of real wages essentially depends positively on factor utilization rates. The second situation characterizes the opposite case, in which case the dynamics of the price level dominate in the formation of real wages (and not the dynamics of the money wage). Table 3.1 summarizes the scenarios that are possible in such an environment and it implies that empirical analysis is needed if definite conclusions are to be drawn with respect to which entry in this table is the relevant one in a particular country at a particular time.

If aggregate demand and the real wage dynamics are wage led and labor-market-led, respectively, we have increasing activity with increasing real wages and in addition a pro-cyclical real wage dynamics (with a quarter phase displacement) and thus get instability from this two-fold positive feedback mechanism. The other cases in Table 3.1 are motivated in a similar way, giving in sum rise to two types of adverse and two types of stabilizing real wage reaction patterns.

In this chapter we will concentrate on situations where the real wage dynamics are labor market-led (for which there is some evidence in the US economy, see Chen *et al.* (2006) and also the on-going debate on -procyclical real wages in this regard). Chen *et al.*

(2006) also provide evidence on profit-led goods market activities, but here the situation is more mixed in the literature, since post-Keynesian authors normally assume wage-led situations in their analysis. In this chapter we shall show in this respect that wage-led situations are always coupled with dynamic multiplier stability, but are – as was argued above – plagued by real wage instability if money wages respond strongly to labor market pressure (in particular inside pressure). Profit-led situations, by contrast, are plagued by dynamic multiplier instability, but imply a stable or convergent partial real wage adjustment mechanism.

We therefore have in both cases instability scenarios – in the first case via the real wage feedback structure and, in the second case, via a goods market quantity adjustment process that works too fast. In the first situation, downward money wage rigidity may be of help in controlling the explosive dynamics of real wages and in the second case a weakening of the multiplier process far off the steady state may allow for bounded dynamics, though not convergent ones. Our model therefore allows for interesting alternative stability scenarios, dependent on the working of the wage-price spiral. This allows also to include Blanchard and Katz type error correction terms, found to be relevant in the case of the US economy in Chen *et al.* (2006)) and employment policies, pursued by firms, in a Keynesian aggregate demand situation where income distribution and the state of the labor market matters.

Moreover, we also get in this model type interesting steady state relationships, underlying the dynamics of the model. On the one hand, we find for the steady state that owners of capital get what they spend, since their profit rate is solely determined by their trend investment behavior. On the other hand, as the model is formulated, we have that the steady state rate of employment on the labor market is determined by the target rate in the investment function solely. Finally, the steady ratio of capacity utilization is generally only equal to the utilization ratio of the capital stock desired by firms. This holds if workers adjust their behavior to the steady state rate of employment set by capitalist firms and if their reaction with respect to the insider utilization ratio of the workforce is the same as in the firms' reaction pattern. This steady ratio of capacity utilization is a fairly complicated function of the parameters of the model and thus dependent on a variety of exogenous magnitudes of our approach to the interaction of goods and labor market dynamics.

There are, however, processes on the nominal side of the model that may modify such situations significantly. If there is accelerating inflation, the interest rate policy pursued by the central bank may not only enforce upper turning points in economic activity, but may also modify its steady state position back to natural rates of employment and capacity utilization, if these rates are known to the central bank. Such monetary policy thus exercises a strong influence on the working of the economy which may not really function without it. Concerning deflationary episodes the role of the central bank may, however, be much more limited, since there is a floor to the setting of the nominal rate of interest. In such a situation, downward money wage rigidity and thus behavior of workers may be of decisive importance for the viability of the economy.

The next section presents the model of this chapter. In '4D steady-stae configuration and reduced-form 3d dynamics' we derive the laws of motion that characterize the considered economy. 'Feedback structures of KMGS and KGR dynamics: a brief comparison' investigates its steady state and basic stability calculations. In 'Local instability and global boundedness' we consider the essential feedback structures of this model type and compare them with other ones.[2] The feedback structures are then used to construct a case where in fact local stability of the steady state arises. We call this a consensus-driven economy that is considered at the end of this section. Section 6 then considers the case of local instability of the steady state solution characterizing a conflict-driven economy. This provides various scenarios that may nevertheless allow for upper as well as lower turning points from a global point of view, i.e. that make the considered dynamics an economically viable one from the global point of view. In the case of a conflict-driven economy the order is established only through large fluctuations in economic activity or economic policy. 'Numerical examples' provides some numerical illustrations of the model. 'Political aspects of the Kaleckian investment and employment cycle' points to some problems on the nominal side of the considered economy that do not yet feedback into the real dynamics, but that demand for the extension of the model concerning interest effects on aggregate demand and a Taylor interest rate policy rule in order to tame the explosive dynamics that is existing in the nominal part of the dynamics. Besides monetary policy we there also briefly consider fiscal policy of a Keynesian type which augments the private sector of our Keynes/Kalecki-Goodwin/Rose economy in a straightforward way. The final section concludes. The employed stability criteria are considered in an appendix to this chapter.

## The model

We here consider the private sector of the macroeconomy in isolation from the government sector (and fiscal and monetary policies). The role and implications of macroeconomic policy for the modeled investment and employment dynamics will be considered in a later section of this chapter. We start from the wage-price dynamics or the aggregate supply side of the model, as it is often called in the literature. For the description of aggregate supply we will employ the following general formulation of a wage-price spiral mechanism (related to both work of Rose (1967, 1990) and Blanchard and Katz (1999):

$$\hat{w} = \beta_{we}(e-\bar{e}) + \beta_{wu}(u_w - \tilde{u}_w(e)) - \beta_{w\omega}\ln(\frac{\omega}{\omega_0}) + \kappa_w\hat{p} + (1-\kappa_w)\pi^c \tag{3.1}$$

$$\hat{p} = \beta_{py}(y-\bar{y}) + \beta_{p\omega}\ln(\frac{\omega}{\omega_0}) + \kappa_p\hat{w} + (1-\kappa_p)\pi^c \tag{3.2}$$

In these equations, $\hat{w}, \hat{p}$ denote the growth rates of nominal wages w and the price level $p$ (their inflation rates) and $\pi^c$ a medium-term inflation-climate expression which however is of no relevance in the following due to our neglect of real interest rate effects on the demand side of the model. We denote by $e$ the rate of employment on the external labor market and by $u_w$ the ratio of utilization of the workforce within firms. This latter ratio of employment is compared by the workforce in their negotiations with firms with their desired normal ratio of utilization $\tilde{u}_w(e), \tilde{u}_w' < 0$ which can and is here assumed to depend negatively on the external rate of employment $e$, since higher employment on the labor market implies demands for lower worktime within firms. We thus have two employment gaps, an external one: $e-\bar{e}$ and an internal one: $u_w - \tilde{u}_w$, which determine wage inflation rate $\hat{w}$ from the side of demand pressure within or outside of the production process. In the wage PC we in addition employ a real wage error correction term $\ln(\omega/\omega_0)$ as in Blanchard and Katz (1999), see Asada *et al.* (2006a) for details, and as cost pressure term a weighted average of short-term (perfectly anticipated) price inflation $\hat{p}$ and the medium-term inflation climate $\pi^c$ in which the economy is operating.

As the wage PC is constructed it is subject to an interaction between the external labor market and the utilization of the workforce within firms. Higher demand pressure on the external labor market translates itself here into higher workforce wage demand pressure within firms (and demand for a reduced length of the normal working day, etc.), an interaction between two utilization rates of the labor force that has to be and will be taken note of in the formulation the employment policy of firms. Demand pressure on the labor market thus exhibits two interacting components, where employed workers may make their behavior dependent upon.

We use the output-capital ratio $y = Y/K$ to measure the output gap in the price inflation PC and again the deviation of the real wage $\omega = w/p$ from the steady state real wage $\omega_0$ as error correction expression in the price PC. Cost pressure in this price PC is formulated as a weighted average of short-term (perfectly anticipated) wage inflation and again our concept of an inflationary climate $\pi^c$. In this price Phillips curve we have three elements of cost pressure interacting with each other: a medium-term one (the inflationary climate) and two short terms ones, basically the level of real unit-wage labor costs (a Blanchard and Katz (1999) error correction term) and the current rate of wage inflation, which taken by itself would represent a constant markup pricing rule. This basic rule is, however, modified by these other cost-pressure terms and in particular also made dependent on the state of the business cycle by way of the demand pressure term $y - \bar{y}$ in the market for goods.

On the demand side of the model we use for reasons of simplicity the conventional dynamic multiplier process (in place of a full-fledged Metzlerian inventory adjustment mechanism) as in Asada *et al.* (2006b), i.e.:

$$\hat{Y} = \dot{Y}/Y = \beta_y(Y^d/Y - 1) + \bar{a} \tag{3.3}$$

where $Y^d, Y$ denote aggregate demand and supply and $\bar{a}$ a trend term in the behavior of capitalist firms to be explained below. Assuming a fixed proportions technology with given output-employment ratio $x = Y/L^d$ and potential output-capital ratio $y^p = Y^p/K$, allows us to determine from the output-capital ratio y the employment $u_w$ of the workforce within firms that corresponds to this activity measure y:

$$u_w = y/(xle), \quad u_w = L^d/L^w, l = L/K, e = L^w/L \tag{3.4}$$

(with $L^d$ hours worked, $L^w$ the number of workers employed within firms and with $L$ denoting labor supply). This relationship represents by and large a technical relationship (to be calculated by 'engineers') and relates hours worked to goods market activity as measured by $y$ in the way shown above.

This technological relationship must be carefully distinguished from the employment (recruitment) policy of firms that reads on the intensive form level:

$$\begin{aligned} \hat{e} &= \dot{e}/e = \beta_{eu}(u_w - \tilde{u}_f(e)) - \beta_{e\omega}(\omega - \omega_o) + \bar{a} - \hat{L}, \text{ i.e.,} \\ \dot{e} &= \beta_{eu}(y/(xl) - \tilde{u}_f(e)e) - \beta_{e\omega}(\omega - \omega_o)e + (\bar{a} - \hat{L})e, \\ &\quad \tilde{u}_f' > 0. \end{aligned} \tag{3.5}$$

Basis of this formulation of an employment policy of firms in terms of the employment rate is – by assumption – the following level form representation of this relationship:

$$\dot{L}^w = \beta_{eu}(L^d - \tilde{u}_f(e)L^w) - \beta_{e\omega}(\omega - \omega_o)L^w + \bar{a}L^w, \; i.e. \tag{3.6}$$

$$\hat{L}^w = \beta_{eu}(L^d/L^w - \tilde{u}_f(e)) - \beta_{e\omega}(\omega - \omega_o) + \bar{a} \tag{3.7}$$

where $\bar{a}$ again integrates the trend term assumed by firms into now their employment policy and where $\tilde{u}_f(e)$ represents the utilization ratio of the workforce of firms that is desired by them. This ratio is here made dependent on the rate of employment on the external labor market in a positive way, since firms will accept higher demand pressure within their workforce employment relationship (in place of the new recruitment of workers), if the external labor market has become tighter. Firms therefore react to both measures of demand pressure (in the labor market and within the production process) by an attempt to obtain some balance in these two types of wage pressure, just as in a physical capillary system. The growth rate of the workforce of firms is thus a positive function of the utilization gap $u_w - \tilde{u}_f$ of the workforce within firms, where the benchmark utilization ratio $\tilde{u}_f$ desired by firms depends positively on the outside employment ratio, since firms are inclined to allow on an average for larger utilization rates within firms when the outside labor market situation is becoming more tense. In order to obtain Equation (3.5) as the resulting law of motion for the rate of employment one simply has to take note of the definitional relationship $\hat{e} = \hat{L}^w - \hat{L}$, where $L$ denotes the labor supply in each moment in time. We have also included into the above recruitment policy a term that says that intended recruitment will be lowered in case of increasing real wage costs of firms.

In order to close the model we assume extremely classical saving habits $(s_w = 0, s_c = 1)$, i.e. the consumption-output ratio is simply given by $\omega/x$. For investment behavior we moreover assume:

$$I/K = i(\cdot) + \bar{a} = i_\rho(\rho - \rho_o) - i_e(e - \bar{e}_f) + \bar{a}, \tag{3.8}$$

with $\rho = y(1 - \omega/x)$ the current rate of profit.[3] In this equation, the magnitude $\bar{a}$ denotes a given trend investment rate, representing investor's 'animal spirits' from which firms depart in a natural way if there is excess profitability (and vice versa). Moreover, firms have a view of what the rate employment should be on the external labor market (Kalecki's (1943, Ch. 12) analysis of why 'bosses' dislike full employment) and thus reduce their (domestic) investment plans (driven by excess profitability) in situations of a tense labor market. They thus take pressure from the labor market in the future evolution of the economy by their implicit collective understanding that high pressure in the capillary system we have considered above will lead to conditions in the capital-labor relationship, unwanted by firms, since persistently high employment rates may give rise to significant changes of workforce participation with respect to firms' decision making, in the hiring and firing decision of firms, in reductions of the workday, etc. not at all liked by 'industrial leaders'.

We view the rate $\bar{a}$, the trend investment decision of capitalist firms as the (mathematically seen) independent variable of the model, whereas any changes in the growth rate $n$ of the labor force, the so-called natural rate of growth, are following the growth rate of the capital stock more or less passively and have in any case little to do with the biological reproduction rate of a given society. There are, of course, many possible ways in which the growth rate of the labor force $\hat{L}$ (not the growth rate of the working population) is governed by the accumulation path of the economy. In this chapter we make two specific (simplifying) assumptions in this regard: first $\hat{L} = \bar{a}$ and later on even $\hat{L} = \hat{K}$, in order to concentrate on the interaction of income distribution with the goods market dynamics and the demand pressures on the labor market these former dynamics give rise to.

The model neglects on the quantity side unintended inventory changes and on the value side windfall profits or losses caused by the assumed possibility of a discrepancy between savings and investment. It describes through its equations a closed economy where we abstract from all government activities and where we ignore the behavior of central banks due to our neglect of real interest effects on the demand side of the model (consisting of workers' consumption and firms' investment demands solely). We also abstract here from the role of financial markets in the financing of investment decisions by assuming that all profits are paid out as dividends and that investment is purely equity-financed with no feedback on the assumed consumption behavior, see Chiarella and Flaschel (2000: Ch. 6) for the budget equations that allow for such flow consistency.

As in earlier work, see Asada *et al.* (2006a) in particular, we can derive as reduced forms from the described wage-price spiral a real wage dynamic $\hat{\omega} = \hat{w} - \hat{p}$, which does not depend on the inflationary climate term $\pi^c$ and an augmented reduced-form price PC where $\pi^c$ has a coefficient of unity. However, since the real rate of interest is no issue in our model, this latter reduced-form equation does not yet play a role in the implied dynamical system to be considered below. In this system we only need to consider the dynamics of real wages $\omega$, of the output-capital ratio $y$ and of the rate of employment $e$ (plus full employment labor intensity $l = L/K$ if the natural rate of growth would be given exogenously).

## The implied dynamics

We now reduce the considered macrodynamic model to a system of four differential equations in the pairs of state variables $y, e$ and $\omega, l$. The first pair can be considered to describe the Keynes-Kalecki goods market and employment dynamics and the second one the Goodwin-Rose growth cycle dynamics, though Kalecki and Rose have also included income distribution effects and goods market effects in their analysis of the capital accumulation process, respectively. Later on in this chapter we assume, by way of a special assumption on labor supply $L$, that the state variable $l$ stays at its steady state level and thus will reduce the dynamics to dimension 3 then.

As the model is formulated we therefore have as laws of motion on its supply side, a law describing the dynamics of real wages and one growth law, describing the capital accumulation induced by the assumed investment behavior. The inflationary tension resulting on the nominal side of the considered dynamics does not yet play a role in their core dynamics, since we do not have any real interest rate effects or wealth effects included in its formulation. On the demand side we have the law of motion for capacity utilization of firms, measured by $y = Y/K$, and the law of motion of the employment rate $e$ on the external labor market implied by the employment policy of firms.

Note that we assume in this section that $\hat{L}$ is given by $\bar{a}$, i.e. this latter trend term also applies to the conditions of labor supply, and thus not only to investment and the dynamic multiplier story that is based on it (and the employment policy of firms). Note, furthermore, that aggregate demand per unit of capital, the Keynesian heart of our accumulation dynamics, is always given by the expression:

$$y^d = (\omega/x)y + i(\cdot) + \bar{a}, \quad i(\cdot) = i_\rho(\rho - \rho_o) - i_e(e - \bar{e}_f), \quad \rho = (1 - \omega/x)y$$

in the following.

### *DAD: multiplier and employment dynamics*

The Disequilibrium AD or DAD part of the model is given by:

$$\begin{aligned} \dot{y} &= -\beta_y(1 - \frac{\omega}{x})y + (\beta_y - y)i(\cdot) + \beta_y\bar{a}, \quad y = Y/K \quad \text{with} \qquad (3.9) \\ \dot{y}_y &= -\beta_y(1 - \frac{\omega}{x}) + (\beta_y - y)(1 - \frac{\omega}{x})i_\rho \\ &= -\beta_y(1 - i_\rho)(1 - \frac{\omega}{x}) - y(1 - \frac{\omega}{x})i_\rho \end{aligned}$$

We assume that $\beta_y > y_o$ holds in all of the following and thus get that the sign of $1 - i_\rho$ is decisive for the sign of $\dot{y}_y$, which is negative if the propensity to invest into capital stock growth from the obtained profit rate is less than one at the steady state.

This law of motion is obtained from:

$$\frac{\dot{Y}}{Y} = \beta_y(\frac{Y^d}{Y} - 1) + \bar{a}, \quad C = \omega L^d = \frac{\omega}{x} Y \quad (s_w = 0, s_c = 1) \quad \text{and}$$
$$\frac{I}{K} = i(\cdot) + \bar{a} = i_\rho(y(1 - \frac{\omega}{x}) - \rho_o) - i_e(e - \bar{e}_f) + \bar{a}.$$

We furthermore have:

$$u_w = \frac{1}{xl}\frac{y}{e} \quad \text{via fixed proportions in production}$$

which represents a static (technological) relationship between the ratio of capital stock utilization $y = Y/K$ and the ratio of workforce utilization $u_w$ within firms.

Finally:

$$\dot{e} = \beta_{eu}(y/(xl) - \tilde{u}_f(e)e) - \beta_{e\omega}(\omega - \omega_o)e - i(\cdot)e, \quad \tilde{u}_f' > 0. \tag{3.10}$$

gives again the law of motion for the employment policy of firms.

The reduced-form dynamic IS-relationship is depending on income distribution (due to the assumed savings behavior) and on the investment decision of firms in a specific way, translated into the time rate of change of the output-capital ratio by means of the adjustment speed in the dynamic multiplier process that is driving the goods market. The utilization ratio of the employed labor force is a linear function of the ratio between the utilization ratio of the capital stock $y$, and the utilization rate of the labor force $e$ on the external labor with a multiplier that is given by the product of the reciprocal values of both labor productivity and the full employment labor-capital ratio (this expression has to be inserted into the laws of motion in various places in order to get an autonomous system of four differential equations describing the evolution of the considered macroeconomy). The expression $u_w$ can be altered by firms through changes in labor productivity (technical change), by manipulating labor supply or the external employment rate or – politically – by enforced changes in income distribution that lead to appropriate changes of Keynesian aggregate demand.

### *DAS: real wage dynamic and capital accumulation*

The Disequilibrium AS or briefly DAS part of the model is given by:[4]

$$\frac{\dot{\omega}}{\omega} = \kappa[(1-\kappa_p)(\beta_{we}(e-\bar{e}) + \beta_{wu}(u_w - \tilde{u}_w(e)) - (1-\kappa_w)\beta_{py}(y-\bar{y})]$$
$$- \kappa[(1-\kappa_p)\beta_{w\omega}\ln(\frac{\omega}{\omega_o}) + (1-\kappa_w)\beta_{p\omega}\ln(\frac{\omega}{\omega_o})], \quad u_w = \frac{1}{xl}\frac{y}{e} \tag{3.11}$$
$$\hat{l} = \hat{L} - \hat{K} = -i_\rho(\rho - \rho_o) + i_e(e - \bar{e}_f) = -i(\cdot) \tag{3.12}$$

if it is assumed that labor force growth is governed by $n = \hat{L} = \bar{a}$ which is an assumption of at least the same ideal type as the assumption of constant labor force growth.

The law of motion for the real wage depends on a variety of demand pressure items, since all cost-pressure terms (relating to the $\kappa$-coefficients) can be reduced to their underlying demand pressure terms when the two linear equations of nominal wage and price dynamics are solved for the two unknowns $\hat{w} - \pi^c, \hat{w} - \pi^c$, from which $\hat{\omega} = \hat{w} - \hat{p}$, $\omega = w/p$ can then be obtained. Of course, demand pressure terms on the labor market influence real wages in a positive fashion and those on the goods market in a negative way. The Blanchard and Katz real wage error correction terms in the WPC and PPC both act on real wages in a negative fashion as suggested by the label that is used for their working.

We assume in a later stability analysis for the law of motion of real wages that the insider term $\beta_{wu}(u_w - \tilde{u}_w(e))$ is of a size that does not alter the positive dependence of real wage growth on the rate of employment $e$ and its negative dependence on the ratio of capacity utilization $y$. Depending on the choice of parameter values it may, however, easily happen that the term $u_w = \frac{1}{xl}\frac{y}{e}$ overthrows the negative influence of $y$ on the growth rate of real wages, in which case the dynamics of real wages is completely dominated by the labor market inside and outside of firms and thus completely labor-market-led. Since $u_w$ depends negatively on the rate of employment $e$ it may, furthermore, also happen that an overall negative dependence of $\hat{\omega}$ on the rate of employment is established. The movement of real wages is thus subject to a variety of influences which may imply that it is not moving in a clear or even in a strictly pro-cyclical fashion.

## 4D steady state configuration and reduced-form 3D dynamics

In this section we will calculate the steady state of the dynamics (3.9)–(3.12). This system is an autonomous one, once the definitions of $u_w$ and $\rho$ have been inserted into it. As steady state solutions we then obtain the following:

### *Steady state solution of the 4D dynamics*

From the conditions $\dot{y} = 0, \hat{l} = -i(\cdot) = 0$ we get as our first steady state result that there must hold for the rate of profit $\rho$:

$$\rho_o = y_o(1 - \omega_o/x) = \bar{a}, \quad i.e., \tag{3.13}$$

capitalists get what they spend in the steady state. Note that the values of $y_o, \omega_o$ are restricted by this steady state condition, but remain to be determined still.

Next we find, by way of $i_\rho(\cdot) = i(\cdot) = 0$, that there holds for the steady state rate of employment on the external labor market:

$$e_o = \bar{e}_f \quad \neq \bar{e} \quad \text{in general.} \tag{3.14}$$

This states that the steady state rate of employment (not at all to be interpreted as an inflation-oriented NAIRU rate of employment)[5]) is solely determined by the investment behavior of firms, i.e. by the benchmark level they set for this rate, beyond which firms believe that the social structure of accumulation (workforce participation in firms' decision making and the like) will change significantly to their disadvantage.

As an intermediate step we, furthermore, get for the value of $(y/l)_o$ by way of the condition:

$$\tilde{u}_f(e_o) = (y/l)_o/(xe_o),$$

i.e. the steady state value:

$$(y/l)_o = \tilde{u}_f(e_o)xe_o$$

and from this for the utilization ratio of the workforce of firms in the steady state

$$u_{wo} = \tilde{u}_f(e_o), \quad \text{i.e.}$$

the steady state utilization rate of the labor force is determined by the benchmark rate in the employment policy of firms which in turn depends on the external rate of employment that firms desire in order to keep workforce relationships within firms under sufficient control.

Making use of the condition $\hat{\omega}(\cdot) = 0$ in the reduced-form expression for real wage dynamics then gives ($\kappa_w < 1$):

$$y_o = \bar{y} + \frac{(1-\kappa_p)(\beta_{we}(e_o - \bar{e}) + \beta_{wu}(\tilde{u}_f(e_o) - \tilde{u}_w(e_o))}{(1-\kappa_w)\beta_{py}} \neq \bar{y} \tag{3.15}$$

since the Blanchard / Katz error correction terms are zero in the steady state (by assumption). We assume that the adjustment parameters in the numerator of this expression are sufficiently small such that – in the case where $e_o - \bar{e}$ or $u_{wo} - \tilde{u}_w(e_o)$ become negative – the steady state output capital ratio $y_o$ stays positive. We note also that increasing labor market flexibility in whatever respect may in this approach have positive or negative effects on steady state capacity utilization $y_o = (Y/K)_o$ depending on the benchmark choices of both workers and firms. We also note, however, that the model is 'ill-defined' (indeterminate) in the case where price inflation does not depend on the demand pressure in the market for goods.

Common inside and outside employment benchmark levels of firms and workers give rise to $y_o = \bar{y}$ (also for $\beta_p y = 0$) and to specific deviations from this simple benchmark case otherwise. We note, however, in addition that there need not exist any pressure around the balanced growth path (and even less far away from it) that tends to harmonize the various benchmarks on the labor and the goods market with each other. Instead, the departure of steady state values from their corresponding benchmark values, in the wage and price Phillips curves in particular, simply means that the steady state inherits some of the problems that govern the course of the economy in general such as upward or downward pressure on wage and price inflation that is neutralized through opposite deviations from the benchmark levels.

On the basis of the steady state value for the output capital ratio $y_o$ we finally get:

$$\omega_o = (1 - \bar{a}/y_o)x \tag{3.16}$$

$$l_o = y_o/(y/l)_o \tag{3.17}$$

where $\omega_o$ is the value used in the dynamic error correction mechanism (and the corresponding $\rho_o$ in the investment equation of firms) as the relevant benchmark values.

All steady state values are positive as long as this holds for the parameter $\bar{a}$. Here it must however also be assumed that $\bar{a} < y_o$ holds true. If this parameter is increased, the steady rate of profit increases while the steady state value of the real wage declines (since output per unit of capital remains constant in such a case). There are no further changes implied by such an increase in trend investment, up to the fact that capitalist firms here always exactly get what they spend. Note, furthermore, that the steady state value of $y$ depends on various adjustment speeds in the wage-price module and is in particular not defined if $\beta_{py}$ becomes zero (unless equal to $\bar{y}$). This problem on the real side of the considered dynamics will disappear, when nominal adjustment problems and a Taylor interest rate policy rule are taken into account in a later section of this chapter.

If – by contrast – the employment rate target of firms is decreased (because they want to exercise further pressure on the behavior of their workforce) we have that the steady state rate of employment on the external labor market is fully adjusting to this new target of firms implying in addition a fall in the steady state values of $y_o, \omega_o$, while the steady rate of profit does not change in such a case. We thus primarily get in such a situation a lower steady state employment rate, a lower steady rate of capacity utilization and a lower steady state share of wages in national income.

### *Reduced-form 3D dynamics*

We now assume for the following stability analysis that even $n := \hat{K}$ holds (for analytical simplicity) and have of course the same steady state solution as before (with $l$ now frozen – by assumption – at its predetermined steady state value $l_o$ at all points in time). The implication of this assumption is a modified law of motion for the employment rate which now integrates the capital accumulation relationship (as represented by the law of motion for full employment labor intensity ratio $l = L/K$) into the law of motion for $e$. The implied DAS-DAD dynamics are now:

$$\dot{y} = f(y,e,\omega) = -\beta_y(1-\frac{\omega}{x})y + (\beta_y - y)i(\cdot) + \beta_y\bar{a}, \tag{3.18}$$

$$\dot{e} = g(y,e,\omega) = \beta_{eu}(\frac{y}{xl_o} - \tilde{u}_f(e)e) - \beta_{e\omega}(\omega-\omega_o)e - i(\cdot)e, \tag{3.19}$$

$$\hat{\omega} = h(y,e,\omega), \quad h_y < 0,\ h_e > 0,\ h_\omega < 0, \quad \text{see eq.}(3.11) \tag{3.20}$$

with $i(\cdot) = i_\rho(\rho - \rho_o) - i_e(e - \bar{e}_f)$, $\rho = (1-\omega/x)y$. Note again that we have assumed in the third law of motion, see (3.11), that real wage growth depends positively on the rate of employment $e$, i.e. we take on a Goodwin (1967) perspective in this matter. However, the influences of changing capacity utilization $y$ are here separated from employment rate changes and act negatively on real wage growth, dominating the positive effect on this growth rate that is caused by the accompanying parallel effect on workforce utilization ratios. Note also that the first equation allows for two cases (and a borderline case), namely:

**Case 1:** $f_y < 0, f_e < 0, f_\omega > 0$ or
**Case 2:** $f_y > 0, f_e < 0, f_\omega < 0,$

respectively. This is implied by the following partial derivatives:

$$\dot{y}_y = c(1-\frac{\omega}{x}), \quad \dot{y}_\omega = -c\frac{y}{x}, \quad c = -\beta_y(1-i_\rho) - yi_\rho = (\beta_y - y)i_\rho - \beta_y.$$

We thus have that a partially stable integrated multiplier process ($i_\rho$ sufficiently small) is necessarily coupled with a wage-led regime in the aggregate demand function and an unstable multiplier process with a profit-led regime in the aggregate demand function. These two cases thereby give rise to two typical stability scenarios in our model of Kalecki-Goodwin-Rose (KGR) accumulation and employment dynamics. The critical condition that separates these two cases from each other is given by: $i_\rho^c = \beta_y/(\beta_y - y_o) > 1$ or $\beta_y^c = y_o i_\rho/(i_\rho - 1)$ as far as steady state stability analysis is concerned. Note that the steady state of the reduced 3D dynamics is the same as the one calculated for the originally 4D dynamics (if their steady state value $l_o$ is inserted into the 3D case).

On the basis of the assumed labor and goods market dominance in the third law of motion we indeed get for the sign structure in the Jacobian of the dynamics at the steady state (under the not very restrictive assumption $\beta_y - y_o > 0$ sufficiently large):

$$J = \begin{pmatrix} + & - & - \\ \pm & \pm & \pm \\ - & + & - \end{pmatrix} \quad or \quad \begin{pmatrix} - & - & + \\ \pm & \pm & \pm \\ - & + & - \end{pmatrix}.$$

We assume for the time being that the entry $J_{23}$ is positive, i.e. that $\beta_{e\omega}$ is chosen sufficiently small.

In the first case we then get instability in particular if the dynamic multiplier process works with sufficient speed ($\beta_y$ sufficiently large in the entry $J_{11}$) and thus obtain a Kaldor (1940) situation with respect to the search for bounding mechanisms (in a profit-led environment). In the other case, we have a wage-led situation in the goods market ($\dot{y}_\omega > 0$) and thus get instability in the assumed case of a labor-market-led real wage dynamics if this feedback structure becomes sufficiently dominant (in the destabilizing interaction resulting from the entries $J_{13}$,$J_{31}$ in the Jacobian $J$). In between these two situations are of course also parameter domains with local stability characteristics. The overall conclusion, however, is that certain bounding mechanisms (like downward money wage rigidity) have to be added in general in order to keep the dynamics an economically viable one.

Summing up, we have on this level of generality a model type where trend investment and target employment of firms basically determine the long-run outcome and where the dynamics around the implied steady state positions is driven in an unstable or stable fashion by a Keynesian dynamic multiplier process that depends on income distribution and by an advanced type of wage-price spiral and the resulting real wage dynamics, with insider and outsider effects and an employment recruitment policy of firms in addition (that links inside employment rates with outside employment rates).

## Feedback structures of KMGS and KGR dynamics: a brief comparison

In this section we briefly compare the model of this chapter with the related K(eynes) M(etzler) G(oodwin) S(teindl) model introduced and investigated in Asada *et al.* (2006a). The purpose of this section is to show how these two related models compare and differ in their feedback channels and what feedback channels of a Kaleckian approach to accumulation dynamics are still missing in the KGR model of the present chapter.

### *Feedback channels in KMGS growth*

The original KMG model, see Chiarella and Flaschel (2000) and Chiarella *et al.* (2005) for its derivation and detailed investigation, contained four important feedback chains, the interest rate channel (Keynes- vs. Mundell-effects), the real wage channel (normal vs. adverse Rose effects) and the Metzlerian inventory dynamics (which is of a multiplier-accelerator type). The KMGS model of Asada *et al.* (2006b) – like the present model – excludes two of these feedback chains (Keynes- and Mundell-effects), but introduces two new feedback chains: a dynamic Harrodian accelerator mechanism in fixed capital formation and a Kalecki-Steindl reserve army mechanism. These feedback chains interact with each other in the full 5D dynamics of the KMGS model and different feedback mechanisms can become dominant, depending on the parameters of the model.

*1. The Keynes and Mundell effects.* Neither the stabilizing Keynes effect nor the destabilizing Mundell effect is present in the KMGS model. The reason is simple: we have excluded there any influence of the real rate of interest on investment and consumption (and also wealth effects on consumption are ignored). Thus, although price inflation appears in the real wage dynamics, it does not affect aggregate demand.

*2. A Metzler type inventory accelerator mechanism.* The Metzlerian inventory adjustment process defines two laws of motion, one for sales expectations and one for inventory changes. The crucial parameters in these adjustment equations are the adjustment speeds of sales expectations and of intended inventory changes, respectively, where the first one tends to be stabilizing and the second one destabilizing.

*Table 3.2* The feedback structure of the KMGS model ($u$ capacity utilization)

| | |
|---|---|
| Metzlerian Accelerator Mechanism: | $y^e \overset{+}{\longmapsto} y \overset{+}{\longmapsto} y^d \overset{+}{\longmapsto} y^e$ |
| Harrodian Accelerator Mechanism: | $u \overset{+}{\longmapsto} \dot{a} \overset{+}{\longmapsto} \dot{u}$ |
| Goodwin/Rose Reserve Army Mechanism: | $\omega \overset{+:C(-:I)}{\longmapsto} u, e \overset{+/-}{\longmapsto} \dot{\omega}$ |
| Kalecki/Steindl Reserve Army Mechanism: | $e \overset{-}{\longmapsto} \dot{a} \overset{+}{\longmapsto} \dot{u} \overset{+}{\longmapsto} \dot{e}$ |

*3. A Harrod type investment accelerator mechanism.* This mechanism works in Asada *et al.* (2006b) through parameters in the investment equations. Increased capacity utilization leads to higher investment (both directly and via the gradual changes in the trend of capital accumulation), thereby leading to an increase in aggregate demand. As a result, sales expectations increase and produce a further rise in output and capacity utilization. Hence, a dynamic Harrodian multiplier-accelerator process here interacts with distribution effects and the Metzlerian inventory adjustment process. Trend investment can be seen as representing an investment climate – like the inflation climate – or as slowly evolving 'animal spirits', and it may be reasonable to assume that the direct effect on current investment is stronger than the indirect effect on trend investment.

*4. A Goodwin/Rose type reserve army mechanism.* There are additional feedback channels of Goodwin-Rose type. The specification of aggregate demand in KMGS implied that the short-term effect of real wages on goods demand is positive (via workers' consumption). Hence, real wages will be further stabilizing if price flexibility with respect to demand pressure on the market for goods is sufficiently high and wage flexibility with respect to demand pressure on the market for labor is sufficiently low (the delayed negative effect of real wages on investment behavior will of course just establish the opposite conclusions).

*5. A Kalecki/Steindl type reserve army mechanism (the conflict about full employment and its consequences).* This conflict is represented in the present chapter by the parameter $i_e$. We here assume, as in Flaschel and Skott (2006), Asada *et al.* (2006b), that 'bosses dislike full employment'. Increases in the rate employment $e$ thus exert a downward pressure in the investment demand function, leading to reduced economic activity and providing a check to further increases in the rate of employment.

The feedback channels described in 2–5 are summarized in Table 3.2.

The full interaction of these feedback chains determines the stability of the interior steady state position of the considered model. Based on our partial analysis of the feedback channels, we expected and have confirmed in Asada *et al.* (2006) that wage flexibility, fast inventory adjustment and fast investment trend adjustment are destabilizing, while price flexibility is stabilizing (if the corresponding Rose effect is tamed by assuming appropriate investment behavior). Manipulating the stabilizing parameters appropriately may thus help to create local stability or allow at least to ensure the boundedness and economic viability of the trajectories in the case of local instability.

## The feedback structure of the KGR model of capital accumulation and employment dynamics

Comparing the feedback chains of the KGR model of this chapter to the feedback channels just discussed first of all shows that Keynes and Mundell effects are ignored here too, since there is not yet a real rate of interest effect in aggregate goods demand (and since monetary policy, be it money supply oriented or interest rate oriented, is not yet an issue here).

Furthermore, we use in KGR growth only a dynamic multiplier story (to describe Keynesian goods market quantity adjustment process) in place of a (possibly accelerating) Metzlerian inventory and sales expectations adjustment process. Nevertheless we can have unstable adjustment processes in the multiplier process too, if we assume that the propensity to spend in aggregate demand is larger than one. Besides no Metzlerian accelerator mechanism we also do not yet allow for Harrodian fixed capital investment accelerator processes.

As in the KMGS approach we have two reserve army mechanisms present in our KGR variant of this approach that are related of the work of Goodwin (1967) and Kalecki (1943) and that interact with Rose (1967) type real wage feedbacks:

$$\omega \overset{\pm}{\longmapsto} y^d \overset{+}{\longmapsto} y \overset{+}{\longmapsto} u_w = \frac{1}{xl_o}\frac{y}{e} \overset{+}{\longmapsto} e \overset{\pm}{\longmapsto} \hat{\omega}.$$

In this feedback channel, we have in addition (via our formulation of Okun's Law) a direct effect of real wages on the rate of employment and also a negative effect of the rate of employment onto its rate of change (via the workforce utilization target of firms) and finally, of course, the influence of the assumed labor supply reaction to capital stock growth. Furthermore there are opposing influences of economic activity $y$ on the growth rate of real wages, via the goods market and price inflation dynamics and via the utilization ratio of the workforce within firms and money wage inflation dynamics. Finally, there is also the ambiguous effect of changes of the rate of employment on the real wage, directly and positive through the external labor market and indirectly and partially negative through changes in workforce utilization within firms.

The Goodwin reserve army mechanism is working in this Keynesian aggregate demand environment if increase in real wages and decreases in profitability decrease aggregate demand (if this demand is profit-led) and if this decreases the rate of employment via decreases in capital stock utilization, thereby providing a check to further real wage increases. Yet, the Goodwin reserve army mechanism was initially a purely supply side phenomenon and is not easily identified in a Keynesian goods demand environment as we will see later on. Furthermore, the alternative reserve army mechanism, the one of Kalecki (1943), works independently of the shown real wage feedback channel, since it postulates that increases in the rate of employment directly decrease the growth rate of the capital stock which decreases aggregate demand, output and thereby provides a check to further increases in the rate of employment. While the real wage channel may give rise to a variety of (un-)stable feedback situations, the Kaleckian mechanism should by and large contribute to the stability of the considered steady state (though it may undermine this stability to a certain degree if labor supply is capital stock growth driven).

In closing this discussion we briefly stress again the importance of the assumed Okun-type two stage links from the goods market to the labor market which translate capital utilization ratio into labor force utilization ratios and changes in the rate of employment on the external labor market. Taking all these feedback mechanisms into account we intend to make use of them in the numerical section such that an assumed locally explosive adjustment process around the balanced growth path is turned into economically viable (bounded) dynamics through appropriate nonlinearities in the adjustment functions of the model. First of all we, however, consider a situation where under strong assumptions indeed a locally asymptotically stable and thus an attracting steady state can be shown to exist.

In the preceding section we have, in addition, investigated minor further destabilizing feedback chains caused by our assumptions on labor force growth that are, however, not of central importance in the present chapter, since they are easily modified by way of other assumptions on this rate of growth. Nevertheless these feedback chains suggest that recruitment policies of firms (acting on the participation rate of the domestic labor force or on foreign labor markets) may indeed contribute to economic instability when coupled with certain further reaction patterns of the model.

## *A feedback-suggested local stability scenario*

We now investigate the interaction of the feedback structures considered in the preceding subsection on the basis of the following additional assumption (besides the ones already made for real wage dynamics: $\hat{\omega}_y < 0, \hat{\omega}_e > 0$ and for the dynamic multiplier process $\dot{y}_y < 0$ $(\beta_y > y_o)$ which implied $\dot{y}_\omega > 0$).

*Assumptions:*

1. We first assume that $\beta_{eu}, \beta_{e\omega}$ are large enough to dominate the signs of the partial derivatives in the law of motion for the employment rate $e$.

2. Furthermore, we assume the parameter $\beta_y$ to be large enough (and $i_\rho < 1$) such that the sign of $b = a_1(\beta_y)a_2(\beta_y) - a_3(\beta_y)$ in the Routh Hurwitz conditions is determined by $a_1(\beta_y)a_2(\beta_y)$, which is a quadratic function of $\beta_y$, while the determinant is only linear in $\beta_y$. The economy is wage led in such a situation and the dynamic multiplier stable from the perspective of the involved partial derivatives.

3. Finally, we assume that the parameters $\beta_{we}, \beta_{wu}$ are small enough and thus not decisive for the sign of the determinant of the system at the steady state (the Rose feedback channel $J_{13}J_{21}J_{32}$ for this wage led economy is assumed as being sufficiently weak).

This in particular means that the influence of the $-i(\cdot)$ term in the equation for the adjustment of the employment rate, describing the effect of the recruitment policy of firms in their search for additional labor force supply, is not so strong that the direct effects of increased capacity utilization, increased external employment and an increasing real wage are overthrown.

For the considered Jacobian this in sum gives:

$$J = \begin{pmatrix} J_{11} & J_{12} & J_{13} \\ J_{21} & J_{22} & J_{23} \\ J_{31} & J_{32} & J_{33} \end{pmatrix} = \begin{pmatrix} - & - & + \\ + & - & - \\ - & \pm & - \end{pmatrix}.$$

In this Jacobian we have in the first row the negative multiplier effect $J_{11} < 0$, the Kaleckian reserve army effect $J_{12} < 0$, and the positive effect of a wage-led economy $J_{13} > 0$. In the second row we have the assumed dominance of the $\beta_e' s$ and a negative effect of real wages on (recruited) labor force growth, represented by $J_{23}$.

Indeed, under the assumed conditions, we can easily derive the validity of the Routh-Hurwitz conditions $(a_1, a_2, a_3, b > 0)$. We obviously have $a_1 > 0$ for the diagonal terms in $J$. With respect to $a_2$ only the term $J_{23}J_{32}$ can create instability problems. This term has, however, been assumed to be neglectable. This same assumption (on $J_{23}$) also allows to ignore a destabilizing effect in the determinant of $J$.

We thus in sum get that the parameters $\beta_y, \beta_e' s$ and $\beta_{w's}, i_\rho$ can be crucial for macroeconomic stability (with the former to be chosen sufficiently large and the latter sufficiently small). Yet, the opposite situation may only be one among many other where no local stability result may hold. It is therefore not unlikely that the steady state may be locally repelling and that the forces that can make such an economy a viable one must therefore be found in certain behavioral nonlinearities that limit the dynamics to economically meaningful domains when it departs too much from its steady state position.

**Remark**: The stability result just achieved will get lost in situations where insiders dominate the evolution of the real wage (both with respect to the rate of employment $e$ and the rate of capacity utilization $y$), in particular if Blanchard and Katz error correction is weak, since an increasing parameter $\beta_{wu}$ will imply a negative value for the $a_2$ Routh-Hurwitz polynomial parameter (if chosen sufficiently large). Insiders may therefore destabilize situation of economic prosperity if they last sufficiently long.

## *Consensus-driven economies: Attraction towards accepted steady state positions*

The Kaleckian reserve army mechanism (like the Goodwinian one) may not be optimal for the stable evolution of modern market economies, both from the economic and the social point of view. Both mechanism correct results that are unwanted by firms and their owners through mass unemployment (and supporting economic policy) with all its consequences for the economic and social evolution of the considered society. We thus now introduce some further assumptions on the parameters of the model that characterize our model economy that imply its stable evolution around an steady state path that is satisfactory both from the workers' and the firms' point of view.

Specifically, we assume that demand pressure in the labor market (both inside and outside of the firm) does not influence the rate of wage inflation very much, i.e. the wage level is a fairly stable magnitude. Furthermore, the Kaleckian reserve army mechanism is absent from the model ($i_e = 0$). Moreover, the benchmark values for demand pressures and the employment policy of firms are all given magnitudes, consistent with each other and all sufficiently high to not imply labor market segmentation and significant disqualification of unemployed workers (this can be coupled with flexible hiring and firing policies then, i.e. the parameter $\beta_{eu}$ may be chosen as large). Finally, but not really necessary, we may assume $\kappa_w, \kappa_p = 0$, i.e. cost-pressure on the market for labor as well as for goods is only relevant if it becomes permanent in nature.

These conditions imply as Jacobian matrix around such a 'satisfactory' steady state:

$$J = \begin{pmatrix} J_{11} & J_{12} & J_{13} \\ J_{21} & J_{22} & J_{23} \\ J_{31} & J_{32} & J_{33} \end{pmatrix} = \begin{pmatrix} - & 0 & + \\ + & - & \pm \\ - & 0 & - \end{pmatrix}.$$

It is easy to show for this case of a wage-led economy that all Routh-Hurwitz conditions are valid in this situation, i.e. the steady state of the economy is not only sufficiently good in nature, but also attracting. We thus have another case here where now a flexible labor market, a balanced workforce participation within firms and a balanced choice of working hours per week may be in harmony with each other and may work satisfactorily well in an environment that is close to balanced growth. Such consensus-driven economies can be usefully compared with economies that are equally flexible in their adjustment mechanisms, but subject to significant reserve army fluctuations as well as with economies where a variety of rigidities are working in addition.[6]

## Local instability and global boundedness

We continue to investigate the 3D dynamics in the state variables $y, e, \omega$:

$$\dot{y} = f(y,e,\omega) = -\beta_y(1-\frac{\omega}{x})y + (\beta_y - y)i(\cdot) + \beta_y\bar{a},$$

$$\dot{e} = g(y,e,\omega) = \beta_{eu}(\frac{y}{xl_o} - \tilde{u}_f(e)e) - \beta_{e\omega}(\omega - \omega_o)e - i(\cdot)e,$$

$$\hat{\omega} = h(y,e,\omega), \quad h_y < 0,\ h_e > 0,\ h_\omega < 0, \qquad \text{see Equation (3.11)}$$

where $i(\cdot) = i_\rho(\rho - \rho_o) - i_e(e - \bar{e}_f), \quad \rho = (1-\omega/x)y$ in order to turn now to the analysis of partial situations (in phases of prosperity or stagnation, respectively) where local steady state instability is sooner or later tamed by certain turning points during the evolution of such boom or busts. We first consider reasons that lead to the instability of the balanced growth path of the investigated economy, before we study factors which may lead to turning points in these phases when the economy departs too much from the balanced growth path scenario.

### *Conflict-driven economies: Repelling steady state configurations*

We here again consider the regime of a stable multiplier process, i.e. also of a wage-led economy, the empirically more relevant one and now indeed consider such a regime close to the steady state of the dynamics. We assume that the Kaleckian reserve army mechanism is not working close to the steady state ($i_e = 0$), that the parameter $\beta_{e\omega}$ in Okun's law is small close to balanced growth and that Blanchard and Katz error correction is weak around the steady state ($\beta_{w\omega} = 0, \beta_{p\omega} = 0$). Furthermore, insider effects are assumed to represent the dominant factor (dominating the $y-$effect) in the real wage dynamics and outsider effects dominate with respect to $e$ in the money wage dynamics. The matrix of partial derivatives $J$ of system (3.18)–(3.20) is therefore then characterized by:

$$J = \begin{pmatrix} J_{11} & J_{12} & J_{13} \\ J_{21} & J_{22} & J_{23} \\ J_{31} & J_{32} & J_{33} \end{pmatrix} = \begin{pmatrix} - & 0 & + \\ + & - & + \\ + & + & 0 \end{pmatrix}.$$

By and large the Rose real wage channel is thus the destabilizing force in the considered situation, augmented by a secondary destabilizing effect caused by the recruitment of labor supply according to the growth rate of the capital stock. These effects make the determinant of $J$ unambiguously positive and thus imply local instability around the steady state by means of the Routh-Hurwitz conditions.

By contrast, a profit-led economy would have a negative determinant in the considered situation, but would in turn be unstable if the parameter $\beta_y$ is chosen sufficiently large (giving rise to a positive trace thereby) or if the $\hat{\omega}_y$ effect is sufficiently weak or even negative (due to a larger parameter $\beta_{py}$), since the minors of order two of the Jacobian $J$ then become all negative. This latter effect is again a destabilizing Rose or real wage effect, now situated in a profit-led environment.

Inspecting the assumptions made above from a broader perspective, the objective to establish divergent dynamics around the steady state is likely met for the considered KGR economy, i.e. that there will be repelling forces around its balance growth path in general (due to a variety of reasons like dominant insider behavior and more).

### Kalecki-type upper turning points

In a situation of strong, but later on weakening economic growth (as it was given in the 1950s, 1960s and the early 1970s) we expect that the following sign structure in the considered Jacobian $J$ is the relevant one (and assume $i_\rho \leq 1$ in particular):

$$J = \begin{pmatrix} J_{11} & J_{12} & J_{13} \\ J_{21} & J_{22} & J_{23} \\ J_{31} & J_{32} & J_{33} \end{pmatrix} = \begin{pmatrix} - & - & + \\ + & - & - \\ - & + & - \end{pmatrix}.$$

We thus consider here the stabilizing role of the Kaleckian reserve army mechanism (via $J_{12}J_{21}$ in particular), a stabilizing interaction between real wages and the rate of employment (via $J_{23}J_{32}$ in particular), a stabilizing feedback established via the dynamics of capacity utilization and wage-led goods demand (via $J_{13}J_{31}$ in particular) and only stabilizing eigen-feedbacks along the diagonal of the matrix $J$.

We again have a wage-led goods market dynamics, the dominance of the $\beta_e$ terms in the employment dynamics and the dominance of the goods market with respect to utilization ratios and of the labor market with respect to employment rates as far as real wage dynamics are concerned. We then have a negative trace and only positive minors of order two for the matrix $J$. The only problematic term in the determinant of $J$ is then given by the term $J_{13}J_{21}J_{32}$ representing again a destabilizing real wage channel within the considered dynamics. The other five products composing the determinant of $J$ are all negative which suggests that the determinant is negative if this real wage channel does not work with extraordinary strength. A value of the parameter $\beta_{ey}$ chosen sufficiently low (i.e. a recruitment policy of the firms that is sufficiently sluggish in the considered situation) may for example generate such a situation. For the Routh-Hurwitz condition:

$$a_1a_2 - a_3 = (-\mathrm{tr}\, J)(J_1 + J_2 + J_3) + \det J$$

we finally get that the only problematic term in this expression is given by $J_{12}J_{23}J_{31}$, since $J_{13}J_{21}J_{32}$ is positive and since all other terms in the determinant are contained in the expressions that form $a_1a_2$. Again, it is very likely that this problematic term is dominated by the many expressions that form the remainder of $a_1a_2$. This is, for example, the case when the Kaleckian reserve army mechanism is working sluggishly ($i_e$ small, i.e. it is only working when high employment rates are becoming persistent). One may assume here that this is coupled with a weak real wage effect on the recruitment policy of firms and also a weak entry. $J_{31}$ in the dynamics of real wages.

If these conditions become established the Routh-Hurwitz conditions would imply local stability of the steady state. Yet we assume these conditions to prevail in a boom phase far off the steady state in which case we can only speculate (and test this speculation numerically) that this contributes to global stability by implying an upper turning point for the considered phase of the long cycle in income distribution and factor utilization ratios.

Of course there may come supply side bottlenecks in existence in addition in the considered situation, given by the conditions $e \leq 1, y \leq y^p$ that may help to enforce upper turning points if these bounds to the employment rate and the ratios of capacity utilization are reached. Furthermore, $\tilde{u}_f(e)$ may become steep at or close to the ceiling of absolute full employment $e = 1$.

### *Goodwin-type upper turning points?*

In the original Goodwin (1967) growth cycle model one considers a Classical profit-led economy where aggregate Keynesian goods demand does not yet play a role and where therefore the term 'profit-led' simply means that reduced profit slow down capital stock growth and the growth rate of the economy (and vice versa). This leads to increasing unemployment which sooner or later corrects income distribution again in favor of higher profitability. The turning points in the classical growth cycle model are therefore solely a consequence of changing income distribution, while production is always at full capacity.

This is different in the model type considered in this chapter, since profit-led here means that the investment parameter $i_\rho$ is so large (measured relative to the adjustment speed $\beta_y$) that at one and the same time we have that real wage increases act negatively on (Keynesian) aggregate goods demand and that the dynamic multiplier process – considered in isolation – is unstable, due to the strong influence of income $y$ on aggregate goods demand. Profit-led economies are therefore in this case plagued by partial multiplier instability which may be so strong that the trace of the Jacobian becomes positive in which case this partial instability dominates the overall outcome.

In the profit-led economy we have the following sign distribution in the Jacobian $J$ in the case of a booming economy (for which we assume that insider-outsider effects are such that real wage growth depends both positively on the utilization ratio of the workforce within firms as well as on the employment rate characterizing the external labor market:[7]

$$J = \begin{pmatrix} J_{11} & J_{12} & J_{13} \\ J_{21} & J_{22} & J_{23} \\ J_{31} & J_{32} & J_{33} \end{pmatrix} = \begin{pmatrix} + & - & - \\ + & - & - \\ + & + & - \end{pmatrix}.$$

Manipulating (reducing appropriately) the speed of adjustment $\beta_y$ characterizing the dynamic multiplier process (and the first row of the above matrix $J$) one can then first of all achieve that the trace of $J$ becomes negative. In the same way one can also ensure that the principle minors of order two are all positive. Concerning the determinant of $J$ we also get in this way (since $J_{11}, J_{13}$ are thereby reduced simultaneously) that the expression $-J_{12}(J_{21}J_{33} - J_{23}J_{31})$ becomes the dominant term in $\det J$. Yet, this remaining term has contradicting signs in its two product expressions (the first one is negative and thus supportive, while the second one is positive and thus dangerous for economic stability). Manipulating the speed term $\beta_y$ is thus not sufficient for stability and the creation of eigenvalues with only negative real parts.

There is finally again the Routh-Hurwitz condition $-trace\, J(J_1 + j_2 + j_3) + \det J$ to be considered. Here only the terms $(J_{12}J_{23}J_{31} + J_{13}J_{21}J_{32})$ in $\det J$ can create problems, since all other ones cancel against some of the all positive terms in the $-trace\, J(J_1 + j_2 + j_3)$ expression. And with respect to these remaining terms only the second one is negative and thus problematic for stability. The two terms $(J_{12}J_{23}J_{31}), (J_{13}J_{21}J_{32})$ must therefore be made small relative to their respective counterparts in order to ensure the stability of the presently considered dynamics beyond which what can be achieved by lowering the adjustment speed of the dynamic multiplier appropriately in the range of a profit-led regime.

Closer inspection, however, again reveals that the size of $J_{13}$ can again be manipulated via an appropriate reduction of the speed parameter $\beta_y$ such that the remaining terms in $-\text{tr}\, J(J_1 + j_2 + j_3)$ will dominate the second of the above problematic terms. Moreover, choosing the parameter $\beta_{e\omega}$ in an appropriate range, may eliminate the final problem for stability and thus turn all real parts of eigenvalues of the Jacobian $J$ into negative magnitudes.

We stress, however, once again that the Jacobian has only been evaluated properly at the steady state and that this therefore only proves the local asymptotic stability of this steady state position. Yet, numerical experience with growth models of this type suggests that such results apply also far off the steady state position and thus at least give rise to the hope that one can enforce turning points in economic activity (in a period of accelerating growth) by assuming the above parameter restrictions to hold sufficiently far above the steady state position.

Overall, however, our finding is that Keynesian profit-led regimes may be plagued by multiplier instability to an extent that does not bring about trajectories that are bounded from above. Policy action – of the type described in Kalecki (1943), but also monetary policy – may therefore be needed to enforce upper turning points in such periods of strong economic growth and the significant changes in the capital-labor relationship that are implied thereby.

### *Rose-type lower turning points*

In situations of a depressed economy we may by contrast find that the following sign structure in the Jacobian $J$ may apply:

$$J = \begin{pmatrix} J_{11} \, J_{12} \, J_{13} \\ J_{21} \, J_{22} \, J_{23} \\ J_{31} \, J_{32} \, J_{33} \end{pmatrix} = \begin{pmatrix} - \; 0 \; + \\ + \; - \; + \\ - \; 0 \; 0 \end{pmatrix}.$$

The Kaleckian reserve army mechanism is surely absent in such a situation ($i_e = 0$) as may be the Blanchard and Katz error correction terms. Furthermore, the dependence of real wages on the rate of employment $e$ may then be weak, since the $\beta'_w s$ are then sufficiently small. In such a situation we immediately get that the coefficients $a_1, a_2, a_3, a_1 a_2 - a_3$ in the Routh-Hurwitz conditions are all positive. The basic stabilizing mechanism is then a normal real wage or Rose effect which stimulates the economy if real wages begin to increase due to falling price levels.

The considered situation would again imply local asymptotic stability around the steady state, but is here taken once again as an indication that there are tendencies for a recovery in the considered depressed state of the economy which give rise to a lower turning point in economic activity. This tentative result must of course be checked by numerical simulations of the model that based on behavioral nonlinearities that establish the considered situations for lower (and upper) turning points far off the steady state.

### *Goodwin-type lower turning points?*

In the profit-led economy in its depressed phase we assume the following sign distribution in the Jacobian $J$:[8]

$$J = \begin{pmatrix} J_{11} \, J_{12} \, J_{13} \\ J_{21} \, J_{22} \, J_{23} \\ J_{31} \, J_{32} \, J_{33} \end{pmatrix} = \begin{pmatrix} + \; 0 \; - \\ + \; - \; + \\ + \; 0 \; 0 \end{pmatrix}.$$

We have assumed in this matrix that the Kaleckian reserve army mechanism is not working in the downward direction (since it only characterizes the economic – and political – aspects of full employment) and that the influence of the rate of employment on the dynamics of the real wage can be neglected in this state of the economy. Furthermore, Blanchard and Katz error correction is assumed to be sufficiently weak in the depression.

Dynamic multiplier instability can then be tamed by assuming that $\beta_y$ is chosen such that the trace of $J$ is negative and such that the term $J_{13}J_{31}$ dominates the principal minors of

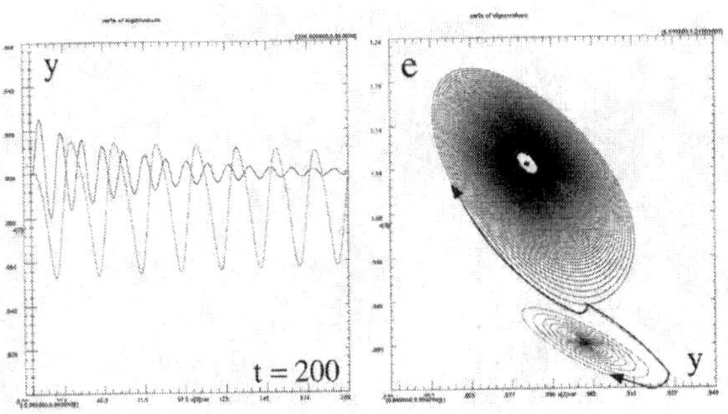


*Figure 3.1* Damped fluctuations in Kaleckian investment and employment dynamics

order two. In the considered situation we moreover always have that the determinant of $J$ is negative and is part of the $a_1a_2$ expressions, implying that the Routh Hurwitz conditions can be fulfilled in this case by an appropriately low choice of the size of the parameter $\beta_y$ within the profit-led goods demand regime. The case of lower turning points is thus easier to handle in this regime than the case of upper turning points, though, here too, much depends on the speed with which firms adjust their output decision towards their observation of aggregate goods demand.

## Numerical examples

We have shown in the preceding section that the steady state of the considered KGR dynamics may likely be an unstable one and that there are a variety of possibilities that may nevertheless keep the resulting dynamics bounded during prosperity or depression and thus economically viable. The actual occurrence of such bounding mechanism may change in time and thus be confined to certain episodes in the evolution of capitalistic market economies. Moreover, monetary or fiscal policy may also be of importance in the factual explanations of the occurrence of such regime changes in the post-war evolution of industrialized economies (for example from the welfare state to Reagonomics and economic and social deregulation), see the next section in this regard. The relevance of the model of this chapter is therefore not so much given by the implication of a unique cyclical pattern of capital accumulation and employment dynamics around its steady state position, but by its flexibility to explain a variety of partial scenarios in the evolution of capitalism after the Second World War. Clearly, though this is welcome from an economic point of view, the mathematical and numerical analysis of the dynamics is thereby made more complicated and unattractive as compared to other cycle models, like the Goodwin (1967) growth cycle dynamics, and thus less appealing from the mathematical point of view.

In this section we briefly consider in addition to our analytical results some numerical simulations of the model of this chapter on its 3D reduced-form level. We simplify the model somewhat by assuming fixed ratios $\bar{e}, \bar{u}_w, \bar{y}, \bar{e}_f, \bar{u}_f$ for the various benchmark comparisons in the wage and price PC, in the investment function and in Okun's law and assume in addition a situation where the steady state value of $y$ is equal to $\bar{y}$. We thus make use in this section of the following parameter set:[9] $\beta_{we} = 0.5, \beta_{wu} = 0.6, \kappa_w = 0.5, \bar{e} = 0.9, \bar{u}_w = 0.9, \beta_{py} = 0.385, \kappa_p = 0.5, \bar{y} = 0.9, \beta_y = 1.2, \beta_{ey} = 0.3, \bar{u}_f = 0.9, \beta_{ew} = 1.5, x = 2, y^p = 1, i_p = 1.5, i_e = 0.1, \bar{a} = 0.3, \bar{e}_f = 0.9$.

In Figure 3.1 we show for wage adjustment speeds $\beta_{we} = 0.5, \beta_{we} = 1$ the damped

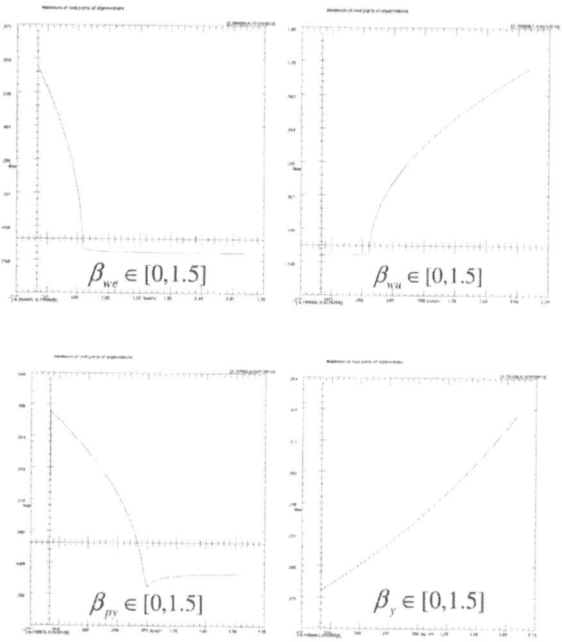


*Figure 3.2* Eigenvalue diagrams for selected speeds of adjustment

oscillations that result from these two adjustment speeds. The unexpected result of this simulation run is that there are indeed multiple stead state solution as the model is formulated, one economically meaningful solution for the lower adjustment speed and one that runs into supply bottlenecks in the labor market and thus cannot remain of the form shown in the fluctuation around the higher steady state value for $e$ in Figure 3.1. We thus get that increasing wage flexibility with respect to demand pressure on the external labor market may destabilize the steady state considered in this chapter and lead to cyclical convergence to another interior steady state with a higher NAIRU level $\bar{e}$ on the labor market and a lower NAIRU level $\bar{y}$ on the market for goods. Such results hold for a large range of adjustment speeds $\beta_y$ on the market for goods and can also occur when the parameter $\beta_{we}$ is decreased instead of its increase considered above. Note, finally, that the movements in capacity utilization and the rate of employment are far from being positively correlated due to our extended formulation of Okun's law.

In Figure 3.2 we consider eigenvalue diagrams – showing the maximum real part of eigenvalues as function of selected adjustment speeds – in order to show where the steady state becomes locally unstable (when the considered real part becomes positive). We can see from this figure that increasing the parameters $\beta_{we}$, $\beta_{py}$ is stabilizing the economy, while we have to decrease the parameter $\beta_{wu}$ in order to achieve this. The parameter $\beta_y$, when increased, is not stabilizing the economy, in contrast to what one would have expected from the partial derivative of $\dot{y}$ with respect to $y$, which is negative. Our base parameter set is chosen such that our steady state solution is unstable – as is indicated by the eigenvalue diagram for $\beta_y$, but leads nevertheless to convergent fluctuations as Figure 3.1 shows, yet convergence to a steady state for which the eigenvalues have not been calculated here.

In Figure 3.3, finally, we show further eigenvalue diagrams, now for the benchmark

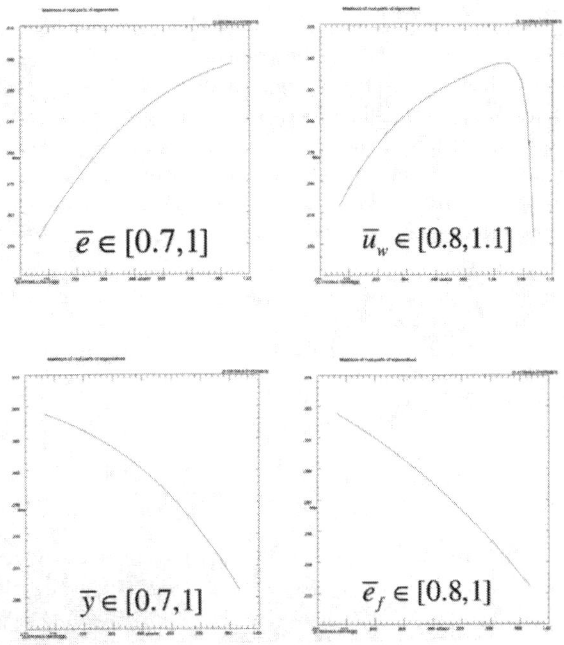


*Figure 3.3* Eigenvalue diagrams for selected benchmark values of the model

levels that define NAIRU-type utilization rates in the labor and in the goods market as well as the benchmark value for the employment rate in firms' investment behavior. We obtain from these figures that higher NAIRU levels in the labor market are destabilizing the economy further, while a higher NAIRU level in the goods market reduces the explosiveness of the steady state considered in this chapter, given through the choice of our base parameter set. Moreover, the result we here obtain for increases in the benchmark level $\bar{e}_f$ by which firms judge whether there is pressure on them due to changing work conditions is in fact stabilizing the economy (while increases in the reaction coefficient $i_e$ – not shown – is not). We conclude that the implications of the dynamics considered in this chapter can be numerous and need not confirm what is suggested through partial reasoning (concerning isolated entries of the Jacobian matrix of the dynamics at the steady state).

## Political aspects of the Kaleckian investment and employment cycle

In this chapter we have shown that the private sector of a capitalist economy may generate long cycles in investment in employment with specific upper and lower turning points, possibly depending on the specific historical period to be investigated by this model type. Missing so far in the model's laws of motion was, however, any influence from monetary or fiscal policy, the first due to our complete neglect of interest rates and financial markets' dynamics, and the second, since government expenditure, taxes or other means of financing this expenditure have not been taken into account so far. Yet, besides the purely economic aspects of full employment and resulting investment and employment cycles, the political aspects of these issues – as they were briefly and brilliantly described in Kalecki (1943) – must also be taken into account in any thorough discussion of such cycle mechanisms.

The analysis of the dynamics of the private sector we have studied in this chapter is moreover in one important respect still partial and thus not yet complete even on this level, since it does not investigate what is happening on the nominal side of the model. We have derived in 'The implied dynamics' the reduced-form real wage dynamics that results from our wage price spiral mechanism, but have not yet considered explicitly the underlying reduced-form equations for money wage and price level inflation rates (from which the real wage dynamics has been derived). With respect to nominal price inflation in particular, the reduced-form expression explaining the forces behind price inflation reads:[10]

$$\hat{p} = \frac{\dot{p}}{p} = \pi^c + \kappa[\beta_{py}(y - \bar{y}) + \beta_{p\omega}\ln(\omega/\omega_o)$$
$$+\kappa_p(\beta_{we}(e - \bar{e}) + \beta_{wu}(u_w - \tilde{u}_w(e)) - \beta_{w\omega}\ln(\omega/\omega_o))]$$

In order to allow for steady inflation rates the term following $\pi^c$ in the above formula must be zero in the steady state which gives for the output capital ratio in such a situation:

$$y_{oo} - \bar{y} = \frac{\kappa_p(\beta_{we}(e_o - \bar{e}) + \beta_{wu}(\tilde{u}_f(e_o) - \tilde{u}_w(e_o))}{\beta_{py}} = \frac{(1-\kappa_w)\kappa_p}{1-\kappa_p}(y_o - \bar{y})$$

A comparison with the steady state value of $y_o$, however, immediately reveals that this output–capital ratio is equal to the steady state ratio only in very special cases (concerning the weights in the cost pressure terms of both wage and price inflation), while we will have smaller or larger values of this $y$ compared to $y_o$ in general (for example $y_{oo} = \bar{y} + 0.5(y_o - \bar{y})$ in the balanced case where $\kappa_w = \kappa_p = 0.5$). If the real part in the economy is in the steady state, we may thus have persistently falling inflation rates ($\hat{p} < \pi^c$) or rising inflation rates ($\hat{p} < \pi^c$) in the nominal part of the economy, a process that surely cannot go on for ever. Political pressure may therefore come into being that may induce an adjustment of $\bar{e}, \bar{e}_f$ and of $\tilde{u}_{wo}, \tilde{u}_{fo}$ towards each other, respectively (or may fail to do so). In this case we then get that:

$$y_o = \bar{y}, \quad \bar{e} = \bar{e}_f, \quad u_{wo} = u_{fo}$$

will be established, i.e. there is only one NAIRU on the external and the internal labor market of firms and also with respect to the capital stock utilization ratio and these common benchmark levels are - as the model is presently formulated and applied – completely determined by the benchmark utilization and employment ratios as they are set by firms, if firms cannot be forced to alter their target levels in this respect.

## *Monetary policy*

We now, however, assume that the monetary authority can influence economic activity, via its interest rate policy, by making investment depending on the actual real rate of interest in the following way:

$$I/K = i(\cdot) + \bar{a} = i_p(\rho - \rho_o) - i_e(e - \bar{e}_f) - i_r((r - \hat{p} - \rho_o) + \bar{a} \tag{3.21}$$

As interest rate policy of the central bank we assume in addition the following classical type of Taylor rule:

$$r^* = \rho_o + \hat{p} + \alpha_p(\hat{p} - \bar{\pi}) \tag{3.22}$$
$$\dot{r} = \alpha_r(r^* - r) \tag{3.23}$$

The target interest rate of the central bank $r^*$ is here made dependent on the steady state real rate of interest (the real rate of profit) augmented by actual inflation back to a nominal rate, and is as usually dependent on the inflation gap. With respect to this target there is then assumed an interest rate smoothing of strength $\alpha_r$. In the present chapter we will only consider an extreme case of such a Taylor interest rate policy rule, namely the limit case $\alpha_r = \infty$ of no interest rate smoothing (the other limit case being an interest rate peg). In this case we have:

$$\begin{aligned} r &= \rho_o + \hat{p} + \alpha_p(\hat{p} - \bar{\pi}) \\ I/K &= i_\rho(\rho - \rho_o) - i_e(e - \bar{e}_f) - i_r\alpha_p(\hat{p} - \bar{\pi}) + \bar{a} \\ \hat{p} &= \pi^c + \kappa[\beta_{py}(y - \bar{y}) + \beta_{p\omega}\ln(\omega/\omega_o) \\ &\quad + \kappa_p(\beta_{we}(e - \bar{e}) + \beta_{wu}(u_w - \tilde{u}_w(e)) - \beta_{w\omega}\ln(\omega/\omega_o))] \end{aligned}$$

The end result of such an extension of the model towards a treatment of monetary policy in its context is that the function $i(\cdot)$ is now extended by a third term whereby the negative influence of the employment rate on the rate of investment is enhanced and augmented by similar effects of $u_w$ and $y$ on it (with the same negative sign) and finally that the inflation climate $\pi^c$ and its adaptive revision given by the law of motion:

$$\dot{\pi}^c = \beta_{\pi^c p}(\hat{p} - \pi^c)$$

is now feeding back into the real part of the economy.

We see that the negative influence of economic activity (measured by the employment rate and now also the utilization ratios of both labor and capital) on the rate of investment is thereby made a stronger one, which possibly adds further stability to the dynamics according to our discussion of its turning points (as a substitute for the traditional Keynes-effect in models of exogenous money supply). Furthermore, the indirect inclusion of the inflation climate among the determinants of the rate of investment now adds a Mundell effect to the considered dynamics, but a stabilizing one, since – due to our formulation of monetary policy – increasing inflation and thus an increasing inflationary climate exercise a negative influence on investment and thus on economic activity and thus provide a check to further inflation. Monetary policy may thus add further stability to the considered dynamics, in particular on the nominal side of its working which is now fully integrated into them.

More important, however, is the impact of the added monetary policy on the steady state behavior of our economy.[11] In order to provide a simple illustration for this assertion we disregard here the Blanchard/Katz error correction terms in the wage and price Phillips curves. The above law of motion for the inflation climate and the law of motion for real wages (3.20) now provide to independent equations for the determination of the steady state values of $e, y$. Assuming for the influence of insider effects on the wage inflation rate:

$$\tilde{u}_w(\bar{e}) = \bar{y}/(xl_o\bar{e}), \quad \text{i.e.}$$

a consistency requirement for the benchmark value of the utilization ratio of the workforce in the steady state, gives for the steady state values of both $e, y$ the values $\bar{e}, \bar{y}$ (since $\rho_o = \bar{a}$ continues to hold true). From the $\dot{e} = 0$-equation we then furthermore get the steady state value for labor intensity $l_o$. Finally, the determination of $e_o$ through the level $\bar{e}_f$ now disappears from the set of steady state conditions, which now imply by means of $i(\cdot) = 0$:

$$i_e(e_o - \bar{e}_f) + i_r(\hat{p}_o - \bar{\pi}) = 0$$

This gives now an equation for the determination of the steady state rate of inflation in its deviation from the target rate of the central bank (and it also provides the steady state value of the nominal rate of interest $i_o$ by $\rho_o + \hat{p}_o$).

The addition of interest rate effects on investment behavior and a specific interest rate policy rule thus imply that steady state levels of the employment rate and the utilization ratios of both workers and capital are now given by their NAIRU levels and no longer by the target rate of firms for their control of the social structure of accumulation. Furthermore, this latter target $\bar{e}_f$ now determines the steady state rate of inflation (together with the NAIRU $\bar{e}$ and the target rate $\bar{\pi}$ of the central bank) and it makes this rate the higher the less strict the employment target of firms in their investment function becomes. Lowering the NAIRU $\bar{e}$ itself can be seen in addition to imply the steady state rate of inflation due to the relationship:

$$\hat{p}_o = i_e(\bar{e}_f - \bar{e})/i_r + \bar{\pi}, \quad \text{i.e.,}$$

the model exhibits a long run Phillips curve that is negatively sloped (and which allows for zero steady state inflation if $\bar{e}_o = \bar{e}_f + i_r\bar{\pi}/i_e$ holds true).

The case of an interest rate policy becomes considerably more complex if a Tobinian portfolio sector is added to the model whose return characteristics influence investment behavior in addition. Monetary policy must then work its way through the portfolio substitution process and it moreover then depends on the way long-term interest, Tobin's $q$ and other important variables determined by portfolio choice and asset accumulation feedback onto the investment decision of firms. Such complications for the conduct of monetary policy must, however, be left for future research here, see Chiarella *et al.* (2006) on these matters. The direct control of investment behavior in this model type as well as in models of the New Keynesian variety represents, however, only a first step into an analysis of the implications of monetary policy for economic activity and capital accumulation.

## *Fiscal policy*

Concerning fiscal policy Kalecki (1943,Cch. 12) gives a variety of reasons why industrial leaders may be opposed to full employment achieved, that is possibly, by it. In view of our model and its formulation of this opposition even on the level of private investment formation it is, however, somewhat astonishing to note that a government expenditure function of fairly Keynesian type may – like monetary policy – provide further strength to the negative impact of the rate of employment on the rate of capital accumulation and may therefore be in line with what the industrial leaders may have instinctively or consciously (through their common insight) established as reaction an increase of the rate of employment towards the rate of (absolute) full employment. In order to substantiate this assertion we assume as fiscal policy rule the following expenditure function:

$$G/Y = (G/Y)_o - \alpha_g(e - \bar{e}_g), \text{ i.e. } \quad g = G/K = (G/Y)_o y - \alpha_g(e - \bar{e}_g)y.$$

where we assume that the component of $(G/Y)_o = (T/Y)_o$ in national income is purely tax-financed (and the remainder through changes in government debt and open market operations of the central bank which again impact on the portfolio choice of asset holders not yet considered in this chapter). Part of the above expenditures may be infrastructure expenditures which expand the capital stock like private investment and can thus be added to the $i(\cdot)$ term again (as in our formulation of monetary policy), while the remainder may represent unproductive government expenditures to be added to the aggregate demand expression $y^d$ directly. In both cases, however, we introduce a term into the goods market dynamics which enhances the working of the term $i_e(e-\bar{e})$, if $bare_g = \bar{e}_f$ is assumed. A proper Keynesian fiscal policy rule (whereby government spending is increased in during periods of stagnation and decreased in periods of prosperity) thus works in principle as industrial leaders would prefer it to work as far as situations of an increasing employment rate is concerned.

The real difference between such policies and the intentions of industrial leaders therefore may be found in the fixing of the benchmark level $\bar{e}_g$ from which onwards government expenditure will be larger than the tax-financed portion. Considering fiscal policy in Germany under Chancellor Willy Brandt, for example, one can even find evidence for a target rate $\bar{e}_g$ equal to '1' and considering the behavior of other governments in this period surely a rate much above the level that industrial leaders will consider as consistent with their view on the evolution of the social structure of accumulation, that does not increase – but will in fact even reduce – workforce participation, does not decrease labor market flexibilities and the like. The opposition of firms and of their managers may be more directed against the level of $\bar{e}_g$, then against the fact that government pursues a Keynesian policy in the ups and downs of the business cycle which may help to stabilize their goods demand around a level compatible with their view of a convenient level of unemployment on the external labor market and his implications for the labor market within firms.

Note that the simplest way to introduce the above fiscal policy into the model is to assume that $(G/Y)_o = (T/Y)_o$ represents government consumption and is financed by taxing wages and the rest of government expenditure is assumed to be debt financed and used for investment purposes, since this leaves total goods consumption unchanged and adds the cyclical component of government expenditures again to the investment behavior without changing its determinants significantly (if $\bar{e}_g = \bar{e}_f$ is assumed). This latter assumption may be justified in steps – by way of a long phase of significant unemployment on the labor market which removes the tendencies concerning workforce participation, workforce firing and workday reductions established during the prosperity phase of the Kaleckian investment and employment cycle. If fiscal policy is moreover conducted symmetrically over the considered cycle the evolution of government debt may only become a problem if downturns are long and upswings are short. In such a case a more conservative (asymmetric) expenditure rule may also be established which does not give depressions less weight than upswings as far as counter-cyclical expenditure management is concerned. In this way the social structure of accumulation may be adjusted towards a growth path that allows again for a prosperity period sooner or later. Note here, however, again that we have so far bypassed all problems that may be implied by the working of the financial markets and the portfolio choice of asset holders – nationally or even more in periods of rapid globalization – for the real macroeconomic activity on the goods and the labor markets.

## Conclusions

We have considered in this chapter a model of the Keynes/Kalecki-Goodwin/Rose variety with an advanced type of wage-price spiral, a simple dynamic multiplier story – based on a theory of aggregate demand that includes Kaleckian (1943, Ch. 12) opposition of industrial leaders to the establishment of long phases of full employment on the labor market – and an advanced type of Okun's law linking goods and labor markets. We have investigated extensively the reduced-form 3D real dynamics implied by the model, their local and global stability features and the partial feedback structures that underlie these stability considerations. Of particular interest was the case of local instability of the steady state solution and the derivation of various scenarios that may allow for upper as well as lower turning points from a global point of view, in order to make the considered dynamics an economically viable one. In 'Numerical example' we, moreover, provided some numerical illustrations of the model. In the preceding section we finally pointed to some problems on the nominal side of the considered economy that were not yet feeding back into the real dynamics and that demanded therefore for an extension of the model concerning interest effects on aggregate demand and a Taylor interest rate policy rule in order to tame the explosive dynamics shown to exist in the nominal part of the dynamics. Besides monetary policy we there also briefly considered the role of fiscal policy of a Keynesian type which augmented the private sector of our Keynes/Kalecki-Goodwin/Rose economy in a simple and straightforward way.

Kalecki's (1943) essay on the political aspects of full employment was thus one of the focal points of this chapter, yet was still treated here in a very basic format, since this chapter was primarily concentrated on the economic aspects of full employment. These concerned the role of longer phased cycles of prosperity and stagnation, as already considered in Asada *et al.* (2006b), based on a theory of aggregate demand that included Kalecki (1943,Ch. 12) opposition of industrial leaders to the establishment of long phases of full employment on the labor market, and cyclical evolutions in the kind and degree of the welfare state and its various aspects, quite in contrast to what is normally investigated under the heading 'business fluctuations'. We by and large view the employed workforce, the insider, to represent the dominant element that destabilizes long-lasting situations of full employment, leading in particular to reactions of industrial leaders and the government (including the central bank) that bring about upper turning points in economic activity and subsequent strong recessions or even depression in such booming economies. Yet, we have seen that a variety of further reasons may be involved in explaining actual pronounced turning points in economic activity, upper as well as lower ones, in particular as whether the real wage dynamics are goods or labor market lead and the goods and labor market dynamics are wage or profit led. There may therefore be specific historical reasons involved that explain lasting changes in labor market and inflation regimes which makes the analysis conducted in this chapter considerably less closed than comparable models of the ordinary business cycle.

An important further topic of this chapter was, once it is assumed that the rate of employment on the labor market is adjusting only gradually to rate of capacity utilization of firms, that one has to introduce the utilization ratio of the workforce in order to get a meaningful chain of events that lead from the utilization of the capital stock of firms to this rate of employment. As in a capillary system there are two labor market pressures for firms, one outside and one inside measure, which may be treated and manipulated in different ways by firms during phases of prosperity or depression. Such an extension of Okun's law is a necessary step in any approach that wants to formulate the link from goods to labor market on a theoretically coherent basis and was thus nearly a compelling step in the present framework. During phases of prosperity, however, the dominance of insiders in the wage-price spiral may lead to the partially destabilizing situation that real wage changes may depend negatively on the rate of employment and positively on the rate of capacity utilization, in contrast to what is expected in a framework that does not allow for insider effects in the dynamics of goods and labor markets, where therefore employment is always immediately adjusted to the activity level implied by the working of the market for goods.

A final issue that was only treated briefly in this chapter concerned the distinction between conflict-driven and consensus-driven economies. The first type of economy exhibits a repelling steady state path and thus demands for nonlinearities a least far off the steady

*Table 3.3* Four types of market economies

| | *High steady state* | *Low steady state* |
|---|---|---|
| Stable steady state | Nordic consensus-driven economy | Kaleckian market economy type I |
| Unstable steady state | Kaleckian market economy type II | Southern conflict-driven economy |

state in order to keep its trajectories bounded. Such economies generate order by more or less large scaled cycles in employment and economic activity, that are endogenously generated and subject to supportive monetary or fiscal policy. The question here is whether this is a socially acceptable way of running the economy (disregarding efficiency issues) or whether ways have to be found to allow the economy to progress to a situation which we have called a consensus-driven economy in this chapter.

Consensus-driven and conflict-driven economies can be further differentiated as shown in the Table 3.3. There we distinguish, besides 'Scandinavian type' consensus-driven economies and strictly conflict-driven countries, between developed economies which are very flexible, but exhibit an unstable steady state position and those which are fairly inflexible around a stable depressed steady state situation.

They may be even further differentiated on the basis of the details of their steady state position. Such and further questions must be left for future research here however. In these and other respects this chapter thus provides an introduction into Kaleckian long phased cycles (not business cycles as he has characterized the situation) with more or less welfare state features in their prosperity phase and more or less deregulation processes in their stagnation phase. We hope that the classifications provided in this chapter will stimulate further work on the Kaleckian (1943) type of reserve army mechanism as it has been distinguished here from a Goodwin (1967) type of reserve army mechanism (that is driven by the conflict about income distribution).

## Appendix: Routh Hurwitz stability conditions

**Theorem** (Routh-Hurwitz stability conditions for a three-dimensional system)

*All of the roots of the characteristic equation of the Jacobian of a dynamical system*

$$\lambda^3 + a_1\lambda^2 + a_2\lambda + a_3 = 0$$

*have negative real parts if and only if the set of inequalities*

$$a_1 > 0, \quad a_3 > 0, \quad b = a_1 a_2 - a_3 > 0 \qquad (3.24)$$

*is satisfied.*

**Remark:**

The inequality $a_2 > 0$ is always satisfied if the set of inequalities (3.24) is satisfied.

## Notes

1 A similar model of Steindlian accumulation dynamics is studied in Flaschel and Skott (2006) and Asada *et al.* (2006b).

2 See, for example, Flaschel and Skott (2006), Asada *et al.* (2006b) for a related model of capital accumulation.

3 An alternative assumption about investment behavior is given by:

$$I/K = i_o(y - \bar{y}) + i_{\rho^m}(\rho^m - \rho_o^m) - i_e(e - \bar{e}_f) + \bar{a}, \quad \rho^m = (1 - \omega/x)\bar{y} \tag{3.25}$$

which separates short-term business cycle utilization rate effects from normal utilization profitability effects $\rho^m$ caused by changing income distribution. Note also that we do not discuss the financing of investment explicitly. A justification for this is that all profits are paid out as dividends and all investment is financed by the issue of new equities, the value of which is not yet feeding back onto the investment decision of firms.

4 $\kappa = 1/(1 - \kappa_w \kappa_p)$.

5 See also the concluding section of this chapter.

6 We add to this consideration that the investment function when estimated for the US economy shows a significant negative influence of the rate of employment on the rate of capital accumulation $I/K$ which indicates that this economy may not be of the type just considered (at least partially).

7 We also assume again that the $\beta_e$-terms are the dominant ones in our formulation of the dynamics of the employment rate.

8 We assume now that only the $\beta_{eu}$-term is dominant in our formulation of the dynamics of the employment rate (but that the role of $\beta_{e\omega}$ is neglectable).

9 We note with respect to this parameter set that the parameter $\bar{a} = \rho_o$ may be considered as much too high from the empirical point of view, though it also represents a profit share of 30 percent. Yet, since this rate also represents the growth rate of the economy it is of course of exceptional size. The model therefore needs reformulation, by adding deductions from profits that drive a sufficient wedge between its rate of profit and the resulting rate of growth.

10 A similar expression applies to the reduced-form wage level inflation rate, but need not be discussed explicitly unless wage policy is taken into account in addition to monetary and fiscal policy.

11 We expect the steady state to be locally unique, since its defining five equations should imply a Jacobian with non-zero determinant, but cannot say anything on global uniqueness for the moment.

## References

Asada, T., Chen, P., Chiarella, C. and P. Flaschel (2006a) AD-AS and the Phillips curve. A baseline disequilibrium approach. In C. Chiarella, P. Flaschel, R. Franke and W. Semmler (eds) *Quantitative and Empirical Analysis of Nonlinear Dynamic Macromodels.* Contributions to Economic Analysis. Amsterdam: Elsevier.

Asada, T., Flaschel, P. and P. Skott (2006b) Prosperity and Stagnation in Capitalist Economies. In C. Chiarella, P. Flaschel, R. Franke and W. Semmler (eds) *Quantitative and Empirical Analysis of Nonlinear Dynamic Macromodels.* Contributions to Economic Analysis. Amsterdam: Elsevier.

Blanchard, O.J. and L. Katz (1999): Wage dynamics: Reconciling theory and evidence. *American Economic Review. Papers and Proceedings* 89: 69–74.

Chen, P., Chiarella, C., Flaschel, P. and W. Semmler (2006) Keynesian Macrodynamics and the Phillips Curve: an estimated baseline macro-model for the U.S. economy. In C. Chiarella, P. Flaschel, R. Franke and W. Semmler (eds) *Quantitative and Empirical Analysis of Nonlinear Dynamic Macromodels.* Contributions to Economic Analysis. Amsterdam: Elsevier.

Chiarella, C. and P. Flaschel (2000) *The Dynamics of Keynesian Monetary Growth: Macrofoundations*. Cambridge: Cambridge University Press.

Chiarella, C., Flaschel, P. and R. Franke (2005) *Foundations for a Disequilibrium Theory of the Business Cycle. Qualitative Analysis and Quantitative Assessment.* Cambridge: Cambridge University Press.

Chiarella, C., Flaschel, P., Hung, H. and W. Semmler (2006) *Portfolio Choice, Asset Accumulation and Macroeconomic Activity: A Tobinian Stock-Flow Approach.* Sydney:University of Technology.

Flaschel, P. and P. Skott (2006) Steindl models of growth and stagnation. *Metroeconomica*, 57, 305–40.

Goodwin, R.M. (1967): A growth cycle. In C.H. Feinstein (ed.) *Socialism, Capitalism and Economic Growth.* Cambridge: Cambridge University Press.

Kaldor, N. (1940) A model of the trade cycle. *Economic Journal*, 50, 78–92.

Kalecki, M. (1943) Political aspects of full employment. Reprinted in M. Kalecki, *Selected Essays on the Dynamics of the Capitalist Economy*, Cambridge: Cambridge University Press, 1971.

Okun, A.M. (1970) *The Political Economy of Prosperity.* Washington, DC: The Brookings Institution.

Rose, H. (1967): On the non-linear theory of the employment cycle. *Review of Economic Studies*, 34, 153–73.

Rose, H. (1990) *Macroeconomic Dynamics: A Marshallian Synthesis.* Cambridge, MA: Basil Blackwell.

# 4 A Goodwin cycle with changing regimes of industrial relations

*Jörg Glombowski and Michael Krüger*

## Introduction

In his seminal growth-cycle contribution (Goodwin 1967), Goodwin did not really offer extensive justifications for the basic assumptions of his model except for a brief hint on the Marxian theory of capital accumulation.[1] To give an example: While it seems to be a plausible assumption to relate the rate of growth of real wages positively to the employment rate, there certainly is no automatic mechanism at work such that there will be an increase in real wages whenever the employment rate rises.

Workers may not be able to ensure wage increases for multiple reasons, e.g. political limits to their freedom of action, divisions among competing fractions of their organizations (multiple unions) or failures to overcome their free rider problem (weak unions or no unions at all). Even if they were capable of enforcing higher real wages due to favorable labor demand conditions, they may resist the temptation due to long-run considerations, say, long-term contracts with the employers, a cooperative stance with respect to employers' organizations or because of their view on electoral perspectives for ruling left-wing political parties, which might be negatively affected by aggressive wage claims. Similar arguments apply to mechanistic assumptions with respect to wage declines or limited increases due to low rates of employment. While we do not seriously raise doubts about the empirical appeal of Goodwin's analysis as a general rule, presumably being valid in principle, we propose a modification which will allow labor unions and employers' organizations to behave more flexibly in the course of time. We shall establish a non-cooperative cyclical path of the economy à la Goodwin, and alternatively we allow for the possibility of cooperative behavior between workers and employers, which gives rise to higher employment rates resulting from wage restraint and high investment rates. These two "regimes" may appear both in a more or less regular pattern, depending on a variety of social, political and institutional circumstances. We will not work out deterministic patterns, but rather we shall refer to stochastic mechanisms giving rise to different sequences of regimes and, therefore, different time paths of the variables under consideration. This procedure may generate, for instance, developments characterized by strong social partnership relations, and, likewise, situations in which workers and capitalists start fighting whenever the economic circumstances offer a chance in their favor. The nature of the stochastic process employed will be discussed below. It should be clear from the outset that the model includes transitory periods, i.e. time paths related to the implementation or breakdown of wage-investment agreements.[2]

*Table 4.1* Notation

| | | |
|---|---|---|
| $\alpha$ | : | accumulation share |
| $\beta$ | : | employment rate |
| $\lambda$ | : | wage share |
| $\rho$ | : | profit rate |
| $\sigma$ | : | capital productivity |
| $w$ | : | real wage rate |
| $y$ | : | labor productivity |
| $A$ | : | labor force |
| $K$ | : | capital stock |
| $L$ | : | employment |
| $Y$ | : | net product |
| $n$ | : | growth rate of the labor force |
| $a_1$, $a_2$, $m_1$, $m_2$ | : | constant, positive parameters |

## The model

### *The non-cooperative regime (Regime I)*

The non-cooperative regime is fairly close, but not identical, to the working of Goodwin's original model. Table 4.1 shows the set of variables and parameters is used in the present chapter. Some additional parameters will be introduced at a later stage.

The model is formulated in discrete time. The first set of equations represents definitions:

$$\beta_t = L_t/A_t$$
$$y_t = Y_t/L_t$$
$$\lambda_t = w_t/y_t$$
$$\sigma = Y_t/K_t$$
$$\rho_t = (1-\lambda_t)\sigma$$

We adopt Goodwin's wage equation in a discrete form, i.e.

$$w_{t+1} = w_t(1 - a_1 + a_2\beta_{t+1}) \tag{4.1}$$

Accumulation is described by:

$$K_{t+1} = K_t(1 + \alpha_{nc}\rho_t) \tag{4.2}$$

Note that the share of accumulation $\alpha$ is assumed to be constant in the non-cooperative regime and this is indicated by the subscript *nc*. Finally, the growth rate of labor productivity $y_t$ is determined by a positive trend value, but in addition it depends on the wage share in income.[3] This means that high wage shares induce an acceleration of the positive labor productivity trend and vice versa. We formalize this assumption by means of:

$$y_{t+1} = y_t(1 + m_1 + m_2\lambda_t) \tag{4.3}$$

This set of equations constitutes the model. It can be reduced to two difference equations in $\beta$ and $\lambda$:

$$\beta_{t+1} = \left[\frac{1 + \alpha_{nc}\sigma(1-\lambda_t)}{(1 + m_1 + m_2\lambda_t)(1+n)}\right]\beta_t \tag{4.4}$$

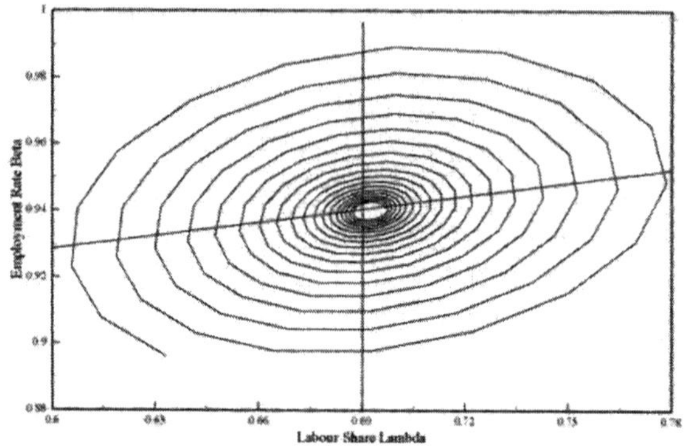


*Figure 4.1* Inward spiralling trajectory: basic model

$$\lambda_{t+1} = \left[\frac{1 - a_1 + a_2\beta_{t+1}}{1 + m_1 + m_2\lambda_t}\right]\lambda_t \qquad (4.5)$$

In a diagram spanned by the variables $\beta$ and $\lambda$ the partial equilibrium curve for $\beta$ is just a vertical line starting at the equilibrium point $\lambda_{nc}$. The partial equilibrium curve for $\lambda$ is the linear relation $\beta = (m_1 + a_1) + m_2\lambda)/a_2$.

Their point of intersection determines the following steady state solution, denoted by the subscript *nc*:

$$\beta_{nc} = \frac{1}{a_2}(a_1 + m_1 + m_2\lambda_{nc}) \qquad (4.6)$$

$$\lambda_{nc} = \frac{1 + \alpha_{nc}\sigma - (1 + m_1)(1 + n)}{\alpha_{nc}\sigma + m_2(1 + n)} \qquad (4.7)$$

The model produces cycles, but the cycles are not closed orbits. Rather the evolution of the variables shows dampened fluctuations as an inward spiralling process towards the long run equilibrium path $(\beta_{nc}, \lambda_{nc})$.

## *The cooperative regime (Regime II)*

Whenever unions or employers' organizations consider improvements of their situations in comparison to the non-cooperative solution or some average performance over a couple of years, they will recognize that there are multiple possibilities for improvement. If the unions try to do better than $\beta_{nc}\lambda_{nc}$, while the employers try to do better than $\beta_{nc}(1 - \lambda_{nc})$, then any agreement to raise the employment rate while keeping the wage share constant, would be beneficial to both parties.[4]

Another simple case would be provided by the Nash-bargaining solution (subscript N). One can show that this would imply $\beta_N = 1$ and $\lambda_N = 0.5$. But the use of the (normative) Nash-bargaining solution does not seem to be a proper assumption for our setting.

We prefer to work with rather pragmatic assumptions when specifying a "cooperative regime". We assume that full employment cannot be reached (except occasionally for small lapses of time) and that both parties are well aware of it. Which reasons may be responsible employment levels below full employment? Employers may feel that the rise in the accumulation share necessary to bring about full employment is too high to acceptable, or some of them may argue that the profit rate compatible with full employment will be not high enough. Both parties may also realize that the stability of a "contract" is negatively related to the ambitions of unions and associations of the entrepreneurs. The higher the permanent rate of employment, the higher the temptation (of parts of the unions) to fight for the realization of its short-run potential to increase wages.

We shall select the steady-state values of our variables for the cooperative regime by applying a random mechanism, to be explained in a minute. Assume, we had found a pair of values $\beta_c$ and $\lambda_c$ defining the steady state, than the behavior of the other variables would follow as:

$$A_{t+1}/A_t = L_{t+1}/L_t = n \tag{4.8}$$

$$y_{t+1}/y_t = 1 + m_1 + m_2\lambda_c \tag{4.9}$$

$$Y_{t+1}/Y_t = K_{t+1}/K_t = (1+n)(1+m_1+m_2\lambda_c) \tag{4.10}$$

$$\rho_c = (1-\lambda_c)\sigma \tag{4.11}$$

$$\alpha_c = \frac{(1+n)(1+m_1+m_2\lambda_c)-1}{(1-\lambda_c)\sigma} \tag{4.12}$$

Note that the parameter $\alpha$ has turned into the variable $\alpha_c$ bearing the burden of supporting the cooperative level of the employment rate.

The random process, referred to above, works as follows. First, a random number $R_2$ is selected from the unit interval. It serves to determine the cooperative level of the employment rate:

$$\beta_c = \beta_{nc} + R_2(1-\beta_{nc}) \tag{4.13}$$

$R_2$ determines the percentage of the non-cooperative steady state unemployment rate to be abolished. Next, we calculate $\lambda_L$ and $\lambda_R$, being the lowest and the highest value of the wage share compatible with $\beta_c$ and the restrictions for advantageous bargaining for both of the parties. $\lambda_L$ follows from the condition that workers' utility, derived from the cooperative regime, must match at least the utility to be derived from the non-cooperative regime, i.e.:

$$\beta_c\lambda_L = \beta_{nc}\lambda_{nc} \quad \text{or} \quad \lambda_L = \beta_{nc}\lambda_{nc}/\beta_c \tag{4.14}$$

Likewise, for the employers the biggest wage share admissible in the cooperative regime must provide the same utility as the non-cooperative regime:

$$\beta_c(1-\lambda_R) = \beta_{nc}(1-\lambda_{nc}) \quad \text{or} \quad \lambda_R = 1-\beta_{nc}(1-\lambda_{nc})/\beta_c \tag{4.15}$$

Again, we select a random number $R_3$ from the unit interval to determine the cooperative wage share:

$$\lambda_c = \lambda_L + R_3(\lambda_R - \lambda_L) \tag{4.16}$$

In other words, we just pick a wage share which favors both parties (or at least one, if $R_3$ refers to the extreme values 0 or 1).[5]

The cooperative steady state growth path can be approached, but need not necessarily be reached in the course of time. One reason is that the parties are either unable and/or do not wish to leave the non-cooperative regime. The second reason might be that attempts to realize the cooperative path are aborted by the behavior of one or even by both organizations during the process of approaching it. In the present version of the model, however, we do not take this possibility into account.

Our next task is to describe a transition path from the non-cooperative to the cooperative regime and to determine how it will possibly get started. Having done this, we will have to discuss which circumstances might eventually lead to the breakdown of a cooperative solution and its consequences.

### *The traverse from the non-cooperative regime to the cooperative steady state (Regime III)*

After the parties have agreed to establish a cooperative regime characterized by $\beta_c$ , $\lambda_c$ and $\alpha_c$, they must also agree on a path leading from a position in the cyclical non-cooperative trajectory to the cooperative position. For the sake of simplicity, we assume that a linear path will be chosen with equal steps taken in a limited period of time.[6] The assumption chosen has the advantage that it offers a real chance to achieve the goal before the process is possibly interrupted.

Let $h$ be the number of periods needed for reaching the cooperative solution and let $t_1$ be the period before the traverse is started.[7] Then we obtain the equations:

$$\beta_{t_1+i} = \beta_{t_1+i} + i(\beta_c - \beta_{t_1})/h \quad \text{for } i = 1, \cdots, h \tag{4.17}$$

$$\lambda_{t_1+i} = \lambda_{t_1+i} + i(\lambda_c - \lambda_{t_1})/h \quad \text{for } i = 1, \cdots, h \tag{4.18}$$

To be sure, this set-up implies that we have to drop the wage determination equation as well as the assumption of a constant share of accumulation and solve the model backwards. Thus we determine the wage development and the path of the accumulation share by reference to the chosen goal and time chosen to achieve it. The result is the following set of three equations:

$$\frac{Y_{t+1}}{Y_t} = \frac{K_{t+1}}{K_t} = (1+n)(1+m_1+m_2\lambda_t)\left(\frac{\beta_{t+1}}{\beta_t}\right) \tag{4.19}$$

$$\alpha(t) = \frac{(1+n)(1+m_1+m_2\lambda_t)}{\sigma(1-\lambda_t)}\left(\frac{\beta_{t+1}}{\beta_t}\right) \quad \text{and} \tag{4.20}$$

$$\frac{w_{t+1}}{w_t} = (1+m_1+m_2)\left(\frac{\lambda_{t+1}}{\lambda_t}\right) \tag{4.21}$$

We do not know in advance, however, at which point in time the random mechanism will trigger the traverse to the cooperative steady state to start and exactly what this state will look like. Assume the traverse starts at a point where the actual prevailing wage share is identical with its cooperative value, while the employment rate has to rise towards its cooperative value. In this case, the transition would imply a constant growth rate of wages, a rising growth rate of output and the capital stock, as well as an increase in the accumulation share. Whenever the wage share would have to rise or to decline during the traverse, this would be welcomed with more or less applause from either side.

We may start off from a point of the cycle from which the transition process would require both a rising wage share and a rising employment rate. This would entail that wages rise during the traverse. The accumulation rate of capital would have to rise which would not necessarily be welcomed by the entrepreneurs. But there may be situations where the capitalists are likely to be more optimistic than the workers. A possible scenario asks for patience from both sides, i.e. when the transition starts at a wage share equal to the cooperative one and the cooperative employment rate being greater than the actually prevailing one at the specific stage of the cycle.

Yet the point of departure from the cycle still has to be determined. There are two plausible reasons motivating such a departure. The first one relies on (growing) dissatisfaction of the two classes, or rather their organizations, with the cyclical character of the movement. The second one is related to the disappointing character of the non-cooperative steady state.[8]

Since the basic model is asymptotically stable, it might make more sense to refer to the ultimate outcome of the process, that is, the absence of cyclical fluctuations in the long run: With some patience, the cyclical nuisance will disappear, while in the long run the unsatisfying character of the non-cooperative steady state will come to the fore ever more clearly. Therefore, we stipulate that there is an environment of the non-cooperative steady state such that whenever the trajectory enters this basin of the steady state, both parties will become ever more convinced that it is worth moving towards a more satisfactory cooperative steady state.

Suppose that the neighborhood is equivalent to a circle with a predetermined radius $\epsilon_1$, we define the distance of a point on the actual trajectory from the non-cooperative state as follows:

$$D(t) = \left[(\beta(t) - \beta_{nc})^2 + (\lambda(t) - \lambda_{nc})^2\right]^{\frac{1}{2}}. \quad \text{whenever} \tag{4.22}$$

$$D(t) < \epsilon_1, \text{ we pick a random number } 0 < R_1 < 1. \tag{4.23}$$

If $R_1 < \epsilon_2$, we select some $(\beta_c, \lambda_c)$ as explained above, together with a period $h$ and enter Regime III.

## *The breakdown of cooperation (Regime IV)*

Let us assume that the system has reached its cooperative steady state growth path and followed it for a while. The question is whether such an outcome may be kept forever. Of course, we restrict ourselves to the discussion of the reasons for a breakdown of cooperation, which are embedded in the limited setting of the model. Whenever cooperation is likely to deteriorate, then it is worth discussing the consequences in terms of the dynamics it generates.[9]

The termination of cooperation may be induced by either (or both) of the parties defecting from the norms of cooperation or the underlying contract.[10]

Entrepreneurs might want to return to lower accumulation shares and/or to higher profit rates, while workers may be tempted to realize higher wage rises than the "contract" permits, but which look justifiable and achievable, given the favorable employment situation. Again, we may apply a random mechanism to describe the possibility of deviations. There are two general ideas we can refer to in the present context. One points to the length of time the cooperative regime has already been operating: On the one hand, the parties may get used to the advantages of cooperation as being "normal", but tend to forget about necessary concessions which they require, and which have been well understood in the past. Therefore, assuming obliviousness, the longer the favorable situation lasts, the higher the likelihood of a defection tends to become. The second idea refers to the distance of the cooperative situation from the non-cooperative steady state (or the point where the traverse started from). Assume, for simplicity, that the wage share is the same in both situations and that only the cooperative employment rate is higher than the average or long-term non-cooperative value. Then their distance is a measure for the (short-term) wage gains to be realized and, moreover, also a measure for the possible reduction of the accumulation share. Thus, the greater the distance from the non-cooperative state, the greater the incentive to defect. We can combine the two ideas to define a probability for defection and we can relate this probability to a random number to eventually trigger a (possible) defection.

But this in only a first step. Once it has been clarified who defects first, we have to work out the chain of reactions and counter reactions. A rigid reaction in the tit-for-tat style would take the very first instance of defection as the end of the cooperation – causing immediate counter reactions and a sudden fall-back to the non-cooperative regime, possibly with slightly changed parameters. A softer reaction would assume the parties take more time to make sure that a defection was not just a one-off accident caused unintendedly by a "trembling hand".

It frequently occurs in model building that there is just one equilibrium situation but a hundred possible distortions. One way to handle this problem is to work out the implications of the simplest story and to leave the other ones to further research activities. This is what we shall do in the remainder of this chapter.

Let us assume in the present exercise that workers will tend to defect by claiming wage increases according to Goodwin's wage formation function, that is, on the basis of the high employment rate brought about by cooperation. Moreover, let us assume that capitalists will immediately react by reducing their share of accumulation.[11] Then we are immediately back to the original non-cooperative regime (or a close relative of it).

Of course, over time, the wish to realize gains from cooperation will gain momentum and start the whole process up again, although modified by all the chance elements determining the switches of regimes.

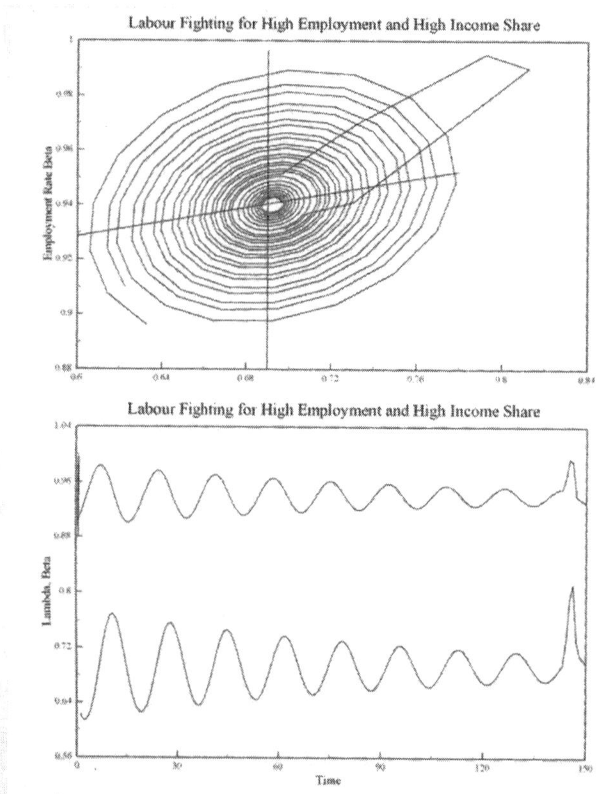


*Figure 4.2* Simulation results I

## Some illustrating examples from the simulations

Model simulations produce lots of varieties, which, nevertheless, retain structural similarities. Let us just consider two different cases here, with two different start-up values

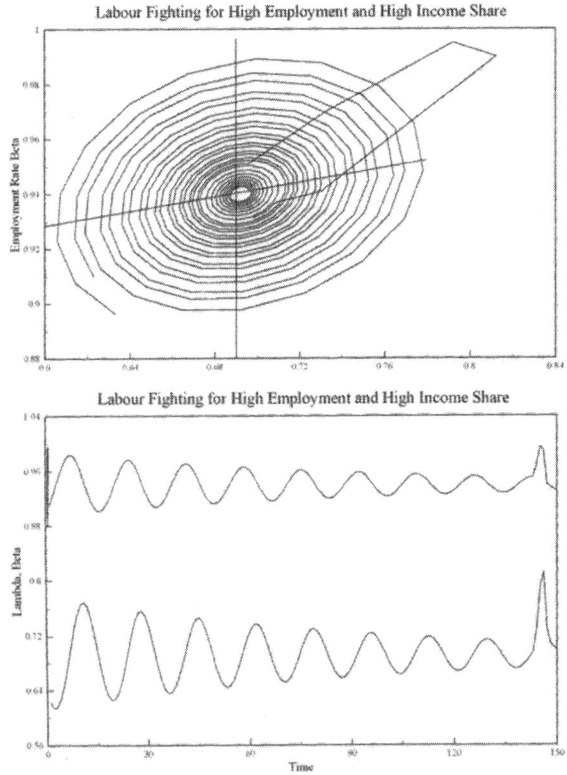


*Figure 4.3* Simulation results II

for the random numbers, while parameters and initial values are identical. In the first case, summarized by the following two graphs in Figure 4.2, we may identify have four phases of non-cooperative regimes, each followed by traverses and cooperative regimes over 150 periods.

The second example, characterized by the next two graphs in Figure 4.3, shows a long-run process of dampened fluctuations towards the equilibrium stage but then there is an attempt of labor at work to improve significantly both the employment and the income position relative to capital. This yields a drastic reduction of the accumulation share and thus reduces the demand for labor to a larger extent. This process also involves some 150 time periods.

Obviously, the chance elements constitute a major difference in the performance of the economy: if the jumps lead to points not too far away from the non-cooperative equilibrium point, there will have more jumps and regime changes.

## Final remarks

Our point of departure refers to a concept of non-cooperation between workers and capitalists. This is in line with the Marxian standpoint about the class structure of capitalist societies. Working out the implications of a perpetual conflict between workers and entrepreneurs for the development of capital accumulation has, without doubt, been a main aim of Goodwin's model. So far, so good. But in the country-specific histories of modern societies we observe a large variety of class behavior. There are cases of long-standing militant conflicts between workers and capitalists and there are also experiences of cooperative behavior between the organizations of both workers and capitalists. Moreover, we may easily find historical examples where both forms of strategy (cooperation and conflict) coexist or alternate. That is to say, there are periods where non-cooperative class strategies determine the rules of the labor market. At some point the strategy is replaced by forms of cooperation. Obviously, it is hard to predict how long a set of strategies may last, because too many social and economic determinants may enter the scene. We tend to believe that it may be an interesting point of departure to develop a model design flexible enough to allow for switching and re-switching processes of the economic strategies of workers and capitalists. Although it is clear that non-cooperative strategies may be at work for many years in a given country, the strategies may not be found appropriate in the long run. This is due to the fact that both workers and capitalists may gain from a cooperative behavior. Depending on their mutual trust, experience, and their expectations about the feasibility of economic and social goals, a social contract describing the elements of the cooperation be may established. Violations of the contract may be tolerated within certain limits. But it is clear that systematic deviations of one partner from the cooperative solution strategy will not be accepted by the other for good.

In this chapter we have made an attempt to study some possible outcomes of changes in strategies. Our simulations serve to describe some sequences of change from a non-cooperative to a cooperative regime and back. Of course, there are several other elements which could – and should – be incorporated, e.g. learning from the experiences and the possible emergence of path dependencies.

## Notes

1 In an enlarged version of the paper (Goodwin 1972) there are some remarks given with respect to the set of assumptions applied in the setup of the model.
2 In the present context the inclined reader may also consult Calmfors and Drifill (1988) and Lancaster (1973).
3 We have applied a similar assumption within a more complicated framework elsewhere. There the wage share enters a "mechanization function", which in turn affects capacity output and labor productivity growth. Cf. Glombowski and Krüger (1987).
4 $\beta_{nc}\lambda_{nc}$ is labor's share in the maximum output achievable, while $\beta_{nc}(1-\lambda_{nc})$ is the share of capital.
5 Note that this procedure allows for the possibility that $\lambda_c < \lambda_{nc}$.
6 Of course, we could also consider other approaches, e.g. the reduction of any remaining distance by a fixed percentage per period.
7 Whenever needed $h$ could be determined at random as well.This is actually done in the simulations of the model to be discussed later.
8 Of course, both could be combined somehow.
9 In the present context the inclined reader may profit from consulting Lancaster (1973).
10 Such a contract could even be an implicit one and should be conceived as unspecified with respect to its duration.
11 The accumulation could be reduced to zero or even below zero until the steady state employment rate of the non-cooperative regime was reached. Moreover, the "new" accumulation share must not necessarily coincide with the "old" one.

## References

Calmfors, L. and Driffill, J. (1988) Bargaining Structure, Corporation, and Macroeconomic Performance. *Economic Policy*, 6, 14–61.

Glombowski, J. and Krüger, M. (1987) Generalizations of Goodwin's Growth Cycle Model, in Batten, D., Casti, J. and Johansson, B. (eds) *Economic Evolution and Structural Adjustment*, Heidelberg: Springer Verlag.

Goodwin, R.M. (1967), A Growth Cycle, in Feinstein, C. (ed.) *Socialism, Capitalism and Economic Growth: Essays Presented to Maurice Dobb*, Cambridge: Cambridge University Press.

Goodwin, R.M. (1972), A Growth Cycle, in Hunt, E.K. and Schwartz, J.G. (eds), *A Critique of Economic Theory*, Harmondsworth: Penguin.

Lancaster, K. (1973), The Dynamic Inefficiency of Capitalism. *Journal of Political Economy*, 81, 1092–109

# 5 Varieties of capitalism

## The flexicurity model

*Peter Flaschel, Alred Greiner, Sigrid Luchtenberg and Edward Nell*

## Social reproduction and the reserve army mechanism

This chapter starts from the observation that Goodwin's (1967) Classical growth cycle does not represent a process of social reproduction that can be considered as adequate for a social and democratic society in the long-run. This chapter therefore derives on this background a basic macrodynamic framework where this form of cyclical growth and social reproduction is overcome by an employer of 'first' resort, added to an economic reproduction process that is highly competitive and flexible and thus not of the type of the past Eastern socialism. Instead, there is high capital and labor mobility (concerning 'hiring' and 'firing' in particular) where fluctuations of employment in the first labor market of the economy (in the private sector) are made socially acceptable through a second labor market where all remaining workers (and even pensioners) find meaningful occupation. The resulting economic system with its detailed transfer payment schemes is in its essence comparable to the flexicurity model developed for the Nordic welfare states and Denmark in particular. We show that this economy exhibits a balanced growth path that is globally attracting. Moreover, credit financed investment can be easily added without disturbing the prevailing situation of full capacity growth. We thus do not get demand-, but only supply-driven business fluctuations in such an environment with both factors of production always full employed. This combines flexible factor adjustment in the private sector of the economy with high employment security for the labor force and thus shows that the flexicurity variety of capitalist reproduction can work in a balanced or at least fairly stable manner.

We start from the (in 1995) still weak empirical evidence for the existence of a long-phase cycle in the state variables $e$ and $v$, the employment rate and the wage share, that we have presented in Flaschel and Groh (1995) for a number of industrialized market economies. We do this on the basis of 15 years of further observations and now also partly based on quite modern econometric techniques. Our brief findings will be that the Goodwin growth cycle model of Flaschel and Groh (1995) provides indeed a useful approach to the explanation of the distributive cycle as it was observed in the US, the UK and in other countries after the Second World War. In Kauermann *et al.* (2007) we have obtained by specifically tailored econometric techniques the graphical representation of the long-phase wage share $v$ / employment rate $e$ cycle (as centers of the business fluctuations around them) for the US economy over the period 1955–2004. Figure 5.1 shows (bottom-right) a single estimated long-phase core cycle (within the scatter plot of $v, e-$observations) for a period length of approximately 50 years and (bottom-left) the six to seven cycles of business cycle frequency (approximately eight years each) that fluctuate around this long-phase cycle. We ignore the shorter cycles in the following and concentrate on the observation that there is

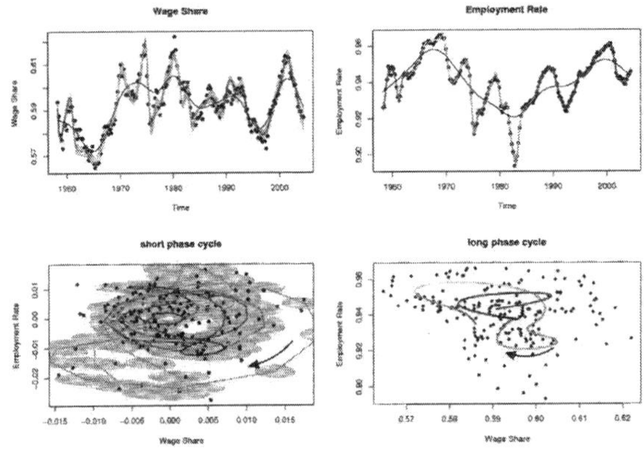


*Figure 5.1* Goodwinian wage share/employment rate dynamics (bottom plots) with estimated long-phase cycle to the right. Top graphs show the data plotted against time

evidence for a long-phase overshooting (non-monotonic) interaction between the share of wages $v$ in national income and the employment rate $e$, the core of which is shown in Figure 5.1, bottom right. This clockwise oriented long-phase cycle appears to be more complex in situations of a high employment rate and is relatively simple structured in the opposite situations. The reader is referred to Kauermann *et al.* (2007) for details on the applied econometric technique and the results that can be obtained from it.

In order to briefly present a simple model of such a long-phase accumulation cycle in the variables $v$ and $e$ we make use of the seminal growth cycle model of Goodwin (1967). From this perspective, the envisaged cycle-generating feedback structure can be based on the following two laws of motion:

$$\hat{v} = \dot{v}/v = \beta_{ve}(e - \bar{e}) - \beta_{vv}(v - \bar{v}), \tag{5.1}$$

$$\hat{e} = \dot{e}/e = -\beta_{ev}(v - \bar{v}), \tag{5.2}$$

where $v$ denotes real unit-wage costs (or the share of wages in GDP) and $e$ the employment rate and the parameters $\beta_{ve} > 0$, $\beta_{ev} > 0$, $\beta_{vv} \geq 0$ determine the speed of adjustment. The coefficients $\bar{e}$ and $\bar{v}$ denote the normal levels of employment and the wage share, respectively, meaning that employment and the wage share are constant at those values. We justify Equation (5.1) by means of the wage dynamics investigated in Blanchard and Katz (1999), with perfect anticipation of price inflation however (implying a real wage Phillips curve) where in addition to demand pressure we have unit wage costs acting as an error correction mechanism on their own evolution. In the second law of motion we focus on a goods market behavior that is profit-led, i.e. increases in unit wage costs act negatively on aggregate demand and thus negatively on the growth rate of the rate of employment $e$.

If $\beta_{vv} = 0$ holds, as Blanchard and Katz assert it for the US economy, we have the cross-dual dynamics of the Goodwin (1967) growth cycle model and thus a center type dynamics that is stable, but not asymptotically stable. In the case $\beta_{vv} > 0$ we can apply Olech's Theorem, see Flaschel (1984), and obtain from it global asymptotic stability of the dynamics in the positive orthant of the phase plane with respect to the uniquely determined interior steady state position $\bar{e}, \bar{v}$. For weak Blanchard and Katz (1999) error correction terms we thus get a somewhat damped long-phased cyclical motion in the wage share/employment rate phase space as shown in Figure 5.2. We have a clockwise rotation in the considered phase space with approximately one cycle in 50 years.[1]

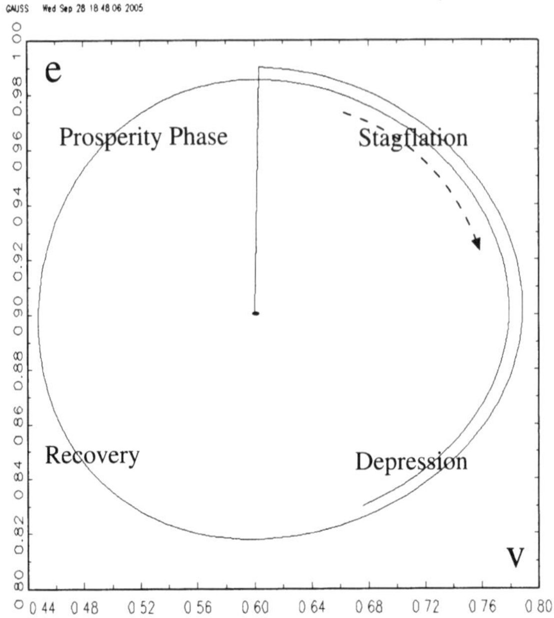


*Figure 5.2* Goodwin-type long-phased wage share/employment dynamic

We can see that the theoretical 2D dynamics mirrors the empirical phase plot to a certain degree. The Goodwin growth cycle mechanism where employment growth depends negatively on income distribution (is profit-led) and where wage share growth depends positively on the state of the labor market thus not only explains the clockwise orientation observed in the data, but also the long-phased nature of the cycle when adjustment speeds are crudely chosen from an empirical perspective. The unique observation of a single long cycle in income distribution and employment that we have available for the US economy after the Second World War is thus in fairly close correspondence to the Classical growth cycle model and its suggestion of a long-phase accumulation cycle.[2]

Generating order and economic viability in market economies by large swings in the unemployment rate (mass unemployment with human degradation of part of the families that form the society), as shown above (see also the next Figure on the growth cycle structure in the British economy), is one way to make capitalism work, but it must surely be critically reflected with respect to its social consequences. Moreover, it must be contrasted with alternative economic systems that allow to combine the situation of a highly competitive market economy with a human rights bill that includes the right (and the obligation) to work, and to get income from this work that at the least supports basic needs and basic happiness. The Danish flexicurity system provides a typical example for such an alternative. By contrast, a laissez-faire capitalistic society that ruins family structures to a considerable degree (through alienated work, mass unemployment and unlimited media programs) cannot stay a democratic society in the long-run, since it produces conflicts that can range from social segmentation to class clashes, racial clashes and more.

In addition to what has been shown above, one should, of course also try to take earlier time period into account than just the 1960s to the present if data – in particular on the wage share – are available. For the UK we have considered in Flaschel and Groh (1995) such

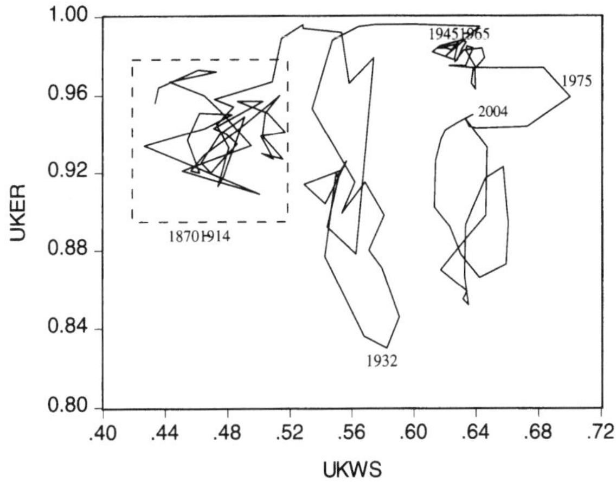


*Figure 5.3* UK income distribution cycles 1870–2004: WS = wage shere; ER = employment rate

long time series from 1855 up to 1965[3] which can here be extended to the following phase plot diagram.[4]

The important insight that can be obtained from these diagrams for the UK (1855–1965) is that the Goodwin cycle – if it really existed – must have been significantly shorter before 1914 (with larger fluctuations in employment during each business cycle), and that there has been a major change in it after 1945. This may be explained by significant differences and changes in the adjustment processes of market economies for these two periods: primarily price adjustment before 1914 and primarily quantity adjustments after 1945. This very tentative judgment must be left for future research, however. Based on Desai's data one could have expected that the growth cycle had become obsolete (and maybe also the business cycle as it was claimed in the 1960s). Yet, extended by the further data from Groth and Madsen (2007), it is now of course obvious that nothing of this sort took place in the UK economy. In fact, we see in Figure 5.3 two periods of excessive employment (in the language of the theory of the NAIRU) which were followed by periods of dramatic unemployment, both started by segments the more or less pronounced occurrence of stagflation.

Such a long-run perspective allows to see to what extent the above shown cycle for the US economy is of a unique nature and therefore possibly representing a specific stage in the social structure of accumulation of capitalist market economies. As Figure 5.3 shows there are indeed two such phases visible in the case of the UK which are clearly separated from each other through the period where the First and Seconde World Wars were taking place. In Flaschel and Groh (1995) we had a long time series from 1855 up to 1965 which when taken in isolation could have suggested what was articulated at that time as 'is the business cycle obsolete' (Bronfenbrenner, 1969). When Flaschel and Groh (1995) was published, the time-bound illusion in such a statement was of course already obvious, yet it is interesting to see (in Figure 5.3) how radically this illusion was disproved by the development that took place in the UK after 1965. There is a Goodwinian distributive cycle after the Second World War in the UK and raises the question of what we will observe in the next 50 years in the UK and elsewhere.

From the perspective of the flexicurity model that we will formulate and investigate in this chapter, the phase plot in Figure 5.3 in our view clearly suggests that the depicted

*Table 5.1* Firms: production and income account

| *Uses* | *Resources* |
|---|---|
| $\delta K$ | $\delta K$ |
| $\omega_1 L_1^d, \quad L_1^d = Y^p/z$ | $C_1 + C_2 + C_r$ |
| $\omega_2 L_{2f}^w$ | $G$ |
| $\Pi \quad (= Y^f)$ | $I \quad (= Y^f)$ |
| $\delta_1 R + \dot{R}$ | $S_1$ |
| $Y^p$ | $Y^p$ |

evolution in the British economy cannot be considered as an ideal for the next stage of the evolution of capitalism. Instead, we will pursue in this chapter the idea that there is a coherent and workable alternative to the depicted distributive cycle in a competitive market environment that mirrors partial as well as macro ideas of the current discussion on the conduct of in particular labor market policies, in particular in the Nordic countries.

In the next section, we augment the Goodwin model by a second labor market where the state acts as the employer of 'first' resort[5] and thus guarantees full employment by specific actions. We show that this extension not only removes the reserve army mechanism from the labor market, despite the possibility of a wage-price spiral mechanism in the first labor market, but also makes the economy convergent to its long-run balanced growth path. The convergence is the faster the more flexible the labor market is adjusting. Apart from the (important) microeconomic problem of how the second labor market that is here added to the Goodwin growth cycle model can work in an efficient and socially acceptable manner, we thus get the result that the macroeconomic performance is not only improved by this reformulation of the Goodwin model, but indeed turned into a state that can be considered as socially superior to the actual working of capitalist market economies such as the US and the UK.

## Flexicurity growth: a baseline model

We have considered from the theoretical and the empirical perspective a long phase growth cycle that in the theoretical model of Flaschel and Groh (1995) was based – as modification of the simple Goodwin growth cycle approach discussed in the preceding section – on a repelling steady state and behavioral nonlinearities far off the steady state that tame the explosive dynamics and make it viable and that is confirmed in its qualitative features through econometric measurements for the US economy after the Second World War. This reserve army mechanism, the distributive cycle as well as the accompanying inflation/unemployment cycle, is obviously a fairly archaic way to provide boundedness and order in an advanced capitalist market economy and its democratic institutions. We are therefore now designing as an alternative to the preceding one a growth model that rests in place of overaccumulation (in the prosperity phase) and mass unemployment (in the stagnant phase) on a second labor market which through its institutional setup guarantees full employment in its interaction with the first labor market, the employment in the industrial sector of the economy that is modeled as highly flexible and competitive.

We therefore first reconsider the sector of firms in such an economy in Table5.1.

This account is a very simple one. Firms use their capital stock (at full capacity utilization as we shall show later on) to employ the amount of labor (in hours): $L_1^d$ in its operation, at

*Table 5.2* Households I and II (primary and secondary labor market)

| *Income Account (Households I):* | |
|---|---|
| *Uses* | *Resources* |
| $C_1 = c_{h1}(1-\tau_h)\omega_1 L_1^d$ | |
| $\omega_2 L_{2h}^w = c_{h2}(1-\tau_h)\omega_1 L_1^d$ | |
| $T = \tau_h \omega_1 L_1^d$ | |
| $\omega_2(L-(L_1^w + L_{2f}^w + L_{2h}^w + L_{2g}^w))$ | |
| $\omega_2 L^r, L^r = \alpha_r L$ | |
| $S_1$ | $\omega_1 L_1^d$ |
| $Y_1^w = \omega_1 L_1^d$ | $Y_1^w = \omega_1 L_1^d$ |

| *Income Account (Households II):* | |
|---|---|
| *Uses* | *Resources* |
| $C_2$ | $\omega_2 L_2^w, L_2^w = L - L_1^w$ |
| $Y_2^w$ | $Y_2^w$ |

the real wage $\omega_1$, the law of motion of which is to be determined in the next section from a model of the wage-price level interaction in the manufacturing sector. They in addition employ labor force $L_{2f}^w = \alpha_f L_1^d, \alpha_f = const$ from the second labor market at the wage $\omega_2$, which is a constant fraction $\alpha_\omega$ of the market wage in the first labor market. This labor force $L_{2f}^w$ is working the normal hours of a standard workday, while the workforce $L_1^w$ from the first labor market may be working overtime or undertime depending on the size of the capital stock in comparison to its own size. The rate $u_w = L_1^d / L_1^w$ is therefore the utilization rate of the workforce in the first labor market, the industrial workers of the economy (all other employment comes from the working of households occupied in the second labor market). Note, finally, that in line with the model of the first section of the chapter, we allow for capital stock depreciation at the rate $\delta$.

Firms produce full capacity output[6] $Y^p + \delta_1 R = C_1 + C_2 + C_r + I + \delta K + G$, that is sold to the two types of consumers (and the retired households), the investing firms and the government. The demand side of the model is formulated here in a way such that indeed this full capacity output can be sold in this way, see the next section on this matter. Deducting from this output $Y^p$ of firms their real wage payments to workers from the first and the second labor market (and depreciation)[7] we get the profits of firms which are here assumed to be invested fully into capital stock growth $\dot{K} = I = \Pi$. We thus have Classical (direct) investment habits in this basic approach to a model with an employer of first resort. There is therefore not yet debt or equity financing of investment in this model type.

We assume a fixed proportions technology with $y^p = Y^p / K$ the potential output–capital ratio and with $z = Y^p / L_1^d$ the given value of labor productivity (which determines the employment $L_1^d$ of the workforce $L_1^w$ of firms).

We next consider the households sector of our social growth model which comprises worker households working in the first labor market and the remaining ones that are all working in the second labor market (Table 5.2).

Households of type I consume manufacturing goods of amount $C_1$ and services from the second labor market $L_{2h}^w$. They pay an (all) income tax $T$ and they pay in addition – via further tax transfers – all workers' income in the labor market that is not coming from firms, from them and government (which is equivalent to an unemployment insurance).

*Table 5.3* Income account (retired households)

| *Uses* | *Resources* |
|---|---|
| $C_r$ | $\omega_2 L^r + \delta_1 R, L^r = \alpha_r L$ |
| $Y^r$ | $Y^r$ |

Moreover, they pay the pensions of the retired households ($\omega_2 L^r$) and accumulate their remaining income $S_1$ in the form a company pension into a fund $R$ that is administrated by firms (with inflow $S_1$, see the sector of households and outflow $\delta_1 R$).

The transfer $\omega_2(L - (L_1^w + L_{2f}^w + L_{2h}^w + L_{2g}^w)$ can be considered as solidarity payments, since workers from the first labor market that lose their job will automatically be employed in the second labor market where full employment is guaranteed by the government (as employer of first resort). We consider this employment as skill preserving, since it can be viewed as ordinary office or handicraft work (subject only to learning by doing when such workers return to the first labor market, i.e, employment in the production process of firms).

The second sector of households is here modeled in the simplest way that is available: Households employed in the second labor market, i.e, $L_2^w = L_{2f}^w + L_{2h}^w + L_{2g}^w$ pay no taxes and totally consume their income. We have thus Classical saving habits in this household sector, while households of type I may have positive or negative savings $S_1$ as residual from their income and expenditures. We here assume that they can accumulate these savings (or dissave in case of a negative $S_1$) from the stock of commodities they have accumulated as inventories in the past.

In order to have a consistent distribution of the funds $R$ that are accumulated by households of type I on the basis of their savings $S_1$, according to the stock-flow relationship $\dot{R} = S_1$ we have to modify this relationship as follows:

$$\dot{R} = S_1 - \delta_1 R$$

where $\delta_1$ is the rate by which these funds are depreciated through company pension payments to the 'officially retired' workers $L^r$ assumed to be a constant fraction of the 'active' workforce $L^r = \alpha_r L$. These worker households are added here as not really inactive, but offer work according to their still existing capabilities that can be considered as an addition to the supply of work organized by the government $L - (L_1^w + L_{2f}^w + L_{2h}^w)$, i.e. the working potential of the officially retired persons remains an active and valuable contribution of the work hours that are supplied by the members of the society. It is obvious that the proper allocation of the work hours under the control of the government needs thorough reflection from the microeconomic and the social point of view, which, however, cannot be a topic in a paper on the macroeconomics of such an economy.

As the income account of the retired households, shown below, shows they receive pension payments as if they would work in the second labor market and they get in addition individual transfer income (company pensions) from the accumulated funds $R$ in proportion to the time they have been active in the first labor market and as an aggregate household group of the total amount $\delta_1 R$ by which the pension funds $R$ are reduced in each period (Table 5.3).

There is finally the government sector which is also formulated in a very basic way (Table 5.4).

The government receives income taxes, the solidarity payments (employment benefits) for the second labor market paid from workers in the first labor market and old-age pension payments. It uses the taxes to finance government goods demand $G$ and the surplus of

*Table 5.4* The government income account

| *Fiscal authority/employer of first resort* | |
|---|---|
| *Uses* | *Resources* |
| $G = \alpha_g T$ | $T = \tau_h \omega_1 L_1^d$ |
| $\omega_2 L_{g2}^w = (1-\alpha_g)T$ | |
| $\omega_2(L - (L_1^w + L_{2f}^w + L_{2h}^w + L_{2g}^w))$ | $\omega_2 L_r^w$ |
| $\omega_2 L^r$ | $\omega_2 \alpha_r L$ |
| $Y^g$ | $Y^g$ |

taxes over these government expenditures to actively employ the core workers in the government sector. In addition, it employs the workers receiving employment benefits from the households in first labor market and it in fact also employs the 'retired' persons to the extent they can still contribute to the various employment activities. We thus have that the total labor force in the second labor market is employed by firms, by households of type I and the remainder through the government as is obvious from the solidarity payments of households working in the first labor market. We thus have that the income payments to workers in the second labor market ($\omega_2 L_2^w$) that are not originating from their services to firms, to households of type I or through an excess of income taxes over government commodity expenditures (base government employment) are paid out of transfers from the household sector that works in industrial production to the government, and that on the basis of these payments the remaining work in the second labor market is organized by government (in the way it does this in the administration of the state in all modern market economies).

In sum, we get that workers are employed either in the first labor market and if not there then by doing auxiliary work within firms, services for households of type I or services in the government sector concerning public administration, infrastructure services, educational services or other public services (in addition, there is potential labor supply $\alpha_r L$ from the retired households, which due to the long life expectancy in modern societies can remain effective suppliers of specific work over a considerable span of time). In this way the whole workforce is always fully employed in this model of social growth (and the retired persons according to their capabilities) and thus does not suffer from human degradation in particular. Of course, there are a variety of issues concerning state organized work that point to problems in the organization of such work, but all such problems exist also in actual industrialized market economies in one way or another.

We thus have a Classical growth model of the economy where full employment is not assumed, but actively constructed. To motivate the behavioral equations of the social growth model of this chapter we derive them as simplification from an advanced Goodwin–Kalecki growth cycle model where indeed the persistent long phase cycle in employment and the wage share we derived and observed in section 1 is augmented by Keynesian goods market dynamics and a Kaleckian reserve army mechanism that concerns the whole social structure of accumulation and in particular an explanation of the rise and the (partial) fall of the welfare state after the Second World War. We will introduce the behavioral equations of our social growth model by contrasting them – as we go along – with what has been assumed in Flaschel *et al.*(2007a) within the Goodwin–Kaleckian growth cycle model of a distributive reserve army mechanism coupled with Kalecki's (1943) political aspects of full employment.

*Table 5.5* Four types of market economies

| | *High steady state* | *Low steady state* |
|---|---|---|
| Stable steady state | Nordic consenus driven economy | Kaleckian market economy type I |
| Unstable steady state | Kaleckian market economy type II | Southern dissent economy |

## Goodwin—Kalecki dynamics: progress towards consensus driven economies and beyond?

In this section we go on from the Goodwinian modeling of the Marxian reserve army mechanism to its extension as a Kaleckian model of the evolution of the welfare state after the Second World War as it was modeled in Flaschel *et al.* (2007a). We progressed in this framework from the case of dissent economies (where in fact a Goodwinian and a Kaleckian type of reserve army mechanism were interacting) to the case of consenus driven economies where we could show the existence of a high and attracting balanced growth path for such an economy. Table 5.5 shows the range of possibilities that was considered in Flaschel *et al.* (2007a).

As conditions for the existence of a consensus driven economy, we assumed Flaschel *et al.* (2007a), see the behavioral equations below, that demand pressure in the labor market (both inside and outside of the firm) does not influence the rate of wage inflation very much, i.e. the wage level is a fairly stable magnitude. Furthermore, the Kaleckian reserve army mechanism was absent from the model ($i_e = 0$). Moreover, the benchmark values for demand pressures and the employment policy of firms are consistent with each other and all sufficiently high to not imply labor market segmentation and significant disqualification of unemployed workers. This can be coupled with flexible hiring and firing policies then, i.e. the parameter $\beta_{eu}$ may be chosen as large as it is desirable.

This modified Kaleckian approach to consensus driven economies is contrasted in the following with the dynamics and the balanced growth path of the model of flexicurity capitalism we introduced in the preceding section. We there compare models of the distributive growth cycle (with more or less conflict between capital and labor) with the flexicurity variant of competitive capitalism. However, the important and difficult topic of the generation of socio-economic progress paths that lead from distributive conflict cycles to consensus driven economies and from there towards the proper functioning of an employer of first resort economy, as the perspective of the flexicurity approach to social growth, must be left for future research.

We derive the behavioral relationships of our model of flexicurity capitalism by contrasting them with the Kaleckian growth cycle model of Flaschel *et al.* (2007a). We represent the laws of motion of the latter economy first in a framework of Goodwin–Kalecki type, before we show how these equations simplify in our model of social growth with an employer of first resort.

We consider first the wage-price dynamics in the first labor market, which is the only labor market in the Goodwin–Kalecki approach. For the description of these dynamics we start from a general formulation of a wage-price spiral as shown below, see Flaschel *et al.* (2007a) for a detailed treatment of its structures.[8]

$$\hat{w} = \beta_{we}(e - \bar{e}) + \beta_{wu}(u_w - \tilde{u}_w) - \beta_{w\omega}\ln(\frac{\omega}{\omega^o}) + \kappa_w\hat{p} + (1 - \kappa_w)\pi^c$$

$$\hat{p} = \beta_{py}(y - \bar{y}) + \beta_{p\omega}\ln(\frac{\omega}{\omega^o}) + \kappa_p\hat{w} + (1 - \kappa_p)\pi^c$$

In these equations, $\hat{w}$, $\hat{p}$ denote the growth rates of nominal wages w and the price level $p$ (their inflation rates) and $\pi^c$ a medium-term inflation-climate expression which however is of no relevance in the following due to our neglect of real interest rate effects on the demand side of the model. We denote by $e$ the rate of employment on the external labor market and by $u_w$ the ratio of utilization of the workforce within firms. This latter ratio of employment is compared by the workforce in their negotiations with firms with their desired normal ratio of utilization $\tilde{u}_w$. We thus have two employment gaps, an external one: $e - \bar{e}$ and an internal one: $u_w - \tilde{u}_w$, which determine wage inflation rate $\hat{w}$ from the side of demand pressure within or outside of the production process. In the wage PC we in addition employ a real wage error correction term $\ln(\omega/\omega_0)$ as in Blanchard and Katz (1999), see Flaschel and Krolzig (2006) for details, and as cost pressure term a weighted average of short-term (perfectly anticipated) price inflation $\hat{p}$ and the medium-term inflation climate $\pi^c$ in which the economy is operating.

As the wage PC is constructed it is subject to an interaction between the external labor market and the utilization of the workforce within firms. Higher demand pressure on the external labor market translates itself here into higher workforce wage demand pressure within firms (and demand for a reduced length of the normal working day, etc.), an interaction between two utilization rates of the labor force that has to be and will be taken note of in the formulation of the employment policy of firms. Demand pressure on the labor market thus exhibits two interacting components, which employed workers may make their behavior dependent upon.

We use the output–capital ratio $y = Y/K$ to measure the output gap in the price inflation PC and again the deviation of the real wage $\omega = w/p$ from the steady state real wage $\omega^o$ as error correction expression in the price PC. Cost pressure in this price PC is formulated as a weighted average of short-term (perfectly anticipated) wage inflation and again our concept of an inflationary climate $\pi^c$. In this price Phillips curve we have three elements of cost pressure interacting with each other, a medium term one (the inflationary climate) and two short term ones, basically the level of real unit-wage labor costs (a Blanchard and Katz (1999) error correction term) and the current rate of wage inflation, which taken by itself would represent a constant markup pricing rule. This basic rule is, however, modified by these other cost-pressure terms and in particular also made dependent on the state of the business cycle by way of the demand pressure term $y - \bar{y}$ in the market for goods.

In our social growth model the above wage-price inflation dynamics simplifies to the following form:

$$\hat{w} = \beta_{wu}(u_w - \tilde{u}_w) - \beta_{w\omega}\ln(\frac{\omega}{\omega^o}) + \kappa_w\hat{p} + (1 - \kappa_w)\pi^c \tag{5.3}$$

$$\hat{p} = \beta_{p\omega}\ln(\frac{\omega}{\omega^o}) + \kappa_p\hat{w} + (1 - \kappa_p)\pi^c \tag{5.4}$$

since we will have – by construction – full employment in this model type (and a NAIRU rate that is zero) and in addition a goods demand that is always equal to the potential output that is produced by firms.

On the demand side of the model the Kaleckian framework used for reasons of simplicity the conventional Keynesian dynamic multiplier process (in place of a full-fledged Metzlerian inventory adjustment mechanism) and extremely classical saving habits together with a

Kaleckian type of investment function, i.e.:

$$\hat{Y} = \dot{Y}/Y = \beta_y(Y^d/Y - 1) + \bar{a}, \quad Y^d = \omega L^d + I(\cdot) + \delta K + G$$

where $Y^d, Y$ denote aggregate demand and supply and $\bar{a}$ a trend term in the behavior of capitalist firms. Assuming a fixed proportions technology with given output–employment ratio $x = Y/L^d$ and potential output–capital ratio $y^p = Y^p/K$, allows us to determine from the output–capital ratio y the employment $u_w$ of the workforce within firms that corresponds to this activity measure y:

$$u_w = y/(xle), \quad u_w = L^d/L^w, l = L/K, e = L^w/L$$

(with $L^d$ hours worked, $L^w$ the number of workers employed within firms and with $L$ denoting labor supply). This relationship represents by and large a technical relationship (to be calculated by 'engineers') and relates hours worked to goods market activity as measured by $y$ in the way shown above.

In the social growth model we always have the relationship $y^d = y = y^p$ per unit of capital and thus no dynamic on the goods market, and get on this basis then:

$$u_w = L_1^d/L_1^w = \frac{y^p}{zle_1} = \frac{y^p}{zl_1^w}, \tag{5.5}$$
$$l = L/K, l_1^w = L_1^w/K, e_1 = L_1^w/L.$$

This technological relationship must be carefully distinguished from the employment (recruitment) policy of firms that reads on the intensive form level:

$$\hat{e} = \beta_{eu}(u_w - \tilde{u}_f) - \beta_{e\omega}(\omega - \omega^o) + \bar{a} - \hat{L}, \ i.e.$$
$$\dot{e} = \beta_{eu}(y^p/(xl) - \tilde{u}_f e) - \beta_{e\omega}(\omega - \omega^o)e + (\bar{a} - \hat{L})e$$

The basis of this formulation of an employment policy of firms in terms of the employment rate is – by assumption – the following level form representation of this relationship:

$$\dot{L}^w = \beta_{eu}(L^d - \tilde{u}_f L^w) - \beta_{e\omega}(\omega - \omega^o)L^w + \bar{a}L^w, \ i.e.$$
$$\hat{L}^w = \beta_{eu}(L^d/L^w - \tilde{u}_f) - \beta_{e\omega}(\omega - \omega^o) + \bar{a}$$

where $\bar{a}$ again integrates the trend term assumed by firms into now their employment policy and where $\tilde{u}_f$ represents the utilization ratio of the workforce of firms that is desired by them. In order to obtain Equation (5.6) as the resulting law of motion for the rate of employment one simply has to take note of the definitional relationship $\hat{e} = \hat{L}^w - \hat{L}$, where $L$ denotes the labor supply in each moment in time. We have also included into the above recruitment policy a term that says that intended recruitment will be lowered in case of increasing real wage costs of firms.

In the social growth model the employment policy of firms (on the first labor market) is by and large the same as above. We stress, however, that the external and the internal labor market and the pressure they are exercising on money wage formation form a capillary system in the Goodwin–Kalecki approach and are handled by firms against this background. Such a situation is no longer present in the social growth model, since there is by construction full employment in this model type and since the second labor market here serves as a buffer for the fluctuations that occur in the employment of workers within firms. Note that the label flexicurity assumes in this regard that firms are completely free in their choice of the hiring and firing parameter $\beta_{eu}$:

$$\hat{e}_1 = \beta_{eu}(u_w - \tilde{u}_w) + \rho^o - \hat{L},\ i.e. \tag{5.6}$$

$$\dot{e}_1 = \beta_{eu}(y^p/(xl) - \tilde{u}_w e_1) + (\rho^o - \hat{L})e_1, \text{or simpler} \tag{5.7}$$

$$\hat{l}_1^w = \beta_{eu}(y^p/(zl_1^w) - \tilde{u}_w) + (\rho^o - \rho) \tag{5.8}$$

since investment is equal to profits in this basic version of the social growth model. Note that we now use a common measure $\tilde{u}_w$ in the money wage PC and the recruitment policy of firms and that we assume now $\rho^o$ to be the trend rate of growth of the economy which is used by firms in their trend labor recruitment policy (in place of the $\bar{a}$ used in the Goodwin–Kalecki model).

In the Keynesian Goodwin–Kalecki framework we assumed extremely classical saving habits ($s_w = 0, s_c = 1$) and for the investment behavior of firms:

$$I/K = i_\rho(\rho - \rho_o) - i_e(e - \bar{e}_f) + \bar{a},$$

with $\rho = y(1 - \omega/x)$ the current rate of profit. In this equation, the magnitude $\bar{a}$ denotes again the given trend investment rate (representing investor's 'animal spirits') from which firms depart in a natural way if there is excess profitability (and vice versa). Moreover, firms have a view of what the rate employment should be on the external labor market (Kalecki's (1943, Ch. 12) analysis of why 'bosses' dislike full employment) and thus reduce their (domestic) investment plans (driven by excess profitability) in situations of a tense labor market. They thus take pressure from the labor market in the future evolution of the economy by their implicit collective understanding that high pressure in the capillary system of internal and external labor markets we have considered above will lead to conditions in the capital-labor relationship, unwanted by firms, since persistently high employment rates may give rise to significant changes of workforce participation with respect to firms' decision making, in the hiring and firing decision of firms, in reductions of the workday etc. not at all liked by 'industrial leaders' in the case of a Kaleckian dissent economy.

In the social growth model, the alternative and extension of this chapter to/of a Kaleckian consensus driven economy, we have already assumed that workers of type II consume their whole income (they pay no taxes). With respect to the other type of workers we assume as their consumption function:

$$C_1 = c_{h1}(1 - \tau_h)\omega_1 L_1^d \tag{5.9}$$

with $c_h$ denoting the propensity to consume and $\tau_h$ the tax rate, and:

$$\omega_2 L_{2h}^w = c_{h2}(1 - \tau_h)\omega_1 L_1^d \tag{5.10}$$

representing the consumption of household services.

Households type I savings is on the basis of our accounting relationships given by:

$$S_1 = \omega_1 L_1^d - C_1 - \omega_2 L_{2h}^w - \omega_2(L - (L_1^w + L_{2f}^w + L_{2h}^w + L_{2g}^w) - \omega_2 L^r) \tag{5.11}$$

due to the assumed solidarity contribution they provide to the second labor market. Investment behavior is in the basic form of the social growth model very simple: all profits of firms are invested and there is no debt or equity financing yet. The growth rate of the capital stock is thus simply given by $\hat{K} = \rho = \Pi/K(\rho^o$ the steady state rate of profit). On the basis of what we have already assumed we thus get:

$$\hat{K} = \rho = y^p[1 - \omega_1(1 + \alpha_\omega \alpha_f)/z] - \delta, \tag{5.12}$$

$$\omega_2 = \alpha_\omega \omega_1, L_{2f}^w = \alpha_f L_1^d \tag{5.13}$$

see below with respect to the parameter $\alpha_f$ which characterizes the employment policy of firms with respect to the second labor market.

For government consumption we finally assume the simple relationship $G = \gamma I$, i.e. government consumption per unit of capital grows at the same rate as the capital stock (which allows to integrate fiscal policy with investment behavior in the intensive form of the model).

Since the government, workers from the second labor market and pensioners do not save, and since all tax transfers are turned into consumption and the savings of households of type I into commodity inventories of firms from which company pensions are to be deducted, and since finally all profits are invested, it can easily be shown from what was presented in accounting form in the preceding section that we must have at all times:

$$Y^p + \delta_1 R = C_1 + C_2 + C_r + I + \delta K + G, \; C_1 = c_{h1}(1 - \tau_h)\omega_1 L_1^d \tag{5.14}$$

if firms produce at full capacity $Y^p = y^p K, L_1^d = Y^p/z$ (which they can and will do in this case). There is thus no demand problem on the market for goods and thus no need to discuss a dynamic multiplier process as in the Goodwin–Kalecki model with which this model was compared here. Note that, moreover, we have by construction of the social growth model at all points in time:

$$L = L_1^w + L_{2f}^w + L_{2h}^w + L_{2g}^w + L_r^w = L_1^w + L_2^w \qquad L_r = \alpha_r L \tag{5.15}$$

We thus assume that households of type I must pay as solidarity contribution (employment benefits) those workers of type II, whose wages are not paid by firms, through households of type II service to households of type I and through the core employment in the government sector. The government employs in addition as administrative workers and infrastructure workers (public work and education) the remaining workforce in the second labor market (plus the $L^r$ services from pensioners). This completes the discussion of the behavioral equations of the social growth model, the intensive form of which will now be derived in the following section. Compared to the Goodwin–Kalecki model of Flaschel *et al.* (2007a) this model type will be shown to function very easily without need of a discussion of conflict-driven upper and lower turning points in economic activity and income distribution which are necessary to keep the locally centrifugal dynamics of the Goodwin–Kalecki approach bounded and thus viable. There are only mildly conflicting income claims in the social growth model and also only mild conflicts about the role and the extent of the welfare state in such a framework (to be discussed below).

In the Goodwin–Kalecki growth cycle model we have (in the dissent situation) conflict-riddled turning points in economic and social activities than can end prosperity phases in a radical fashion and then lead the society into long-lasting depressions, processes that are harmful and wasteful with respect to human and physical capital and that may not work towards a recovery under all circumstances. The need for an alternative to such a situation is therefore a compelling one from the perspective of a social and democratic society and the potential it may contain for the evolution of mankind. We have already introduced in the previous and this section the economic contours of such an alternative. This alternative model of social reproduction will be analyzed in its macrodynamic features in the next two sections.

## Flexicurity growth: full capacity convergence towards balanced reproduction

### *The dynamics and their balanced growth path*

Inserting the equations of the social growth model appropriately into each other gives rise to the following 3D dynamics in the state variables $\omega_1 = w/p, l_1^w = L_1^w/K$ and $l = L/K$ where the last variable does, however, not feedback into the first two laws of motion due to the construction of the labor markets of the model:[9]

$$\hat{\omega}_1 = \kappa\left[(1-\kappa_p)(\beta_{wu}(\frac{y^p}{zl_1^w}-\tilde{u}_w)-\beta_{w\omega}\ln(\frac{\omega_1}{\omega_1^o})) -(1-\kappa_w)\beta_{p\omega}\ln(\frac{\omega_1}{\omega_1^o})\right] \quad (5.16)$$

$$\hat{l}_1^w = \beta_{eu}(\frac{y^p}{zl_1^w}-\tilde{u}_w)+n-\rho, \quad (5.17)$$

$$\rho = y^p[1-\omega_1(1+\alpha_\omega\alpha_f)/z]-\delta \quad (5.18)$$

$$\hat{l} = n-(y^p[1-(1+\alpha_\omega\alpha_f)\omega_1/z]-\delta) = y^p[(1+\alpha_\omega\alpha_f)(\omega_1-\omega_1^o)/z] \quad (5.19)$$

However, in order to get a stationary value of $l$ in the long-run we must assume a special value for $\omega_1^o$ in the first two equations (as the steady state reference real wage in the first labor market), which is determined by:

$$\hat{l}=0, \quad \text{i.e.} \quad y^p[1-(1+\alpha_\omega\alpha_f)\omega_1/z]=\delta+n. \quad (5.20)$$

The reference wage used in the first two laws of motion must therefore be chosen such that the capital stock grows with the natural rate $n$ in the steady state which is one of the conditions needed for steady growth in the Harrod (1939) growth model. Since our model is based on Say's law the other conditions of the Harrod model do not apply here.

Based on this assumption we get for the interior steady state or balanced growth path of the social growth economy the equations ($\tilde{u}_w = 1$ in the following for reasons of simplicity):

$$l_1^{wo} = \frac{y^p}{\tilde{u}_w z} = \frac{l_1^{do}}{\tilde{u}_w} = y^p/z \quad (5.21)$$

$$\omega_1^o = \frac{1-\frac{n+\delta}{y^p}}{1+\alpha_f\alpha_\omega}z < z \quad (5.22)$$

$$l^o = \text{arbitrary} \quad (5.23)$$

Since we have a zero determinant for the 3D Jacobian of the above dynamics (since the third law of motion only depends on the first state variable) we have zero root hysteresis in the 3D system which in the given form allows to treat and solve the first two equations independently of the third one which when appended can converge to any value of $l$, depending on shocks to labor supply, capital formation and the like. Note, however, that this only applies if there is social consensus with respect to the steady state real wage $\omega_1^o$ as the benchmark for real wage negotiations in the first labor market. Choosing in addition (and for example) as parameter values[10] $\alpha_w = 0.5, n = 0.05, \delta = 0.1, y^p = 0.5$ gives for the ratio $v_1 = \omega_1/z$, the wage share in the first labor market, the approximate value $v_1 = 0.64$ and for the profit share $\Pi^o/Y^p$ the value $0.1$ which in sum implies for the shares of wages and government expenditures the value 90 percent. Note, finally, that the living standards in this society, as measured by real wages, depend of course on the value of the labor productivity of workers in the first labor market.

## *Monotonic convergence towards balanced growth*

For the Jacobian of the 3D dynamics evaluated at the steady state we get from the laws of motion:

$$J^o = \begin{pmatrix} J^o_{11} & J^o_{12} & 0 \\ J^o_{21} & J^o_{22} & 0 \\ J^o_{31} & 0 & 0 \end{pmatrix}$$

with:

$$J^o_{11} = -\kappa[(1-\kappa_p)\beta_{w\omega} + (1-\kappa_w)\beta_{p\omega}]$$

$$J^o_{12} = -\kappa(1-\kappa_p)\beta_{wu}\frac{y^p}{z}(l_1^{wo})^{-2}\omega_1^o$$

$$J^o_{21} = \frac{y^p(1+\alpha_\omega\alpha_f)}{z}l_1^{wo}$$

$$J^o_{22} = -\beta_{eu}\frac{y^p}{zl_1^{wo}}$$

$$J^o_{31} = \frac{y^p(1+\alpha_\omega\alpha_f)}{z}l$$

Since we only have to investigate the first two laws of motion, it suffices to consider the following matrix with respect to its eigenvalues:

$$J^o = \begin{pmatrix} J^o_{11} & J^o_{12} \\ J^o_{21} & J^o_{22} \end{pmatrix} = \begin{pmatrix} - & - \\ + & - \end{pmatrix}$$

From the sign structure in this matrix it is obvious that we always have locally asymptotically stable dynamics (i.e. trace $J^o < 0, \det J^o > 0$). Furthermore, the condition trace $J^o = 4\det J^o$, i.e.:

$$(J^o_{11} + J^o_{22})^2 = 4(J^o_{11}J^o_{22} + J^o_{21}J^o_{12})$$

separates monotonic convergence (for parameters $\beta_{eu}$ sufficiently large) from cyclical convergence (parameters $\beta_{eu}$ sufficiently small). Reformulated, this condition reads:

$$|J^o_{22}| = |J^o_{11}| + 2\sqrt{|J^o_{21}J^o_{12}|}, \quad i.e. \quad \beta^H_{eu} = \frac{zl_1^{wo}}{y^p}[|J^o_{11}| + 2\sqrt{|J^o_{21}J^o_{12}|}]$$

We thus get for the bifurcation value $\beta^H_{eu}$ that separates monotonic from cyclical convergence:

$$\beta^H_{eu} = \kappa[(1-\kappa_p)\beta_{w\omega} + (1-\kappa_w)\beta_{p\omega}] + 2\sqrt{(1+\alpha_\omega\alpha_f)\kappa(1-\kappa_p)\beta_{wu}\omega_1^o l_1^{wo}} \tag{5.24}$$

This critical parameter for the hiring and firing speed parameter in our social growth economy is therefore in particular the larger, the larger the reaction of money wage inflation with respect to workforce utilization, i.e. the larger the parameter $\beta_{wu}$ becomes. We thus get that economic fluctuations can be avoided in this type of economy if wages in the first labor market respond relatively sluggishly to demand pressure in this market (as measured by the utilization rate of the insiders) and if hiring and firing is a sufficiently flexible process as envisaged by the concept of flexicurity capitalism.

## *Global viability*

For the investigation of global asymptotic stability we will now analyze the core dynamical system by means of so-called Liapunov functions. For this purpose we represent the 2D dynamics of the preceding section as follows:

$$\hat{\omega}_1 = G^1(\omega_1) + G^2(l_1^w), \quad G^{1'} < 0, G^{2'} < 0 \tag{5.25}$$

$$\hat{l}_1^w = H^1(\omega_1) + H^2(l_1^w), \quad H^{1'} > 0, H^{2'} < 0 \tag{5.26}$$

The Liapunov function to be used in the stability proof then reads as follows:

$$V(\omega_1, l_1^w) = \int_{\omega_1^o}^{\omega_1} H^1(\tilde{\omega}_1)/\tilde{\omega}_1 d\tilde{\omega}_1 + \int_{l_1^{wo}}^{l_1^w} -G^2(\tilde{l}_1^w)/\tilde{l}_1^w d\tilde{l}_1^w$$

This function describes by its graph a 3D sink with the steady state of the economy as its lowest point, since the above integrates two functions that are negative to the left of the steady state values and positive to their right. For the first derivative of the Liapunov function along the trajectories of the considered dynamical system we moreover get:

$$\begin{aligned}
\dot{V} &= dV(\omega_1(t), l_1^w(t))/dt = \left(H^1(\omega_1)/\omega_1\right)\dot{\omega}_1 - \left(G^2(l_1^w)/l_1^w\right)\dot{l}_1^w \\
&= H^1(\omega_1)\hat{\omega}_1 - G^2(l_1^w)\hat{l}_1^w \\
&= H^1(\omega_1)(G^1(\omega_1) + G^2(l_1^w)) - G^2(l_1^w)(H^1(\omega_1) + H^2(l_1^w)) \\
&= H^1(\omega_1)G^1(\omega_1) - G^2(l_1^w)H^2(l_1^w) \qquad (5.27) \\
&= -H^1(\omega_1)(-G^1(\omega_1)) - (-G^2(l_1^w))(-H^2(l_1^w)) \qquad (5.28) \\
&\leq 0 \qquad [=0 \quad \text{if and only if} \quad \omega_1 = \omega_1^o, l_1^w = l_1^{wo}]
\end{aligned}$$

since the multiplied functions have the same sign to the right and to the left of their steady state values and thus lead to positive products with a minus sign in front of them (up to the situation where the economy is already sitting in the steady state). We thus have proved that there holds:

**Proposition 5.1**
*The interior steady state of the dynamics:*

$$\hat{\omega}_1 = \kappa[(1-\kappa_p)(\beta_{wu}(\frac{y^p}{zl_1^w} - \tilde{u}_w) - \beta_{w\omega}\ln(\frac{\omega_1}{\omega_1^o})) - (1-\kappa_w)\beta_{p\omega}\ln(\frac{\omega_1}{\omega_1^o})] \tag{5.29}$$

$$\hat{l}_1^w = \beta_{eu}(\frac{y^p}{zl_1^w} - \tilde{u}_w) + \rho^o + (y^p[(\omega_1 - \omega_1^o)(1 + \alpha_\omega\alpha_f)/z] - \delta) \tag{5.30}$$

*is a global sink of the function $V$, defined on the positive orthant of the phase space, and is attracting in this domain, since the function $V$ is strictly decreasing along the trajectories of the dynamics in the positive orthant of the phase space.*

From the global perspective there may, however, be supply bottlenecks in the second labor market. Here we assume that the economy is working always in a corridor around the steady state where the government as the employer of first resort has still a sufficient amount of workforce working in the range of activities that is organized by it. Due to the stability results obtained in the present and the preceding section this is not a very restrictive assumption under the normal working of the economy.

## Company pension funds: law of motion and steady state position

There is a further law of motion in the background of the model that needs to be considered in order to provide an additional statement on the viability of the considered model of flexicurity capitalism. This law of motion describes the evolution of the pension fund per unit of the capital stock $\eta = \frac{R}{K}$ and is obtained from the defining equation $\dot{R} = S_1 - \delta_1 R$ as follows:

$$\hat{\eta} = \hat{R} - \hat{K} = \frac{\dot{R}}{K}\frac{K}{R} - \rho = \frac{S_1 - \delta_1 R}{K}/\eta - \rho, \quad \text{i.e.:}$$
$$\dot{\eta} = \frac{S_1}{K} - (\delta_1 + \rho)\eta = s_1 - (\delta_1 + \rho)\eta$$

with savings of households of type I and profits of firms per unit of capital being given by:

$$s_1 = (1 - (c_{h1} + c_{h2})(1 - \tau_h) - \tau_h)\omega_1 y^p / z - \alpha_\omega \omega_1 (l_x^w + l^r),$$
$$l_x^w = l - (l_1^w + l_{2f}^w + l_{2h}^w + l_{2g}^w)$$
$$l^r = \alpha_r l,$$

i.e. due to the financing of the employment terms $l_{2h}^w + l_{2g}^w$:

$$s_1 = (1 - c_{h1}(1 - \tau_h) - \alpha_g \tau_h)\omega_1 y^p / z - ((1 + \alpha_r)l - (l_1^w + l_{2f}^w))\alpha_\omega \omega_1,$$
$$l_{2f}^w = \alpha_f y^p / z$$
$$\rho = y^p[1 - (1 + \alpha_\omega \alpha_f)\omega_1 / z] - \delta$$

For reasons of analytical simplicity we now assume that the government pursues an immigration policy that ensures for the total growth rate of the labor force the condition $n = \hat{K}, i.e.$ the total labor supply grows by this migration policy with the same rate as the capital stock. This keeps the ratio $l = L/K$ constant, a simplifying assumption that must be accompanied by the assumption that the actual $\bar{l}$ must be chosen in a certain neighborhood of a base value $\bar{l}_o$ that is to be determined later on. Since we are now no longer able to determine the steady state value of the real wage $\omega_1$ from the law of motion for $l$, we have to supply it from the outside now: $\omega_1^o = \bar{\omega}_1 =$ given. This also provides us with the steady state value of the rate of profit $\rho^o = \bar{\rho} = y^p[1 - (1 + \alpha_\omega \alpha_f)\bar{\omega}_1 / z] - \delta$ which also determines the steady value of natural growth $n_o = \bar{\rho}$. Moreover, we also assume for simplicity $\delta_1 = \delta$ for the depreciation rates of the capital stock and the stock of pension funds.

This gives for the law of motion of the pension fund to capital ratio the differential equation:

$$\dot{\eta} = (1 - c_{h1}(1 - \tau_h) - \alpha_g \tau_h)\omega_1 y^p / z$$
$$-((1 + \alpha_r)\bar{l} - (l_1^w + \alpha_f y^p / z))\alpha_\omega \omega_1 - [y^p - (1 + \alpha_\omega \alpha_f)\omega_1 y^p / z]\eta$$

We thus get that the trajectory of the pension fund ratio $\eta$ is driven by the autonomous evolution of the state variables $\omega_1, l_1^w$ that characterize the dynamics of the private sector of the economy and that has been shown to be convergent to the steady state values $\bar{\omega}_1, l_1^{wo} = y^p / z$ as usual). Assuming that these variables have reached their steady state positions then gives:

$$\dot{\eta} = (1 - c_{h1}(1 - \tau_h) - \alpha_g \tau_h)\bar{\omega}_1 y^p / z$$
$$-((1 + \alpha_r)\bar{l} - (l_1^{wo} + \alpha_f y^p / z))\alpha_\omega \bar{\omega}_1 - (\delta + \bar{\rho})\eta$$

which gives a single linear differential equation for the ratio $\eta$. This dynamic is globally asymptotically stable around its steady state position ($l_1^{wo} = y^p/z$):

$$\eta_o = \frac{(1-c_{h1}(1-\tau_h)-\alpha_g\tau_h)\bar{\omega}_1 y^p/z - ((1+\alpha_r)\bar{l}-(1+\alpha_f)y^p/z)\alpha_\omega\bar{\omega}_1}{\delta+\bar{\rho}}$$

In this simple case we thus have monotonic adjustment of the pension-fund capital ratio to its steady state position, while in general we have a non-autonomous adjustment of this ratio that is driven by the real wage and employment dynamics of the first labor market. The steady state level of $\eta$ is positive iff there holds for the full employment labor intensity ratio:

$$\bar{l} < \frac{(1-c_{h1}(1-\tau_h)-\alpha_g\tau_h)\bar{\omega}_1 y^p/z + ((1+\alpha_f)y^p/z)\alpha_\omega\bar{\omega}_1}{(\delta+\bar{\rho})(1+\alpha_r)\alpha_\omega\bar{\omega}_1}$$

We now assume, moreover, that the additional company pension payments to pensioners should add the percentage $100\cdot\alpha_c$ to their base pension $\omega_2\alpha_r\bar{l}$ per unit of capital. We thus have as further restriction on the steady state position of the economy, if there is an $\alpha_c$ target given:

$$\delta\eta_o = \alpha_c\omega_2^o\alpha_r\bar{l}, \quad \omega_2^o = \alpha_\omega\bar{\omega}_1$$

Inserting the value for $\eta_o$ then gives:

$$\alpha_c = \delta\frac{(1-c_{h1}(1-\tau_h)-\alpha_g\tau_h)\bar{\omega}_1 y^p/z - ((1+\alpha_r)\bar{l}-(1+\alpha_f)y^p/z)\alpha_\omega\bar{\omega}_1}{(\delta+\bar{\rho})\omega_2^o\alpha_r\bar{l}}$$

We thus get that a target value for $\alpha_c$ demands a certain labor intensity ratio $\bar{l}$ and vice versa. For a given total labor intensity ratio there is a given percentage by which company pensions compare to base pension payments. This percentage is the larger the smaller the ratio $l_1^{wo}/\bar{l}$ due to the following reformulation of the $\alpha_c$ formula:

$$\begin{aligned}\alpha_c = &\frac{\delta}{(\delta+\bar{\rho})\alpha_r\alpha_\omega\bar{\omega}_1}\\ &[((1-c_{h1}(1-\tau_h)-\alpha_g\tau_h)\bar{\omega}_1+(1+\alpha_f)\alpha_\omega\bar{\omega}_1)l_1^{wo}/\bar{l}\\ &-(1+\alpha_r)\alpha_\omega\bar{\omega}_1]\end{aligned} \quad (5.31)$$

If this value of the total employment labor intensity ratio prevails in the considered economy (where it is of course as usually assumed that $c_{h1}(1-\tau_h)+\alpha_g\tau_h < 1$ holds) we have that core pension payments to pensioners are augmented by company pension payments by a percentage that is given by the parameter $\alpha_c$ and that these extra pension payments are distributed to pensioners in proportion to their contribution to the time that they have worked in the private sector of the economy. There is thus a negative trade-off between the ratios $\bar{l}, \alpha_c$, as expressed by the relationship (5.31). This also shows that the total working population must have a certain ratio to the capital stock in order to allow for a given percentage of extra company pension payments. Due to $\delta\eta_o = \alpha_c\omega_2^o\alpha_r\bar{l}$ and $s_1^o = (\delta+\bar{\rho})\eta_o$ we also have the equivalence between positive savings per unit of capital of households of type I and positive values for $\alpha_c, \eta_o$. Moreover, these values are in fact positive if there holds:[11]

$$\bar{l} < \frac{(1-c_{h1}(1-\tau_h)-\alpha_g\tau_h)\bar{\omega}_1 y^p/z + (1+\alpha_f)y^p/z)\alpha_\omega\bar{\omega}_1}{(\delta+\bar{\rho})(1+\alpha_r)\alpha_\omega\bar{\omega}_1}$$

This inequality set limits to the total labor-supply capital-stock ratio $\bar{l}$ which allows for positive savings of households of type I in the steady state and thus for extra pension

*Table 5.6* Firms: production and income account

| *Uses* | *Resources* |
|---|---|
| $\delta K$ | $\delta K$ |
| $\omega_1 L_1^d = \omega_1 Y^p/z$ | $C_1 + C_2 + C_r$ |
| $\omega_2 L_{2f}^w = \alpha_\omega \omega_1 \alpha_f Y^p/z$ | $G$ |
| $rD$ | |
| $\Pi$ | $I = (i_\rho(\rho - \rho_o) - i_d(d - d_o) + \bar{a})K$ |
| $Y^p$ | $Y^p$ |

*Table 5.7* Investment and credit account

| *Uses* | *Resources* |
|---|---|
| $\delta K$ | $\delta K$ |
| $I = (i_\rho(\rho - \rho_o) - i_d(d - d_o) + \bar{a})K$ | $\Pi$ |
| | $\dot{D} = I - \Pi$ |
| $I^g$ | $I^g$ |

payments to them later on. Households of type I are by and large financing the second labor market through taxes and employment benefits (besides their contribution to the base income of the retired people). Since firms have a positive rate of profit in the steady state, since the government budget is always balanced and since only households of type I save in this economy, we have thus now established the condition under which such an economy accumulates not only capital, but also pensions funds – under appropriate restrictions on labor supply – to a sufficient degree. We get from the above expressions that the extra pension payment ratio $\alpha_c$ will increase if $y^p, \alpha_f$ is increasing and it will decrease (among others) if the levels of $z, \bar{\omega}_1, \bar{l}, c_{h1}$ are increasing.

## Pension funds and credit

In this section we will investigate the implications of the situation where pension funds are used for real capital formation instead of remaining idle except of being used for company pension payments (of amount $\delta R$ at each point in time). The productive use of part of the pension fund $R$ is here assumed to be rewarded at the constant interest rate $r$ applied to the debt level $D$ accumulated by the firms in the private sector of the economy.

### *Accounting relationships*

Pension funds as quasi commercial banks which give credit to firms out of their funds and thus allow firms to invest in good times far beyond their retained earnings, i.e. profits net of interest payments on loans (Table 5.6).

The behavior and financing of gross investment is shown in Table 5.7.

We assume as investment behavior of firms the functional relationship:

$$I/K = i_\rho(\rho - \rho_o) - i_d(d - d_o) + \bar{a}.$$

This investment schedule states that investment plans depend positively on the deviation of the profit rate from its steady state level and negatively on the deviation of the debt to

*Table 5.8* Firms' net worth

| *Assets* | *Liabilities* |
|---|---|
| $K$ | $D$ |
| | *Real net worth* |
| $K$ | $K$ |

*Table 5.9* Pension funds and credit (stocks)

| *Assets* | *Liabilities* |
|---|---|
| $R$ | $sR$ |
| | $D$ |
| | $X$ excess reserves |
| $R$ | $R$ |

capital ratio from its steady state value. The exogenous trend term in investment is $\bar{a}$ and it is again assumed that it represents the influence of investing firms 'animal spirits' on their investment activities (Table 5.8).

In the management of pension funds we assume that a portion $sR$ of them is held as minimum reserves and that a larger portion of them has been given as credit $D$ to firms. The remaining amount are idle reserves $D^s$, not yet allocated to any interest bearing activity (Table 5.9).

Pension funds receive the savings of households of type I (the other households do not save) and they receive the interest payments of firms. They allocate this into required reserve increases, payments to pensioners, new credit demand of firms and the rest as an addition or substraction to their idle reserves (Table 5.10).

The above representation of the flows of funds in the pension funds system implies for the time derivative of accumulated funds $R$ the relationship:

$$\dot{R} = S_1 - \delta R - (I - \Pi) = S_1 + \Pi - \delta R - I, \quad \text{i.e.:}$$

it is given by the excess of savings of households of type I over current company pension funds payments to retired households and the new credit that is given to firms to finance the excess of investment over retained profits (Table 5.11).

Households in the first labor market consume with a constant marginal propensity out of the income after primary taxes and they employ household services in constant proportion to consumption habits. They pay the wages of the workers in the second labor market that are not employed by firms, by them and the government as a quasi unemployment benefit insurance (a generational solidarity contribution) and they pay the common base rent of all

*Table 5.10* Pension funds and credit (flows)

| *Resources* | *Uses* |
|---|---|
| $S_1$ | $s\dot{R}$ |
| $rD$ | $\delta R + rD$ |
| | $\dot{D} = I - \Pi$ |
| | $\dot{X}$ |
| $S_1 + rD$ | $S_1 + rD$ |

*Table 5.11* Households of types I and II (primary and secondary labor market: income account (Households I))

| *Uses* | *Resources* |
|---|---|
| $C_1 = c_{h1}(1-\tau_h)Y_1^w$ | |
| $\omega_2 L_{2h}^w = c_{h2}(1-\tau_h)Y_1^w$ | |
| $T = \tau_h Y_1^w$ | |
| $\omega_2(L-(L_1^w+L_{2f}^w+L_{2h}^w+L_{2g}^w))$ | |
| $\omega_2 L^r$ | |
| $S_1$ | $\omega_1 L_1^d$ |
| $Y_1^w$ | $Y_1^w$ |

*Table 5.12* Scheme to fund excess employment and pensioners

| *Income account (Households II)* | |
|---|---|
| *Uses* | *Resources* |
| $C_2$ | $\omega_2 L_2^w$ |
| $Y_2^w$ | $Y_2^w$ |

| *Income account (Retired Households)* | |
|---|---|
| *Uses* | *Resources* |
| $C_r$ | $\omega_2 L^r + \delta R + rD$ |
| $Y^r$ | $Y^r$ |

| *The government: income account – Fiscal Authority/Employer of First Resort* | |
|---|---|
| *Uses* | *Resources* |
| $G = \alpha_g \tau_h Y_1^w$ | $T = \tau_h Y_1^w$ |
| $\omega_2 L_{2g}^w = (1-\alpha_g)\tau_h Y_1^w$ | |
| $\omega_2 L_x^w$ | $\omega_2(L-(L_1^w+L_{2f}^w+L_{2h}^w+L_{2g}^w))$ |
| $\omega_2 L^r$ | $\omega_2 L^r$ |
| $Y^g$ | $Y^g$ |

pensioners (as intergenerational contribution). The remainder represents their contribution the pension scheme of the economy, from which they will receive $\delta R + rD$ when retired. We consider this as a possible scheme of funding the excess employment and the pensioners, not necessarily a just one however (Table 5.12) .

Government gets primary taxes and spends them on goods as well as services in the government sector (which are here determined residually). It administrates the common base rent payments as well as the payments of those not yet employed in the sectors of the economy. Its workforce consists of all workers that are not employed by firms of households of type I and also of all pensioners that are still capable to work. The model therefore assumes not only that there is a work guarantee for all, but also a work obligation for all members in the workforce, with the addition of those that are retired but still able and willing to work.

### *Investment and credit dynamics in flexicurity growth*

For simplicity we here again assume that the government pursues an immigration policy that ensures for the growth rate of the labor force the condition $n = \hat{K}, i.e.$ the total labor supply grows by this migration policy with the same rate as the capital stock. This again keeps the ratio $l = L/K = \bar{l} =$ constant. Since we are again no longer able to determine the steady state value of the real wage $\omega_1$ from the law of motion for $l$, we have to supply it again from the outside: $\omega_1^o = \bar{\omega}_1 =$ given. This, however, no longer also provides us with the steady state value of the rate of profit, since profits are now to be determined net of interest payments: $\rho = y^p[1-(1+\alpha_\omega\alpha_f)\bar{\omega}_1/z] - \delta - rd$, where $d = D/K$ denotes the indebtedness of firms per unit of capital. We assume again as trend term in Okun's law the growth rate of the capital stock (i.e. this part of the new hiring is just determined by the installation of new machines or whole plants (under the assumption of fixed proportions in production)). The normal level of the rate of employment of the workforce employed by firms is again set equal to '1' for simplicity.

On the basis of these assumptions we get from what was formulated in the preceding subsection (where investment was assumed to be given now by $I/K = i_\rho(\rho-\rho_o) - i_d(d-d_o) + \bar{a}$):

$$\begin{aligned}
\hat{l}_1^w &= \beta_{eu}\left(\frac{y^p}{zl_1^w} - 1\right) \\
\hat{\omega}_1 &= \kappa\left[(1-\kappa_p)\left(\beta_{wu}\left(\frac{y^p}{zl_1^w} - 1\right) - \beta_{w\omega}\ln\left(\frac{\omega_1}{\bar{\omega}_1}\right)\right) - (1-\kappa_w)\beta_{p\omega}\ln\left(\frac{\omega_1}{\bar{\omega}_1}\right)\right] \\
\dot{d} &= [i_\rho(\rho-\rho_o) - i_d(d-d_o) + \bar{a}](1-d) - \rho \\
\hat{\eta} &= s_1 + \rho - (\delta\eta + (1+\eta)[i_\rho(\rho-\rho_o) - i_d(d-d_o) + \bar{a}]) \\
&= (1-c_{h1}(1-\tau_h) - \alpha_g\tau_h)\omega_1 y^p/z \\
&\quad -((1+\alpha_r)\bar{l} - (l_1^w + \alpha_f y^p/z))\alpha_\omega\omega_1 \\
&\quad +[y^p[1-(1+\alpha_\omega\alpha_f)\bar{\omega}_1/z] - \delta - rd] \\
&\quad -(\delta\eta + (1+\eta)[i_\rho(\rho-\rho_o) - i_d(d-d_o) + \bar{a}])
\end{aligned}$$

The introduction of debt financing of firms thus makes the model considerably more advanced in its economic structure, but not so much from the mathematical point of view, due to the recursive structure that characterizes the dynamical system at this level of generality. We note that there is not yet an interest rate policy rule involved in these dynamics, but the assumption of an interest rate peg: $r = const.$

We make use in the following of the following abbreviations:

$$s_1^o = (1-c_{h1}(1-\tau_h) - \alpha_g\tau_h)\bar{\omega}_1 y^p/z - ((1+\alpha_r)\bar{l} - y^p/z(1+\alpha_f))\alpha_\omega\bar{\omega}_1$$

and:

$$\rho_{max} = y^p[1-(1+\alpha_\omega\alpha_f)\bar{\omega}_1/z] - \delta.$$

On the basis of such expressions we then have:

**Proposition 5.2**

*The interior steady state of the considered dynamics is given by:*[12]

$$l_1^{wo} = \frac{y^p}{z},\ \omega_1^o = \bar{\omega}_1,\ \eta_o = \frac{s_1^o + \rho_o - \bar{a}}{\delta + \bar{a}},$$

*where $d_o, \rho_o$ have to be determined by solving the two equations:*

$$\rho_o = \rho_{max} - rd_o, \quad \rho_o = \bar{a}(1-d_o)$$

*which gives for the steady state values of $d, \rho, \eta$ the expressions:*

$$d_o = \frac{\bar{a}-\rho_{max}}{\bar{a}-r}, \quad \rho_o = \bar{a}\frac{\rho_{max}-r}{\bar{a}-r},$$

$$\eta_o = \frac{s_1^o + \bar{a}\frac{\rho_{max}-r}{\bar{a}-r}}{\delta+\bar{a}} = \frac{s_1^o(\bar{a}-r) - \bar{a}(\bar{a}-\rho_{max})}{(\delta+\bar{a})(\bar{a}-r)}.$$

We assume that both the numerator and the denominator of the fraction that defines $d_o$ are positive, i.e. the trend term in investment is sufficiently strong (larger than the rate of profit before interest rate payments $\rho_{max}$ and larger than the rate of interest $r$). Moreover, it is also assumed that $\rho_{max} > r$ holds so that all fractions shown above are in fact positive. In the case where $\bar{a} = \rho_{max} = y^p[1-(1+\alpha_\omega\alpha_f)\bar{\omega}_1/z] - \delta$ holds we have $d_o = 0$ and $\rho_o = \bar{a}$ in which case the value of $\eta_o$ is the same as in the sections on investment without debt financing. Nevertheless the dynamics around the steady state remain debt financed and are therefore different from the one of the preceding section. We thus can have a 'balanced budget' of firms in the steady state while investment remains driven by $I/K = i_\rho(\rho-\rho_o) - i_d(d-d_o) + \bar{a}$ outside the steady state position.

For the fraction of company pension funds divided by base pension payments we now get as relationship in the steady state:

$$\alpha_c = \frac{\delta\eta_o + rd_o}{\alpha_\omega\alpha_r\bar{\omega}_1\bar{l}}$$

an expression that in general does not give rise to unambiguous results concerning comparative dynamics. In the special case $d_o = 0$ we, however, can state that this fraction depends positively on $s_o^1$ (also in general) and negatively on $\bar{a}, \delta, \bar{l}$.

The Jacobian at the interior steady state of the here considered 4D dynamics reads:

$$J^o = \begin{pmatrix} J_{11} & 0 & 0 & 0 \\ ? & J_{22} & 0 & 0 \\ ? & ? & J_{33} & 0 \\ ? & ? & ? & J_{44} \end{pmatrix}$$

with:

$$\begin{aligned} J_{11} &= -\beta_{eu}/l_1^{wo} \\ J_{22} &= -\kappa[(1-\kappa_p)\beta_{w\omega} + (1-\kappa_w)\beta_{p\omega}] \\ J_{33} &= -(i_\rho + i_d)(1-d_o) - (\bar{a}-r) \\ J_{44} &= -\bar{a}(1+\delta) \end{aligned}$$

This lower triangular form of the Jacobian immediately implies that the elements on the diagonal of the matrix $J^o$ are just equal to the four eigenvalues of this matrix which are therefore all real and negative. This gives:

**Proposition 5.3**

*The interior steady state of the considered dynamics is locally asymptotically stable and is characterized by a strict hierarchy in the state variables of the dynamics.*

Due to the specific form of the considered laws of motion we conjecture that the steady state is also a global attractor in the economically relevant part of the 4D phase space. We then would get again monotonically convergent trajectories from any starting point of this part of the phase space and thus fairly simple adjustment processes also in the case where investment is jointly financed by profits (retained earnings) and credit.

The stability of the steady state is increased (i.e. the eigenvalues of its Jacobian matrix become more negative) if the speed parameter characterizing hiring and firing is increased, if Blanchard and Katz type error correction becomes more pronounced and if the parameters $i_\rho, i_d, \bar{a}$ in the investment function are increased.

Summing up, we thus can state that the adjustment processes and their stability properties remain very supportive for the working of our model of flexicurity type which is generally monotonically convergent with full capacity utilization of both capital and labor to a steady state position with a sustainable distribution of income between firms, our three types of households and the government. We conclude that flexicurity capitalism may be a workable alternative to current forms of capitalism and can avoid in particular severe social deformations and human degradations caused by the reserve army mechanism and the mass unemployment it implies for certain stages in a long-phase distributive and welfare state cycle, in the US and the UK more of a neoclassical cold turkey type and in Germany and in France more gradualistic in nature.[13]

## Outlook: Keynesian demand problems

As an outlook we here briefly sketch a situation where capacity utilization problems as well as stability problems may arise within the flexicurity variant of a capitalistic economy. We modify the baseline model in 'Flexicurity growth: a baseline model' above in a minimal way in order to obtain such results. In place of pension funds, as well as the credits they give to firms, we now consider the situation where firms finance their investment plans through their profits and through the issuing of corporate bonds. We assume these bonds to be of the fixed price variety and we also keep the rate of interest that is paid on these bonds fixed for simplicity.

The amount of such bonds that firms have issued in the past is denoted by $B$ and their price is 1 in nominal units. Firms thus have to pay $rB$ as interest at the current point in time and they intend to use their real profits net of interest rate payments and in addition the issue $\dot{B}^s/p$ to finance their rate of investment $I/K = i_\rho(\rho - \rho_o) - i_b(\frac{B}{pK} - (\frac{B}{pK})_o) + \bar{a}$. This rate of investment is assumed to depend positively on excess profitability compared to the steady state rate of profit and negatively the deviation of their debt from its steady state level (Table 5.13).

Households of type I behave as was assumed so far, but attempt to channel their real savings now into corporate bond holdings as shown below. They will be able to exactly satisfy their demand for new bonds when there is goods market equilibrium prevailing ($I = S$), since only firms and these households act on this market, while all other economic units just spend what they get (with balanced transfer payments organized by the government). The real return from savings in corporate bonds $rB/p$, at each moment in time, will be added below to the base rent payments of retired households, which receive these benefits in proportion to the bonds they have allocated during their working life in the private sector of the economy. The bonds allocated in this way thus only generate a return when their holders are retired and then – as in the pension fund scheme of 'Flexicurity growth: a baseline model' above – at the then prevailing market rate of interest (which is still

*Table 5.13* Firms: production and income account

| Uses | Resources |
|---|---|
| $\delta K$ | $\delta K$ |
| $\omega_1 L_1^d, L_1^d = Y/z$ | $C_1 + C_2 + C_r$ |
| $\omega_2 L_{2f}^w, \omega_2 = \alpha_\omega \omega_1, L_{2f}^w = \alpha_f L_1^d$ | $G$ |
| $rB/p$ | $I = i_\rho(\rho - \rho_o)K - i_b(\frac{B}{p} - (\frac{B}{p})_o) + \bar{a}K$ |
| $\Pi(= Y^f)$ | $[I = \Pi + \dot{B}^s/p]$ |
| $Y$ | $Y$ |

*Table 5.14* Income account: Households I (primary labor market) and Retired Households

| *Households I* | |
|---|---|
| *Uses* | *Resources* |
| $C_1 = c_{h1}(1-\tau_h)\omega_1 L_1^d$ | |
| $\omega_2 L_{2h}^w = c_{h2}(1-\tau_h)\omega_1 L_1^d$ | |
| $T = \tau_h \omega_1 L_1^d$ | |
| $\omega_2(L - (L_1^w + L_{2f}^w + L_{2h}^w + L_{2g}^w))$ | |
| $\omega_2 L^r, L^r = \alpha_r L$ | |
| $S_1 [= \dot{B}^d/p]$ | $\omega_1 L_1^d$ |
| $Y_1^w = \omega_1 L_1^d$ | $Y_1^w = \omega_1 L_1^d$ |

| *Retired Households* | |
|---|---|
| *Uses* | *Resources* |
| $C_r$ | $\omega_2 L^r + rB/p, L^r = \alpha_r L$ |
| $Y^r$ | $Y^r$ |

determined exogenously). The pension fund model is therefore here only reformulated in terms of nominal paper holdings (coupons) and thus no longer based on the storage of physical magnitudes. Hence, corporate bonds are here not only of a fixed-price variety, but also provide their return only after retirement. This is shown in the income account of retired persons (Table 5.14). The income account of the workers in the second labor market is unchanged and therefore not shown here again.

The government income account (not shown) is also kept unchanged and in particular balanced in the way used in the preceding model types. The modifications of the model of 'Flexicurity growth: a baseline model' above are therefore of a minimal kind, largely concerning a different type of investment behavior of firms and a new type of organizing the formerly assumed company pension funds. However, the assumed flexicurity system becomes now of real importance, since we here will get demand determined (Keynesian) business cycle fluctuations in the dynamics implied by the model, whereas firms did not face capacity under- or over-utilization problems in the earlier model types. Keynesian IS-equilibrium determination has to be considered now and gives rise to the following equation for the effective output per unit of capital (characterizing goods market equilibrium):[14]

$$\begin{aligned}
y &= Y/K \\
&= C_1/K + C_2/K + C_r/K + \delta + I/K + G/K \\
&= c_h(1-\tau_h)\omega_1 \frac{y}{z} + \alpha_\omega \omega_1 (\bar{l} - l_1^w) + \alpha_\omega \alpha_r \omega_1 \bar{l} + rb \\
&\quad + \delta + i_\rho(\rho - \rho_o) - i_b(b - b_o) + \bar{a} + \alpha_g \tau_h \omega_1 y/z \\
\rho &= y - (1 + \alpha_f \alpha_\omega)\omega_1 y/z - \delta - rb, \qquad b = B/(pK)
\end{aligned}$$

which taken together gives:

$$y = \frac{\alpha_\omega \omega_1 (\bar{l} - l_1^w) + \alpha_\omega \alpha_r \omega_1 \bar{l} + (rb + \delta)(1 - i_\rho) - i_\rho \rho_o - i_b(b - b_o) + \bar{a}}{1 - [c_h(1-\tau_h) + \alpha_g \tau_h - i_\rho(1 + \alpha_f \alpha_\omega)]\omega_1/z - i_\rho}$$

$$= y(l_1^w, \omega_1, b, \ldots)$$

Note that we have modified the investment function in this section to $i(\cdot) = i_\rho(\rho - \rho_o) - i_b(b - b_o) + \bar{a}$. Note also that we have again assumed that natural growth $n$ is always adjusted to the growth rate of the capital stock $\hat{K}$. We also assume that the denominator in the above fraction is positive and now get the important result that output per unit of capital is no longer equal to its potential value, but now depending on the marginal propensity to spend as well as on other parameters of the model. This is due to the new situation that firms use corporate bonds to finance their excess investment (exceeding their profits) or buy back such bonds in the opposite case and that households of type I buy such bonds from their savings. They buy fewer consumption goods, thus reducing the tax revenue from taxing consumption and, consequently, the pension fund that is financed through taxes. We thus have independent real investment and real savings decisions, which – when coordinated by the achievement of goods market equilibrium as shown above – lead to a supply of new corporate bonds that is exactly equal to the demand for such bonds at this level of output and income. This simply follows from the fact that only firms and households of type I are saving, while all other budgets are balanced. Households of type I thus just have to accept the amount of the fixed price bonds offered by firms and are thereby accumulating these bonds (whose interest rate payments are paid out to retired people according to the percentage they have achieved when retiring).

Assuming the accumulation of corporate bonds in the place of real commodities and an investment function that is independent from these savings conditions thus implies that the economy is subject to Keynesian demand rationing processes (at least close to its steady state). These demand problems are here derived on the assumption of IS-equilibrium and thus represented in static terms in place of a dynamic multiplier approach that can also be augmented further by means of Metzlerian inventory adjustment processes. We stress once again that the possibility for full capacity output is here prevented through the Keynesian type of under-consumption assumed as characterizing the household type I sector and the fact that there is then only one income level that allows savings in bonds to become equal to bond-financed investment in this simple credit market that is characterizing this modification of the flexicurity model, due to the now existing effective demand schedule $y(l_1^w, \omega_1, b, \ldots)$. We assume that the parameters are chosen such that we get for the partial derivatives of the effective demand function $y$:

$$y_{l_1^w}(l_1^w, \omega_1, b, \ldots) < 0, \quad y_{\omega_1}(l_1^w, \omega_1, b, \ldots) > 0, \quad y_b(l_1^w, \omega_1, b, \ldots) < 0$$

holds true. This is fulfilled for example if the expression in the denominator of the effective demand function is negative and if the parameter $i_b$ is chosen sufficiently large. Effective demand is then wage led and flexible wages therefore dangerous for the considered economy.

As now significantly interacting laws of motion we have in the considered case:

$$\hat{l}_1^w = \beta_{eu}(\frac{y}{zl_1^w} - 1)$$

$$\hat{\omega}_1 = \kappa\left[(1-\kappa_p)\left(\beta_{wu}\left(\frac{y}{zl_1^w} - 1\right) - \beta_{w\omega}\ln(\frac{\omega_1}{\omega_1^o})\right)\right.$$
$$\left. - (1-\kappa_w)\left(\beta_{pu}\left(\frac{y}{y^p} - \bar{u}_c\right) + \beta_{p\omega}\ln\left(\frac{\omega_1}{\omega_1^o}\right)\right)\right]$$

$$\dot{b} = (1-b)(i_\rho(\rho-\rho_o) - i_b(b-b_o) + \bar{a}) - \rho + \hat{p}b$$

$$\hat{p} = \kappa\left[\beta_{py}\left(\frac{y}{y^p} - \bar{u}_c\right) + \beta_{p\omega}\ln\left(\frac{\omega_1}{\omega_1^o}\right) + \kappa_p\left(\beta_{wu}\left(\frac{y}{zl_1^w} - 1\right)\right.\right.$$
$$\left.\left. - \beta_{w\omega}\ln\left(\frac{\omega_1}{\omega_1^o}\right)\right)\right] + \pi^c$$

$$\dot{\pi}^c = \beta_{\pi^c p}(0 - \pi^c)$$

where $\hat{p}$ has to be inserted into the other equation (where necessary) in order to arrive at an autonomous system of four ordinary differential equations. This particular formulation of the debt financing of firms thus makes the model considerably more advanced from the mathematical as well as from an economic point of view. We note that there is not yet an interest rate policy rule involved in these dynamics, but that the assumption of an interest rate peg is maintained still: $r = const.$

The laws of motion describe again (in this order) our formulation of Okun's law, the real wage dynamics as it applies in a Keynesian environment (see'Goodwin–Kalecki dynamics' above), the debt dynamics of firms and a simple regressive expectations scheme concerning the inflationary climate surrounding the wage-price spiral where it is assumed (and, in fact, also taking place) that inflation converges back to a constant price level. There is, therefore, not yet an inflation accelerator present in the formulation of the dynamics of the four state variables of the model. Nevertheless, price level inflation is now explicitly taken account of, indeed for the first time in this chapter.

Steady state and stability analysis is no longer straightforward in this Keynesian variant of flexicurity capitalism. With respect to steady state positions we have to solve now a simultaneous equation system in the variables $\omega_1, \rho, b$. Due to the structure of the effective demand function we have, moreover, no longer zero entries in the Jacobian of the dynamics at the steady state of the first three state variables (the last law of motion is a completely trivial one). As economic mechanism we can identify a real wage channel as in the Kaleckian dynamics (working here in a wage led environment by assumption). There is, furthermore, the dynamic of the debt to capital ratio of firms. These feedback channels can be tamed through appropriate assumptions, but are even then working in an environment that gives no straightforward economically plausible stability assertions, due to the strong interactions present in the dynamics. We therefore have to leave the stability analysis for future research.

The conclusion of this section, therefore, is that effective demand problems can make flexicurity capitalism significantly more difficult to analyze and therefore demand a treatment of much more depth – including inflation and interest rate policy rules, government deficits and fiscal policy rules, etc. – than was possible in this concluding section. Moreover, credit relationships may be looked for that avoid the increase in complexity of the dynamics of this concluding section.

## Acknowledgements

We have to thank the participants of seminars held in Chemnitz University, Bielefeld University and the IMK, Düsseldorf and in particular Gangolf Groh for very helpful suggestions that improved this chapter significantly. Of course, the usual caveats apply.

## Notes

1 The parameters underlying this simulation are: $\beta_{ve} = 0.06; \bar{e} = 0.9; \beta_{vv} = 0.01; \beta_{ev} = 0.1; \bar{v} = 0.6.$ and are approximately obtained from simple OLS estimates of these dynamics (with no good statistical properties however, but definitely more appropriately chosen compared to the case without any empirical reference).

2 Note with respect to Figure 5.2 that it is assumed there that an increasing wage share is accompanied by inflationary pressure as it is suggested by the conflicting income claims approach. Note furthermore that – as is shown in Flaschel *et al.* (2007b) – this cycle can be more complicated in nature if empirically observed nonlinearities in the money wage Phillips curve are taken into account which in fact move the cycle of the theoretical model already fairly close to what is shown in Figure 5.1, bottom right.

3 See Desai (1984) for the sources of these data and for an econometric approach on the basis of these data with respect to the Goodwin growth cycle model.

4 We have to thank C. Groth and J. Madsen for providing access to these data, they have collected for their paper on 'Medium-term fluctuations and the "Great Ratios" of economic growth" (unpublished).

5 And thus not yet of last resort, since this latter approach has been rightly criticized as being too passive and inventory like in nature.

6 Augmented by company pension payments $\delta_1 R$.

7 The term $S_1$ is equal to $\delta_1 R + \dot{R}$.

8 The considered wage-price spiral will imply a law of motion for real wages which in simplified form also appears in the flexicurity model. As these models are formulated, their dynamics are, however, independent of the nominal levels of wages and prices, i.e. everything can be expressed in real terms. For the introduction of the monetary sector see Flaschel *et al.* (2007a).

9 The steady state value, see below, is here assumed to underlie Blanchard and Katz (1999) type error correction in the first labor market.

10 The value of $n$ must be chosen that high since technical change is still ignored in this baseline social growth model.

11 Note that the numerator is easily shown to be not only positive, but even larger than 1 under standard Keynesian assumptions on expenditure and taxation rates.

12 The steady state value of $s_1^o$ is the same as in the preceding section.

13 We refer the reader back to what is shown in Figure 5.3 where the post-war period up into the 1960s seemed to suggest that the working of the reserve army mechanism had been overcome, a suggestion that was disproved in the subsequent years in a striking way.

14 Standard Keynesian assumptions will again ensure that $y^o > 0$ holds true.

## References

Blanchard, O.J. and L. Katz (1999) Wage dynamics: reconciling theory and evidence. *American Economic Review. Papers and Proceedings*, 89: 69–74.

Bronfenbrenner, M. (ed.) (1969) *Is the Business Cycle Obsolete?* New York: Harper & Row.

Desai, M. (1984) An econometric model of the share of wages in national income: UK 1855–1965. In R.M. Goodwin *et al.* (eds): *Nonlinear Models of Fluctuating Growth.* Heidelberg: Springer, 253–77.

Flaschel, P. (1984) Some stability properties of Goodwin's growth cycle model. *Zeitschrift für Nationalökonomie*, 44, 63–9.

Flaschel, P. and G. Groh (1995) The classical growth cycle: reformulation, simulation and some facts. *Economic Notes*, 24, 293–326.

Flaschel, P. and H.-M. Krolzig (2006) Wage-price Phillips curves and macroeconomic stability: basic structural form, estimation and analysis. In C. Chiarella, P. Flaschel, R. Franke and W. Semmler (eds): *Quantitative and Empirical Analysis of Nonlinear Dynamic Macromodels.* Contributions to Economic Analysis. Elsevier, Amsterdam.

Flaschel, P., R. Franke and W. Semmler (2007a) *Kaleckian Investment and Employment Cycles in Postwar Industrialized Economies.* Working paper. New York: SCEPA, New School University.

Flaschel, P., D. Tavani, L. Taylor and T. Teuber (2007b): *A structuralist model of the wage-price spiral with non-linear demand pressure terms.* Workling paper. New York: SCEPA, New School University.

Goodwin, R. (1967) A growth cycle. In C.H. Feinstein (ed.) *Socialism, Capitalism and Economic Growth.* Cambridge: Cambridge University Press, 54–8.

Groth, C. and J. B. Madsen (2007) Medium-term fluctuations and the "Great Ratios" of economic growth. Copenhagen: mimeo.

Harrod, R. (1939) An essay in dynamic economic theory. *The Economic Journal* XLIX, 14–33.

Kalecki, M. (1943) Political aspects of full employment. Reprinted in M. Kalecki (1971) *Selected Essays on the Dynamics of the Capitalist Economy*, Cambridge: Cambridge University Press.

Kauermann, G., T. Teuber, and P. Flaschel (2007) *Exploring US Business Cycles with ivariate Loops using Penalized Spline Regression.* Working paper. Bielefeld: CEM.

Solow, R. (1956) A contribution to the theory of economic growth. *Quarterly Journal of Economics*, 70, 65–94.

# Part II

# Nonlinear macrodynamics: empirical analysis

# 6 Goodwin cycles and the US economy, 1948–2004

*Simon Mohun and Roberto Veneziani*

## Introduction

Goodwin's predator-prey model (Goodwin 1967, 1972) is a formalization of Marx's account of class conflict over distributive shares in his theory of capitalist accumulation. Distribution and accumulation are modeled by means of a non-linear dynamic Lotka-Volterra mechanism, yielding growth cycles. As employment grows the bargaining strength of the working class increases, yielding an increase in the wage share; the falling profit share reduces accumulation and hence the rate of employment; the bargaining strength of the working class weakens, recreating the profitability conditions necessary for accumulation. This mechanism repeats itself forever, unchanged, yielding conservative oscillations with a fixed period in the two main variables, the wage share $(u)$, and the employment rate $(v)$. A large number of authors have analyzed the model, extending it in many directions. This chapter contributes to the much smaller literature investigating the empirical evidence for Goodwin cycles. The theoretical presumption is that because the model captures some fundamental insights of the functioning of capitalist economies, its cycles should be found in the data.

However, the empirical and econometric evidence is mixed. In the US post-war $(u, v)$ plot, Solow identified 'a suggestion of predominantly clockwise motion, but in three separate episodes' (Solow, 1990: 39) and 'a bare hint of a single large long-period clockwise sweep' (ibid: 40). Flaschel and Groh (1995) and Harvie (2000) found a similar pattern in the post-war plots of, respectively, eight and ten OECD countries, with shorter (10–15 years) clockwise cycles around an incomplete long-period (50–70 years) clockwise motion. In the UK data considered by Desai (1984), the post-war period is also characterized by a similar pattern. There is, moreover, no common methodology of measurement across these studies. All of this raises the issues of whether Goodwin cycles exist and what they are.

*A priori* theoretical considerations and the absence of stable short-run cycles have led most authors (e.g. Desai 1984; Farkas and Kotsis 1992; Harvie 2000) to interpret Goodwin cycles as long-run secular waves and to adopt an 'approach which attempts to argue for a large phase length and amplitude of this growth cycle' (Flaschel and Groh 1995: 295). From this perspective, the Goodwin cycle is seen as modeling a long-run conflict between workers and capitalists, influenced by secular forces such that shorter-run factors are averaged out. The main idea is that 'under modern post-war conditions ... the large changes in income distribution among capital and labour which this reproduction process calls for will use up an amount of time which can be drastically higher than the 8-10 years that Solow calculated ...' (ibid. 1995: 294).

This interpretation is not entirely convincing. First, it is unclear that there is a long-run empirical regularity to be explained. In several countries the long-run motion is not well shaped. Moreover, 'one cycle is not a periodic motion' (Solow 1990: 40) and much less so the 'three-quarter cycle' (Harvie 2000: 357) that emerges from the post-1945 data. When longer time series are analyzed, however, the existence of stable long-run cycles is questionable, as shown in the UK 1855–1965 data by the 'steady shift to the right (rising $u$)' (Desai 1984: 259). Second, the behavioural foundations of such secular motions are not obvious, and the role of structural breaks, such as that in all developed countries around 1980, seems underestimated.

The chapter argues that the Goodwin cycle isolates *in vitro* the main forces underlying distributive conflict, but because of endogenous forces that modify the balance of power between classes and the structure of the bargaining process, the symbiotic mechanism described is fragile. This feature is captured by the structural instability of the model (Veneziani and Mohun 2005). Goodwin cycles are then the shorter-run cycles that appear around the long-run trend.

If correct, this interpretation suggests that the long-run behaviour of the wage share and the employment rate is mainly the product of structural change, which in turn implies that the econometric results obtained under the assumption that the model describes long-run secular motions should be interpreted with caution. For example, Desai (1984) embeds the cyclical mechanism in a more general model with money wage bargaining and adaptive expectations, in order to test the parameter restrictions that yield the structurally unstable Lotka-Volterra specification. Analysis of the UK data over the century 1865–1965 leads him to reject such restrictions and thus to reject Goodwin's original specification. Similar results are obtained by Harvie (2000) for ten OECD countries for the post-war period. If structural changes dominate the long-run motion of the wage share and the employment rate, these results are not surprising because they reflect underlying structural changes.[1] Hence this chapter attempts a careful distinction between long-run structural changes and short-run cycles.[2]

A further contribution of this chapter concerns the appropriate definitions of the variables for empirical analysis. This involves issues such as the appropriate treatment of the self-employed (both with respect to wage share and employment share), the appropriate definition of profits (which involves decisions about data such as the rental income of persons, indirect business tax and non-tax liabilities, and capital consumption), and the sectoral coverage of the statistics (corporate and non-corporate, private and public, total and non-farm). Precise and informed definitions are desirable both to exclude data that are essentially extraneous to the issue at hand and to capture the behavioural assumptions underlying a model of distributive conflict. Much of the existing literature is not satisfactory in either of these regards, and this chapter pays some attention to the issues involved.

This chapter is organized in the following way. The next section 'Marx and Goodwin' explores the inspiration from Marx's *Capital* for Goodwin's model, outlines the model itself and suggests how it might be interpreted. 'Measurement issues' are then discussed, and the following section describes long-run trends in the US corporate economy from 1948 to 2004. The focus throughout is on the USA, the leading capitalist country, and therefore the most important test for the model. 'Empirical evidence for Goodwin-type cycles' considers the detrended shorter-run data. Two main conclusions are drawn which contrast with the existing empirical literature.[3] First, the long-run trends show a sharp structural change at the beginning of the 1980s, but there are no long-run cycles. Second, the model captures some remarkable regularities in the short-run $(u, v)$ cycles, which coincide, in period and timing, with the NBER dating of (the troughs of) business cycles. 'Wages, the working class and distributive conflict' then discusses some of the requirements that the model makes of the data in order that distributive conflict be appropriately measured. This issue is pursued by disaggregating the data, dividing non-farm private industry employees into two groups, supervisory and non-supervisory employees, and focusing on the latter. The same two conclusions apply. However, this analysis throws up some interesting new puzzles. One is that there is a very large shift in wage share away from the four-fifths who are non-supervisory employees to the one fifth who supervise. A second is that the combination of these wage shares apparently produces *one* long-run cycle in the trend data in a way that does *not* show up in the corporate sector. After a suggestion as to why this difference might be more apparent than real, an overall conclusion summarizes, and the data, sources and methods are described in an appendix, such that the results of this chapter can be replicated.

## Marx and Goodwin

Marx's account of the relation between accumulation and wage fluctuations was developed in two stages. First, he assumed a fixed proportions technology, a constant 'technical composition of capital' whereby 'a definite mass of the means of production continued to need the same mass of labour-power to set it in motion' (Marx 1976: 763). Then if investment in new means of production was greater than the growth of the employed labour force, excess demand for labour-power would generate wage rises. Either this would have no effect on accumulation (because the rate of surplus value was so large that capitalists could absorb rising wages), or accumulation would slacken, reducing the demand for labour-power and hence wages to whatever levels were compatible with the rate of accumulation. Thus his causation went from the rate of accumulation to changes in the demand and supply of labour-power, and thence to changes in wages. In this manner, wages were forced to adjust to the requirements of accumulation.

This could only generate cyclical movements if there were a persistent tendency for the rate of accumulation to outstrip the growth of the labour force. But the historical era of an approximately constant composition of capital was characterized by slow development of capitalist relations on the basis of pre-existing technologies. 'Manu-factories' were only slowly developing, for markets were localized because of transport difficulties, and regulated with legacies inherited from an earlier feudal era. In such nascent capitalist conditions, the market for labour-power was undeveloped, and accumulation depended not upon technological dynamism, but upon increasing the total amount of labour time available for exploitation (the production of 'absolute surplus value'). In this sense, the exploitable working population constituted a 'barrier' to accumulation, to be overcome through a (physically and economically coercive) 'primitive accumulation' that separated the direct producers from their means of production so that they could be transformed into wage labour. Without this, the cycles of developed capitalism could not exist.

The second stage of Marx's argument related to a later historical phase of the development of capitalism, with the production of 'relative surplus value' predominating. That is, once capitalist relations began to generate their own technologies (rather than just appropriating existing ones), 'the development of the productivity of social labour becomes the most powerful lever of accumulation' (ibid.: 772). This occurred through the general introduction of means-of-production-using, labour-saving technologies, raising the technical composition of capital. Through technologically generated unemployment, changing industrial composition, and the growth of unstable and insecure employment, post-industrial-revolution capitalism in effect created its own labour supply,

> a disposable industrial reserve army, ... a mass of human material always ready for exploitation ... The path characteristically described by modern industry, which takes the form of a decennial cycle ... of periods of average activity, production at high pressure, crisis, and stagnation, depends on the constant formation, the greater or less absorption, and the re-formation of the industrial reserve army or surplus population. In their turn, the varying phases of the industrial cycle recruit the surplus population, and become one of the most energetic agencies for its reproduction. (ibid. pp. 783–5)

There is, however, an unresolved tension in Marx's argument. He insisted both that

> the rate of accumulation is the independent, not the dependent variable; the rate of wages is the dependent, not the independent variable (ibid.: 770)

and that

> general movements of wages are exclusively regulated by the expansion and contraction of the industrial reserve army, and this in turn corresponds to the periodic alternations of the industrial cycle (ibid.: 790)

It is not obvious that these two statements are compatible. On the one hand, changes in wages are determined by changes in the industrial reserve army in a cyclical mechanism. For the existence of cycles, there has to be feedback from wage changes to changes in the rate of accumulation and hence changes in the industrial reserve army. On the other hand, that feedback is simultaneously denied by the assertion of one way causation from changes in the rate of accumulation to changes in wage rates.

But suppose capitalism has causal mechanisms that operate with very different timescales. In a long-run timescale, the rate of accumulation is determined by capitals competing through innovations of product and process, generating a technical progress which is typically (although not universally) labour-saving and means-of-production-using. Long-run wages respond to whatever these productivity increases allow. Technical progress determines profitability, so that the long-run rate of profit is associated with particular profiles of technology and distribution, which in turn determine the long-run rate of accumulation and thence the long-run rate of employment.[4] Accordingly, associated with the long-run evolution of the rate of profit, there will be some long-run relationship between the wage share and the employment rate.

There are also shorter-run cyclical patterns between wage share and employment rate. An increase in accumulation puts upward pressure on wages in the labour market; rising wages both depress profitability and hence investment and the rate of accumulation, and stimulate (generally labour-saving) technical change; demand-side pressures in the labour market subside partly because the demand for labour falls and partly because the rise in unemployment increases the supply of labour; profitability recovers as real wage rises lag productivity growth, investment increases, increasing the rate of accumulation and the labour market tightens again.

These short-run cyclical fluctuations in employment rate and wage share were formalized by Goodwin (1972) 'to give more precise form to an idea of Marx's - that . . . [capitalist cycles] can be explained by the dynamic interaction of profits, wages and unemployment' (ibid.: 442). Goodwin proposed, in a summary of the Marxian approach,

> a homeostatic mechanism which functions by means of variations in distributive shares but does so in such a way as to keep them constant in the long run. If real wages go up, profits go down: if profits go down, saving and investment lag, thus slowing up the creation of new jobs. But the labour force is continually growing both through natural increase and through men 'released' by technological progress. The reserve

> army of labour grows, wages lag behind the growth of productivity, profits rise and accumulation is accelerated back up to a high level. This in turn gradually reduces unemployment, wages rise, and so it goes on, indefinitely. (ibid.)

His model elegantly and parsimoniously expresses an interpretation of the cycle mechanism that Marx had in mind.[5]

Goodwin began with two homogeneous and non-specific factors of production, labour and 'capital' (plant and equipment). Focusing on real net quantities, he made the following assumptions.

1. Steady disembodied technical progress, such that labour productivity $a$ grows at a constant rate $\alpha$, and hence $a = a_o e^{\alpha t}$.
2. Steady exogenous growth in the labour force, so that labour supply $n$ grows at a constant rate $\beta$, and hence $n = n_o e^{\beta t}$.
3. A constant capital–output ratio $\sigma = k/q$, with all wages $wl$ consumed and all profits $q - wl$ saved and invested. Then the wage share $u$ is $wl/q$, or $w/a$, where labour productivity is $a = q/l$, and the profit share is $1 - w/a$. So profits are $(1 - w/a)q$, which is investment $\dot{k}$. Hence the profit rate is $\dot{k}/k$ which is $\dot{q}/q = (1 - w/a)/\sigma$.
4. A real wage rate that rises in the neighborhood of full employment. For simplicity, he assumed a linear approximation $\dot{w}/w = -\gamma + \rho l/n$, with both $\gamma$ and $\rho$ positive and where $l/n \equiv v$.

Putting all this together and focusing on the wage share $u$ and the employment rate $v$, the model describes closed orbits in $(u, v)$ space according to the following equations:

$$\frac{\dot{u}}{u} = -(\alpha + \gamma) + \rho v \tag{6.1}$$

$$\frac{\dot{v}}{v} = \left\{\frac{1}{\sigma} - (\alpha + \beta)\right\} - \frac{u}{\sigma} \tag{6.2}$$

These equations describe the short-run cyclical dynamics.[6]

These short-run cyclical dynamics are *growth* cycles. In the long run, income shares are constant, so that, setting equation (6.1) to zero, the long-run employment rate is:

$$v = \frac{\alpha + \gamma}{\rho} \tag{6.3}$$

which implies from the wage equation that in the long-run real wage growth is equal to the growth of labour productivity:

$$\frac{\dot{w}}{w} = \alpha \tag{6.4}$$

Similarly, setting equation (6.2) to zero, the long-run wage share is:

$$u = 1 - \sigma(\alpha + \beta) \tag{6.5}$$

Consider the long-run behaviour of the US economy over the 57 years from 1948 to 2004. In the non-farm business sector, the average annual growth of real output per hour (a proxy for $\alpha$) was 2.2 per cent, and that of real hourly compensation in non-farm business (a proxy for $\frac{\dot{w}}{w}$) was 1.8 per cent. Thus equation (6.4) is not descriptively satisfied. Neither is equation (6.5). The long-run average value of the capital–output ratio in the corporate sector (a proxy for $\sigma$) is 2.1, and of (whole economy) labour force growth (a proxy for $\beta$) is 1.6 per cent. Substituting these values into equation (6.5) gives a long-run wage share of 92.1 per cent, whereas the average (corporate sector) wage share between 1948 and 2004 was rather lower, at 78.9 per cent.[7]

Goodwin recognized the descriptive problems of his assumptions. He characterized his model as 'starkly schematized and hence quite unrealistic', with assumptions that are 'too simple and too crude to represent reality'. But he also asserted that the assumptions were chosen to represent 'the most essential dynamic aspects of capitalism'. If this is accepted, then one way in which the model can be made 'more realistic is by incorporating additional, empirically valid assumptions' (ibid. pp. 442–3). This is the path taken by much of the literature commenting on and developing Goodwin's model (for example, Desai 1973; Flaschel 1988; Skott 1989). The following sections take a different approach. They focus on whether the model does indeed succeed in capturing 'the most essential dynamic aspects of capitalism', and they do so by exploring the differences between cycle and trend.

## Measurement issues

### *The measurement problem*

There is no common methodology of measurement in those earlier studies that attempted empirically to investigate Goodwin cycles. Consider for example the wage share. Vercelli (1977: 66) used the ratio of compensation of employees to net national income. But this allocates to the profit share all self-employed income and all rental income of persons. These are substantial categories at best of doubtful relevance to the Goodwin model. Desai (1984) analyzed a theoretical model in which 'the share of wages in national income' is 'the ratio of the real wage to the average product per worker', and then conceded that in order to estimate the model:

> we have to somehow pretend that our highly aggregative model with one good, homogeneous labour, malleable capital stock, constant rates of growth of labour force and productivity, no government sector is in some sense an approximation to the UK economy ... (ibid.: 259).

Solow (1990, pp. 39–40) used data for the US non-farm business economy, had a wage share that for the period 1947–86 varied between 0.94 and 1.07, and gave no details on how the wage share was measured. Flaschel and Groh (1995: 308) used the ratio of compensation of employees to GDP, which includes in the implicit profits share all self-employed income, and rental income of persons (as with Vercelli); it also includes *inter alia* indirect business tax and non-tax liabilities, and capital consumption. Finally, Harvie (2000: 356) used the ratio of compensation of employees to the sum of compensation of employees and operating surplus, which is more meaningful. But his compensation of employees data included armed forces pay, and his operating surplus data included self-employed income and the operating surplus of general government.

If the data are to be investigated for evidence of Goodwin cycles, that data has to be appropriate for the phenomena under investigation. The remainder of this section outlines the main issues involved.

### *The relevant sectors*

The mechanism of distributive conflict described in the Goodwin model would not be expected to apply to general government, because general government produces negligible marketed output. Moreover, at least in the US, the government sector that does produce marketed outputs (government enterprises) is very small. Hence the scope of the economy should be restricted to private industries.

Two datasets (both excluding the government sector) are used in this chapter. Dataset 1 focuses on the corporate sector (which includes the corporate farm sector). Dataset 2 is broader, covering (corporate and non-corporate) non-farm private industries; ideally private households and not-for-profit institutions serving households should also be excluded, but the data do not consistently allow it.

### *The employment rate*

The civilian labour force comprises the unemployed plus those in employment, the latter comprising employees (wage and salary earners), the self-employed (active proprietors or partners who devote a majority of their working hours to their unincorporated businesses), and unpaid family helpers. While the latter are not relevant here, the self-employed are a difficulty. They amounted to 20.3 per cent of all employment in 1949 (10.1 million people). Their share of employment halved by 1970, and then remained fairly stable at 10-11 per cent of employment until 1994 (increasing in number from 7.1 million in 1970 to 10.6 million in 1994 as overall employment rose), before falling back to 8.8 per cent by the end of the century (10.3 million in 2003). Hence the self-employed are both significant in number and non-constant in their share of rising total employment.

If the employment rate is defined as:

$$v = \frac{\text{All employment}}{\text{Civilian labour force}} = \frac{\text{Employees + Self-employed}}{\text{Employees + Self-employed + Unemployed}} \tag{6.6}$$

then compositional changes in the labour force between employees and self-employed will not matter (as long as there is no significant movement between self-employed and unemployed). But leaving the self-employed out of the numerator, or out of both numerator and denominator will generate bias in $v$ because of the non-constant movement of self-employed into employee status.

Dataset 1 uses the overall national employment rate, and so includes the self-employed in both numerator and denominator. Indeed, since the employment rate is defined to be the percentage of all in employment to the civilian labour force, it also includes such categories as employees in general government and in households and non-profit institutions. Hence it has to be assumed that the economic trends that affect corporate sector employment and unemployment sufficiently dominate the data that the national employment rate can be used to proxy the unavailable corporate sector employment rate. While this is not unreasonable, it is a significant assumption since one-third of employees are located outside the corporate sector.

Dataset 2 uses an employment rate restricted to non-agriculture private industry adult employees, and so excludes the self-employed, employees in general government and private households from both numerator and denominator.

### *The wage share*

There are three issues with respect to the wage share. First, what wages should count? Second, how should the income of the self-employed be treated? And third, what is the wage share a share of?

*Table 6.1* Compensation of employees by sector and legal form of organization as a percentage of total compensation of employees, 1948–2004

| | *Mean* | *Standard deviation* | *Coefficient of variation (%)* |
|---|---|---|---|
| Corporate business | 65.6 | 1.55 | 2.4 |
| Non-corporate business | 11.4 | 3.47 | 30.4 |
| Sole proprietors and partnerships | 9.0 | 3.59 | 40.0 |
| Other private business | 0.5 | 0.07 | 15.5 |
| Government enterprises | 2.0 | 0.21 | 10.5 |
| Non-business | 23.0 | 2.33 | 10.1 |
| Households and NPIs serving households | 5.6 | 1.28 | 22.9 |
| General government | 17.4 | 1.57 | 9.1 |

### *What wages should count?*

Wages are taken to be 'compensation of employees', including both wage and salary accruals and employer contributions for social insurance. However, not all such wages should be included if the cyclical mechanism as a model of class conflict is taken seriously.

Table 6.1 describes the proportions in which the compensation of employees in the US economy is distributed by sector and legal form of organization.The proportion of total compensation of employees in corporate business is about two-thirds of the total, and fairly stable over the period. That in non-corporate business (sole proprietors and partnerships, other private business and government enterprises) averages about one-ninth of the total, but is 15 times as variable. And that in households, non-profit institutions serving households, and general government averages about two ninths of the total, a share that is five times as variable as that of corporate business. In a Goodwin cyclical mechanism, compensation of employees in such non-business sectors is clearly not relevant, and should be excluded. But the variability of share in non-corporate business is a difficulty if employees are drifting between non-corporate business and non-business occupations.

A further issue is that because the Goodwin model is a model of class conflict over distributional shares, 'wages' represent the labour income of the working class. However, not all 'compensation of employees' accrues to the working class (unless the latter category is defined so broadly as to lose any analytical content). The use of Dataset 2 below attempts to take this into account.

### *What is the labour income of sole proprietors and partnerships?*

Sole proprietors and partnerships not only employ wage workers; they earn an income ('proprietors' income') which is not differentiated between wages and profits. This income is substantial, averaging 9.3 per cent of national income over the period. (It was 16.2 per cent in 1948, almost halves by the mid-1960s - mostly owing to the decline of proprietors' income in the farm sector - and fluctuates thereafter between 6.2 per cent and 8.6 per cent.) For most purposes, this income has to be treated entirely as profit (which it is not), or entirely as labour income (which it is not), or split by some imputation procedure into elements of both (which might be true but entails in a model of class struggle that the self-employed exploit themselves).

In Dataset 1 the corporate sector does not have any self-employed, so the self-employed are irrelevant to the measurement of wages. But since they are in the employment rate, this chapter assumes that the relation between the compensation of employees and employees in employment dominates the data. In Dataset 2, the self-employed are excluded from both wage share and employment rate.

### *What is the wage share a share of?*

The third issue with regard to the wage share is difficult because NIPA aggregates (whether GDP or National Income) are much more than the sum of wages and profits. In addition to wages (compensation of employees) and corporate profits, GDP, for example, also includes proprietors' income, net interest, rental income of persons, indirect business tax and non-tax liabilities, the current surplus of government enterprises less total subsidies, and capital consumption, and excludes net income receipts from the rest of the world. Moreover, both corporate profits and proprietors' income include inventory valuation and capital consumption adjustments, and the rental income of persons incorporates the latter as well. The same issues are relevant with respect to National Income. So taking the wage share as compensation of employees to GDP or National Income hugely exaggerates the implied profits share, and it is very difficult then to relate the latter to the behavioural hypotheses suggested by Goodwin. Hence these behavioural hypotheses require an appropriate definition of 'profits'.

In both Datasets 1 and 2, the denominator of the wage share is measured as that net value added category most (approximately) appropriate to the coverage of the wage data in the numerator.

## Long-run trends in the US corporate sector 1948–2004

Consider the corporate sector in the US economy. Net value added is the sum of compensation of employees, net operating surplus and taxes on production and imports less subsidies. In order to focus directly on distributive conflict, corporate net value added $(Y)$ is considered in what follows as just the sum of compensation of employees and net operating surplus $(\Pi)$. (Taxes on production and imports less subsidies are thereby excluded.) The corporate rate of profit $(r)$ is defined conventionally as the ratio of corporate profits to the corporate capital stock $(K)$, where profits are identified as the net operating surplus of domestic corporate business in current dollars, and the capital stock as the sum of the current-cost net stock of private non-residential fixed assets (equipment, software and structures) and the non-farm inventories of non-financial corporate business. Decompose this rate of profit into the product of corporate profit share and corporate capital productivity (the inverse of the corporate capital–output ratio),

$$r = \frac{\Pi}{Y}\frac{Y}{K} \tag{6.7}$$

and consider the long-run time path of this decomposition.

The discussion following equations (6.3)–(6.5) above merely took log differences of the various series and divided each by the relevant number of years. A more sophisticated approach to establishing long-run trends is to filter the data using the Hodrick-Prescott procedure (1997 (1980)). Suppose that a series $y_t$ can be considered as the sum of a growth component $g_t$ and a cyclical component $c_t$ whose average in the long run is close to zero.

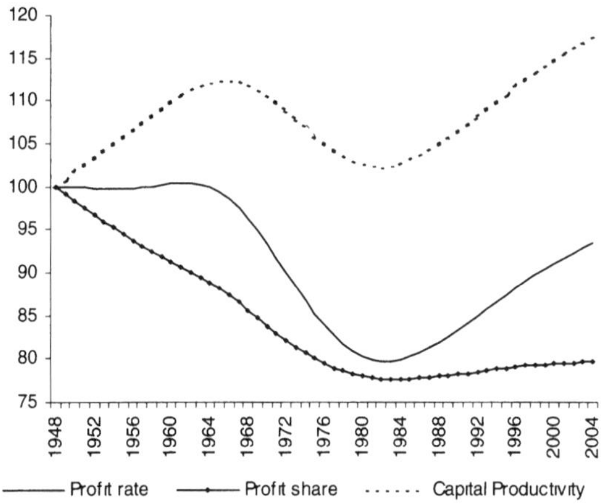


*Figure 6.1* Long-run trends: profit rate, profit share and capital productivity, corporate sector, USA, 1948–2004

Then the HP filter chooses the $g_t$ to minimize:

$$\sum_{t=1}^{t=T} (y_t - g_t)^2 + \lambda \sum_{t=1}^{t=T} [(g_t - g_{t-1}) - (g_{t-1} - g_{t-2})]^2 \tag{6.8}$$

Here $\lambda$ is a positive number which 'penalizes variability' (Hodrick and Prescott 1997: 3) in the trend; the larger is $\lambda$, the closer the solution of the programming problem (6.8) to a least squares fit of a linear time trend. Choice of $\lambda$ is then a compromise between the distance of the variable from its trend (the first term in equation (6.8)) and the curvature of the trend (the second term). Hodrick and Prescott originally suggested values for $\lambda$ of 100 for annual series and 1600 for quarterly series. More recently, Ravn and Uhlig (2002) have argued that *if* a value of $\lambda$ of 1600 is appropriate for quarterly series, then the value for the corresponding annual series should not be 100 but rather 6.25. On the other hand, Duménil and Lévy (1993: 223) have suggested that, for 100 years of annual data, in order to obtain what they called a 'more rigid trend' a higher value of $\lambda$ was necessary, and they set $\lambda$ at 5,000. There is no 'correct' value; the choice entirely depends upon what the research is trying to do. In what follows, $\lambda$ is set at 1000 for annual data, and for the corresponding quarterly data, at 256,000.

The long-run trends for the decomposition of equation (6.5) are shown in Figure 6.1, each series being indexed to 1948. In terms of trend, the profit share falls by just over one-fifth from 1948 to 1982, and then is approximately constant. But trend capital productivity rises by about 12.5 per cent from 1948 to 1966, a rise sufficient to prevent any significant fall in the trend rate of profit up to 1964. The fall in trend capital productivity after 1966 combines with the falling trend profit share to produce a precipitate decline in the trend rate of profit from 1964 to 1982. Its recovery thereafter to the end of the century is primarily associated with rising trend capital productivity.

Thus for the corporate sector, neither the profit share (and hence the wage share) nor capital productivity (and hence the capital output ratio) are constant in long-run terms. If they were, Figure 6.1 would depict a single horizontal straight line. In terms of the broad spirit of the Marxian approach to the long run sketched earlier, one would expect a positive

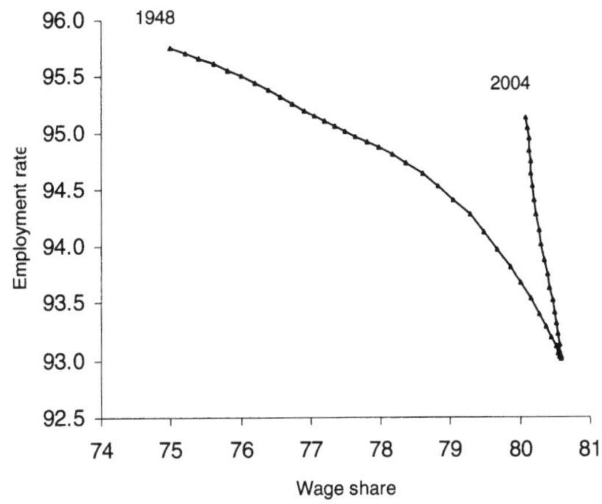


*Figure 6.2* National employment rate and corporate wage share in corporate net value added, long-run trends, USA, 1948–2004

long-run relationship between the profit rate and the employment rate, and, to the extent that the profit share tracks the profit rate, a negative one between the wage share and the employment rate. Figure 6.2 shows the corporate wage share, defined as the ratio of corporate employee compensation to corporate net value added, and the employment rate as the percentage ratio of total employment to total employment and unemployment, defined across all sectors of the economy.

There are two noteworthy features:

1 In trend terms there is in general a strong negative relationship between wage share and employment rate, until 1982. The gradient is much steeper after 1982 than before, indicating a fundamental change in the early 1980s. Thereafter only a small fall in wage share is sufficient to generate a comparatively large rise in the employment rate (because of rising capital productivity).
2 There are no cycles in the long-run trend data.

Thus the Goodwin model, as measured by the corporate sector, does not capture well the long-run dynamics of US capitalism.

## Empirical evidence for Goodwin-type cycles

Leave aside the issue of whether the addition, rather than the substitution, of more realistic assumptions will help the model, and focus instead on the claim that the underlying assumptions and hence equations (6.1) and (6.2) represent in the short run 'the most essential dynamic aspects of capitalism'. If this claim were valid, then, in however attenuated a form, it should show up in the data. The issue is whether there are identifiable short-run cycles that equations (6.1) and (6.2) might 'essentially' represent.

Figure 6.3 displays the cyclical relationship between the corporate wage share and the national employment rate (in annual data).

A cyclical pattern is apparent, but relative to equations (6.1) and (6.2) stochastic perturbations are altering the period, amplitude and position. This is clearer in Figures 6.4 and 6.5, which depict the individual cycles separately using quarterly data. While quarterly

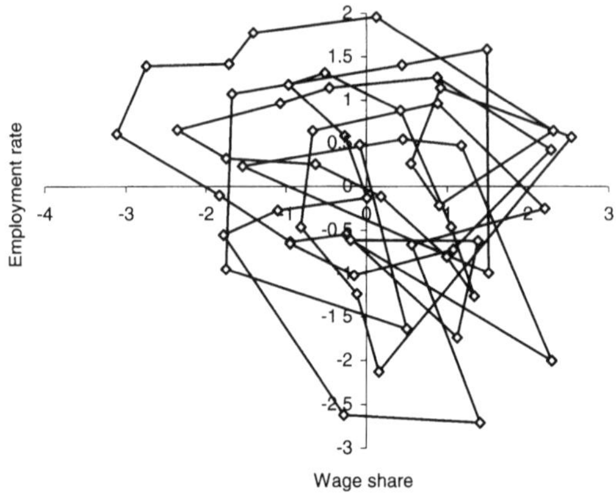


*Figure 6.3* Detrended cycles, national employment rate and corporate sector wage share, USA, annual data, 1948–2004

data enable greater precision in the dating of individual cycles, and show more clearly the effects of perturbations, they do not essentially alter the qualitative $(u, v)$ results found from the annual data. The cycles are broadly coterminous with NBER trough dates (about four quarters later than NBER peak dates), except for that ending in 1974Q4 (the NBER trough being one quarter later). Also the short NBER 1980Q3–1982Q4 cycle is amalgamated with its successor 1982Q4–1991Q3.

Conformity with the NBER dates is better before the structural turning point of the early 1980s than after. The left hand picture in Figure 6.5 shows four quarters following 1980Q3 which seem transitional in that they do not appear to belong to any cycle at all. Thereafter, there is some visual indication that the 1980s cycle in fact comprises two cycles: from 1981Q3 to 1986Q2, entirely below the horizontal axis, and then from 1986Q2 to 1991Q1, mostly above the horizontal axis. Moreover, the 1990s cycle is also odd in that from 1991Q1 through to 1994Q2 it is hard to discern a cyclical movement at all. This is in marked contrast to the second half of the 1990s when the 'normal' cyclical pattern was re-established.

Thus examination of the data for the US corporate sector provides strong *prima facie* evidence that there are (detrended) cycles in the wage share and the employment rate, approximately identifiable with NBER trough to trough dates. All of the cycles are clockwise in direction, as the underlying causal argument would predict. But each cycle is different in position, amplitude and duration, so that the economic relationships generating detrended cycles do so in a way that is both systemic (cycles exist) and historically contingent (no two cycles are the same).

## Wages, the working class and distributive conflict

### *Wages and the working class*

The Goodwin model is a 'predator-prey' dynamic system in which, by equation (6.1), the more the prey population (the employment rate), the faster the growth of the predator population (the wage share), and, by equation (6.2), the smaller the number of predators, the faster the growth of the prey population. Goodwin commented that while this

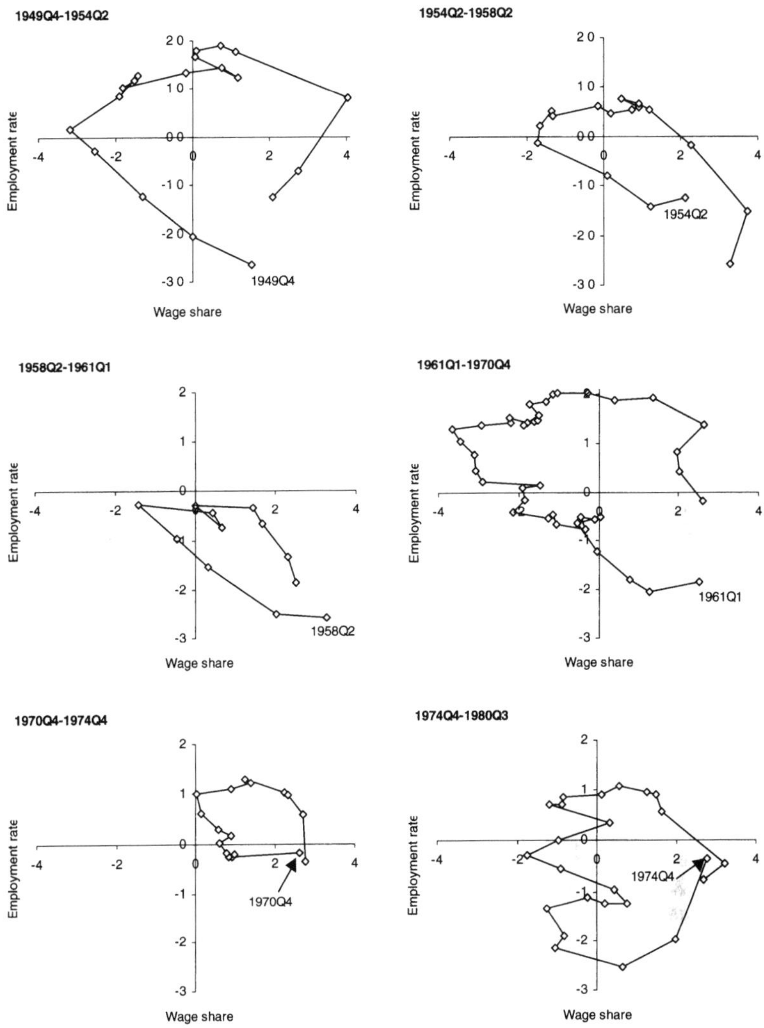


*Figure 6.4* Detrended corporate sector cycles, USA, quarterly data, 1949–1980

characterization is 'to some extent ... purely formal', the analogy with 'the symbiosis of two populations - partly complementary, partly hostile - is helpful in the understanding of the dynamical contradictions of capitalism, especially when stated in a more or less Marxian form' (Goodwin 1972: 445). For Goodwin, the cyclical mechanism described by equations (6.1) and (6.2) is 'essentially what Marx meant by the contradiction of capitalism and its transitory resolution in booms and slumps' (ibid.: 448). The two classes depend upon each other in an antagonistic relationship.

In the *model*, wages (and hence the wage share) accrue to the working class and profits (and profit share) to the capitalist class. But in the *data* this is not true. Wages in Dataset 1 are identified with compensation of employees, which covers everyone employed by the

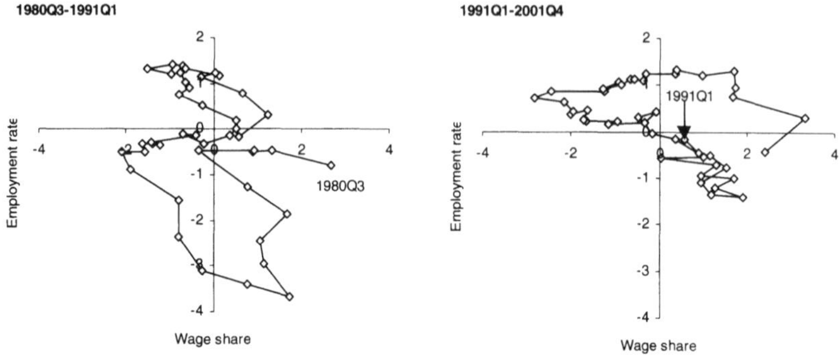


*Figure 6.5* Detrended corporate sector cycles, USA, quarterly data, 1980–2001

corporate sector. If the earnings of all corporate employees are classified to wages, this leaves the corporate capitalist class with no obvious membership. If the earnings of the mightiest CEO and those of the humblest shop-floor worker are both 'wages', it is not easy to see how structural class relations can be personified. Yet they must be so personified for the Goodwin cyclical mechanism to work.

One way in which this issue might be approached is through a focus on hierarchy within the firm. Those lower down the hierarchy are hired and fired by those higher up; negotiations around wage increases are between those lower down the hierarchy and those above them; those lower down 'strike', and those higher up 'lock out'. Subordination to hierarchy is the pervasive experience of employment in capitalist firms; some people supervise, while most people are supervised.

Data on those who are supervised are available ('production and related workers' in Mining and Manufacturing, 'construction workers' in Construction, and 'non-supervisory employees' in Private Service-Producing industries). The questionnaires eliciting the raw data in the establishment survey define production and related workers and construction workers to include 'working supervisors or group leaders who may be 'in charge' of some employees, but whose supervisory functions are *only incidental* to their regular work', and non-supervisory workers to include 'every employee *except* those whose *major* responsibility is to supervise, plan, or direct the work of others' (emphases added). The production and related workers and construction workers categories exclude those employed in financial and trade functions, plus a small miscellany of other functions.[8] Therefore amalgamating production and related workers, construction workers and non-supervisory workers into a proxy measure of the working class is very approximate (although improving through time as the employment weight of the service sector increases). Imperfect though it is, it enables a better measure of 'wages' than the standard category of all employees who receive wages and salaries.

Henceforth 'non-supervisory workers' refers to the aggregate of production and related, construction and non-supervisory workers, and 'supervisory workers' refers to the residual aggregate of those whose major responsibility is supervision. The coverage is broadly all non-farm private industry.[9] In 1948, 87.9 per cent of all non-farm private industry employees were classified as non-supervisory. This proportion falls to 82.6 per cent in 1970, and thereafter fluctuates within a two percentage point band. Hence for most of the period some 81–82 per cent of employees in non-farm private industry are a proxy measure

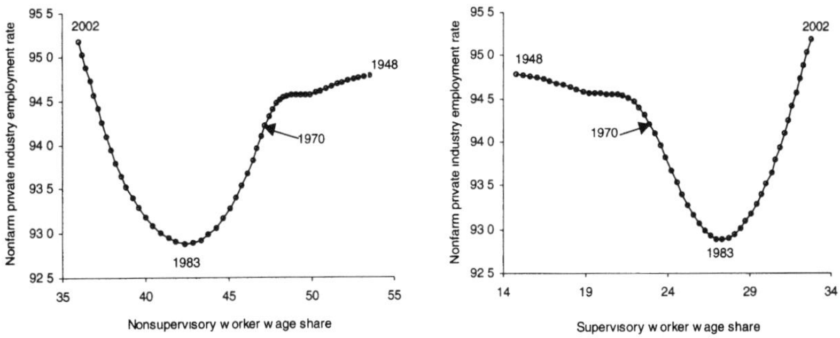


*Figure 6.6* Employment rate and wage shares in net value added, non-supervisory and supervisory workers, non-farm private industry, long run trends, USA, 1948–2002

for the working class, and some 18–19 per cent of employees supervise them. As just mentioned, some of these latter are engaged in low-level finance and trade functions, and it is obviously stretching credulity to call such office employees (in mining, construction and manufacturing) agents of capital. However, this is not too important: because of the highly skewed wage and salary distribution, the trend in the labour income of supervisory workers will be dominated by the trend of the higher labour income earners.

## *Non-Farm private industry: long-run trends*

Figure 6.6 is the analogue of Figure 6.2, and shows the overall non-farm private industry employment rate against non-supervisory and supervisory wage shares taken separately.

Each graph in Figure 6.6 displays a roughly similar U-shape as that in Figure 6.2, with a similar turning point (1983 instead of 1982). But for non-supervisory workers, the direction is reversed, so that 1948–83 exhibits declines in both their wage share and the overall employment rate; thereafter the non-supervisory wage share continued to decline as the overall employment rate rose. Part of the decline was due to the falling proportion of non-supervisory workers, but that was primarily confined to the years before 1970.[10] By contrast, for the much smaller number of supervisory workers, 1948–83 shows a large increase in their wage share as the overall employment rate fell; after 1983, the long-run relationship between supervisory worker wage share and the overall employment rate was positive. For both supervisory and non-supervisory workers, as with corporate sector employees in Figure 6.2, there are no cycles in the long run data.

## *Non-farm private industry: short-run cycles*

Dating of the short-run cycles is more approximate, because of the lack of quarterly data. Figures 6.7 and 6.8 are drawn starting with the NBER trough dates, and then adjusting visually.

If the years 1991–4 are ignored (analogous to 1991Q1–1994Q3 for the corporate sector), then all the cycles are clockwise in direction. The dating is close to that in Figures 6.4 and 6.5, but is not exactly the same, and this is summarized in Table 6.2.

For the corporate sector, the transitional dates of 1980Q3–1981Q3, and 1991Q1–1994Q3 are omitted, and similarly the transitional years 1991-4 for the non-supervisory employees

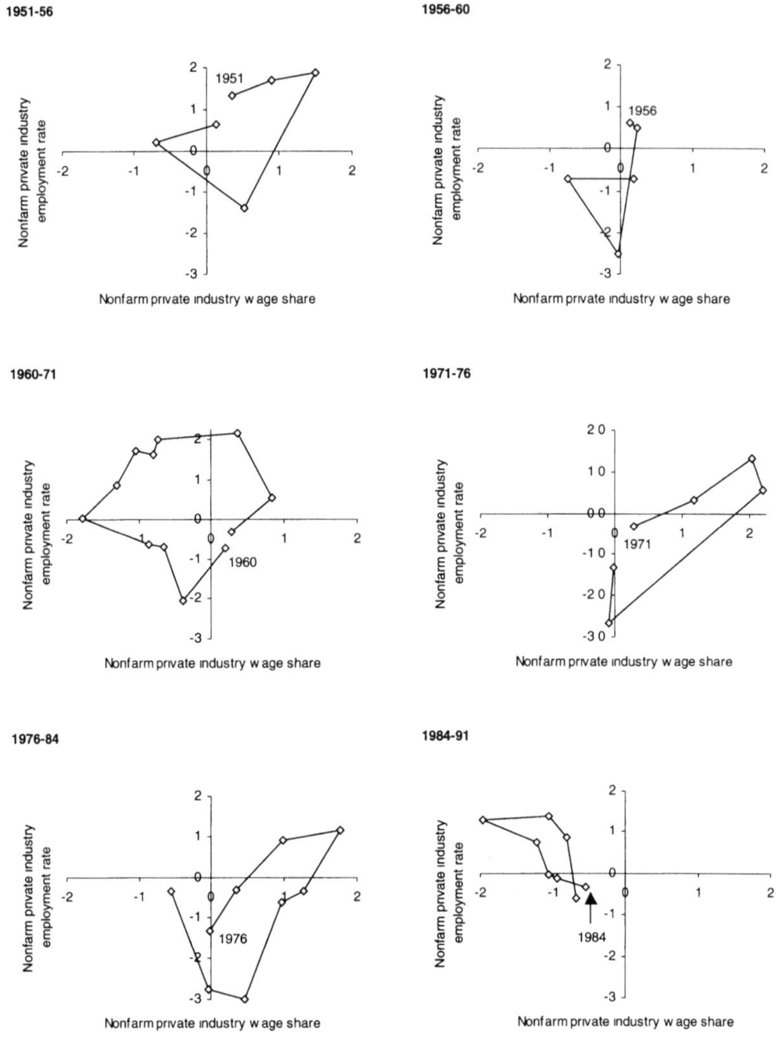


*Figure 6.7* Non-supervisory employees, detrended cycles, non-farm private industry, USA, quarterly data, 1951-1991

in non-farm private industry. Thus the data display a similar pattern: Goodwin-type cycles exist, they are clockwise in direction, short-run rather than long-run, and similar to NBER business cycles. They are not constant in either period or amplitude or position, consistent with an interpretation of continuous displacement. While the results show some sensitivity in dating and shape to the choice of dataset, the qualitative conclusions are unambiguous.

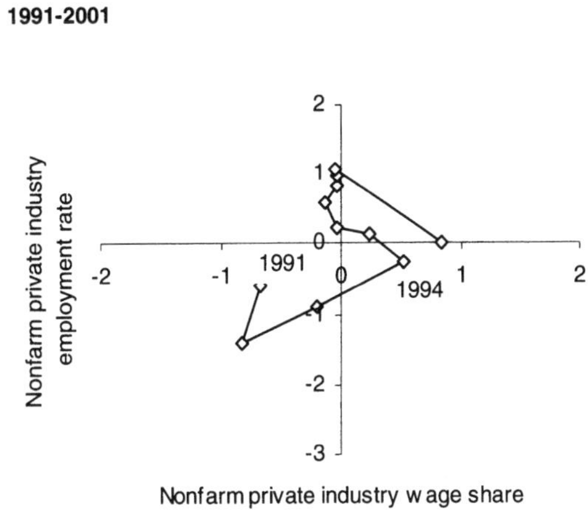


*Figure 6.8* Non-supervisory employees, detrended cycle, non-farm private industry, USA, quarterly data, 1991(1994)–2001

*Table 6.2* Cycle date comparisons

| *NBER trough to trough* | *Corporate sector all employees* | *Non-farm private industry non-supervisory employees* |
|---|---|---|
| 1949Q4-1954Q2 | 1949Q4-1954Q2 | 1951-56 |
| 1954Q2-1958Q2 | 1954Q2-1958Q2 | 1956-60 |
| 1958Q2-1961Q1 | 1958Q2-1961Q1 | |
| 1961Q1-1970Q4 | 1961Q1-1970Q4 | 1960-71 |
| 1970Q4-1975Q1 | 1970Q4-1974Q4 | 1971-76 |
| 1975Q1-1980Q3 | 1974Q4-1980Q3 | 1976-84 |
| 1980Q3-1982Q4 | 1981Q3-1986Q2 | |
| 1982Q4-1991Q1 | 1986Q2-1991Q1 | 1984-91 |
| 1991Q1-2001Q4 | 1994Q3-2001Q4 | 1994-2001 |

## *An anomalous picture*

If supervisory wages are added to non-supervisory wages in order to derive an all employee wage share for non-farm private industry, a rather different long-run picture emerges. Figure 6.9 shows that from 1953 to 1999 there is one complete long-run cycle in the trend data in a clockwise direction. The difference with Figure 6.2 showing the analogous picture for all employees in the corporate sector is marked. While the different employment rate definitions (whole economy trend versus non-farm private industry trend) do have some effect, it is quantitative rather than qualitative.[11] The qualitative difference is caused by the different wage share definitions (affecting both numerator and denominator). Why then does the addition of the non-corporate wage share to the corporate wage share produce such

*Figure 6.9* Employment rate and all employee wage share, non-farm private industry, trends, USA, 1948–2002

a contrast with the trend of the corporate wage share alone, producing a cyclical pattern when there is no such pattern in the trend wage share in the corporate sector alone? Three related comments suggest themselves.

First, the variation in the trend employment rate is small, at just 1.8 percentage points. Similarly, that in long-run wage share is just 1.65 percentage points.[12] But as was shown above, this small variation in long-run wage share conceals a very large wage share shift from non-supervisory to supervisory workers. Amalgamating these two categories alters the focus in a Goodwin model from distributive conflict between classes to an un-theorized conflict in the functional distribution of income. It is not obvious that such an alteration of focus is desirable either from an interpretative point of view or from the perspective underlying this chapter, for it runs counter to the spirit of Goodwin's model, and it renders the notion of class and class conflict opaque.

Second, Figure 6.9 could be interpreted as not showing a cycle at all in any meaningful sense. Rather, it shows a long-run negative and elastic relationship between employment share and wage share from 1948 to the early 1970s, characterizing the 'golden age' of the post-war boom. This is followed by a decade of transition from the early 1970s to the early 1980s, with its attendant well-known instabilities, which culminated in the change of monetary policy in 1979 and a decisive shift away from the social and economic parameters of the 'golden age' as the balance of class power tilted towards capital. What was thereby established after 1983 was a different long-run negative and inelastic relationship between employment share and wage share. Hence Figures 6.2 and 6.9 tell the same story of a shift from an elastic to an inelastic negative relationship, but differently nuanced because of the different underlying data. Decomposing Figure 6.9 into the two graphs of Figure 6.6 then allows a more detailed description of the underlying class struggle.

Third, the non-corporate sector raises notorious difficulties in classification terms. Obvious candidates for investigation in the measure of net value added are first, proprietors' income, raising the issues surrounding self-employment, and second, the inclusion of net interest, because the receipt of net interest by the largely unincorporated real estate sector dominates the category, and increasingly so through time. For example in 2002 the component of the net operating surplus 'net interest and miscellaneous payments' was about five times larger for private industry than it was for the corporate sector. Thus further research is necessary on whether the components of the wage share of the non-corporate sector are appropriate for the exploration of Goodwin cycles of distributional conflict.

In sum, functional measures of aggregate income distribution are not categories of class income. Since the latter are the focus in a Goodwin model, considerable care is required in the construction and interpretation of the wage data. In particular, a more detailed class analysis is required of both the 'compensation of employees' in the corporate sector, and the income categories of the non-corporate sector. For the most casual inspection of Figures 6.2, the left hand side of 6.6, and 6.9 shows that different definitions matter.

## Conclusion

This chapter has attempted to interpret the US economy in terms of long-run trends and short-run cycles within an overall perspective of class conflict. The evidence for short-run cyclical behaviour involving the wage share and the employment rate is strong. These short-run cycles are 'Goodwin cycles' in the sense that they describe a cyclical relation between the latter variables. They are little different from the NBER business cycle. Moreover, the Goodwin mechanism is a 'pure' mechanism of distributive conflict that is structurally unstable. Hence again it is not surprising that the cycles are different in period, amplitude and position. As noted by Solow 'the displacements [of the shorter-run cycles] are quite large and they suggest that the Goodwin model cannot be the only mechanism governing the relation between the wage share and the employment rate' (Solow, 1990: 39).

This chapter finds no evidence that long-run Goodwin cycles exist, at least in the corporate sector. This result is arguably sensitive to the choice of data, for there is apparently one 46-year cycle for non-farm (corporate and non-corporate) private industries. The previous section has suggested that such a cycle is more apparent than real, but substantiating this at a level beyond suggestion requires further investigation of the national accounts categories of the corporate and non-corporate sectors. Indeed, no previous study has investigated the adequacy of the category 'compensation of employees' to measure the 'wages' required to construct the wage share needed by the Goodwin model. For the latter is a model of class conflict, but national accounts do not (unsurprisingly) distinguish classes. While the recipients of labour income include the classically defined working class, they are also rather more than this. Using the distinction between non-supervisory and supervisory employees to proxy relations of hierarchy and control in a class-divided society, this chapter documents the extraordinary trend shift in labour income away from non-supervisory employees. Nevertheless, detrended short-run Goodwin cycles remain.

This raises a number of issues. Given the very large fall in the non-supervisory trend wage share shown in the left hand graph of Figure 6.6 of 17.5 percentage points, why did supervisory wages rise by 17.9 percentage points to produce a long-run approximate constancy in trend total wage share? And why did the same huge redistribution produce such a small variation in the long-run trend of the aggregate wage share? What were the forces making for redistribution? Were they separate from the Goodwin-type cyclical mechanism, or were they in some as yet unspecified manner tied up with it? Hence the final conclusion of this chapter is both to validate a short-run Goodwin-type mechanism and to raise a rich research agenda concerning the theoretical and empirical significance of the decomposition of employees into more class-delineated categories.

## Appendix

This chapter uses two different data sets, called Dataset 1 and Dataset 2.

### *Electronic sources*

For business cycle dates: National Bureau of Economic Research (NBER), 'Business Cycle Expansions and Contractions'.
Available HTTP: <http://www.nber.org/cycles/cyclesmain.html>

For wage share data in Dataset 1: National Income and Product Accounts (NIPA), US Department of Commerce.
Available HTTP:<http://www.bea.gov/>

For all employment rate statistics, for wage share data in Dataset 2, and for the *Handbook of Methods*: Bureau of Labor Statistics (BLS), US Department of Labor.
Available HTTP:< http://www.bls.gov/>

For the capital stock data for the rate of profit in Dataset 1: Fixed Assets Tables (FAT): Bureau of Economic Analysis, US Department of Commerce.
Available HTTP: < http://www.bea.gov/ > and

Flow of Funds Accounts (FoF), Federal Reserve Board.
Available HTTP: < http://www.federalreserve.gov/ >

### *The long-run averages*

In the discussion following equation (6.5), the data for the long-run averages were calculated as log differences. The capital–output ratio is the inverse of capital productivity, which is the ratio of the capital stock to net value added in the corporate sector. For the corporate capital stock, see below. labour force growth is calculated from the BLS series LNU01000000, labour productivity growth from the BLS series PRS85006093, and real wage rate growth from the BLS series PRS85006153.

### *The rate of profit*

Profits are the net operating surplus of the corporate sector (NIPA Table 1.14 line 8, W322RC1). For the profit share, see the wage share below. The capital stock is corporate equipment, software and structures (FAT Table 4.1 line 13) plus non-farm, non-financial corporate business inventories (FoF Table B102, line 5).

### *The employment rate*

#### *Dataset 1*

There is no employment rate that is confined to the corporate sector, and so a national employment rate is used. The data are taken from BLS, Table A1 of the Employment Situation News Release, constructed from the Current Population Survey (CPS) and cover those who are aged 16 or over. In terms of the series identifiers, the annual employment rate (not seasonally adjusted) is measured as the percentage ratio of the total in employment (LNU02000000) to the total labour force (LNU01000000). The (seasonally adjusted) quarterly employment rate is measured as the ratio of LNS12000000Q to LNS11000000Q.

*Dataset 2*

The employment rate is one for non-agriculture, private industries wage and salary workers (16+), constructed from Table A5 of the Employment Situation News Release as the ratio of Employment (LNU02032189) to Employment (LNU02032189) plus Unemployment (LNU03032229). Note that 'non-agriculture' is a slightly broader category than 'non-farm'.

The different employment rates make little difference to the results (the largest difference in the rates being in the early years of the period).

### The wage share

*Dataset 1*

The wage share is defined with respect to the corporate sector (NIPA Table 1.14, annual and quarterly), and is the ratio of compensation of employees (line 4, series A442RC1) to the sum of compensation of employees and net operating surplus, where the net operating surplus is taken as the sum of net interest and miscellaneous payments (line 9, series A453RC1), business current transfer payments (line 10, series W323RC1), and corporate profits with inventory valuation and capital consumption adjustments (line 11, series A445RC1). Note that the sum of compensation of employees and net operating surplus is less than net value added because taxes on production and imports less subsidies are excluded. (The quarterly line numbers and series identifiers are the same.)

*Dataset 2*

Wages of non-supervisory workers are collected from the Current Employment Statistics (CES) Survey, which is a payroll or establishment survey. This creates issues of comparability. Whereas the CPS counts people, the CES counts jobs. The former counts multiple jobholders once, whereas the latter counts every job. This is significant, because between 4.5 per cent (in 1974) and 6.4 per cent (in 1995) of those in employment were multiple job-holders. There are also differences in employment definitions: CPS includes the unincorporated self-employed, agricultural and related workers, private household workers, and workers absent without pay, and excludes people under 16; the CES survey excludes these categories of employment (except for the logging industry) and has no age restriction. Moreover, the CES Survey excludes employees on leave without pay for the entire pay period and employees on strike for the entire pay period. Finally, in June 2003, the CES survey underwent a complete industry reclassification, changing from the 1987 Standard Industrial Classification System (SIC) to the 2002 North American Industry Classification System (NAICS). NAICS-based data is only available back to 1964; SIC-based annual data goes back to 1948 (for the relevant categories of this chapter, but is no longer produced, and is available to 2002 only. Quarterly data can be determined from the CES Survey by averaging seasonally adjusted monthly data, but only from 1964. Because of this, only annual data are used.

This chapter tries to overcome the issues of comparability as follows. Use the SIC-based data, and for all private industry, take the ratio of non-supervisory workers (EEU00500003) to all employees (EEU00500001). Apply this ratio to the NIPA series of full-time equivalent employees for all private industry less farms (NIPA Table 6.5 line 3 (A4303C0) minus line 5 (B4305C0)). This will not be completely accurate for a number of reasons: for example, multiple job-holding may be unequally distributed between supervisory and non-supervisory employees; the NIPA data includes private households and non-farm agricultural industries. The hope is that given the level of aggregation of this chapter, the inaccuracies thereby imported are not large.

Total wages of non-supervisory employees are calculated as average weekly earnings (EEU00500004), multiplied by the NIPA ratio (for private industry less farms) of employee compensation (NIPA Table 6.2 line 3 (A4003C0) minus line 5 (H4005C0)) to wage and salary accruals (NIPA Table 6.3 line 3 (A4103C0) minus line 5 (B4105C0)), multiplied by the constructed number of non-supervisory employees (described in the preceding paragraph), multiplied by 52. Total wages of supervisory employees are calculated as the difference between NIPA employee compensation (private industry less farms) and the constructed total wages of non-supervisory employees.

The operating surplus component in the denominator of these constructed wage shares of supervisory and non-supervisory employees is the NIPA net operating surplus of private industry (NIPA Table 1.10 line 12 (W260RC1) less farms (Table 7.3.5 line 23 (W251RC1)), less the rental income of persons (NIPA Table 1.10 line 16 (A048RC1)). It thereby includes non-farm proprietors' income, (otherwise there would be no profit component in non-corporate industry), but since this is included in all three wage shares (non-supervisory, supervisory, and both together), it should not distort the comparisons made in this chapter.

## Acknowledgements

We are grateful for helpful comments from Alessandro Vercelli, from participants at the Goodwin Workshop, Bremen, 11–12 November 2005, and at the Analytical Political Economy Workshop, Queen Mary, London, 1–2 June 2007, and from two anonymous referees.

## Notes

1 Indeed, if the data are characterized by significant structural changes over the period, a straightforward estimation of the main equations of the model under a long-run interpretation is liable to produce puzzling results. Thus, for instance, in Harvie (2000) in all countries the estimated average values of the wage share and the employment rate lie outside the plot, the estimated period of the cycle is one year, and the estimates of the parameters of the Phillips curve are unrealistically high (Harvie 2000: 362 Table 2).

2 This is also broadly consonant with the approach suggested by Vercelli (1977), although his quantitative procedures were different.

3 Despite different theoretical and econometric approaches, this chapter shares some features with the literature on the cyclical profit squeeze (Goldstein 1996, 1999), in particular the emphasis on the distinction between trend and cycles and on structural changes. The results, too, are broadly consistent.

4 Duménil and Lévy (1993, 2002) have written extensively in these terms.

5 It is worth noting in passing that Marx's historically specific concept of an 'industrial reserve army or surplus population' is much broader than the historically more recent concept of 'unemployment' (ibid.: 794–7).

6 Goodwin (1972: 445–8). For a more detailed formal analysis of the Goodwin model, see Gandolfo (1997), Section 24.4: 449–64.

7 The variables are more precisely defined, and their coverage discussed, in the following sections. Restricting the coverage to the years of NBER peaks (1948–2000) makes only a negligible difference.

8 For more descriptive detail, see US Department of Labor, Bureau of Labor Statistics 1994: 1221. In Mining, and Construction, the production worker category excludes individuals working in accounting or finance, advertising, cafeterias, collection and credit, executive, professional and technical (including legal and medical) positions, personnel, purchasing and sales; in Manufacturing it excludes in addition people working in force account construction, product installation and servicing, record-keeping not related to production, and delivery. See the BLS *Handbook of Methods*, ch. 2 for further detail and definitions. Sample questionnaires are in the appendix to this chapter.

9 Further details are given in the Appendix.

10 If the proportion of non-supervisory to all employees is held at its 1948 level, and the resulting non-supervisory trend wage share compared with the actual trend, for all years to 1967, between 50 and 56 per cent of the decline is attributable to the falling proportion. This proportion then declines sharply (47 per cent in 1970, 32 per cent in 1982, and 13 per cent in 2002).

11 A similar pattern (not shown in this chapter) is obtained from a long-run scatter of the non-farm private industry all employee wage share against the economy-wide employment rate.

12 In Figure 6.9, the $(u, v)$ data points for 1953 and 1999 are effectively the same, being the co-ordinates of where the time-path crosses itself. Hence the variation in $u$ between 1953 and 1975 is the same as that between 1975 and 1999. Similarly for the variation in $v$ between 1953 and 1983, and 1983 and 1999.

## References


Desai, Meghnad (1973) 'Growth Cycles and Inflation in a Model of the Class Struggle'. *Journal of Economic Theory* 6: 527–45

Desai, Meghnad (1984) 'An Econometric Model of the Share of Wages in National Income: UK 1855–1965'. In R. M. Goodwin, M. Krüger and A. Vercelli (eds), *Nonlinear Models of Fluctuating Growth*. Lecture Notes in Economics and Mathematical Systems 228, Berlin: Springer-Verlag

Duménil, Gérard and Dominique Lévy. (1993) *The Economics of the Profit Rate*. Aldershot: Edward Elgar

Duménil, Gérard and Dominique Lévy. (2002) 'The Profit Rate: Where and How Much Did It Fall?. Did It Recover? (USA. 1948–1997).' *Review of Radical Political Economics* 34: 437–61

Farkas, M. and M. Kotsis, (1992) 'Modelling Predator-Prey and Wage-Employment Dynamics'. In G. Feichtinger (ed.), *Dynamic Economic Models and Optimal Control*, Amsterdam: North Holland

Flaschel, Peter (1988), 'Fiscal Policy in an Accelerator-Augmented Classical Growth Cycle'. In Peter Flaschel and Michael Kruger (eds), *Recent Approaches to Economic Dynamics*, Frankfurt: Peter Lang

Flaschel, Peter and Gangolf Groh (1995), 'The Classical Growth Cycle: Reformulation, Simulation and Some Facts'. *Economic Notes* 24: 293–326

Gandolfo, Giancarlo (1997). *Economic Dynamics*,3rd edn. Berlin: Springer Verlag

Goldstein, Jonathan (1996) 'The Empirical Relevance of the Cyclical Profit-Squeeze: A Reassertion'. *Review of Radical Political Economics* 28: 55–92

Goldstein, Jonathan (1999) 'Predator-Prey Model Estimates of the Cyclical Profit Squeeze'. *Metroeconomica* 50(2): 139–173

Goodwin, Richard M. (1972) 'A Growth Cycle'. In E. K. Hunt and Jesse G. Schwartz,

*A Critique of Economic Theory*, Harmondsworth: Penguin, 442–449. A revised and enlarged version of R. M. Goodwin, 'A Growth Cycle', in C. H. Feinstein (ed.), *Capitalism and Economic Growth*, Cambridge: Cambridge University Press, 1967, 54–8

Gordon, David M. (1996) *Fat and Mean. The Corporate Squeeze of Working Americans and the Myth of Corporate 'Downsizing'.* New York: Martin Kessler Books

Harvie, David (2000) 'Testing Goodwin: Growth Cycles in Ten OECD Countries'. *Cambridge Journal of Economics* 24: 349–76

Hodrick, Robert J. and Edward C. Prescott (1997) 'Postwar US Business Cycles: An Empirical Investigation'. *Journal of Money, Credit and Banking*, 29(1): 1–16. Originally published as Discussion Paper No. 451, Carnegie Mellon University, 1980

Marx, Karl (1976, originally 1867) *Capital* Volume 1. Harmondsworth: Penguin

Mohun, Simon (2006) 'Distributive Shares in the US Economy, 1964–2001'. *Cambridge Journal of Economics* 30(3): 347–70

Ravn, Morton O. and Harald Uhlig (2002) 'On Adjusting the Hodrick-Prescott Filter for the Frequency of Observations'. *Review of Economics and Statistics* 84(2): 371–80

Skott, Peter (1989), *Conflict and Effective Demand in Economic Growth.* Cambridge: Cambridge University Press

Solow, Robert M. (1990) 'Goodwin's Growth Cycle: Reminiscence and Rumination'. In K. Vellupillai (ed.), *Nonlinear Multisectoral Macrodynamics: Essays in Honour of Richard Goodwin*, Basingstoke: Macmillan

U.S. Department of Labor, Bureau of Labor Statistics (1994) *Employment, Hours, and Earnings. United States, 1909–94.* Two volumes. Bulletin 2445. Washington, DC: U.S. Government Printing Office

Veneziani, Roberto and Simon Mohun (2005) 'Structural Instability and Goodwin's *A Growth Cycle*'. *Structural Change and Economic Dynamics* 17(4): 437–51

Vercelli, Alessandro (1977), 'The Phillips Dilemma: A New Suggested Approach'. *Economic Notes* VI(1): 14–76

# 7 The classical growth cycle after fifteen years of new observations

*Peter Flaschel, Gangolf Groh, Göran Kauermann and Timo Teuber*

## Introduction

In this chapter, we reconsider the simple empirical evidence for the existence of a long-phased cycle in the state variables $e$ and $v$, the employment rate and the wage share, that we have collected in Flaschel and Groh (1995) for a number of industrialized market economies. We do this on the basis of fifteen years of further observations and to a certain degree now also with quite modern econometric techniques. Our findings will be that – in the case of the US economy – the only 3/4 closed long-phase loops we observed in this earlier paper can now be confirmed as by and large closed, giving in sum an approximately 50-year-long cycle in employment and the wage share that was interacting with six to seven business cycles observed in the US economy between 1960 and 2006.

As basic theoretical explanation for the occurrence of such long-phased cycles the reference to the seminal papers by Richard Goodwin (1967), augmented by Rose (1967) type limit cycle considerations, and the many papers that are based on this work suggests itself. By and large this means that we consider a growth cycle model where the steady state in the linear center of the model is repelling and where there are forces far off this steady state which imply constant or falling employment rates at the full employment ceiling $e = 1$ and falling wage shares in situations where income distribution squeezes profitability to a significant degree. We have supplied in Flaschel and Groh (1995) a model example for such a situation and will recapitulate in this chapter only the absolutely necessary ingredients that make a Goodwin-Rose growth cycle dynamics repelling at their interior steady state and bounded within the phase space $[0, 1]^2$. The implication of such a scenario will often be a clockwise motion of the state variables $(v, e)$ in the phase space $[0, 1]^2$ as it has been observed for a number of countries in Flaschel and Groh (1995).

Another example for such an observation is Solow's (1990) contribution to a collection of essays in honor of R. Goodwin where he not only provides a characterization of the merits and weaknesses of this prototype model, but also briefly discusses whether this employment–cycle model of the conflict over income distribution 'fits the facts' (and what such a question may mean here). One of Solow's findings in this article (ibid.: 39) is that there is a suggestion in the data of a predominantly clockwise motion, but in three separate episodes as far as the phase plot of annual US-data, 1947–1986 of the share of wages and the rate of employment is concerned. He adds:

> It is also worth noting that the phase diagram contains the bare hint of a single large long–period clockwise sweep. It is only a hint, at best a hint. One cycle is not a periodic motion. (ibid.: 40)

There are many authors who have stressed the empirical relevance of the period length that is implied by Goodwin's growth cycle model, when its parameters are given empirical content, see in particular Atkinson (1969). Solow himself calculates a period length of 8 to 10 years, however for (linear) Phillips curves that are very steep. He then concludes (ibid.: 38) that:

> Goodwin cycles are something else . What could that something be? Here I presume that we must take seriously the story that the model tells: . . .

The conclusions of this brief chapter will be the same as in Solow's article (we quoted above) and which he continuous as follows (ibid.: .40):

> There may be work for Goodwinians here too, theoretical as well as applied. It would make more sense to me if the Goodwinian mechanism were to apply on a time scale considerably longer than the ordinary business cycle. Since the model determines its own period, there is room for some interplay between facts and the theoretical structure.

Last but not least, in addition to the theoretical considerations the model's contribution to economic policy issues should be recognized as well. Up to the present day, the question regularly comes up in political discussions whether rising wages and an increasing wage share are good or bad for employment. On the one hand, there is the traditional view which claims a negative relationship between both magnitudes due to higher production costs or a lower investment demand which additionally reduces the growth of the capital stock in the future. This is also the view adopted by the Goodwin model and its successors (see below). The opposite view, normally put forward by trade unions, is that in a demand-constrained economy an increasing wage share leads to more purchasing power for those people who have a higher propensity to consume. This effect is perceived to be stronger than the adverse effect on investment demand, provided that the latter is taken into account at all.

The interesting point is now, that the "long-period clockwise sweep" described above contains four different phases two of which supporting the first and the other two supporting the second view, at least at the first glance:

- Phase 1: declining $v$ and rising $e$
- Phase 2: rising $v$ and rising $e$
- Phase 3: rising $v$ and declining $e$
- Phase 4: declining $v$ declining $e$

Obviously, the first and the third phase – if considered in isolation – are in line with the first view, while the second and the fourth seem to support the second standpoint. Given such a cycle without the concrete "background story" provided by the Goodwin model, one might be tempted to conclude that there are – or have been – times in which the "purchasing-power-effect" dominates and other periods in which the "cost-effect" (or "Rose-effect") overcompensates the former. In the light of the approach considered here, however, the Rose-effect is dominant all of the time and the apparently deviating phases have quite a different explanation. During the second phase, characterized by $v\uparrow$ and $e\uparrow$, the growth rate of effective demand – triggered, among others, by high multiplier effects caused by supernormal investment demand (due to the low wage rate) – is still higher than the growth rate of labor supply, despite the fact, that the increasing wage share already has a dampening effect on the demand side. In the fourth phase, in which $v\downarrow$ and $e\downarrow$ can be observed, aggregate demand is already stimulated by the increasing investment, but its growth rate is still too weak to cope with that of labor supply (caused, as in the previous case, by a constant rate of Harrod-neutral technical progress or population growth).

Against this background, the question about the empirical relevance of the model considered here is of utmost importance. If it turns out not to contradict the data, a straightforward policy implication is that there exists no cogent reason to abandon a restrictive wage policy even in times where a falling wage share goes hand in hand with a further increasing rate of unemployment. This follows because the true reason – according to the model – for the ongoing deterioration on the labor market is not the decline of the wage share, but the fact that the latter does not decline sharply enough! Consequently, policy makers would be well-advised to resist the political pressure resulting from an apparent failure of moderate wage policy, at least as far as the link between wage share and unemployment is concerned.[1] This view is further underpinned by the fact, that due to the long-run nature of the model also prolonged phases with falling $v$ and falling $e$ are not at odds with the model's predictions.

On this background, we shall introduce in the next section a general formulation of the Goodwin growth cycle model. "Exploring growth cycles for the US economy" then summarizes some time series evidence for the Goodwin cycle from the work of Flaschel and Groh (1995). In "The US economy" we provide basic econometric evidence for the existence of this cycle. "Business cycles and long-phase cycles in the US economy" makes use of more refined techniques that establish evidence for the Goodwin growth cycle and its mirror image, the unemployment – inflation cycle. The final section concludes.

## The growth cycle model: basic ingredients for a limit cycle result

In this section we sketch the bare essentials that allow for the derivation of a stable limit cycles in the state space $(0,1)^2$. We start from a general 2D dynamical system[2] of the form:[3]

$$\hat{v} = \dot{v}/v = f(v,e) \tag{7.1}$$

$$\hat{e} = \dot{e}/e = g(v,e) \tag{7.2}$$

where the state variables $v, e$ denote the wage share and the rate of employment, respectively, and where $\hat{x}$ is used to denote the growth rate of a variable $x$. In this general form the model can be interpreted in the spirit of the original Goodwin model as well as in terms of an approach where the demand constraint determines output and employment. Thus, in the case of $f_v = 0$ and $g_e = 0$ one might think of the classical variant with Say's law applying and a fixed proportions technology which makes employment dependent on the current capital stock. Combined with classical saving behavior (i.e. with savings only stemming from capital income while all wage earnings are devoted to consumption) this leads to the well-known profit-squeeze which occurs if a rising wage share does no longer allow for enough savings and thus investment in order to let the capital stock increase by a sufficient amount to absorb labor supply. The resulting higher unemployment will then exert a dampening effect on further increases of the wage share. Alternatively, as already mentioned, one can interpret the above model in terms of a demand-constrained economy with the wage share affecting consumption and investment demand; this is also the variant pursued here.

Equation (7.1) can be derived from the general two wage/price Phillips curve approach of Chiarella *et al.* (2005) and we may assume that $f_v < 0$ holds true if a Blanchard and Katz (1999) error correction approach is chosen as foundation of the employed wage and price Phillips curves. The other partial derivative, $f_e$, is due to the role which employment plays in conjunction with the wage Phillips curve. Since, however, increases of the nominal wage rate have a corresponding impact on the development of prices (via the price Phillips curve), the net effect on the development of the wage share is not unique. Thus, one might think of

*Table 7.1* Four types of real wage or wage share feedback mechanisms

| | Wage-led goods demand | Profit-led goods-demand |
|---|---|---|
| Labor-market-led real wage adjustment | Adverse = divergent | Normal = convergent |
| Goods-market-led real wage adjustment | Normal = convergent | Adverse = divergent |

situations where the wage-effect is dominant and others where the price-effect is stronger. In the following, we will call the case $f_e > 0$ a labor market led situation (since real wage movement is then dominated by nominal wage movements) and the opposite case (where price movements dominate) a goods market led situation.

Equation (7.2) can be interpreted as a dynamic IS-relationship where income distribution matters in aggregate demand and where the dynamic multiplier process is characterized by the derivative $g_e$ (which can be positive or negative). The case $g_v > 0$ mirrors a situation in which the "purchasing-power-effect" of higher wages (i.e. higher consumption demand due to a higher income share of people with a higher propensity to consume) dominates the "cost-" or "Rose-effect", according to which higher real wages lead to a decline in investment demand. We call the case where $g_v > 0$ holds wage-led and the opposite case profit-led, in line with what is used in the literature.

In sum, we thus get the scenario of basically four different interactions of the rate of employment with income distribution shown in Table 7.1.[4]

From a partial perspective we thus get two cases where real wage or wage share adjustment is stable and two cases where it is not, see Chen and Flaschel (2006) for details on this.

We assume for the phase plot of the considered dynamical system that $e = 1$ is the full employment rate ceiling and that the motion along this ceiling is horizontal for low wage shares and pointing inwards to lower rates of employment for all $v$ sufficiently large, as shown in Figure 7.1. Similarly, we assume that the rate of change of the wage share is negative (latest) for wage shares equal to one, see again Figure 7.1. The basic implication of these two assumptions is that $[0, 1]^2$ is an invariant set of the considered dynamics (cannot be left by it), since the vertical as well as the horizontal axis cannot be crossed by it (are invariant set themselves).

Next we assume that there is an interior steady state – representing a balanced situation for the economy – around which the right hand sides of the above dynamics can be considered as (locally) linear. We assume for this steady state position that the dynamic multiplier is unstable there ($g_e > 0$) and that the economy is as in Goodwin's original model a labor market led and profit-led one ($f_e > 0, g_v < 0$). Moreover, the Blanchard and Katz error correction terms, see Flaschel and Krolzig (2005) for their discussion, are still absent around this steady state, i.e. $f_v = 0$ holds.[5] For the Jacobian matrix at the steady state we get in this situation:

$$J = \begin{pmatrix} 0 & + \\ - & + \end{pmatrix}.$$

The considered steady state is therefore unstable and of the type shown in Figure 7.1. It then follows from the Poincaré-Bendixson theorem, see Hirsch and Smale (1974), that each trajectory which does not have a steady state as limit point must converge to a closed orbit.

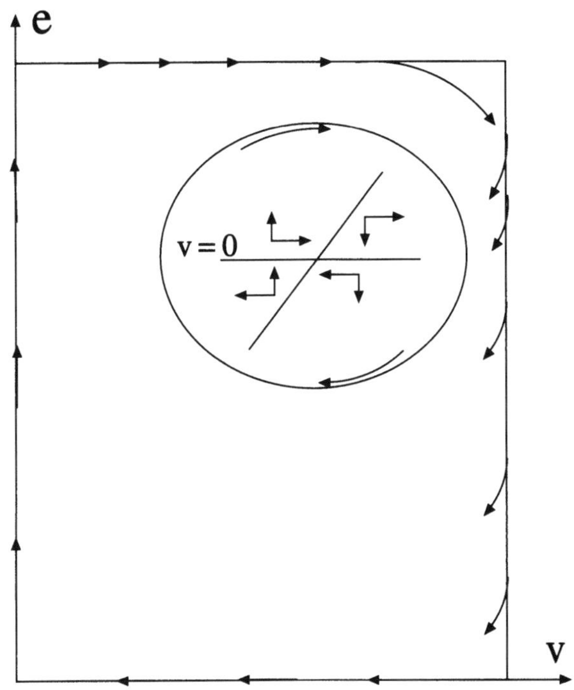


*Figure 7.1* Basic ingredients for persistent and attracting growth cycle dynamics

In particular, if there is no further steady state than the one considered in Figure 7.1, this statement holds true for every trajectory that starts in the invariant domain $(0, 1)^2$ of positive wage shares and positive rates of employment. An example of such a situation was provided in Flaschel and Groh (1995).[6]

## Exploring growth cycles for the US economy: a brief reconsideration

In Flaschel and Groh (1995) we have confronted the behavior of the state variables $v, e$, the wage share and the rate of employment, in their bounded phase space with corresponding yearly data for the eight OECD–countries FRG, France, Italy, Belgium, UK, Ireland, USA and Japan. We repeat their results here for the case of the US economy in order to show in subsequent sections how these still tentative results have indeed been further confirmed by the evolution in the USA over the past 15 years.

The plot on the left hand side of Figure 7.2[7] shows the US time series phase plot that corresponds to Figure 7.1. There is the indication of a long clockwise loop with one-quarter of the loop however still missing. Nevertheless, the figure suggests that the Goodwin growth cycle model and its reformulation in the present chapter is not contradicting the data. In Flaschel and Groh (1995) we have in addition also considered the unemployment/inflation loop as it is generally investigated even in basic textbooks, see Mankiw (1992) for an example. The idea was that price inflation is by and large generated by a constant markup over wage inflation. If this is correct, the Goodwin cycle should be accompanied by a similar nominal cycle in (un)employment and inflation, since the wage share can be reinterpreted as unit real wage costs. We show this loop – following textbook presentations – in the $(1 - e, \hat{p})$

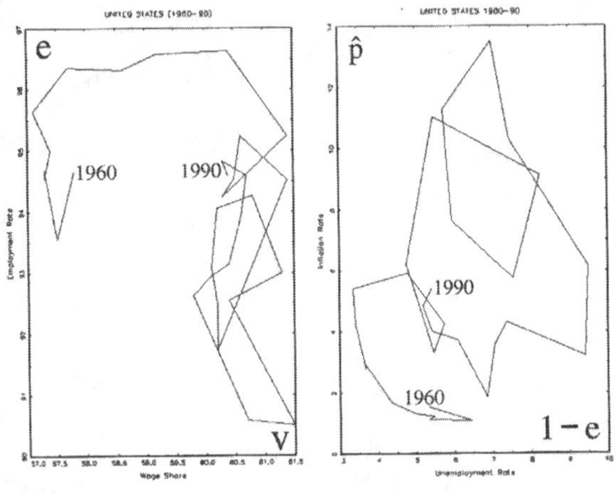


*Figure 7.2* Time series phase plots: the Goodwin growth cycle and the inflation-unemployment nexus

phase space in the right hand plot in Figure 7.2 and see indeed even on this simple phase plot an also clockwise orientation that follows the left hand cycle to a certain degree.

We conclude from these plots as in Flaschel and Groh (1995) that both phenomena are worthwhile to be considered further and will indeed pursue exactly this in the now following sections.

## The US economy: extended data set and basic econometric testing

In this section we will only consider the Goodwin growth cycle model. We will again consider its mirror image, the unemployment–inflation nexus, in the next section where more powerful econometric techniques will be applied to study both cycle mechanisms. Let us here however first consider a simple 2SlS estimate of a linear version of the Goodwin model (7.1)–(7.2). In this way we estimate the model linearly over the whole phase space and expect that its global features will dominate the outcome, and not its local instability presentation in Figure 7.1. The estimation result is shown in Figure 7.3 and it is based on the data set (U.S. Department of Labor: Bureau of Labor Statistics) employed in the empirical study of Kauermann *et al.*(2007), see also the next section.

The estimation shown in Figure 7.3 exhibits an acceptable t-statistics, but may be considered as insufficient as far as R-squared and the Durbin Watson coefficient (in the second equation) is concerned. Yet, with this estimate we only intend to provide a first insight into parameter signs and sizes in the case where the typical nonlinearity in our reformulation of the Goodwin growth cycle model is ignored. The estimated coefficients give rise to the following Jacobian matrix for the 2D dynamics in the state variables $v, e$ :[8]

$$J = \begin{pmatrix} -0.23 & 0.56 \\ -0.51 & -0.22 \end{pmatrix} = \begin{pmatrix} - & + \\ - & - \end{pmatrix}.$$

Since the linear model represents the average behavior of the original nonlinear model (7.1)–(7.2) we see that stability is characterizing the matrix $J$ ($\det J > 0$, trace $J < 0$. The Blanchard and Katz (1999) error correction mechanism is working with significant strength ($J_{11} < 0$) and the dynamic multiplier process behind the reduced form presentation of the law

Sample: 1958:2 2004:3

Included observations: 186

Total system (balanced) observations 372

| | Coefficient | Std. Error | t-Statistic | Prob. |
|---|---|---|---|---|
| C(11) | 0.229038 | 0.142975 | 1.601940 | 0.1100 |
| C(12) | 0.562955 | 0.136181 | 4.133876 | 0.0000 |
| C(13) | -0.371814 | 0.177445 | -2.095377 | 0.0368 |
| C(21) | 0.510863 | 0.071240 | 7.171027 | 0.0000 |
| C(22) | 0.223516 | 0.067854 | 3.294048 | 0.0011 |
| C(23) | 0.563353 | 0.088415 | 6.371704 | 0.0000 |

| | |
|---|---|
| Determinant residual covariance | 1.10E-07 |

Equation: 4*@DLOG(V1)=-C(11)*V1(-1)+C(12)*E1(-1)+C(13)

Instruments: E1(-1) V1(-1) C

Observations: 186

| | | | |
|---|---|---|---|
| R-squared | 0.113698 | Mean dependent var | -0.000480 |
| Adjusted R-squared | 0.104011 | S.D. dependent var | 0.027606 |
| S.E. of regression | 0.026131 | Sum squared resid | 0.124959 |
| Durbin-Watson stat | 1.785956 | | |

Equation: 4*@DLOG(E1)=-C(21)*V1(-1)-C(22)*E1(-1)+C(23)

Instruments: E1(-1) V1(-1) C

Observations: 186

| | | | |
|---|---|---|---|
| R-squared | 0.230329 | Mean dependent var | 0.000198 |
| Adjusted R-squared | 0.221918 | S.D. dependent var | 0.014761 |
| S.E. of regression | 0.013020 | Sum squared resid | 0.031024 |
| Durbin-Watson stat | 1.013713 | | |

*Figure 7.3* The Goodwin growth cycle: two-stage least-squares estimation

of motion (2) is stable ($J_{22} < 0$). The eigen feedback effects thus indeed work in this overall fashion in a stabilizing way. In the off-diagonal of the matrix $J$ we have the typical sign structure of the Goodwin growth cycle model which is working with considerable strength. With regard to $J_{21}$ the negative sign indeed confirms the dominance of the "Rose-effect" over the "purchasing-power-effect" and thus gives a first answer to one of the key questions raised in the introduction.

On the basis of this matrix $J$ and the estimated constants we can moreover calculate the interior steady state position of this numerical example of the Goodwin model and get approximately $(v_o, e_o) = (0.70, 0.93)$. This is a sensible steady state position, though one whose confidence interval may be large. Nevertheless our system estimate provides us with an idea of how the numerical magnitudes behind a linearized version of model (7.1)–(7.2) may look like.

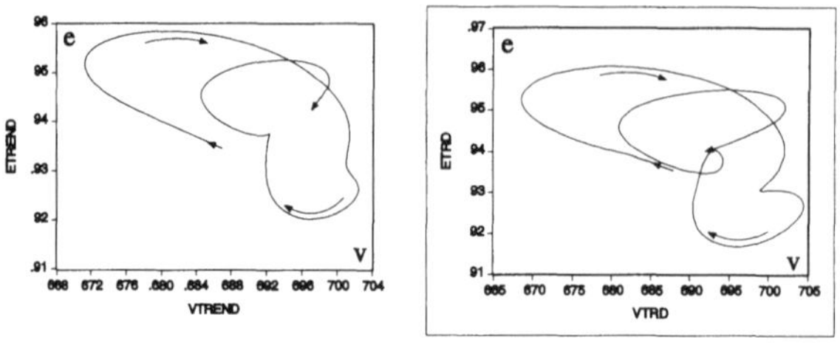


*Figure 7.4* The Goodwin growth cycle: HP-trend visualization

We next consider the Hodrick-Prescott decomposition into trend and cycle in order to remove the business cycle component from the data. This should allow us to see how the empirical Goodwin cycle indicated in Figure 7.2 looks like in the case of our extended data set. However determining cyclical trends by means of the Hodrick-Prescott filter leads to the loss of data and this the more the larger the parameter $\lambda$ in this procedure is set. In Figure 7.4 we show on its left the usual choice $\lambda = 1600$ and on its right the choice $\lambda = 4800$. By and large we see in both figures a Goodwin growth cycle that is significantly more closed than the one shown in Figure 7.2.

We conclude from these basic econometric treatments that the vision of the Goodwin (1967) growth cycle model – when augmented as in Rose (1967) to lead to attracting limit cycle results as described in "The growth cycle model" above – is further confirmed when now available data for the US economy after the Second World War are employed.

## Business cycles and long-phase cycles in the US economy: bivariate p-spline testing

Econometric studies often investigate on the methodological level as well as in empirical research the problem of how to separate the business cycle from the trend in important macroeconomic time series. Yet, economic growth theory in its advanced form provides us with insights on which economic ratios may exhibit a secular trend (like capital intensity when not measured in efficiency units) and which ones will not (like the output capital ratio or the rate of employment as two measures of macroeconomic factor utilization). In contrast to a variety of econometric studies macrodynamic theory therefore uses appropriate ratios or growth rates in its analytical investigations and there in particular the ones that allow for the determination of steady state positions and which therefore should not exhibit a trend in the very long run when the macrodynamic theory is formulated in a sufficiently general way.

In applying a methodology developed in Kauermann *et al.* (2007) we will in line with the formulation of the Goodwin growth cycle model (7.1)–(7.2) use secularly trendless magnitudes, namely the employment rate on the external labor market, the wage share in national income and the inflation rate (here of producers' prices). There are a variety of smaller as well as larger macrodynamic models in the tradition of Goodwin (1967) and Friedman (1968) which show the existence of persistent cycles in the interaction between the employment rate and the wage share on the one hand and the employment rate and the inflation rate on the other hand which tend to be long-phased when simple constant parameter estimates are used for their numerical investigation. In these models the usual business cycle fluctuations must therefore be explained by systematic variations in the parameters of the model which then add cycles of period lengths of about eight years to the

50-year cycles these models generate when used with average constant parameter values.

We have considered in Flaschel *et al.* (2007) models of the employment/income distribution cycle and the employment/inflation cycle in isolation as well as in their direct interaction or more indirect ones in a five dimensional model of goods market, labor market and interest rate dynamics and have calculated numerically the long-phase cycles these models generate under plausible parameter values. We take from these models and from the earlier sections of this chapter the working hypothesis that there should be long-phase cycles interacting with business cycles in the data as far as employment, income distribution and inflation is concerned. The method developed in Kauermann *et al.* (2007) now in fact allows us to test this hypothesis in a way much more refined than just by using Hodrick-Prescott filters with an arbitrarily given $\lambda$ parameter. Moreover, it can do this by using an econometric approach that is close in spirit to the two-dimensional phase plots of the employment – income distribution and the employment – inflation cycle of the literature on the Goodwin growth cycle and the Friedman inflation cycle, see Flaschel *et al.* (2007) for details. The technique developed in Kauermann *et al.* (2007) can be sketched in the following way. We decompose wage share $v$ and employment rate $e$ in a long-phase cycle and business cycle model, that is $v = c_v(t) + b_v(t)$ and $e = c_e(t) + b_e(t)$, with $c(t)$ as long-phase cycle and $b(t)$ as business cycle. The cycles themselves are understood as functions in time, which ought to be estimated. We pursue a so called non-parametric approach by assuming smoothness for $c(t)$ and $b(t)$, but no specified parametric structure. The functions are then estimated using the technique of penalized splines (p-splines) as generally described in Ruppert *et al.* (2003). This means, a high dimensional basis is used to capture the shape of the functions, but for fitting a penalty is imposed which leads to smooth fits as those shown in Figures 7.5 and 7.6. The business cycle itself is fitted in radial basis coordinates, which in fact allows to decompose long-phase and business cycle accordingly. Both cycles are shown in Figures 7.5 and 7.6.

With respect to the long-phase real cycle model, the Goodwin (1967) growth cycle model, we have in Figure 7.5 the following situation. As far as the evolution of the wage share, shown top-left, is concerned we have more volatility as is the case with the inflation rate. This may be due to the involvement of labor productivity as constituent part of the definition of the wage share. Nevertheless one can see a single long-phase cycle in the solid line shown in the time series presentation of the wage share. The employment rate is leading with respect to this long phase cycle in the wage share. We know from Goodwin (1967) and the numerous articles that followed his approach that the interaction of the employment rate with the wage share is generating a clockwise motion in the $v, e$ phase space, see again Flaschel *et al.* (2007) for details. In Figure 7.5 we can in this regard see that the cycles of business cycle frequency are also moving in a clockwise fashion (bottom left plot). We see (if minor cycles are neglected) by and large seven business cycles overlaid over the long-phase cycles as they are also shown in the figure top-right. Figure 7.5 bottom right shows the long-phase cycle in isolation.

We stress that our extraction of the business cycle component (the 'short' cycle) as shown in Figure 7.5 is an integral part of our treatment of the long-phase evolution of the economy. This differs significantly from the Hodrick-Prescott trend vs cycle separation shown in Figure 7.4 which is enforced by an exogenous choice of the parameter $\lambda$ used in this cycle extraction procedure.

With respect to the mirror image of the real growth cycle, the inflation – unemployment dynamics, we see that the unemployment rate is also leading compared to the inflation rate in the long phase cycle (the solid lines in the two time series plots top-left in Figure 7.6).

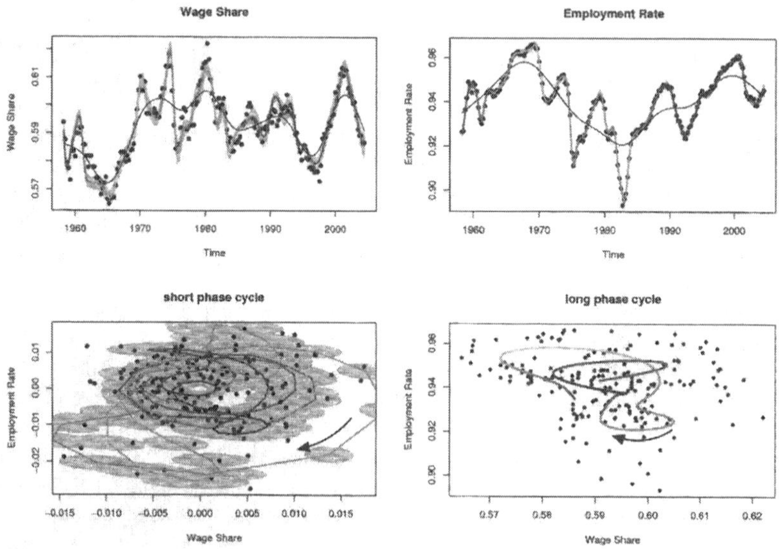


*Figure 7.5* Exploring US income distribution cycles with bivariate loops using penalized spline regression

Looking closer to the business cycle plot (bottom left), as done in Kauermann *et al.* (2007), we see moreover that there are now approximately six business cycles surrounding these long-phase cycles, in line with what is shown to hold for the US economy in Chiarella *et al.* (2005). We also get that the clockwise rotation of the long-phase cycle is by and large also characterizing the business cycles surrounding it, though there are exceptions to this rule, see also the figure top-right in this regard. We note we use, as is usual, the unemployment rate in place of the employment rate on the horizontal axis. Using the latter would give rise to an anti-clockwise orientation of the business and the long-phase cycles shown in these figures. Figure 7.6 in the present section also shows for better visibility the long-phase cycle in isolation and it indicates that indeed 50 years of data are needed in order to at least indicate the existence of such a cycle.

As in the preceding sections we therefore see again a cycle that is nearly closed (and thus approximately 50 years long) and that is moving clockwise as suggested by the simple Goodwin (1967) growth cycle model when extended by markup inflation procedures and the like, see Desai (1973) for an early example. The same cyclical pattern therefore holds true for the accompanying unemployment – inflations cycle, the Friedmanian nominal side of the real cycle so to speak. We conclude that the method developed in Kauermann *et al.* (2007) provides an important approach to the separation of long-phased cycles that describe the evolution from high to low inflation regimes and from high to low wage share regimes from cycles of business cycle frequency. This method therefore allows in a distinct way the discussion of long waves in inflation and income distribution in modern market economies after the Second World War.

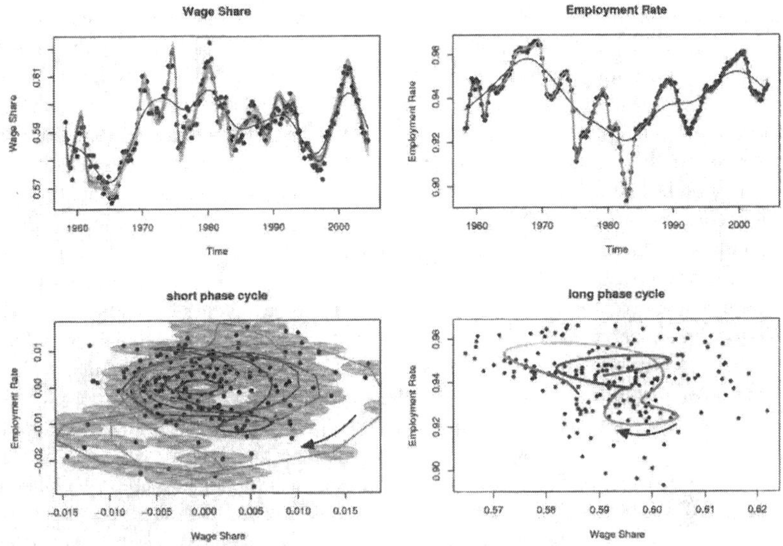


*Figure 7.6* Exploring US inflation cycles with bivariate loops using penalized spline regression

## Conclusions

In this chapter we have provided new empirical evidence for the existence of a long-phased cycle concerning the wage share and the employment rate after the Second World War along the lines of the original Goodwin (1967) model and later modifications of it. Taking an approach of Flaschel and Groh (1995) as a starting point, the time horizon for the investigation was now extended to 50 years, based on data for the US economy. For the empirical analysis three different techniques have been applied. First, the two dynamic equations constituting the model have been estimated in their linearized form around the steady state by means of a two-stage LS-estimation. It turned out that at least the signs of the model's "core", the two off-diagonal elements of the Jacobian, have in fact the signs suggested by the model. This means that the assumptions of a "labor-market-led" real wage adjustment as well as of "profit-led" goods demand are not rejected by the data.

In a second step, a Hodrick-Prescott decomposition into trend and cycle was applied in order to remove the business cycle component from the data. As a result, a cycle emerged that was already closed to a higher degree than the one presented in Flaschel and Groh (1995). Thus, the use of new observations led to a further confirmation of the underlying growth cycle model. The issue of separating the business cycle from the trend was then further investigated in a third step by means of a technique developed in Kauermann *et al.* (2007). It turned out that a single long-phased cycle in the wage share and the employment rate could be detected which was overlaid by approximately seven business cycles. Furthermore, the long-period cycle was indeed characterized by a clockwise motion of the two variables just mentioned in the phase plane as predicted by the theoretical model.

A similar picture emerged with regard to the interaction between unemployment and inflation. Once again, a closed long-phased cycle, moving in a clockwise way, could

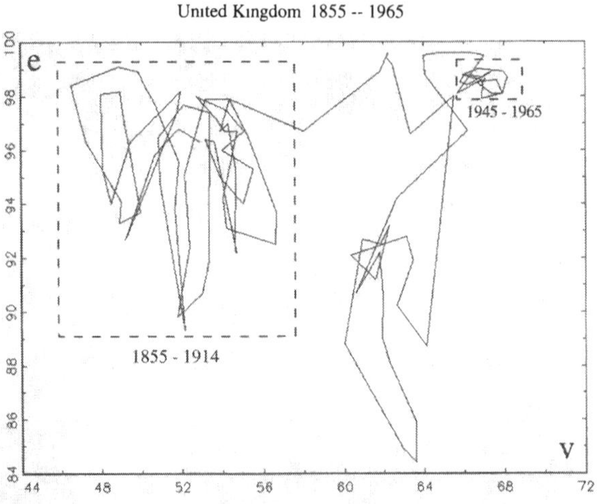


*Figure 7.7* UK Income distribution cycles 1855–1965

be established with about six business cycles surrounding it. Thus, earlier theoretical approaches in the tradition of Friedman (1968) could be confirmed as well as recent empirical findings by Chiarella *et al.*(2005). Furthermore, it turned out that a time horizon of 50 years is indeed necessary to derive the results just mentioned.

In addition to what has been shown in this chapter, one should, of course, also try to take earlier time periods into account than just the 1960s to the present if data – in particular on the wage share – are available. For the United Kingdom there exist such long time series[9] from 1855 up to 1965 which are summarized by the phase plot diagram in Figure 7.7.

These data[10] seem to indicate that there have been two different types of dynamics with respect to the interaction of the rate of employment and the share of wages:

- the period before 1914 where the employment rate exhibits significant fluctuations of less than 10 years in phase length;
- the period after the Second World War (1945–1965) where no such fluctuations can be observed any more.

The important insight that can be obtained from these diagrams for Great Britain (1855–1965) is that the Goodwin cycle – if it exists – must have been significantly shorter before 1914 (with larger fluctuations in employment during each cycle), and that there has been a major change in it after 1945. This may be explained by significant differences and changes in the adjustment processes of market economies for these two periods: primarily price adjustment before 1914 and primarily quantity adjustments after 1945. This very tentative judgment must be left for future research however.

## Acknowledgements

We have to thank Lance Taylor for various clarifying comments on the concepts used in this and related papers. Of course, usual caveats apply.

## Notes

1 This does not deny that restrictive wage policy (if not accompanied by additional measures) might have side-effects which are not desirable with regard to its social or distributional consequences.
2 See Barbosa Filho and Taylor (2006) and Taylor (2004) for detailed analyzes of systems of this type.
3 The model underlying these two differential equations is typically formulated such that it includes natural growth as well as Harrod-neutral technical change, assumptions that are not visible in the reduced form we use here as a starting point.
4 A labor market led situation is basically of a Marx-Goodwin-Kalecki profit squeeze type and is the generally observed situation in the literature, see also the discussion on pro-cyclical real wages (here real wage growth).
5 Blanchard and Katz (1999) error correction is only one possibility to justify a negative influence of the wage share on its rate of growth, see for example Barbosa Filho and Taylor (2006) and Taylor (2004) in this regard.
6 Note, however, that the model in the general form presented here may allow for a variety of further dynamic outcomes.
7 From Data Source & Information GmbH (1992): *International Statistical Yearbook 1992* (on CD–ROM).
8 See Barbosa Filho and Taylor (2006) for estimates of the here considered growth dynamics that can be usefully contrasted with the results of this chapter.
9 See Desai (1984) for the sources of these data and for an econometric approach on the basis of these data with respect to the Goodwin growth cycle model.
10 Note that they do not – at least on the surface – support one of Kaldor's famous stylized fact of growth theory (the constancy of the wage share in the long run).

## References

Atkinson, A.B. (1969) The timescale of economic models: how long is the long run? *Review of Economic Studies*, 36, 137–52.

Barbosa Filho, N.H. and L. Taylor (2006) Distributive and demand cycles in the US economy: a structuralist Goodwin model. *Metroeconomica*, 57, 389–411.

Blanchard, O.J. and L. Katz (1999) Wage dynamics: reconciling theory and evidence. *American Economic Review. Papers and Proceedings*, 69–74.

Chen, P. and P. Flaschel (2006) Measuring the interaction of wage and price Phillips curves for the US economy. *Studies in Nonlinear Dynamics and Econometrics*, 10(3).

Chiarella, C., P. Flaschel and R. Franke (2005): *Foundations for a Disequilibrium Theory of the Business Cycle. Qualitative Analysis and Quantitative Assessment.* Cambridge: Cambridge University Press.

Desai, M. (1973) Growth cycles in a model of the class struggle. *Journal of Economic Theory*, 6, 527–45.

Desai, M. (1984) An econometric model of the share of wages in national income: UK 1855–1965. In: R.M. Goodwin *et al.* (eds) *Nonlinear Models of Fluctuating Growth.* Heidelberg: Springer.

Flaschel, P. and G. Groh (1995) The classical growth cycle: reformulation, simulation and some facts. *Economic Notes*, 24, 293–326.

Flaschel, P. and H.-M. Krolzig (2005): Wage-price Phillips curves and macroeconomic stability: basic structural form, estimation and analysis. In C. Chiarella, P. Flaschel, R. Franke and W. Semmler (eds) *Quantitative and Empirical Analysis of Nonlinear Dynamic Macromodels.* Contributions to Economic Analysis. Elsevier, Amsterdam.

Flaschel, P., G. Kauermann and T. Teuber (2007) Long cycles in employment, inflation and real unit wage costs: qualitative analysis and quantitative assessment. *American Journal of Applied Sciences*.

Friedman, M. (1968) The role of monetary policy. *American Economic Review* 58, 1–17.

Goodwin, R. (1967) A growth cycle. In C.H. Feinstein (ed.) *Socialism, Capitalism and Economic Growth*. Cambridge: Cambridge University Press.

Hirsch, M. and S. Smale (1974) *Differential Equations, Dynamical Systems and Linear Algebra*. London: Academic Press.

Kauermann, G., T. Teuber and P. Flaschel (2007) *Exploring US Business Cycles with Bivariate Loops using Penalized Spline Regression*. Working paper. Bielefeld: CEM.

Mankiw, G. (1992) *Macroeconomics*. New York: Worth Publisher.

Rose, H. (1967) On the non-linear theory of the employment cycle. *Review of Economic Studies*, 34, 153–73.

Ruppert, D., M. Wand and D. Carroll (2003) *Semiparametric Regression*. Cambridge: Cambridge University Press.

Solow, R. (1990) Goodwin's growth cycle: reminiscence and rumination. In K. Velupillai (ed.): *Nonlinear and multisectoral macrodynamics. Essays in Honour of Richard Goodwin*. London: Macmillan.

Taylor, L. (2004) *Reconstructing Macroeconomics: Structuralists Proposals and Critiques of the Mainstream*. Cambridge, MA: Harvard University Press.

# 8 Debt–equity cycles in the twentieth century

## Empirical evidence and a dynamic Keynesian model

*Lance Taylor and Codrina Rada von Arnim*

## Introduction

Distributive-demand cycles along Goodwin's (1967) lines show up clearly in short- to medium-run macroeconomic data for industrial economies (Barbosa-Filho and Taylor 2006). In this chapter we take up long-term oscillations in business debt and equity which may well be influenced by distributive and debt dynamics. Such cycles can be discerned in financial numbers for the US, UK, and Japan, although it is fair to say that if each cycle is interpreted as a "data point," far from enough points are available to enable compelling statistical analysis. Evidence regarding the cycles is presented in this section using numbers obtained mostly from the Flow of Funds Accounts for these countries. The data show that equity–capital and debt–capital ratios fluctuate over wide ranges and do not sum to one. The latter observation reflects the fact that business net worth is not equal to zero in flows of funds and associated balance sheets which are based on current values of enterprise assets and "liabilities" including the value of both equity and debt.

As with the financial ratios, capacity utilization in the US has fluctuated significantly – over a range of eight percentage points since the Second World War and more than 30 points during the Great Depression. In a chronological "long run" neither the Modigliani-Miller Theorem (with its underlying assumption that business net worth is zero) nor Say's Law seems to apply. For these reasons we choose to model debt–equity cycles from the macroeconomic demand side, with both business net worth and capacity utilization treated as endogenous variables.

To a first approximation, cyclical dynamics of the form the data demonstrate can arise from a system of two differential equations based on a Wicksellian financial framework with balance sheets set out in "Debt–equity cycles". A bare bones Keynesian model for short-term macro equilibrium and demand-driven capital stock growth follows in "The accounting basis for a debt—equity cyccle model" . In the model, the flow of new loans is set by firms' needs to finance investment. Outstanding credit determines the level of financial system liabilities ("money") held by households.

"A short-term macro model" is about the differential equations themselves. One is for the change in the ratio of the value of corporate equity to capital stock, $q$, and follows from the standard intertemporal arbitrage equation for the return to holding shares. The other is for the ratio of debt to capital,$\lambda$, and follows from the corporate sector's flow of funds. In "Differential equations for the debt—capital and equity–capital ratios", it is shown that under appropriate conditions, perfect foresight positive feedback of the equity price into its own change over time and indirectly into the debt–capital ratio can generate long-run predator-prey dynamics with contrasting clockwise and counterclockwise oscillations as demonstrated by the data for the US and UK on one hand and Japan on the other.

However, the model as based on two "slow" differential equations for securities–capital ratios suffers from a problem with turning points. When cycles are clockwise, for example, it predicts that at the trough the equity–capital ratio starts to rise because the increase in share prices outstrips the growth rate of capital, while at the top the ratio begins to fall because capital grows more rapidly than prices. This scenario is consistent with the data at a cyclical low, but not at a peak where asset prices continue to grow more rapidly than capital and then begin to decrease "on their own" (with credit and capital falling in train). Based on Keynes's ideas about the cycle (especially in the *Treatise on Money*), a simple bifurcation involving the "required" return to equity as it responds to "fundamentals" is set up in "Dynamics of the model" to allow the model to approximate the data better. The bifurcation has "faster" dynamics than the equations for the equity–capital and debt–capital ratios, and shows how the rapid ascents and descents of the former can take place. "More volatile dynamics" summarizes the main results.

## Debt-equity cycles: stylized facts

Over the past 50–100 years, six secular debt–equity cycles appear in data for the US, UK, and Japan.

Post-Second World War data for the US and UK (Figures 8.1 and 8.2 and 8.3 respectively) demonstrate clockwise cycles between the value of equity outstanding and the value of business debt, both normalized by the value of the capital stock as an indicator of the size of the sector. In the diagrams we plot the ratio of net debt of non-financial corporations, $L$, to the value of their capital stock, $PK$, on the horizontal axis against the ratio of outstanding equity, $P_eE$, to capital (a standard measure of Tobin's $q$)[1] on the vertical. As noted above, the two ratios do not add up to one since there is non-zero corporate worth.

For the post-war period we observe two clockwise cycles in both economies: a first oscillation ends in 1979 after hitting a bull market peak in 1967. The years 1979–80 mark the start of the next cycle, which goes into a downswing two decades later with the 1999–2000 crash following the 1990s boom. In Figure 8.1 for the US and Figure 8.2b for the UK, the highest value of $q$ in the second cycle is substantially above the maximum in the first, and the run-up to the peak during the 1990s is more rapid.[2] Post-2000 both debt– and equity–capital ratios declined, and at the end of 2005, US price–earnings ratios were still 40 per cent above historical mean values. Another downswing in the offing?

It can be seen visually that stock prices lead the cycles, or in more allegorical terms the value of equity is a prey variable with debt as a predator. Seemingly, optimistic expectations are fueled by the rise in the price of equity, and in turn higher equity prices are sustained by better access to loans.

A good description of the macroeconomics for the US can be found in Figure 8.3, which shows changes in net claims among the major NIPA sectors normalized by trend GDP and the NBER cycles. During the 1990s, negative net financial claims for both business and households are on the rise, with the government and rest of the world sector supporting their accumulation of debt. Business net borrowing also rises in the 1960s in the run-up to the peak of the earlier cycle, and then drops off sharply in the 1970s after equity prices begin to fall. A similar collapse in borrowing by corporations (this time accompanied by households) also shows up after 1999. In other words, predator-prey dynamics is observed in both cyclical upswings and downswings.

Normalizing equity and debt by the value of capital stock leads to diagrams in which cycles are easy to visualize. However, in both economies there appears to be a long-term

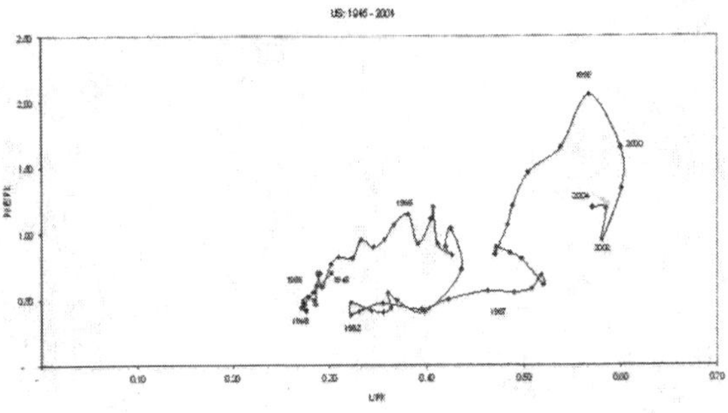

*Figure 8.1* Post-war debt–equity cycles in the US

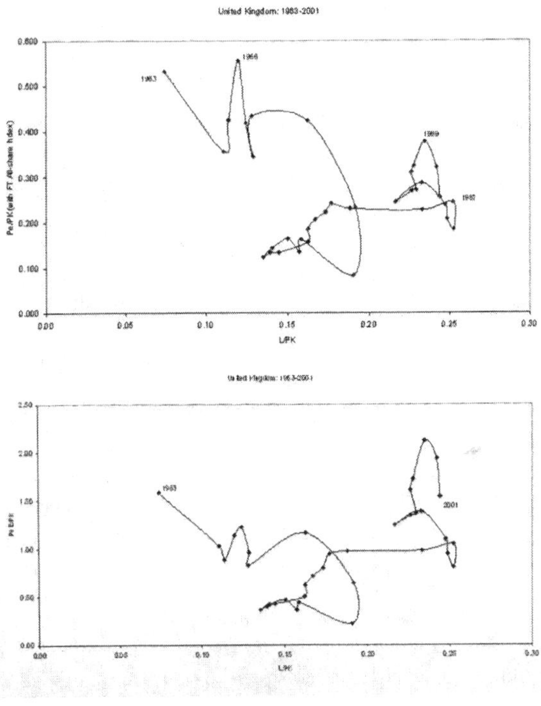


*Figure 8.2* Post-war debt–equity cycles in the UK

tendency for the debt–capital and possibly the equity–capital ratio to rise. Whether these trends persist in future decades of course remains to be seen.

Data are less readily available for the pre-Second World War period, but at least in the US the same cyclical pattern emerges from benchmark years for which Goldsmith and Lipsey (1963) calculated values of business capital, equity, and debt.

Figure 8.4b is based on their estimates, which satisfy the relationship $PK = P_eE + L$, thereby unrealistically setting corporate net worth to zero. Figure 8.4a instead uses the S&P 500 as the indicator of equity valuation. In both versions a clockwise cycle between the

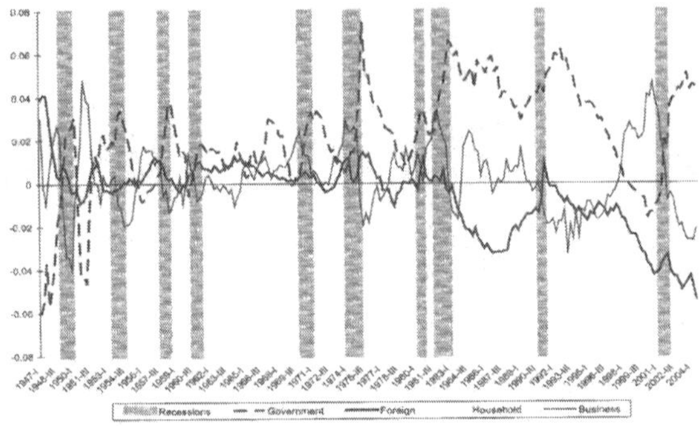


*Figure 8.3* NIPA-based financial needs of the government, foreign sector, household and the business sectors normalized by trend GDP and NBER reference cycles

early 1900s and the 1930s emerges, with the former years probably representing the high point of a cyclical upswing during the late 1800s.

Japan provides an interesting contrast to the US and UK, as shown in Figure 8.5 where we plot the outstanding debt to capital ratio against the ratio of an equity price index to capital stock in the upper diagram and against the ratio of outstanding value of equity to capital stock in the lower. Japan's characteristic financial structure is reflected in its relatively high values of the debt–capital ratio (between 0.7 and 1.4), in contrast with levels well below one for the US and UK. When accumulation of debt is on the rise, the equity–capital ratio goes down. Vice versa, when the ratio of debt to capital stock is decreasing, the stock market follows an upward trend. In Japan, it seems that the debt–capital ratio leads the equity–capital ratio. Several small cycles also show up – the first in the second half of 1950s, the second during 1970s and the last in the late 1980s. However, they are far from being as definite as in the US and UK and do not detract from the general tendency for Japanese debt to be the prey variable and equity the predator.

The observed pattern also points to differences in the institutional framework of Japan as compared to the US or the UK. Between the 1950s and 1970s, Japan is rapidly catching up with the richer economies by pursuing an aggressive industrial policy aimed at building strong corporations. The stock market is not developed, so high rates of investment must be supported by accumulation of debt. Thereafter comes the famous "bubble" as portfolios shift from debt toward equity and then the bust with the debt–capital ratio still in decline.

In all three countries, the cycles show up in the balance sheets for the non-financial corporate sector, and reflect changes in the structure of assets and liabilities as driven by financial market dynamics. In the next section we describe an accounting framework for a debt–equity model.

## The accounting basis for a debt–equity cycle model

Our specification builds upon Lavoie and Godley (2001–2). It presupposes that the main institutional sectors of the economy – households, business, and the financial sector or "banks" – satisfy their balance sheet and flows of funds restrictions at all times. The balance sheets are set out in Table 8.1, in which in addition to terms previously defined, $M$ is the

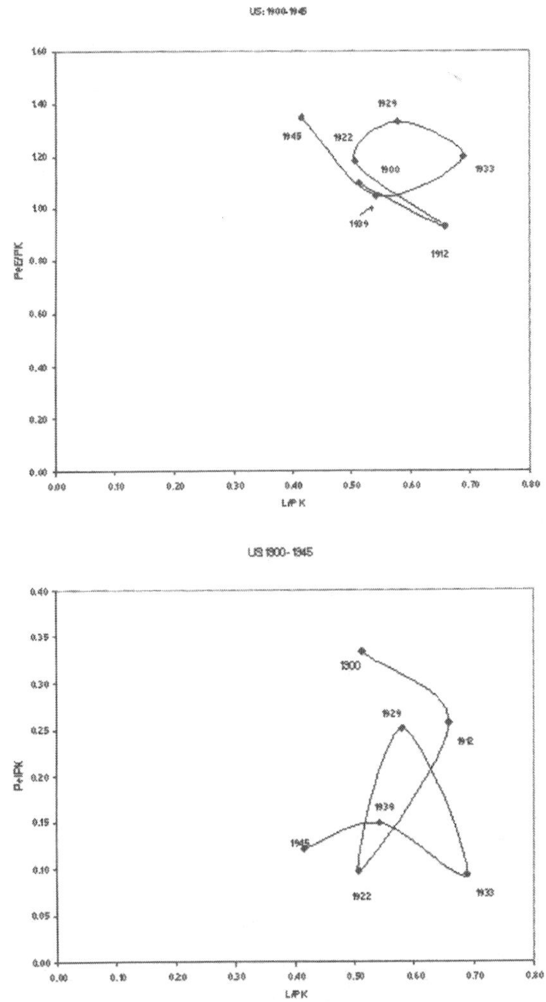


*Figure 8.4* Pre-war debt–equity cycles in the US

money supply and $\Omega_h$and $\Omega_f$stand for levels of net worth of households and business firms respectively.

The household balance sheet is consistent with the flow of funds relationship Household Savings = Change in Money Holdings + Change in Equity Holdings at Current Prices (or $S_h = \dot{M} + P_e\dot{E}$ where a "dot" over a variable signifies its derivative with respect to time) and the statement that Change in Net Worth = Savings + Capital Gains ($\dot{\Omega}_h = S_h + \dot{P}_e E$). The capital gains can be substantial: "Between 1994 and the first quarter of 2000, the market capitalization of shares held by households snowballed from \$4 trillion to \$12.2 trillion" (Brenner 2002). Moreover, American households, so well described by Keynes (1936) as constituting a "stock-minded public . . . where a rising stock-market may be an almost

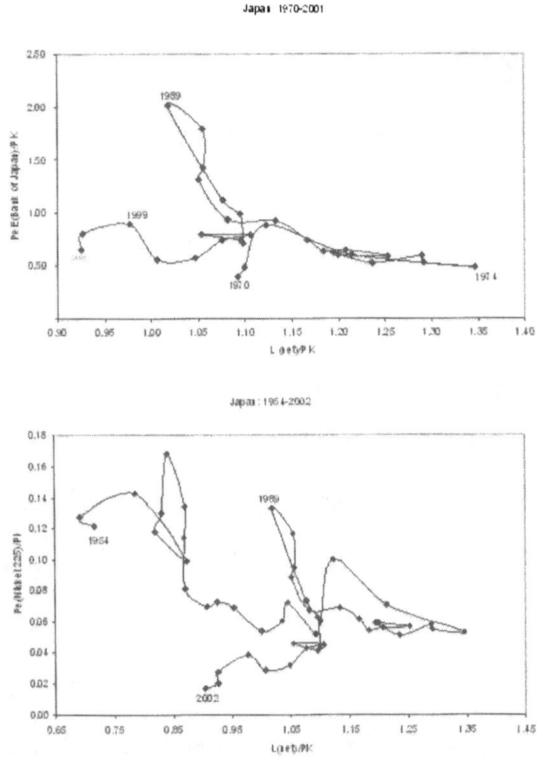


*Figure 8.5* A post-war debt–equity cycle in Japan

*Table 8.1* Balance sheets underlying the debt–equity model

| *Households* | | *Corporations* | | *Banks* | |
|---|---|---|---|---|---|
| $M$ | $\Omega_h$ | $PK$ | $L$ | $L$ | $M$ |
| $P_eE$ | | | $P_eE$ | | |
| | | | $\Omega_f$ | | |

essential condition of a satisfactory condition to consume", opted for a dramatic change in their saving behavior with the personal net saving rate decreasing from 8.7 per cent in 1992 to -0.12 per cent in 2000 (Brenner 2002). These linkages are built into the macro model presented below.

The corporate sector's assets include the value of capital stock only. Liabilities comprise net debt and equity at market value, with net worth as the balancing item which can take either sign.[3] In effect, a change of a firm's asset valuation does not lead instantaneously into a change in equity prices. Endogenous net worth creates room for independent dynamics (including possible jumps) for $q$ due to Keynes's "animal spirits" or the forces producing "financial fragility" à la Hyman Minsky (1975).[4]

As we have seen, debt–equity cycles in the US and UK reveal increases in the ratios of both debt and equity to capital stock during the boom which points to a positive relationship between the propensity to borrow/lend and stock market dynamics. As discussed in "Dynamics of the model", the theoretical underpinnings of this argument are Keynesian in essence. They were clearly stated by Minsky in his analysis of the investment and financial instability. He says that "whenever, as a result of an improvement in confidence and credit, the leveraging of investment increases, the owners of the inherited stock of capital assets, whose liability structure is compatible with a previous stage of confidence, find themselves with an unused margin of 'borrowing power"' (ibid.: 120). During the last boom in the US, non-financial corporations financed 22 per cent of their investment in fixed assets through new borrowing (Brenner 2002: 200).

For the financial sector's balance sheet we use a simple Wicksellian or pure credit "banking" formula: Loans = Bank Assets = Bank Liabilities = Money Supply. We assume that "loans create money" in the sense that banks satisfy loan demand coming from the non-financial business sector's flow of funds and that the household balance sheet adjusts to absorb the corresponding increase in the money supply. This specification is compatible with the view expressed by scholars such as Kindleberger (2000) that "endogenous" expansion of net credit often underlies financial cycles.

On the basis of the balance sheets, we next set out a short-term demand-driven macro model with the output–capital ratio $u = X/K$ as the adjusting variable in the short run. The model will be used to fill in the details of differential equations for the debt–capital ratio $\lambda = L/PK$ and the equity–capital ratio $q = P_e E/PK$.

## A short-term macro model

In part to keep the algebra within bounds, we assume that the real interest rate $j$ on both money and loans is pre-determined. The model's financial sector boils down to a banking system in which demand for loans is met by an accommodating supply at an interest rate that cannot differ from the one in the money market if the banks are to stay in business with zero pure profits. From Table 8.1, the value of firms' capital stock, $PK$, is exhausted by their outstanding loans $L$, the value of their equity $P_e E$, and their net worth $\Omega_f$.

Gross corporate income is $rPK$ with $r$ as the profit rate that can also be written as $r = \pi PX/PK = \pi u$ where $\pi$ is the profit share. As noted above, we treat $u$ as an indicator of the level of economic activity and also assume that $\pi$ stays constant.[5] Business pays real interest $jL$ on its outstanding debt and also dividends $D$ to households. We scale dividends to the capital stock, $D = \delta PK$. In intensive form, business net income thus becomes $\xi_f = r - j\lambda - \delta$. Other sources of funds for firms are new borrowing $\dot{L}/PK = \lambda\hat{L}$ (with $\hat{L} = \dot{L}/L$) and issuance of equity. A working hypothesis (again aimed at keeping the model uncluttered) is that they finance a share $\chi$ of their capital formation $g = I/K$ with new shares, so that $P_e\dot{E}/PK = \chi g$.[6] Firms' flows of funds thus become:

$$(r - j\lambda - \delta) + \lambda\hat{L} - (1 - \chi)g = 0 \quad . \tag{8.1}$$

The profit rate $r$ and growth rate $g$ are determined on the real side of the model, so in (8.1) the change in the supply of bank loans $\lambda\hat{L}$ has to be endogenous to allow firms to carry through their investment plans.

In standard fashion, household consumption is assumed to depend on income and wealth. Again scaled to the capital stock, their income $\xi_h$ comprises wage payments $(1 - \pi)u$, interest $j\lambda$ that firms pay to the financial sector which is then transferred to households via payments on their deposits, and dividends $\delta$. Because $(1 - \pi)u = u - r$, we have that $\xi_h = u - (r - j\lambda - \delta)$. For future reference, note that $\xi_h$ rises when the corporate debt burden

$j\lambda$ and distributed profits $\delta$ go up, the former because the financial sector pays its higher interest receipts over to households.

Money is a fairly small share of household net worth and the capital stock so again to simplify we use just $q$ as an indicator of wealth.[7] Household consumption $\gamma_h$ (scaled to $PK$) becomes $\gamma_h = (1 - s_h)\xi_h + \phi q$ where $s_h$ is the household saving rate and the parameter $\phi$ measures the wealth effect. As discussed above, households use their saving to acquire new bank deposits $\dot{M}/PK$ and new equity $\chi g$ issued by firms. Their flows of funds (scaled to the value of capital) thus become:

$$s_h[u - (r - j\lambda - \delta)] - \phi q - \chi g - \lambda\hat{M} = 0 \quad . \tag{8.2}$$

Because $L = M$ and $\hat{L} = \hat{M}$ from the Wicksellian financial system's balance sheet, accounting consistency ensures that households raise their net worth by picking up the flow of new deposits that new bank lending creates.

Ignoring depreciation, the growth rate of the capital stock permitted by available saving, $g^s$, is the sum of (8.1) and (8.2),

$$g^s = s_h u + (1 - s_h)(r - j\lambda - \delta) - \phi q = [s_h + (1 - s_h)\pi]u - (1 - s_h)(j\lambda + \delta) - \phi q \quad . \tag{8.3}$$

By reducing the saving of firms a bigger debt burden $j\lambda$ cuts into $g^s$ but the effect is attenuated by the $(1 - s_h)$ term which reflects the boost to household income from $j\lambda$ mentioned above.

Post-Keynesian investment functions of the sort estimated by Fazzari and Mott (1986-87) and Ndikumana (1999) emphasize cash-flow considerations. If the interest burden $j\lambda$ increases, firms are likely to cut back on capital formation $g^i$. For symmetry with the saving function (8.3) it is convenient (and conventional) to make $g^i$, the growth rate of capital stock produced by investment demand, depend on $q$, and we also carry an accelerator term $\beta u$ in the output–capital ratio or "capacity utilization":

$$g^i = g_0 + \beta u + \eta q - \psi j\lambda \quad . \tag{8.4}$$

The short-term macro equilibrium condition is $g^i - g^s = 0$, or:

$$g_0 - (1 - s_h\delta) + (\eta + \phi)q + (1 - s_h - \psi)j\lambda - [s_h + (1 - s_h)\pi - \beta]u = 0 \quad . \tag{8.5}$$

Solving for $u$ in (8.5) we obtain the expression:

$$u = \frac{g_0 - (1 - s_h\delta) + (1 - s_h - \psi)j\lambda + (\eta + \phi)q}{\Delta} \tag{8.6}$$

with $\Delta = s_h + (1 - s_h)\pi - \beta$.

The usual short-run stability condition is $\Delta > 0$, or saving rises more than investment in response to an increase in $u$. Assuming that this condition is satisfied, note the ambiguous effect of $j\lambda$ on $u$. A bigger debt burden reduces investment demand through the coefficient $-\psi$ but also cuts into overall saving through the coefficient $1 - s_h$ as discussed above. If the saving effect dominates, $1 - s_h > \psi$, effective demand can be said to be "debt-led." Otherwise, a large enough investment response $\psi$ will make demand "debt-burdened." There is an obvious analogy to wage-led and profit-led effective demand in contemporary Goodwin-style models of the medium-term business cycle (Barbosa-Filho and Taylor 2006). The remaining term in (8.6) involves $q$. Through both investment and saving effects, a higher $q$ increases the level of economic activity. How $q$ itself gets determined is taken up below.

Capital stock growth is set from the demand side in this model. To get a final expression for $g$ we plug (8.6) into the investment demand function (8.4):

$$g = [\frac{s_h + (1-s_h)\pi}{\Delta}]g_0 - \frac{\beta(1-s_h)}{\Delta}\delta$$
$$+[\frac{\beta}{\Delta}(1-s_h) - (1+\frac{\beta}{\Delta})\psi]j\lambda + [\eta(1+\frac{\beta}{\Delta}) + \phi\frac{\beta}{\Delta}]q \qquad (8.7)$$

The relation between the growth rate of capital and the debt–capital ratio is not as straightforward as is the case for $u$. The sign of the partial derivative of $g$ with respect to $\lambda$ depends on the expression $\frac{\beta}{\Delta}(1-s_h) - (1+\frac{\beta}{\Delta})\psi$. If this term is positive, we have debt-led capital stock growth; otherwise $g$ is debt-burdened.

Some rough numbers may help clarify the distinction. Taking into account taxes net of transfers, imports, etc., the gross household saving rate for the US in the late 1990s was in the range of 0.12. Profits were around a quarter of value-added at factor cost. The profit rate was about 0.075. Net interest, dividend payments, and corporate taxes were all close to one percent of the value of the capital stock, giving retained earnings $\pi u - j\lambda - \delta$ of 0.045.

For $\pi = 0.25$ and $\beta = 0.2$, we get $\Delta = 0.14$ and $\beta/\Delta = 1.4286$. For these numbers, $\frac{\beta}{\Delta}(1-s_h) - (1+\frac{\beta}{\Delta})\psi > 0$ so long as $\psi < 0.52$, a condition that estimated investment functions suggest is likely to be satisfied. Although this sort of back of the envelope calculation is far from definitive, it does show that debt-led growth is a clear possibility.

## Differential equations for the debt–capital and equity–capital ratios

Whether growth is debt-led or debt-burdened becomes of interest in discussing the evolution of the equity–capital ratio $q$. But since it follows directly from the short-run model, we first take up the dynamic behavior of the debt–capital ratio $\lambda$. From the business sector's flow of funds (8.1), a differential equation can be written as:[8]

$$\dot{\lambda} = (j-g)\lambda + \delta + (1-\chi)g - \pi u \quad . \qquad (8.8)$$

Is this equation locally stable in the sense that $\partial\dot{\lambda}/\partial\lambda < 0$? With regard to the lead term $(j-g)\lambda$, real interest rates can exceed growth rates for extended periods of time (for example, during the last two to three decades of the twentieth century, a situation that then reversed and as of early 2006 may be reversing again). However, there are also effects of $\lambda$ on $u$ and $g$ to be considered. From the discussion above, they can take either sign. To keep possible outcomes of the model within limits, we simply assume local stability in (8.8).

Turning to the effects on $\dot{\lambda}$ of $q$, in (8.8) note that an increase in $q$ will raise $u$ and $g$ from (8.7) and (8.8) respectively. The former shift increases corporate saving $\pi u - j\lambda - \delta$ and thereby reduces new borrowing $\dot{\lambda}$. More investment, however, increases the need to borrow. To see which effect dominates we can use the expression:

$$\frac{\partial\dot{\lambda}}{\partial q} = \frac{[-\pi + \beta(1-\chi-\lambda)](\eta+\phi)}{\Delta} + (1-\chi-\lambda)\eta \quad . \qquad (8.9)$$

We can say that there is an "equity-accelerated" debt ratio if $\partial\dot{\lambda}/\partial q > 0$, and an "equity-decelerated" ratio otherwise. Because $\Delta << 1$, the most important term is $-\pi + \beta(1-\chi-\lambda)$. With $\chi < 0$ and $\lambda$ a fraction, it can be positive if the accelerator term $\beta$ is relatively strong. On the other hand, if $\lambda$ is in the range of one or greater as in Japan, we can have $\partial\dot{\lambda}/\partial q < 0$.

The next step is to bring in a differential equation for $q$. Following Diamond (2000) and ultimately Gordon (1962) the return to equity $\rho$ depends via intertemporal arbitrage on capital gains and dividends in a formula such as:

$$\rho P_e E = \dot{P}_e E + D \tag{8.10}$$

in which at least myopic foresight regarding the equity price change $\dot{P}_e$ is presupposed and $D$ is the level of dividend payments. It is convenient to set $D = \delta PK$ and for the moment we hold $\rho$ constant as a "required" return.[9] On these hypotheses we have that:

$$\rho = \hat{P}_e + \frac{\delta}{P_e E/PK} = \hat{P}_e + \frac{\delta}{q}$$

which immediately provides an equation for the growth rate of the equity price (independent of the corporate debt position $\lambda$),

$$\hat{P}_e = \rho - \frac{\delta}{q} \tag{8.11}$$

Because $q = P_e E/PK$, we have $\partial \hat{P}_e/\partial P_e > 0$in (8.11). The asset return equation (8.10) incorporates positive feedback of the equity price into its own growth rate, as is well known.

New issues of equity are $P_e \dot{E}/PK = \chi g$ so that:

$$\hat{E} = \frac{\chi g}{q} \quad . \tag{8.12}$$

Differentiating the definition $q = P_e E/PK$gives $\dot{q} = q[\hat{P}_e + \hat{E} - (\hat{P} + g)]$. Plugging in (8.11) and (8.12) with $\hat{P} = 0$ shows that

$$\dot{q} = (\rho - g)q + \chi g - \delta \quad . \tag{8.13}$$

The effect of $q$ on $\dot{q}$ is given by:

$$\partial \dot{q}/\partial q = (\rho - g) + (\chi - q)\partial g/\partial q \quad . \tag{8.14}$$

In the first term, the real long-run equity return $\rho$ is famously in the range of 7 per cent , higher than any reasonable growth rate. In the second term, $\chi$is small in absolute terms and recently negative in the US. Because $\partial g/\partial q > 0$, we can have $\partial \dot{q}/\partial q < 0$ for sufficiently large values of $q$. The intuition is that the positive feedback of $P_e$ into $\hat{P}_e$ just mentioned makes $\partial \dot{q}/\partial q > 0$ for low values of $q$. But if a higher equity–capital ratio pushes up $g$ in a demand-driven growth model by reducing *ex ante* saving and stimulating investment demand, then with a high enough value of $q$, the derivative $\partial \dot{q}/\partial q$ will change signs and $q$ will not tend to infinity.

The effect of $\lambda$ on $\dot{q}$ comes in via the term in $g$in equation (8.12) for $\hat{E}$ and (more importantly) the presence of capital stock $K$ in the denominator of $q$. It assumes a critical role in the expression:

$$\partial \dot{q}/\partial \lambda = (\chi - q)\frac{\partial g}{\partial \lambda} \quad . \tag{8.15}$$

If capital stock growth is debt-led, the derivative of $\dot{q}$ with respect to $\lambda$ will be negative since $\frac{\partial g}{\partial \lambda} > 0$ and $\chi - q < 0$. If growth is debt-burdened then we have $\partial \dot{q}/\partial \lambda > 0$.

Along with the contrast between an equity-accelerated and equity-decelerated debt ratio, this distinction has important implications for the dynamics of $q$ and $\lambda$ over time. For example, if capital stock growth is debt-led, the turning point at the top of a cycle would happen when rising $q$ and $\lambda$ push up $g$ enough in (8.13) to satisfy the condition $g >$

*Table 8.2* Four Possible Scenarios for the two differential equation system

| | *Debt-led growth* | *Debt-burdened growth* |
|---|---|---|
| Equity-decelerated | Saddlepoint if $\partial\dot{q}/\partial q > 0$ | Counter-clockwise cycle if $\partial\dot{q}/\partial q > 0$ |
| | $\lambda$ $q$ | $\lambda$ $q$ |
| debt ratio | $\dot{\lambda}$ − − | $\dot{\lambda}$ − − |
| | $\dot{q}$ − ± | $\dot{q}$ + ± |
| Equity-accelerated | Clockwise cycle if $\partial\dot{q}/\partial q > 0$ | Saddlepoint if $\partial\dot{q}/\partial q > 0$ |
| | $\lambda$ $q$ | $\lambda$ $q$ |
| debt ratio | $\dot{\lambda}$ − + | $\dot{\lambda}$ − + |
| | $\dot{q}$ − ± | $\dot{q}$ + ± |

$-(\rho-\delta)/(\chi-q)$ so that $\dot{q}<0$. In practice, the cyclical turning points in Figures 8.1–8.5 are dominated by rises and falls in $P_e$ as opposed to acceleration in $g$(though the latter may also be observed as in the US in the late 1990s).[10] In the following section we extend the basic model to take such "fast" equity price dynamics into account.

## Dynamics of the model

Equations (8.4) and (8.13) combine to give a 2 x 2 dynamical system which can generate an equity–debt cycle:

$$\begin{cases} \dot{\lambda} = (j-g)\lambda + \delta + (1-\chi)g - \pi u \\ \dot{q} = (\rho - g)q + \chi g - \delta \end{cases} \quad . \tag{8.16}$$

Its Jacobian is:

$$J = \begin{pmatrix} (j-g) - \pi\frac{\partial u}{\partial \lambda} + (1-\chi-\lambda)\frac{\partial g}{\partial \lambda} & -\pi\frac{\partial u}{\partial q} + (1-\chi-\lambda)\frac{\partial g}{\partial q} \\ (\chi - q)\frac{\partial g}{\partial \lambda} & (\rho - g) + (\chi - q)\frac{\partial g}{\partial q} \end{pmatrix}$$

$$J = \begin{pmatrix} a_{11} \; a_{12} \\ a_{21} \; a_{22} \end{pmatrix} \tag{8.17}$$

and the slopes of the loci along which $\dot{\lambda}=0$ and $\dot{q}=0$ are given by $\frac{\partial q}{\partial \lambda}\big|_{\dot{\lambda}=0} = -\frac{a_{11}}{a_{12}}$ and $\frac{\partial q}{\partial \lambda}\big|_{\dot{q}=0} = -\frac{a_{21}}{a_{22}}$ respectively.

Two points should be recalled about the Jacobian. One is that the partial derivative $\partial\dot{q}/\partial q$ can change sign. As noted above, the term $a_{22}$ in the SE corner of the Jacobian is likely to be positive for low values of $q$ but then may become negative at some higher value. This switch gives rise to interesting dynamic possibilities. Second, appropriate permutations of an equity-accelerated or equity-decelerated debt ratio with debt-led or debt-burdened growth can give rise to cycles. Table 8.2 summarizes possible scenarios. Two of them are consistent with the stylized facts presented in the Introduction. The one in the SW section of Table 8.2 involves an equity-accelerated debt ratio and debt-led growth. It applies to the US and the UK cases. Figures 8.6a and 8.6b depict the movements of the two state variables.

Figure 8.6a presupposes that $\partial\dot{q}/\partial q > 0$. It shows movements of the variables around the steady-state loci along which $\dot{\lambda}=0$ and $\dot{q}=0$. Both nullclines are upward sloping curves, with the one for $\dot{q}=0$ demonstrating local instability and the one for $\dot{\lambda}=0$ stability. As can be seen from the signs of the entries in the Jacobian in the SW corner of Table 8.2, the equity–capital ratio is the prey variable feeding positively into itself as well as into the predatory debt–capital ratio. The resulting clockwise cycles will be convergent or divergent depending on whether the trace of the Jacobian is negative or positive.

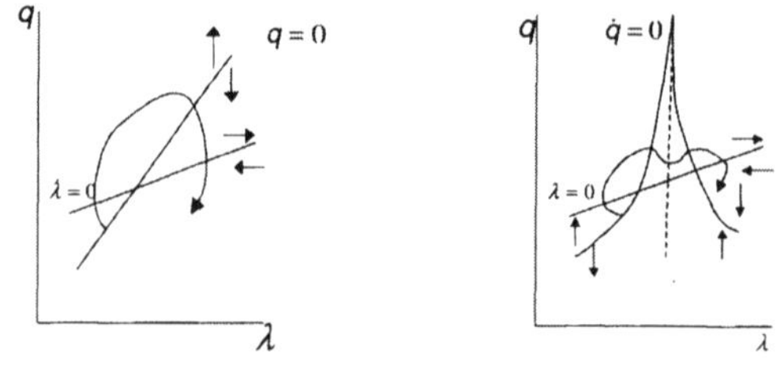


*Figure 8.6* Dynamics with an equity-accelerated debt ratio and debt-led growth

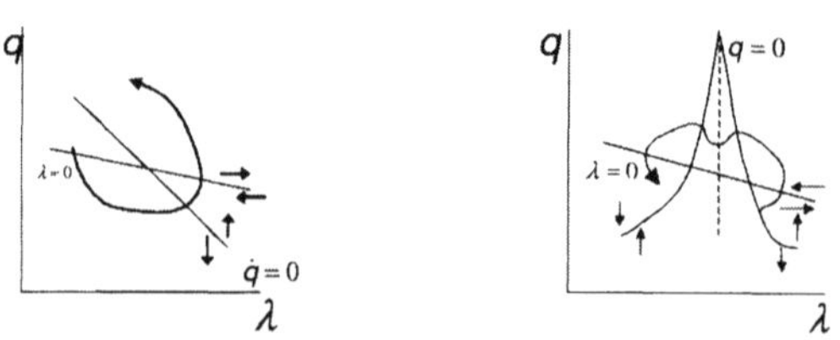


*Figure 8.7* Dynamics with an equity-accelerated debt ratio and debt-burdened growth

Figure 8.6b illustrates the implications of a switch in the sign of $a_{22}$ induced by an increase in $q$. Because the slope of the $\dot{q} = 0$ locus is $-a_{21}/a_{22}$, the sign change gives a nullcline with two branches separating at a cusp at which $\partial\dot{q}/\partial q \to \pm\infty$as $a_{22} \to \mp 0$. The branch to the right, with high values of $q$ and $\lambda$, is locally stable and would give rise to a steady state with high equity and debt ratios unless other dynamic forces intervened. Possibilities are discussed in the following section.

Figures 8.7a and 8.7b show what happens when there is an equity-decelerated debt ratio and debt-burdened growth from the NE section of Table 8.2. The former condition is more likely when $\lambda$ is high and the latter when there is high household saving and a strong drag on investment demand as business debt rises. This configuration plausibly applies to Japan, and the counterclockwise cycles in the diagrams are consistent with the data plotted in Figure 8.6.

## More volatile dynamics

What we have found so far is that a simple demand-driven financial growth model can generate cycles of the sort illustrated in the Introduction. One reason why the model works is that both the flow of funds balance (8.8) and the differential equation for $q$ in (8.13) rest upon relationships that by construction are satisfied by the data. The model maintains stock-flow consistency with this accounting so it is not surprising that it can produce results compatible with Figures 8.1–8.6.

On the other hand, one significant feature of observed real-financial oscillations is left out. As noted above, around a cyclical peak $P_e$ tends to rise and then fall more rapidly than the capital stock – the upper turning point does not occur because $K$ starts growing faster than $P_eE$ as equation (8.13) would predict. Rather, in Kindleberger's (2000) terminology

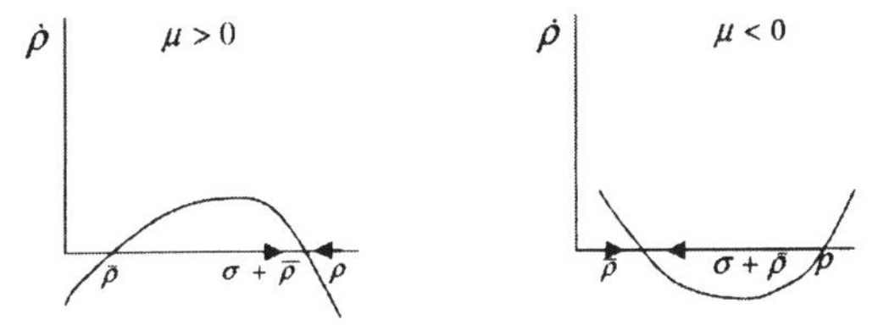


*Figure 8.8* "Fast" dynamics and bifurcations in the bull–bear cycles

a share price "mania" may begin, to be followed by a "panic" and then a "crash". The mania is characterized by rapid increases in the price of equity. It presumably continues until retarding factors such as doubts about the sustainability of a high debt–capital ratio and/or a high price–earnings ratio begin to mount. At some point a flight toward liquidity ensues, eventually causing a sharp decrease in equity prices and as a result a crash of the market. But how does the market become bullish in the first place? How does this theory fit our model?

Kindleberger's answer to the first question is that there is a "displacement" (from Figure 8.1, somewhere around 1990 in the latest US cycle?) that kicks off an asset price spiral, propelled by positive feedback.[11] His appendix presents historical examples, to which we can add nothing here. We can, however, say something about process, drawing heavily upon Keynes. As Erturk (2001) points out, Keynes sets out similar but not identical descriptions of the financial side of business cycles in his *Treatise on Money* (1930) and *General Theory* (1936).[12]

The latter's discussion is summarized in Chapter 22: the upswing is characterized by expectations-driven shifts upward in the schedule for the marginal efficiency of capital and the consumption function, and a shift downward in liquidity preference. Reversals in these movements (especially for the marginal efficiency of capital) provoke panic and crisis. With an emphasis on the role of the interest rate and shifts in the quality of balance sheets (with "hedge" changing to "speculative" and ultimately "Ponzi" financial positions), Minsky (1975) presents a similar model.

The *Treatise* version focuses more on asset prices. As an upswing begins, there is a decreasing bear position, roughly indicated by a fall in the volume of savings deposits as portfolios switch toward securities – this is a "bull market with a consensus of opinion" which shifts toward a "bull market with a difference of opinion" in which liquidity preference (in *General Theory* language) starts to rise even though asset prices are still increasing. As more and more traders join the bear brigade and portfolio preferences move strongly against equity, the downswing gets going.

So why do the traders change their views? Presumably at the macro level they are responding to shifts in observable "fundamental" indicators such as the debt–capital ratio $\lambda$ and the current price–earnings ratio $R = P_e/[(r - j\lambda)PK/E] = q/(r - j\lambda)$. Both fundamentals increase with $\lambda$ and $R$ rises with $q$ as well. In a short hand description, confidence erodes as they approach "critical" or "unsustainable" levels, say $\bar{\lambda}$ and $\bar{R}$ respectively.

In the present set-up, a way to model such shifts in sentiment is through changes in the "required" return to equity $\rho$, heretofore held constant in equation (8.13). When the displacement happens and the liquidity preference schedule shifts downward, $\rho$ must rise in response to greater equity demand. For the reasons just mentioned, at some point this process will reverse. A simple formulation is to set:

$$\dot{\rho} = \mu(\bar{R} - R, \bar{\lambda} - \lambda)(\rho - \bar{\rho})(\bar{\rho} + \sigma - \rho) \tag{8.18}$$

in which the function $\mu(\bar{R} - R, \bar{\lambda} - \lambda)$ is positive when both its arguments are positive. Depending on the channel(s) one wishes to emphasize, it switches sign when one or perhaps both arguments become negative. Since a US/UK-style boom is accompanied by increases in both $R$ and $\lambda$, at some point this sign change will occur (analogous Japanese-style dynamics are presumably driven by variables such as $R$ or perhaps $q$ itself).

In a bit more detail, when $\mu > 0$ the right hand side of (8.18) looks like Figure 8a. A positive value of $\mu$ pushes $\rho$ toward an upper bound $\bar{\rho} + \sigma$ where $\bar{\rho}$ is a base level return to equity and $\sigma$ reflects market exhilaration. The implication is that a high value of $\rho$ makes $q$ rise rapidly until $R$ and/or $\lambda$ exceeds its crisis level. The equity–capital ratio passes a cyclical turning point, and then drops off quickly as Figure 8.8b comes into effect. This is the beginning of the panic phase with economic agents rushing to exit the stock market and selling their share holdings en masse. Bankers behave in a similar manner and stop lending, making the crash inevitable. Economic agents, now bears, switch asset demands from shares toward liquidity.

Sooner or later investment drops substantially, slowing the capital stock growth rate enough to set up a turnaround in $q$ as recovery gets underway. If a mechanism like the one in (8.18) works strongly enough on the downswing in conjunction with a low $\bar{\rho}$, it could conceivably drive the system from the high-$q$ toward the low-$q$ cyclical attractor in Figure 8.6b or 8.7b, prolonging the downswing.[13]

## Conclusions

In summary:

Long-term oscillations involving the equity–capital and debt–capital ratios ($q$ and $\lambda$ respectively) exist in data for the US, UK, and Japan. They follow a broadly clockwise pattern in the first two economies and run counterclockwise in Japan.

By construction, the data satisfy the non-financial business sector's flows of funds and a standard asset return equation. These relationships can be formulated as ordinary differential equations for $\lambda$ and $q$ that can be analyzed in a phase diagram in the $(\lambda, q)$ plane. Under appropriate restrictions on the Jacobian, the dynamical system can generate long-term predator-prey cycles like those apparent in the data.

A simple demand-driven post-Keynesian model can be set up to rationalize the cycles. The clockwise variant (with $q$ as the prey variable and $\lambda$ the predator) arises when capital stock growth is "debt-led" along lines suggested by Minsky (1975) and the debt ratio is "equity accelerated." "Debt-burdened" growth and "equity-decelerated" debt can produce counter-clockwise oscillations. The clockwise scenario bears a strong family resemblance to Goodwin's original distributive growth cycle.

Around a cyclical peak, short-term dynamics of the equity price can be modeled using a transcritical bifurcation involving changes in the "required" return to equity $\rho$ in response to shifting "fundamentals" such as the debt–equity and price–earnings ratios.

## Appendix on sources of data

### *1) United States:*

The main sources for outstanding debt and corporate equities at market value for the United States are the *Flow of Funds Accounts* published by the Federal Reserve Bank. Corporate equities are the time series FL103164003 and outstanding debt is the time series LA104104005. Available HTTP: <www.federalreserve.gov/releases /Z1/Current/data.htm>.

Capital stock is taken from BEA, NIPA Table 6.1. Current-Cost Net Stock of Private Fixed Assets by Industry Group and Legal Form of Organization, and represents the capital stock of the corporate non-financial sector. The same pattern can be observed running the plot with both gross and net capital stock. In Figure 8.1 we used gross capital stock.

The data for the pre-war debt–equity cycle for the US were obtained from Goldsmith and Lipsey (1963). They appear in the national balance sheet, Table 1a (pp. 72–85, Vol. II). We used the S&P index from Shiller (2000) for the benchmark years in the upper diagram of Figure 8.4.

### *2) United Kingdom:*

The London Stock Exchange (available HTTP: <www.londonstockexchange.com/market/ historic.asp>) publishes the market value of equities for UK and Irish companies used in Figure 8.3. In Figure 8.2 we used the FTSE All Shares stock price index, provided by Global Financial Data
(HTTP: <http://www.globalfindata.com>). The Cambridge Endowment for Research in Finance, at Cambridge University, provided data for capital stock and outstanding debt for the non-financial corporate sector.

### *3) Japan:*

Data for capital stock and outstanding debt (or financial liabilities) are taken from *Financial Statements Statistics of Corporations by Industries*, Quarterly, Japanese Ministry of Finance, HTTP: <www.mof.go.jp/english/ssc/historical.htm>. For capital stock we used the time series for fixed assets after removing land in order to avoid the problem of real estate speculation. In order to obtain the value of outstanding debt we added liquid financial liabilities – time series no. 23 (short-term financial liabilities) – to the value of fixed liabilities – time series no. 29 (long-term financial liabilities).

For estimates on the value of equity we used data released by the Bank of Japan for 1970–1999, supplemented for 2000–2001 with data from the Flow of Funds Accounts for 2000–2001 (HTTP:<www2.boj.or.jp/en/dlong/dlong.htm>). The Nikkei 225 obtained from Global Financial Data was another estimate for the value of equity that we used to calculate $q$ (upper diagram of figure 8.5).

## Acknowledgements

The authors are grateful to The Ford Foundation for research support and to Per Berglund, Serguey Braguinsky, Duncan Foley, Alex Izurieta, Marc Lavoie, Leonce Ndikumana, Barkley Rosser, and Richard Sylla for helpful inputs.

## Notes

1 That is, $P_eE$ = outstanding corporate equity with $P_e$ as an equity price index and $E$ the corresponding volume. Tobin (1969) defined $q$ as the ratio between a firm's market value and the replacement costs of its tangible assets. Expressed mathematically this ratio can take various forms, one version being the ratio of outstanding equity $P_eE$ to the current value of capital stock $PK$ which we employ here.

2 Data sources are described in the appendix. In Figure 8.2a, we use the FTSE all-shares index as the equity valuation indicator for the UK (that is, just $P_e$ as opposed to $P_eE$ is used in the numerator of $q$). A similar pattern with a higher peak value for $q$ in the second cycle shows up in Figure 8.2b where a measure of total corporate valuation in the UK is used in the numerator. The latter diagram is somewhat problematical because available data on outstanding equity include not only UK corporations but Irish corporations as well for 1970–1994.

3 In round numbers, net worth of the non-financial corporate sector at the end of 1999 in the US was -$9.6 trillion with the sector's stock market valuation at $19.8 trillion. Tangible assets were valued at $12 trillion, and other net financial liabilities were $1.8 trillion. Non-financial business had -$3.7 trillion in "holding losses" on financial paper (basically equity) during that year, while households enjoyed $4.3 trillion of "holding gains" (mostly on shares issued by domestic non-financial and financial business and the rest of the word).

4 In contrast to our approach, the Modigliani-Miller theorem does not allow for non-zero corporate net worth, thereby resembling a full employment or Say's Law assumption on the real side. These hypotheses lead naturally to models in which prices of goods and services (on the real side) and rates of return to asset and liability claims (on the financial side) adjust smoothly to remove any incipient market disequilibria, with the importance of quantity adjustments correspondingly curtailed.

5 It can be shown that a constant value of $\pi$ in the present model is equivalent to stating that the price level $P$ is set by a constant mark-up over wage costs. For more on the modeling framework being used, see Taylor (2004).

6 For the last two or three decades of the twentieth century in the US, $\chi$ was negative due to stock buybacks.

7 Net holdings of broad money make up about one-sixth of households' net financial assets and one-eighth of their total assets (including residential housing) in the US.

8 Equation (8.8) is derived the following way. We differentiate the ratio of outstanding corporate debt to capital stock with respect to time and obtain $\dot{\lambda} = \lambda\hat{L} - \lambda g$. Using equation (8.1) we get an expression for $\hat{L}$ that we plug into this equation for $\dot{\lambda}$ and thus obtain equation (8.8) for the rate of change in the ratio of debt to capital.

9 This assumption will be relaxed when we take up short-term dynamics in the following section. Alternatively, $\rho$ could be interpreted as the observed return averaged over several decades.

10 The turning point at the top of the last cycle in the US was driven by a fall in the growth rate of equity prices (using the S&P price index) from 30 per cent observed in 1999 to 14 per cent in 2000 and further to an absolute decrease in prices of –6 per cent in 2001. The growth rate of capital followed a similar pattern but with a one-year lag. It started to decrease only in 2001, when it grew at 4 per cent relative to the peak of 7 per cent observed in 2000. At the bottom of the previous cycle at the end of 1970s for the US, equity prices were extremely volatile but then began to outstrip capital stock growth in 1983. There was a pause after the 1987 stock market decline and then a strong price surge in the 1990s.

11 Although our differential equation (8.13) for $q$ incorporates positive feedback of the equity price $P_e$ into its own increase $\dot{P}_e$, it does not generate a rational expectations bubble of the sort investigated by many people in the 1970s and 1980s. Bubbles involving saddlepoints do not show up in the SW and NE corners of Table 8.2 because of

$q$'s cross-dynamics with $\lambda$. Blanchard and Fischer (1989) and Rosser (2000) summarize the now largely forgotten bubble literature.

12 With the exception of Minsky and other post-Keynesians, most business cycle modelers did not take Keynes's emphasis on interactions between the real and financial sectors on board. The *General Theory*'s shifts in the marginal efficiency of capital perhaps influenced multiplier-accelerator formulations but they vanished along with that class of models. Bulls, bears, and liquidity preference do not figure in contemporary formulations of financial dynamics which feature rational bubbles, feedback, and models with different types of actors such as "fundamentalists" and "chartists." Again, see Rosser (2000) for a review.

13 In the jargon, (8.18) generates a "transcritical bifurcation" for $\rho$. A slightly fancier variant could be based on a "cusp catastrophe" as in Zeeman (1974) and Varian (1979).

## References


Barbosa-Filho, Nelson H., and Lance Taylor (2006) "Distributive and Demand Cycles in the US Economy – A Structuralist Goodwin Model," *Metroeconomica*, 57: 389–411

Blanchard, Olivier and Stanley Fischer (1989) *Lectures on Macroeconomics*, Cambridge MA: MIT Press

Brenner, Robert (2002) *The Boom and the Bubble: The US in the World Economy*, London: Verso

Diamond, Peter (2000) "What Stock Market Returns to Expect for the Future?" *Social Security Bulletin* , 63(2): 38–52

Erturk, Korkut (2001) "Asset Prices, Liquidity Preference, and the Business Cycle," Salt Lake City UT: Department of Economics, University of Utah

Fazzari, Steven M., and Tracy L. Mott (1986-87) "The Investment Theories of Kalecki and Keynes: An Empirical Study of Firm Data, 1970–82," *Journal of Post Keynesian Economics* 9: 171–87

Goldsmith, Raymond W. and Robert E. Lipsey (1963) *Studies in the National Balance Sheet of the United States*, New York: National Bureau of Economic Research

Goodwin, Richard M. (1967) "A Growth Cycle," in C. H. Feinstein (ed.) *Socialism, Capitalism, and Growth*, Cambridge: Cambridge University Press

Gordon, Myron (1962) *The Investment, Financing, and Valuation of the Corporation*, Homewood, IL: Irwin

Keynes, John Maynard (1930) *A Treatise on Money*, London: Macmillan

Keynes, John Maynard (1936) *The General Theory of Employment, Interest, and Money*, London: Macmillan

Kindleberger, Charles P. (2000) *Manias, Panics, and Crashes: A History of Financial Crises*, New York: John Wiley & Sons

Lavoie, Marc, and Wynne Godley (2001-2002) "Kaleckian Models of Growth in a Coherent Stock-Flow Monetary Framework: A Kaldorian View," *Journal of Post Keynesian Economics* 24: 277–311

Minsky, Hyman P. (1975) *John Maynard Keynes*, Columbia University Press

Ndikumana, Leonce (1999) "Debt Service, Financing Constraints, and Fixed Investment: Evidence From Panel Data", *Journal of Post Keynesian Economics*, 21(3): 455–78.

Rosser, J. Barkley Jr. (2000) *From Catastrophe to Chaos: A General Theory of Economic Discontinuities*, New York: Kluwer Academic Publishers

Shiller, Robert J. (2000) *Irrational Exuberance*, New York: Broadway Books.

Taylor, Lance (2004) *Reconstructing Macroeconomics: Structuralist Proposals and Critiques of the Mainstream,* Cambridge, MA: Harvard University Press

Tobin, James (1969) "A General Equilibrium Approach to Monetary Theory," *Journal of Money, Credit, and Banking,* 1: 15-29

Varian, Hal (1979) "Catastrophe Theory and the Business Cycle," *Economic Inquiry,* 17: 14–28.

Zeeman, Christopher E. (1974) "On the Unstable Behavior of the Stock Exchange," *Journal of Mathematical Economics* 1, 39–44

# 9 Monetary policy rules in small open economies

## A Keynesian perspective

*Christopher Malikane and Willi Semmler*

## Introduction

This chapter presents an integrated Keynesian monetary model for a small open economy. Our aim is to investigate the quantitative implications of alternative policy rules for the stability properties of such economies. As pointed out by McCallum (1999), there is no consensus on the target variables that should characterize the feedback policy rule of the central bank. In this chapter we specifically seek to investigate the stability properties of policy rules that react to exchange rate and stock price fluctuations, and to investigate the impact of stronger reaction by the central bank to inflation and capacity utilization gaps.

Since all these questions have been approached disparately, using small macro-models whose structure is similar to those of Svensson (1997) and Ball (1999), the contribution of this chapter is to provide an integrated framework in which all these issues can be addressed. In relation to the central bank's response to capacity utilization, McCallum (2001) recommends against policies that react strongly to utilization gaps. Bernanke and Gertler (1999, 2001) and Gilchrist and Leahy (2002) among others recommend against policies that respond to movements in asset prices, which includes exchange rate movements. They argue that such policies do not improve macroeconomic performance, and instead lead to increased aggregate volatility. Yet Kent and Lowe (1997), Cecchetti *et al.* (2000, 2002), Genberg (2001) and Semmler and Zhang (2007) argue that a response of the central bank to asset price fluctuations may improve economic performance by reducing aggregate volatility. Borio and Lowe (2002) also advance the same view on the grounds that a low inflationary environment can lead excess demand to appear in credit aggregates and asset prices, and may thus threaten macroeconomic stability.

For small open economies exchange rate stability is of special importance. Mohanty and Klau (2004) find that in most of these economies the short-term interest rate responds significantly to exchange rate fluctuations. In small open economies, Mishkin (2000) argues that monetary authorities should smooth exchange rates. Ball (1999, 2002) finds that if the exchange rate features in the policy rule in the form of the monetary conditions index-which is a weighted average of the real interest rate and the real exchange rate, it tends to improve macroeconomic performance. Yet, Clarida et. al. (2001) argue that central banks should target domestic inflation and allow the exchange rate to freely float. In the presence of partially dollarized liabilities, Bernanke and Gertler (1999) further argue that positive interest rate movements in response to exchange rate depreciation may worsen the balance sheet of firms and make economic contraction severe. Lastly, studies reviewed by Taylor (2001) find no significant improvement in macro-economic performance when the exchange rate is included in the policy rule.

Our model is made up of four components. On the supply-side, it features two Phillips curves and a Harrod-neutral technical progress production function following Flaschel *et al.* (2001) among others. On the demand side it features the wage share and exhibits Kaldorian consumption habits. The transmission mechanism of monetary policy operates through three financial markets; the foreign exchange, bond, and equities markets. For simplicity, the model follows Taylor (1995) in that monetary policy propagates shocks through asset prices than through portfolio reallocations as in Tobin (1969). The central bank follows a Taylor-type rule interest rate policy rule to maintain macro-stability in the face of shocks. The labor and goods markets are linked through an investment-based Okun's law. At the core, the dynamics of the model are driven by the classical conflict cycle of Goodwin (1967).

This model is then estimated using South African data from 1960:1–2006:4. We find that wage-setting is to a large extent backward-looking, and rigidities appear to emanate more from the goods market than the labor market. On this basis, through simulations, we further find that an interest rate policy rule that reacts more to fluctuations in the employment rate than the goods market conditions is good for stability. In addition, sufficiently strong policy responses to asset price fluctuations ensure macroeconomic convergence.

## Outline of the model

Our point of departure is an open economy wage-price spiral formulation along the lines of Flaschel *et al.* (2001) and Asada *et al.* (2006) among others. This specification of the supply-side of the model, in its reduced-form, exhibits: a) separate demand pressures from the goods and labor markets; b) exchange rate effects that capture the impact of import prices on domestic inflation; and c) a slow moving measure that captures the inflationary climate within which prices and nominal wages are set. Recent formulations from the dynamic stochastic general equilibrium perspective such as Erceg *et al.* (2000), Huang and Liu (2002), Amato and Laubach (2003), and Christiano and Eichenbaum (2005), recognize the significance of separating wage and price adjustment in reproducing observed persistence of monetary shocks on real economic activity. The following equations describe the wage-price spiral:

$$\widehat{p} = \kappa_p(\widehat{w} - n_x) + (1 - \kappa_p)\pi + \beta_p(U - U_0) + \beta_e(\widehat{e} + \widehat{p}^f) \tag{9.1}$$

$$\widehat{w} = \kappa_w \widehat{p} + (1 - \kappa_w)\pi + \beta_w(V - V_0) + n_x \tag{9.2}$$

$$\dot{\pi} = \beta_\pi(\widehat{p} - \pi) \tag{9.3}$$

In (9.1) the price inflation rate is determined by a weighted average between nominal wage inflation in excess of labor productivity $(\widehat{w} - n_x)$, and a slow-moving inflation measure that captures the inflationary climate, which we denote by $\pi$. Labor productivity growth is exogenous. It therefore follows from this formulation that $0 \leq \kappa_p \leq 1$. The price inflation rate is also driven by excess demand pressure $(U - U_0)$. Lastly, the sum of nominal exchange rate depreciation and foreign price inflation determines domestic inflation via import prices. In (9.2) the productivity-adjusted nominal wage inflation rate is determined by a weighted average between the price inflation rate and the inflationary climate, the employment rate gap denoted by $(V - V_0)$. In (9.3) the inflationary climate is modeled as an adaptively evolving process.

The foreign price inflation rate is exogenously driven. We shall therefore, for simplicity, set it to zero in our theoretical exposition. It is useful to express the above system in reduced-form:

$$\widehat{p} - \pi = \lambda[\kappa_p \beta_w(V - V_0) + \beta_p(U - U_0) + \beta_e \widehat{e}] \tag{9.4}$$

$$\widehat{w} - \pi = \lambda \left[ \kappa_w \beta_p (U - U_0) + \kappa_w \beta_e \widehat{e} + \beta_w (V - V_0) \right] + n_x \tag{9.5}$$

$$\dot{\pi} = \lambda \beta_\pi \left[ \kappa_p \beta_w (V - V_0) + \beta_p (U - U_0) + \beta_e \widehat{e} \right] \tag{9.6}$$

Where $\lambda = \frac{1}{1-\kappa_p \kappa_w}$. Using (9.4) and (9.5) to derive the law of motion for the labor share we obtain the following differential equation:

$$\widehat{u} = \lambda \left[ (\kappa_w - 1) \left[ \beta_p (U - U_0) + \beta_e \widehat{e} \right] + \beta_w (1 - \kappa_p)(V - V_0) \right] \tag{9.7}$$

We close the supply-side of the model with a Harrod-neutral production technology which is used in our economy to produce potential output $Y^p$. This allows us to conveniently derive the rate of capacity utilization and its NAIRU-type level as follows:

$$Y^p = y^p K, \qquad U = \frac{y}{y^p}, \qquad U_0 = 1 \tag{9.8}$$

Where $K$ is the fixed capital stock and $y$ is the output–capital ratio, and $y^p$ is the constant potential output–capital ratio. The labor and goods markets are linked via an Okun-type relationship. Specifically when the slack in the goods market translates into investment cutbacks. As a result firms reduce their employment rate. This implies an Okun-type law that is based on the rate of fixed investment, and therefore imparts on the employment rate a sluggishness that is associated with adjustment costs in fixed capital investment. In fact, our formulation is a generalization of Okun's law. It allows for explicit consideration of the traditional effects of the goods market on the labor market, which operate via the accelerator effect in investment expenditure. In addition, this formulation explicitly and in a direct way integrates Goodwin (1967) effects on the labor market, which operate via the rate of profit.

Therefore even if the goods market were slack, but profitability relatively high, firms would cautiously adjust their employment rates by engaging in activities such as labor-hoarding during business cycle downswings and over-time work during upswings. This means that if firms perceive demand conditions to improve sustainably, they would invest in fixed capital and therefore expand employment. However, if firms do not perceive demand improvements to be sustainable, they would not increased fixed capital investment and consequently they would over-employ existing labor. The modified version of Okun's law, in growth rate form, can be written as follows:

$$\widehat{V} = \beta_V (i - i_0) \tag{9.9}$$

Where $i$ is the investment-capital ratio and $\beta_V$ is the adjustment speed of the employment rate to fixed capital investment. This completes our specification of the supply-side of the model.

We model aggregate demand in a disaggregated way. Following Taylor (1995), we assume that the long rate, rather than the short rate, determines aggregate demand. Furthermore from (9.8) we observe that $y = y^p U$. This allows us to specify aggregate demand in terms of the rate of capacity utilization. Consumption in (9.10) exhibits Kaldorian savings habits wherein the savings propensity of pure profit-earners exceeds that of pure wage-earners, i.e. $s_c > s_w$. The real long-term interest rate $\left(r^l - \widehat{p}\right)$ negatively affects consumption expenditure via the credit channel. The stock price $p_e$ positively affects consumption through the wealth effect. In (9.11) firms use both internal and external sources to fund investment expenditure. The decision to reinvest internal funds is determined by the spread between the rate of profit and the real long rate. Firms' access to external funds is captured by the stock price. Exports in (9.12) and imports in (9.13) are determined in a conventional way by the real exchange rate, domestic and foreign income levels.

$$c = (s_c - s_w)y^p uU + (1 - s_c)y^p U - \psi\left(r^l - \widehat{p}\right) + \omega p_e \tag{9.10}$$

$$\begin{aligned} i = {} & i_\rho\left[(1-u)y^p U - \left(r^l - \widehat{p}\right)\right] + i_U\left(U - U_0\right) \\ & + i_{p_e}\left(p_e - p_{e0}\right) + i_0 \end{aligned} \tag{9.11}$$

$$x = x_q\left(\frac{ep^f}{p}\right) + x_{y^f} y^f \tag{9.12}$$

$$m = -m_q\left(\frac{ep^f}{p}\right) + m_y y^p U \tag{9.13}$$

$$U^d = U^d\left(u, U, r^l, p, e, p_e, r, \pi\right) \tag{9.14}$$

$$\dot{U} = \beta_U\left(U^d\left(u, U, r^l, p, e, p_e, \pi\right) - U\right) \tag{9.15}$$

Equation (9.14) is the aggregate demand identity, which sums the components in (9.10)–(9.13). This reduced-form expression of aggregate demand requires some brief elaboration, focusing on a few variables. The labor share has contradictory effects on aggregate demand through the consumption and investment channels as in Chiarella and Flaschel (2000: 196). Assuming relatively small import propensity, capacity utilization positively affects aggregate demand through for example the consumption and investment channels. As will be elaborated below, nominal exchange rate depreciation, which comes from the reduced-form price inflation equation (9.4), is determined partly and negatively by the differential between the short- and long-term interest rates. Hence we have explicitly included the nominal short-term interest rate $r$ in (9.14). Goods market adjustment occurs via a dynamic multiplier process in (9.15), since $y^p$ is a constant parameter.

Having specified the determination of investment expenditure, substituting (9.11) into (9.9) we obtain the following law of motion for the employment rate:

$$\widehat{V} = \beta_V\left(i_\rho\left[(1-u)y^p U - \left(r^l - \widehat{p}\right)\right] + i_U\left(U - U_0\right) + i_{p_e}\left(p_e - p_{e0}\right)\right) \tag{9.16}$$

From (9.4) we observe that this law of motion contains some potentially destabilizing force that emanates from the price inflation rate. An increase in the employment rate puts upward pressure on prices, reduces the real long rate, and further accelerates employment expansion. This destabilizing force can nevertheless be overcome if wage flexibility measured by $\beta_w$, is sufficiently small, among other factors. Equation (9.16) generalizes Okun's law, since it now features non-conventional terms such as profitability, the stock price and the real long-term interest rate.

Asset prices adjust with finite speeds to discrepancies in rates of return to capture frictions in capital markets. In (9.17) the rate of nominal stock price appreciation rises in proportion to the gap between the rate of profit and a slow moving component of the stock price $\pi_e$ that captures the investment climate in the equities market on the one hand, and the real short-term interest rate on the other. The term $\xi$ is the risk premium associated with holding equities. Note that when $\widehat{p}_e = 0$, the equilibrium in the equities market resembles the arbitrage relation in Blanchard (1981). In (9.18) we assume that the equities market climate moves adaptively following the stock price inflation. Following Chiarella and Flaschel (1999), we assume in (9.19) that the nominal exchange rate depreciates in response to discrepancies in the capital account as in Ball (1999) and net exports, denoted by $nx = x - m$. We here also assume a slow moving component $\varepsilon$ in the foreign exchange market to capture the environment within which the foreign exchange market operates, which evolves in an adaptive fashion described by (9.20).

Equation (9.21) links the bond and money markets, the latter represented by the short-term interest rate controlled by the central bank. As in Blanchard (1981), bonds traded are consols with yield $r^l$ and price $\frac{1}{r^l}$. Therefore (9.21) gives the adjustment law of the bond market, which is also augmented by a sentiment term that evolves in an adaptive fashion in (9.22).

$$\widehat{p}_e = \beta_{p_e}\left[(1-u)y^p U + \pi_e - (r - \xi - \widehat{p})\right] \tag{9.17}$$

$$\dot{\pi}_e = \beta_{\pi_e}(\widehat{p}_e - \pi_e) \tag{9.18}$$

$$\widehat{e} = \beta_e\left[\beta_c(r^* - r + \varepsilon) - (x - m)\right] \tag{9.19}$$

$$\dot{\varepsilon} = \beta_\varepsilon(\widehat{e} - \varepsilon) \tag{9.20}$$

$$\widehat{r}^l = \beta_{r^l}\left[r - (r^l - \xi - \pi_{r^l})\right], \quad \left(p_b = \frac{1}{r^l}\right) \Rightarrow (\widehat{p}_b = -\widehat{r}^l) \tag{9.21}$$

$$\dot{\pi}_{r^l} = \beta_{\pi_{r^l}}(\widehat{r}^l - \pi_{r^l}) \tag{9.22}$$

This completes the outline of the equations driving the model. From the above, it follows that there are three channels through which monetary policy affects real economic activity. The first is via the long-term interest rate, which affects consumption and investment expenditures. The second channel is through the stock market, which also affects both these components of aggregate demand. The third channel operates via the exchange rate, which enters price inflation, labor share and aggregate demand determination through net exports. The accelerators, which operate via the slow-moving sentiment terms across these financial markets, serve to accentuate the effects of relatively small shifts in the monetary policy stance on aggregate activity. And yet, these accelerators are potentially destabilizing.

We close the model with a generalized Taylor rule, which takes the following form:

$$r = r_0 + \beta_{r\widehat{p}}(\widehat{p} - \pi_0) + \beta_{rU}(U - U_0) + \beta_{rV}(V - V_0) + \beta_{re}(e - e_0) + \beta_{rp_e}(p_e - p_{e0}) \tag{9.23}$$

Where $\beta_r$ is a reaction parameter of the central bank. The first term is the steady state nominal interest rate. The second term says the central bank reacts by raising the short-term interest rate when inflation rate exceeds the target rate $\pi_0$. The third and fourth terms capture the fact that the central bank also reacts to real economic activity gaps. As (4)–(6) shows if $\beta_p = 0$, which implies complete price rigidity, the goods market does not play a significant role in the determination of price and nominal wage inflation rates. Under these conditions responding to the goods market gap fails to stabilize the economy. Conversely if $\beta_w = 0$, it helps to respond to the goods market gap. In paraphrasing Blanchard (2003), if both flexibility parameters are non-zero, (9.23) says the central bank should set $\beta_{rU}$ and $\beta_{rV}$ in accordance with the sources of rigidities in the economy.

The last two terms are asset prices, to which the central bank reacts by raising interest rates when the nominal exchange rate and the stock price are above some long run value it perceives. There are of course alternative ways of inserting asset prices in the policy rule. For example, we may instead specify the rule in terms of reactions to the rate of exchange rate depreciation and rate of stock price appreciation.

## Feedback stability analysis

Stability analysis is conducted with reference to the basic feedback channels that characterize the dynamics of the economy. The dynamics of our economy are characterized by six feedback mechanisms. These mechanisms are associated with Goodwin (1967), Rose (1967), Dornbusch (1976), Blanchard (1981) and Taylor (1993). Based on the above description of the model, the following system drives the dynamics of our economy:

$$\widehat{u} = \lambda\left[(\kappa_w - 1)\left[\beta_p (U - U_0) + \beta_e \widehat{e}\right] + \beta_w (1 - \kappa_p)(V - V_0)\right] \tag{9.24}$$

$$\widehat{V} = \beta_V \left(i_\rho \left[(1-u)y^p U - \left(r^l - \widehat{p}\right)\right] + i_U (U - U_0) + i_{p_e} (p_e - p_{e0})\right) \tag{9.25}$$

$$\dot{U} = \beta_U \left(U^d \left(u, U, V, r^l, p, e, p_e, \pi\right) - U\right) \tag{9.26}$$

$$\widehat{p} = \lambda\left[\kappa_p \beta_w (V - V_0) + \beta_p (U - U_0) + \beta_e \widehat{e}\right] + \pi \tag{9.27}$$

$$\dot{\pi} = \lambda \beta_\pi \left[\kappa_p \beta_w (V - V_0) + \beta_p (U - U_0) + \beta_e \widehat{e}\right] \tag{9.28}$$

$$\widehat{p}_e = \beta_{p_e}\left[(1-u)y^p U + \pi_e - (r - \xi - \widehat{p})\right] \tag{9.29}$$

$$\dot{\pi}_e = \beta_{\pi_e}(\widehat{p}_e - \pi_e) \tag{9.30}$$

$$\widehat{e} = \beta_e \left[\beta_c (r^* - r + \varepsilon) - (x - m)\right] \tag{9.31}$$

$$\dot{\varepsilon} = \beta_\varepsilon (\widehat{e} - \varepsilon) \tag{9.32}$$

$$\widehat{r^l} = \beta_{r^l}\left[r - \left(r^l - \xi - \pi_{r^l}\right)\right], \quad \left(p_b = \frac{1}{r^l}\right) \Rightarrow \left(\widehat{p}_b = -\widehat{r^l}\right) \tag{9.33}$$

$$\dot{\pi}_{r^l} = \beta_{\pi_{r^l}}\left(\widehat{r^l} - \pi_{r^l}\right) \tag{9.34}$$

Given the high-dimensional structure of the model and the fact that, our approach to analyzing its stability properties will involve slowing down some speeds of adjustment in order to weaken the potentially destabilizing forces. This method of analysis is to a large extent suitable to the structure of our model given that all the dynamic equations are multiplied either by some adjustment speed parameter, or a combination of parameters of other parameters.

The first mechanism that we consider is due to Goodwin (1967), and it interacts the wage share and the employment rate. This mechanism is described by the sub-system (9.24) and (9.25), freezing all the other variables at their steady state. This mechanism can be shown to generate a sign structure of the Jacobian that implies complex eigenvalues. Yet, in response to a minor perturbation the economy displays cyclical divergence. By allowing the short rate to respond to the employment rate, the destabilizing feedback of the employment rate to its own growth rate in (9.25) can be overcome – leading to the emergence of negative real parts in the eigenvalues.

By integrating the goods market in this set-up, we have now the interaction of the Goodwin cycle with that of Rose (1967), where we interpret the latter link the goods market (9.26) and the wage share. The resultant dynamic system exhibits the following sign structure:

$$J^{(3)} = \begin{bmatrix} 0 & + & - \\ - & 0 & + \\ \pm & + & - \end{bmatrix}$$

It can be observed from evaluating the determinant of this Jacobian that a profit-led system, wherein a rise in the wage share leads to a reduction in aggregate demand, tends to be stable. However in the case of a wage-led system, predominantly forward-looking behavior in price-setting measured by a high $\kappa_p$ or nominal rigidity in nominal wage inflation measured by a low $\beta_w$ would be stabilizing. Furthermore high price flexibility tends to be destabilizing in this context. Adding the price inflation rate yields the following Jacobian:

$$J^{(4)} = \begin{bmatrix} 0 & + & - & - \\ - & 0 & + & + \\ \pm & + & - & + \\ 0 & + & + & + \end{bmatrix}$$

This sign structure reveals that the interaction between price inflation and the wage share is stable. Yet the interaction between price inflation and the rate of capacity utilization is stable if the interest rate effect on aggregate demand is small, and the stabilizing multiplier effect is strong. Nevertheless, if nominal wages and prices are sufficiently sluggish and exchange rate adjustment to balance of payments disequilibria is slow, the economy remains stable since then the determinant of the 4D sub-system becomes positive. Therefore, in general, we may conclude at this level of dimension that stability requires a sufficiently small $\beta_e$ since it is mainly through exchange rate depreciation that prices affect the rest of the 4D system. Adding the inflationary climate to this sub-system, multiplying (9.26) by $\beta_\pi$ and subtracting the resultant (9.25) from (9.2) results in the following sign structure:

$$J^{(5)} = \begin{bmatrix} 0 & + & - & - & 0 \\ - & 0 & + & + & + \\ \pm & + & - & + & + \\ 0 & + & + & + & + \\ 0 & 0 & 0 & 0 & - \end{bmatrix}$$

It is then easy to see, by expanding through the fifth row, that the determinant of this Jacobian is negative. In the next steps we incorporate financial markets in this setup and again show that sluggish adjustment these markets tend to be stabilizing. We incorporate the stock price by multiplying (9.29) by $\beta_V i_\rho$ and (9.25) by $\beta_{p_e}$ and then subtract the resultant (9.25) from the resultant (9.29) to obtain the following Jacobian:

$$J^{(6)} = \begin{bmatrix} 0 & + & - & - & 0 & 0 \\ - & 0 & + & + & + & + \\ \pm & + & - & + & + & + \\ 0 & + & + & + & + & 0 \\ 0 & 0 & 0 & 0 & - & 0 \\ 0 & 0 & - & 0 & 0 & - \end{bmatrix}$$

From which it is clear that for sufficiently small accelerator effect $i_U$ would promote stability as it would make the determinant of this Jacobian positive. Incorporating the climate within which equities trading takes place by multiplying (9.30) by $\beta_{\pi_e}$ and (9.31) by $\beta_{p_e}$ and doing the appropriate elimination we obtain:

$$J^{(7)} = \begin{bmatrix} 0 & + & - & - & 0 & 0 & 0 \\ - & 0 & + & + & + & + & 0 \\ \pm & + & - & + & + & + & 0 \\ 0 & + & + & + & + & 0 & 0 \\ 0 & 0 & 0 & 0 & - & 0 & 0 \\ 0 & 0 & - & 0 & 0 & - & + \\ 0 & 0 & 0 & 0 & 0 & 0 & - \end{bmatrix}$$

Where the bottom right negative entry holds if $\beta_{p_e} < 1$. It is therefore straightforward to ascertain that this 7D sub-system is stable. The Blanchard effect involves the interaction between the stock market and output. This interaction is here stable provided there are sufficiently weak accelerator effects in the investment function and stock price adjustment to discrepancies between the rate of profit and the real short rate are sufficiently small. Next we include exchange rate effects, the resultant sub-system becomes:

$$J^{(8)} = \begin{bmatrix} 0 & + & - & - & 0 & 0 & 0 & + \\ - & 0 & + & + & + & + & 0 & + \\ \pm & + & - & + & + & + & 0 & + \\ 0 & + & + & + & + & 0 & 0 & - \\ 0 & 0 & 0 & 0 & - & 0 & 0 & 0 \\ 0 & 0 & - & 0 & 0 & - & + & 0 \\ 0 & 0 & 0 & 0 & 0 & 0 & - & 0 \\ 0 & 0 & + & + & 0 & 0 & 0 & 0 \end{bmatrix}$$

Stability in this system is established if the response of the current account to the rate of domestic capacity utilization and the real exchange rate is small, and in turn allow the short-term interest rate to react positively when the nominal exchange rate changes. The latter policy rule ensures that some negative feedback of the exchange rate to its rate of depreciation is established. Incorporating the climate term in these dynamics, and performing the necessary eliminations we have the following structure:

$$J^{(9)} = \begin{bmatrix} 0 & + & - & - & 0 & 0 & 0 & + & - \\ - & 0 & + & + & + & + & 0 & + & 0 \\ \pm & + & - & + & + & + & 0 & + & + \\ 0 & + & + & + & + & 0 & 0 & - & + \\ 0 & 0 & 0 & 0 & - & 0 & 0 & 0 & 0 \\ 0 & 0 & - & 0 & 0 & - & + & 0 & 0 \\ 0 & 0 & 0 & 0 & 0 & 0 & - & 0 & 0 \\ 0 & 0 & + & + & 0 & 0 & 0 & 0 & + \\ 0 & 0 & 0 & 0 & 0 & 0 & 0 & 0 & - \end{bmatrix}$$

It is also easy to show that the determinant of this sub-system is negative. Incorporating the bond market in this framework leads to the following structure:

$$J^{(10)} = \begin{bmatrix} 0 & + & - & - & 0 & 0 & 0 & + & - & 0 \\ - & 0 & + & + & + & + & 0 & + & 0 & - \\ \pm & + & - & + & + & + & 0 & + & + & - \\ 0 & + & + & + & + & 0 & 0 & - & + & 0 \\ 0 & 0 & 0 & 0 & - & 0 & 0 & 0 & 0 & 0 \\ 0 & 0 & - & 0 & 0 & - & + & 0 & 0 & 0 \\ 0 & 0 & 0 & 0 & 0 & 0 & - & 0 & 0 & 0 \\ 0 & 0 & + & + & 0 & 0 & 0 & 0 & + & 0 \\ 0 & 0 & 0 & 0 & 0 & 0 & 0 & 0 & - & 0 \\ 0 & 0 & 0 & 0 & 0 & 0 & 0 & 0 & 0 & - \end{bmatrix}$$

This sub-system is stable since the determinant is negative. Incorporating the climate in the bond market and performing the appropriate eliminations we have the following structure:

$$J^{(11)} = \begin{bmatrix} 0 & + & - & - & 0 & 0 & 0 & + & - & 0 & 0 \\ - & 0 & + & + & + & + & 0 & + & 0 & - & 0 \\ \pm & + & - & + & + & + & 0 & + & + & - & 0 \\ 0 & + & + & + & + & 0 & 0 & - & + & 0 & 0 \\ 0 & 0 & 0 & 0 & - & 0 & 0 & 0 & 0 & 0 & 0 \\ 0 & 0 & - & 0 & 0 & - & + & 0 & 0 & 0 & 0 \\ 0 & 0 & 0 & 0 & 0 & 0 & - & 0 & 0 & 0 & 0 \\ 0 & 0 & + & + & 0 & 0 & 0 & 0 & + & 0 & 0 \\ 0 & 0 & 0 & 0 & 0 & 0 & 0 & 0 & - & 0 & 0 \\ 0 & 0 & 0 & 0 & 0 & 0 & 0 & 0 & 0 & - & + \\ 0 & 0 & 0 & 0 & 0 & 0 & 0 & 0 & 0 & 0 & - \end{bmatrix}$$

This sub-system is also stable. We thus conclude that modest reactions of the central bank to the employment rate tend to stabilize the Goodwin cycle. In addition slow adjustment speeds for nominal wages and prices in response to demand pressures together with sufficiently small exchange rate flexibility promote stability. We have also found that small accelerator effects in the investment function and a sufficiently small adjustment speed of the stock market promote stability. In the analysis above, we have not included the policy rule (9.23). However it is clear from our analysis that a response by the central bank to exchange rate fluctuations creates a stronger error-correction force that is stabilizes the Dornbusch effect in the foreign exchange market. Similarly, if the central bank responds to stock price fluctuations it creates an error-correcting term that tends to stabilize the Blanchard effects in the stock market. Destabilizing Rose effects can be weakened depending on whether price setting or wage setting is forward-looking.

## Estimation and simulation

In order to calibrate the model, we use South African quarterly data from 1960:1–2006:4. Most of the variables were taken from the IMF database, whilst some were taken from the database of the South African Reserve Bank. We should mention that some of the data series were annual, and so an interpolation technique was used to get corresponding quarterly series. Specifically, data on the fixed capital stock and the employment rate were interpolated into quarterly series. The series on the employment rate was taken from survey reports by the South African Institute of Race Relations.

The estimation strategy we adopt follows closely the approach taken by Flaschel *et al.* (2001). The model is estimated partly as a sub-system and partly in single-equation form. The wage-price dynamics were estimated using 2SLS. The climate variables were measured as four-quarter moving averages of the relevant variables, i.e.:

$$x_t = \frac{1}{4}\sum_{j=0}^{3} x_{t-j} \tag{9.35}$$

Variables such as the exchange rate and the stock price were estimated as indices, with the base year being 2000. This scaling allows for comparison of the estimated parameters associated with these variables to the rest of the parameters in the relevant equations. The usual econometric diagnostics were conducted for each equation, especially serial correlation and parameter stability tests. In some cases, dummy variables were used to

*Table 9.1* Estimated parameters (standard errors in parentheses)

| | | | |
|---|---|---|---|
| Wage-price | $\beta_p = 0.037\ (0.016)$ | Current account | $x_q = 0.03\ (0.00)$ |
| | $\beta_w = 0.64\ (0.11)$ | | $x_{y^f} = 0.05\ (0.00)$ |
| | $\beta_e = 0.03\ (0.01)$ | | $m_q = 0.05\ (0.00)$ |
| | $\beta_\pi = 0.50\ (0.02)$ | | $m_y = 0.43\ (0.01)$ |
| | $\kappa_p = 0.57\ (0.08)$ | Financial markets | $\beta_{p_e} = 0.70\ (0.04)$ |
| | $\kappa_w = 0.0\ (0.00)$ | | $\beta_{\pi_e} = 0.55\ (0.03)$ |
| Production | $y^p = 0.46\ (0.00)$ | | $\beta_e = 0.79\ (0.20)$ |
| | $\beta_V = 1.58\ (0.13)$ | | $\beta_c = 1.05\ (0.27)$ |
| | $\beta_U = 0.01\ (0.006)$ | | $\beta_\varepsilon = 0.60\ (0.03)$ |
| Consumption | $s_c = 0.86\ (0.06)$ | | $\beta_{r^l} = 0.76\ (0.05)$ |
| | $s_w = 0.79\ (0.08)$ | | $\beta_{\pi_{r^l}} = 0.52\ (0.02)$ |
| | $\psi = 0.013\ (0.01)$ | Policy rule | $\beta_{r\widehat{p}} = 0.10\ (0.026)$ |
| | $\omega = 0.00\ (0.00)$ | | $\beta_{rU} = 0.02\ (0.008)$ |
| Investment | $i_\rho = 0.024\ (0.00)$ | | $\beta_{rV} = 0.74\ (0.08)$ |
| | $i_U = 0.034\ (0.00)$ | | $\beta_{re} = 0.03\ (0.006)$ |
| | $i_{p_e} = 0.01\ (0.00)$ | | $\beta_{rp_e} = -0.03\ (0.004)$ |

control for well known episodes such as the 1997/98 emerging market crisis and South African specific events. Table 9.1 gives the estimates of the parameters of the model.

We remark that in estimating the wage-price spiral, we used a detrended employment rate for the wage-price estimation, which shows that shows $\beta_w$ is statistically significant, and greater than $\beta_p$. Thus, according to our estimation rigidities are more in price-setting than in wage-setting in South Africa. This finding is in line with Flaschel *et al.* (2001) and contrasts with Fair (2000) in relation to US data. The implication of this estimation for monetary policy is that the central bank should be more aggressive against labor market pressures than the goods market. This view is supported by the estimated interest rate policy rule in Table 9.1, where $\beta_{rU} = 0.02$ while $\beta_{rV} = 0.74$. In addition the wage-price estimation suggests that workers are backward-looking in the approach, since $\kappa_w = 0$.

The production bloc of the model shows very sluggish adjustment of the goods market to demand fluctuations with $\beta_U = 0.01$. We estimate the employment rate adjustment equation in two stages. In the first stage, we estimate the growth rate of employment as determined by the investment-capital ratio. In the second stage, we insert the estimated growth rate of employment into the growth rate of the employment rate $\widehat{V}$. Our estimation shows that the growth rate of employment is very sensitive to the growth rate of fixed capital, with $\beta_V = 1.58$. The estimated policy rule exhibits central bank accommodation of stock price fluctuations, given the wrong sign for $\beta_{rp_e}$. This is problematic as it potentially accentuates the destabilizing forces of the Blanchard real-financial interaction. Indeed simulations of the model under the estimated policy rule results in explosive behavior which can nevertheless be tamed by increasing the aggressiveness of the central bank to endogenous variables. The rest of the parameters are self-explanatory.

The key mechanism that drives fluctuations in our monetary model is the Goodwin cycle. As a starting point towards considering in detail the types of policy rules that can stabilize the economy, we simulate a partial model based on our estimations in order to show in a simple way what monetary policy can achieve in the presence of the Goodwin mechanism. This partial model is constituted by elements of (9.7) and (9.16), having frozen the other

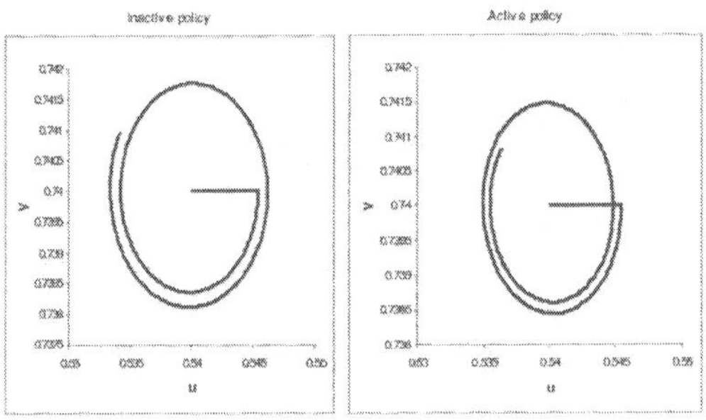


*Figure 9.1* The Goodwin cycle in a partial framework: the role of policy

variables in this sub-system at their steady state. This partial model is then subjected to a temporary shock to the wage share. Figure 9.1 illustrates two cases; one wherein monetary policy is completely inactive and the other wherein monetary policy is active.

In the first case the initial shock sets off a cyclical interaction between the wage share and the employment rate, which turns out to be explosive. However by allowing for an active monetary policy, wherein the short-term interest rate adjusts with sufficient strength to fluctuations in the employment rate, the initial shock to the labor share no longer produces explosive cyclical responses. Figure 9.1 illustrates these results. In the case of an active monetary policy against employment rate fluctuations, the cycle ultimately converges towards the steady state. We could, of course, have formulated a simple policy rule that reacts to the wage share as explored in Asada *et al.* (2006). In such a case stability would arise via the exchange rate channel, which is a channel through which the short rate features, thus creating an error-correction type term in the law of motion of the wage share.

The observation that an appropriately activist Taylor-type monetary policy is capable of ensuring stability in a Goodwin setting lays the basis for a discussion of the types of policy rules that can stabilize the economy. The inertial response of price inflation relative to nominal wage inflation to labor market and goods market demand gaps implies intuitively, that the destabilizing forces from the Goodwin cycle can best be combated by a relatively more aggressive policy response against fluctuations in the employment rate. In order to now explore the stabilizing properties of monetary policy for the whole model given the estimated parameters, we proceed by first specifying a rule that responds more aggressively to asset prices than estimated:

$$\tilde{r} = 0.1\tilde{\hat{p}} + 0.02\tilde{U} + 0.74\tilde{V} + 0.14\tilde{e} + 0.012\tilde{p}_e \tag{9.36}$$

We explore the behavior of the economy when subjected to a temporary and expansionary monetary policy action. Figure 9.2 illustrates the response of the economy under this shock. We have plotted in Figure 9.2 the phase portrait of the Goodwin cycle which is the core cyclical process in our model. Although explosive, we observe that at relatively low levels of the wage share $u$, the rate of profit is high and investment expenditure rises, leading to an expansion in the employment rate. However, as the rate of employment rises workers gain bargaining power and the labor market gets progressively tight. This ultimately squeezes the rate of profit, which discourages investment and therefore lowers the rate of employment.

The other plot in Figure 9.2 shows the impulse responses of the nominal wage and price inflation rates to an expansionary monetary shock, which are both explosive over time. We now increase the response of the central bank to the stock price in (9.36) to $\beta_{rp_e} = 0.15$. This

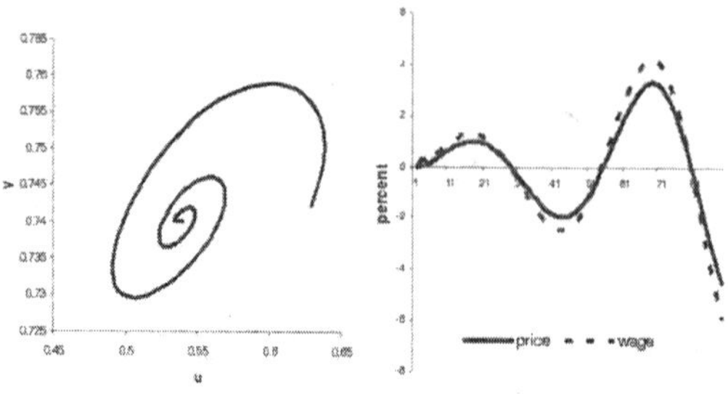


*Figure 9.2* Macro-instability under temporary expansionary monetary shock

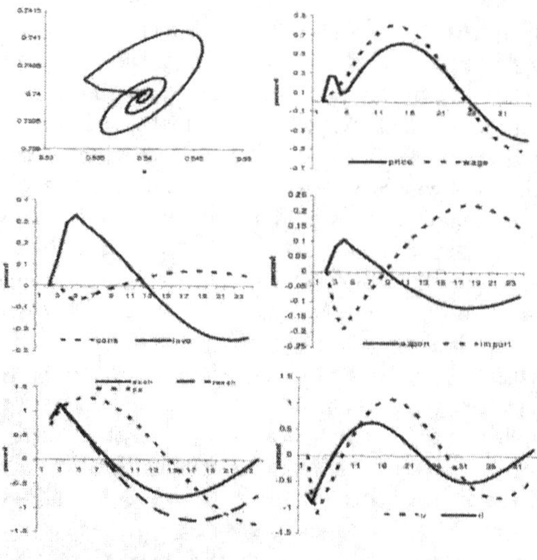


*Figure 9.3* Macro-instability with more aggressive response to stock price fluctuations

more aggressive stance against stock price fluctuations tends to enforce stability, implying that the Blanchard destabilizing forces are relatively strong in this model. The stable results are summarized in Figure 9.3.

The nominal wage and price inflation rates initially rise in response to a temporary reduction in the short-term interest rate, as expected. There are various channels through which this result is produced, here we only explain two of these. First, because of the fall in the short rate, the nominal exchange rate weakens. This puts upward pressure on price and nominal wage inflation via the import channel. Second, the fall in the short rate increases the stock price and also lowers the long rate, these two developments in financial markets push investment expenditure upwards. As a result the employment rate rises. The rise in the employment rate increases both the nominal wage and price inflation rates.

Consumption and investment expenditure respond as expected. In response to a fall in the short rate, investment initially rises via the domestic financial market channel. Because this policy shift also weakens the currency and creates inflationary pressures, the wage share falls initially and consequently increases the rate of profit. However, the fall in the wage share lowers consumption expenditure because of Kaldorian consumption habits. Because of a weak currency exports rise, and imports decline, leading to an improvement in the current account balance.

In response to a fall in the short rate, the real and nominal exchange rates jump, but only reach their maximum after approximately one quarter and thereafter they appreciate because of the improvement in the current account balance. Since there is inertial price inflation adjustment, the impact of the nominal short rate on the real exchange rate is much more persistent than on the nominal exchange rate. Although there is some small delay before the exchange rate reaches its maximum, the size of the exchange rate jump makes our model to be closer to that of Dornbusch (1976) than the "delayed overshooting" effect observed by Christiano and Eichenbaum (1995). Our impulse responses nevertheless resemble those found by Cushman and Zha (1997). The stock price reaches its maximum after six quarters. Thereafter, the stock price disinflates under pressure from the tightening of monetary policy over the period among other factors.

In a different set of simulations not reported here, we have reduced the response of the central bank the exchange rate fluctuations and found that monetary policy then fails to maintain stability. Increasing the reaction of the central bank against inflation fluctuations tends to increase the volatility of macro-aggregates. And finally, increasing the reaction of the central bank to the capacity utilization gap does not produce significant changes in the response of the economy. Based on the above model specification and estimated parameters, our model does not support the proposals by Bernanke and Gertler (2001) and Clarida *et al.* (2001), and point towards the importance of incorporating asset prices in the policy-setting process. Instead these results support the proposal by Kent and Lowe (1997), Cecchetti *et al.* (2000, 2001), and Genberg (2001) among others.

At this stage it is important to mention that our framework is designed to analyze the implications of monetary policy rules in the context of a Keynes-Goodwin model. The results derived above may therefore be sensitive to model specification. Our framework is practically oriented in the sense proposed by Taylor (1995) in that it ignores asset accumulation and instead focuses on asset prices. In particular, our model does not take into account Blanchard-Katz (1999) type error-correction terms in the wage-price spiral as explored in Asada *et al.* (2006). This mechanism may play a significant stabilizing role, requiring only minor reactions of the central to ensure stability.

## Conclusion

This chapter has sought to develop a Keynesian framework for practical policy analysis in small open economies. At the core of our model is a Goodwin cycle, according to which the employment rate falls at high wage share levels and recovers at low wage share levels. In order to clearly bring forward this mechanism in a monetary model, we formulated an investment-based Okun's law through which the growth rate of the employment is directly dependant on the rate of investment. In addition to this mechanism we have incorporated three asset prices that adjust with finite speeds, through which monetary policy actions are propagated to real economic activity.

Given the existence of two Phillips curves in our model, our finding is that the degree to which the central bank responds to demand pressure should be informed by the sources and nature of rigidities that prevail in the economy. In general, the central bank should not respond to a demand pressure term associated with a market that is to a large extent characterized by rigidities. Instead monetary policy should focus on the market characterized to a large extent by flexibility. Through our stability analysis, and model simulations, we found that a policy rule that is indifferent to asset price fluctuations may fail to ensure stability.

## Acknowledgments

We would like to acknowledge Likeleli Pitso for excellent research assistance.

## References

Amato, J.D. and Laubach, T. (2003) Estimation and control of an optimization-based model with sticky prices and wages, *Journal of Economic Dynamics and Control* 27, 1181–215.

Asada, T., Chen, P., Chiarella, C. and Flaschel, P. (2006) Keynesian dynamics and the wage-price spiral: A baseline disequilibrium model, *Journal of Macroeconomics* 28, 90–130.

Ball, L. (1999) Policy for open economies, in Taylor, J.B. (ed.) *Monetary Policy Rules*. University of Chicago Press: Chicago.

Ball, L. (2002) Policy rules and external shocks. In Loayza, N. and Schmidt-Hebbel, K. (eds), *Monetary Policy: Rules and Transmission Mechanisms*. Central Bank of Chile: Santiago.

Bernanke, B. and Gertler, M. (1999) Monetary policy and asset price volatility. *Federal Reserve Bank of Kansas City Economic Review*, 84, 17–52.

Bernanke, B. and Gertler, M. (2001) Should central banks respond to movements in asset prices? *American Economic Review Papers and Proceedings* 91, 253–7.

Blanchard, O.J. (1981)Output, the stock market and interest rates. *American Economic Review* 71, 132–43.

Blanchard, O.J. (n.d) Comments on "Inflation targeting in transition economies; Experience and prospects", by Jiri Jonas and Frederic Mishkin. http://econ-www.mit.edu/files/733. (accessed 07 August 2007).

Blanchard, O.J. and Katz, F. (1999) Wage dynamics: Reconciling theory and evidence, *American Economic Review* 89, 132–43.

Borio, C. and Lowe, P. (2002) *Asset Prices, Financial and Monetary Stability.* BIS Working Paper no. 114.

Cecchetti, S. *et al.* (2000) *Asset Prices and Central Bank Policy*. Geneva Report on the World Economy 2, Centre for Economic Policy Research and International Centre for Monetary and Banking Studies.

Cecchetti, S. *et. al.* (2002) Asset prices in a flexible inflation targeting framework. Paper prepared for the conference on "Asset Price Bubbles: Implications for monetary policy, regulatory, and international policies", Federal Reserve Bank of Chicago and the World Bank.

Chiarella, C. and Flaschel, P. (1999) Keynesian monetary growth dynamics in open economies, *Annals of Operations Research* 89, 35–59.

Chiarella, C. and Flaschel, P. (2000) *The Dynamics of Keynesian Monetary Growth.* Cambridge: Cambridge University Press.

Christiano, L.J. and Eichenbaum, M. (2005) Nominal rigidities and the dynamic effects of a shock to monetary policy, *Journal of Political Economy* 113, 1–45.

Clarida R., Gali., J. and Gertler, M. (2001) Optimal monetary policy in open versus closed economies: An integrated approach. *American Economic Review Papers and Proceedings* 2001, 248–52.

Cushman, D.O. and Zha, T. (1997) Identifying monetary policy in a small open economy under flexible exchange rates, *Journal of Monetary Economics* 39, 433–48.

Dornbusch, R. (1976) Expectations and exchange rate dynamics, *Journal of Political Economy* 84, 1161–75.

Eichenbaum, M. and Evans, C.L. (1995) Some empirical evidence on the effects of shocks to monetary policy on exchange rates, *Quarterly Journal of Economics* 110, 975–1009.

Erceg, C.J., Henderson, D.W., and Levin, A.T. (2000) Optimal monetary policy with staggered wage and price contracts, *Journal of Monetary Economics* 46, 281–313.

Fair, R. (2000) Testing the Nairu model for the United States, *Review of Economics and Statistics* 82, 64–71.

Flaschel, P., Gong, G. and Semmler, W. (2001) A Keynesian macroeconometric framework for the analysis of monetary policy rules. *Journal of Economic Behavior and Organization* 46, 101–36.

Genberg, H. (2001) Asset prices, monetary policy and macroeconomic stability, *De Economist* 149, 433–53.

Gilchrist, S. and J.V. Leahy (2002) Monetary policy and asset prices, *Journal of Monetary Economics*, 49, 75–97.

Goodwin, R. A growth cycle, in Feinstein, C.H. (ed.) *Socialism, Capitalism and Economic Growth*, Cambridge University Press: Cambridge.

Huang, X.D. and Liu, Z. (2002) Staggered price-setting, staggered wage-setting, and business cycle persistence, *Journal of Monetary Economics* 49, 405–33.

Kent, C. and Lows, P. (1997) *Asset Price Bubbles and Monetary Policy*, Research Discussion Paper 9707, Reserve Bank of Australia.

McCallum, B.T. (1999) Issues in the design of monetary policy rules. In Taylor, J.B. and Woodford, M. (eds) *Handbook of Macroeconomics 1C*, North-Holland: Amsterdam.

McCallum, B.T. (2001) Should monetary policy respond strongly to output gaps? *American Economic Review Papers and Proceedings* 91, 258–62.

Mishkin, F.S. (2000) Inflation targeting in emerging-market countries. *American Economic Review* 90, 105–9.

Mohanty, M.S. and Klau, M. (2004) *Monetary Policy Rules in Emerging Market Economies: Issues and Evidence*, BIS Working Paper no. 149

Pindyck, R.S. and Rubinfeld D.L. (1994) *Econometric Models and Economic Forecasts* 3rd edn. McGraw-Hill Inc.: New York.

Rose, H. (1967) On the non-linear theory of the employment cycle, *Review of Economic Studies* 34, 153–73.

Semmler, W. and Zhang, W. (2007) Asset price volatility and monetary policy rules, *Economic Modelling* 24, 411–30.

Svensson, L.E.O. (1997) Inflation forecast targeting: Implementing and monitoring inflation targets, *European Economic Review* 41, 1111–46.

Taylor, J.B. (1993) Discretion versus policy in practice. *Carnegie-Rochester Conference Series on Public Policy* 39, 195–214.

Taylor, J.B. (1995) The monetary transmission mechanism: An empirical framework, *Journal of Economic Perspectives* 9, Fall, 11–26.

Taylor, J.B. (2001) The role of the exchange rate in monetary policy rules. *American Economic Review Papers and Proceedings* 91, 258–62.

Tobin, J. (1969) A general equilibrium approach to monetary theory, *Journal of Money, Credit and Banking* 1, 15–29.

# 10 Semi-structural Keynes–Goodwin modeling

## Elaboration and calibration of a baseline theoretical framework

*Reiner Franke, Peter Flaschel and Christian R. Proaño*

## Introduction[1]

The present chapter is related to current work on modern macroeconomic modeling in a, broadly speaking, Keynesian (but not New-Keynesian) tradition. It particularly draws on the disequilibrium approach advanced in Chiarella *et al.* (2005), which refers to Keynes, Metzler, Goodwin and Taylor as its patron saints. 'Goodwin' indicates that income distribution plays a crucial role in the dynamics. In the form of the wage share, it is determined by the interplay of a wage as well as a price Phillips curve, and in turn impacts positively on aggregate demand *via* workers' consumption and negatively *via* profit-oriented investment. The Metzlerian part is a consequence of goods market disequilibrium, which is absorbed by inventories, while the evolution of the latter feeds back on planned inventory investment and thus aggregate supply. 'Taylor' takes account of monetary policy and follows the general consensus reached over the last decade that the central bank adopts an interest rate rule, most often specified as a variant of the Taylor rule responding to inflation and the output gap. Though modeled in a parsimonious way, when combined with sales and inflation expectations the dynamic system obtained in the end is six-dimensional. This means limited prospects for an analytical treatment, so that the model has to be studied by means of numerical simulations, an endeavor for which numerical values have to be assigned to the parameters. Chiarella *et al.* (2005, Ch. 5 and 6) use calibration methods for the parameter search, which amounts to an extensive investigation that requires judgement and dealing with a great variety of details.[2]

Nevertheless, since the "Keynes-Metzler-Goodwin-Taylor model" cannot be easily estimated by econometric methods due to some components which are too differentiated and some of the disequilibrium adjustment rules which include composed variables whose empirical counterparts, or their behavior, are problematic, a good strategy is to take a step backward and simplify the model at the cost of sacrificing some of its structure. The equations thus arising will no longer meet all standards one can demand from a consistent theoretical model, although they still have more structure than many other theoretically motivated estimation equations. In effect, what such a simplification will arrive at can be best described as a *semi-structural* model.

The remainder of this chapter is organized as follows. In the next section we describe the theoretical model as a closed dynamic system consisting of four-dimensional deterministic differential equations, and formulate its discrete-time analogue. We estimate and calibrate the model by means of an impulse-response analysis in "Econometric estimation and calibration of the model". "Wage and price flexibilities" is devoted to a deeper analysis of the properties of the system and the numerical coefficients on which we thus settle down, and investigates whether *ceteris paribus* variations of a parameter are stabilizing or destabilizing by means of an eigen-value analysis. "Variabilities in the stochastic economy" is concerned with the stochastic economy, where the expressions refer to a decrease or increase of the standard deviations of the model-generated time series. As an upshot of these investigations, both sections present a table that succinctly classifies the parameters in the wage–price dynamics as stabilizing, destabilizing or ambiguous. "Wage—price dynamics and income distribution" focuses on the effects of the wage and price inflation dynamics for income distribution by analyzing a scenario which seeks to reflect the increasing pressure under which the position of workers has come in recent years. Here as well as in the following the distinction between a profit-led and wage-led regime becomes relevant. This notion means that a rise in the wage share induces a negative reaction of capacity utilization (as estimated) or a positive reaction, respectively. The final section concludes.

## A semi-structural Keynes–Goodwin framework

In this section we formulate a semi-structural Keynesian macroeconomic framework in the line of Chiarella *et al.* (2005) and Asada *et al.* (2006). Due to the easy growth rate formulations for composed variables we set up our model in a deterministic, continuous time framework. The time derivative of a dynamic variable $x = x(t)$ is denoted $\dot{x} = dx/dt$, and its growth rate $\hat{x} = \dot{x}/x$. The underlying unit of time is to be thought of as a year. Hence a term $\hat{x}$ in the continuous-time framework approximately equals $4 \cdot d\ \ln(x_t)$ if it is related to its counterpart in the estimated quarterly model. The steady state value of $x$ is designated $x^o$.

### *Output and employment adjustments*

We start the description of our theoretical model with the specification of the goods and labor market dynamics. Taking the rate of capacity utilization $y$ as a proxy for the output gap, we can formulate a type of dynamic IS equation where the growth rate in the rate of capacity utilization of the economy is determined by:

$$\hat{y} = -\beta_{yy}(y-1) - \beta_{yi}[i - \hat{p} - (i^o - \hat{p}^o)] - \gamma_{yv}(v - v^o)/v^o. \qquad (10.1)$$

As Equation (10.1) is formulated, the growth rate of capacity utilization depends negatively on the deviations of capacity utilization, the real interest rate $i - \hat{p}$, and the wage share $v$ from their respective steady state values. Note nevertheless that the effect of the wage share might be positive in the case where the goods market dynamics are wage- and not profit-led.

Since Equation (10.1) views output as demand-driven, employment has to adjust accordingly. In this respect we do not refer to an explicit production function but specify the changes in the rate (not the volume) of employment as an empirical regularity, as a version of Okun's law with distributed lags. For its translation into continuous time, these lags on the right-hand collapse and we get $\hat{e} = \beta_{ey}\hat{y}$. However, this quite simple formulation of the labor market dynamics, once gathered with the other dynamic equations, would give rise to a continuum of equilibrium points. The critical issue is not so much multiplicity as such, but the feature that the equilibrium values of several variables will generally depart from their target or benchmark values.[3] In order to avoid this inconsistency we add to the changes in utilization the influence of the wage share. Our idea is that in times of rising capacity utilization the creation of new jobs is a little delayed if wages are already relatively high. To evaluate the current wage share as relatively high or low, its steady state value $v^o$ is used as a benchmark. This leads us to augment Okun's law as:

$$\hat{e} = \beta_{ey}\hat{y} - \beta_{ev}(v - v^o)/v^o \tag{10.2}$$

where $\beta_{ey}$ is a small 'error correction' coefficient. In the following calibration of the model, we set $\beta_{ey} = 0.30$ according to Okun's rule of thumb, after which the unemployment rate changes inversely 1:3 with the output gap; production must rise by three percent in order to reduce the unemployment rate by one percentage point.

## *Labor productivity as an endogenous variable*

Now we come to a first attempt to endogenize the growth rate of labor productivity $\hat{z}$ which, together with the wage and price Phillips Curves to be introduced below, will deliver a law of motion for the wage share $v = wL/pY = (w/p)/z$, by way of the growth rates $\hat{v} = \hat{w} - \hat{p} - \hat{z}$.

It should first of all be made explicit that although the model considers variable growth rates of labor productivity, it neglects the distinction between movements in hours and the number of jobs. We just write $L$ for employment and express by $z = Y/L$ the ratio of output to the number of current jobs. Nevertheless, since "output–employment ratio" would be an unfamiliar expression, we continue to call $z$ labor productivity.

As an initial step in the determination of the productivity growth rate, observe that if the changes of productive capacity $Y^c$ in the expression for utilization $y = Y/Y^c$, and the changes of the labor force $L^s$ in the employment rate $e = L/L^s$, are given, then, with $\hat{y} = \hat{Y} - \hat{Y}^c$ and $\hat{e} = \hat{L} - \hat{L}^s$, productivity growth results as:

$$\hat{z} \;=\; \hat{Y} - \hat{L} = (\hat{y} + \hat{Y}^c) \;-\; (\hat{e} + \hat{L}^s)$$

Two options can be considered to integrate this open expression into the present framework. In a first specification, productive capacity $Y^c$ can be viewed as being given by the firms' stock of fixed capital, $Y^c = u^n K$, where the constant $u^n$ is the output–capital ratio that would prevail under 'normal' conditions (in the presence of Harrod-neutral technical progress). In this way, $\hat{Y} = \hat{y} + \hat{Y}^c = \hat{y} + \hat{K}$. Here, on the one hand, we could introduce more structure into the model by not only making aggregate demand explicit but also the component of net investment ($I = \hat{K}$).

On the other hand, the labor force $L^s$ may not be regarded as an exogenously growing part of the population but as responding to the general economic climate. While this is certainly a relevant phenomenon, these adjustments will take some time in the real world. As a theoretical short-cut we might nevertheless proxy the economic climate by the growth rate of the capital stock, less the (constant) growth rate of trend productivity $g_z$, and assume that the adjustments of the labor force are instantaneous, which provides us with $\hat{L}^s = \hat{K} - g_z$. With these specifications, the above equation for the actual growth rate of labor productivity becomes:

$$\hat{z} = \hat{y} \;-\; \hat{e} \;+\; g_z \tag{10.3}$$

If the assumption on the labor force is felt to be too restrictive, one can alternatively proxy productive capacity by the concept of potential output, which grows at a constant rate $\hat{Y}^c = g^o$. In fact, $(y-1)$ could then be referred to as the output gap, which is the usual representation of economic activity in most of the small-scale models of the 'new consensus in macroeconomics'. Suppose, furthermore, that also the labor force grows at a constant rate, $\hat{L}^s = g_\ell$. The two rates $g^o$ and $g_\ell$ are linked by the growth rate $g_z$ of trend productivity; without suggesting any causal direction the steady state relationship between output, labor force and productivity reads $g^o - g_\ell - g_z = 0$.[4] The implication for the changes in actual productivity is $\hat{z} = (\hat{y} + g^o) - (\hat{e} + g_\ell) = \hat{y} - \hat{e} + (g^o - g_\ell) = \hat{y} - \hat{e} + g_z$, which coincides with (10.3).

## *The wage and price Phillips curves*

The separate modeling of the wage and price dynamics is one of the main building blocks of theoretical approach by Chiarella *et al.* (2005), which takes into account that the dynamics of the two variables are likely to be influenced in a direct manner by the situations of different markets (labor and goods markets, respectively), but nevertheless also be interdependent. Note that this approach is diametrically opposite to the DSGE (Dynamic Stochastic General Equilibrium) approach to the modeling of wage–price dynamics, as discussed for example in Erceg *et al.* (2000) and Christiano *et al.* (2005), where adjustments of these variables are the result of a monopolistic, intertemporal optimal wage and price setting by households (!) and firms, respectively, under a Calvo (1983) type of staggered contracting environment. In these types of models, labor and goods market conditions, as well as institutional agents such as trade unions, do not play a role for the dynamic behavior of wages and prices.

By contrast, in Chiarella *et al.* (2005), the main driving variable of the wage Phillips curve (WPC) is the employment rate, with additionally the wage share affecting negatively the dynamic behavior of nominal wages. The negative influence of the wage share in (10.4) can be interpreted as arising from a wage bargaining process where the parties also have an eye on the general distribution of total income. At relatively low values of the wage share, workers seek to catch up to what is considered a normal, or 'fair', level, and they succeed in including this aspect in the wage bargaining. By the same token, workers are somewhat restrained in their wage claims if $v$ is currently above normal. Another theoretical (and perhaps more fashionable) underpinning could be borrowed from Blanchard and Katz (1999). They specify a wage curve argument in which the tighter the labor market, the higher the level (!) of the real wage, given the workers' reservation wage. The wage share enters this scenario in a logarithmic form by assuming that the reservation wage depends on labor productivity and lagged wages. A detailed translation of this approach into Equation (10.4) is given in Chiarella, Flaschel and Franke (2005, pp.170ff). Blanchard and Katz quote evidence from macroeconomic as well regional data that, for the United States, (their counterpart for) the coefficient $\beta_{wv}$ is close to zero (in contrast to most European countries). Proaño *et al.* (2006), using a more up-to-date methodology, a system GMM approach, find nevertheless that, while the coefficient of the labor share is indeed significant and numerically higher than in the US estimation, in the latter it also turns out to be significantly bounded away from zero.

The fully structural wage Phillips curve is given by:

$$\hat{w} = [\kappa_{wz}\hat{z} + (1-\kappa_{wz})g_z] + [\kappa_{wp}\hat{p} + (1-\kappa_{wp})\pi^c] + f_w(e,v) \tag{10.4}$$

$$f_w(e,v) = \beta_{we}(e - e^o) - \beta_{wv}(v - v^o)/v^o$$

where the two first terms in square brackets provide additional benchmarks for neutral wage adjustments, in the sense that wages increase in line with productivity and (current and expected) prices. The functional expression $f_w$ summarizes the two driving variables, employment and the wage share. As already indicated in note 3 above, $e^o$ is here treated as an exogenously given 'natural' rate of employment, the counterpart of the usual NAIRU specification. Regarding the coefficient $\kappa_{wz}$ on labor productivity growth, the steady state condition $\hat{v} = \hat{w} - \hat{p} - \hat{z} = 0$ has to be observed. Hence, with $\pi^c = \hat{p}$ in this position, the steady state condition implies $\hat{p}+\hat{z}=\hat{w}=\kappa_{wp}\hat{p}+(1-\kappa_{wp})\pi^c+\kappa_{wz}\hat{z}+(1-\kappa_{wz})g_z$, where $g_z$ denotes the growth rate of trend productivity.

With respect to the price Phillips curve (PPC), besides capacity utilization as the main driving variable, again the wage share takes effect in this relationship in a positive manner though. Cost push terms are contemporaneous wage inflation and the inflation climate, whereas productivity growth may have a negative effect.

When assigning the weights of these variables, it has to be noted that benchmark inflation is formed as a weighted average, not of the inflation climate $\pi^c$ and wage inflation, but of $\pi^c$ and wage inflation corrected for productivity growth. Regarding the latter, it is only natural to assume that the growth of actual and trend productivity is weighted in the same manner as in the wage Phillips curve. The price Phillips curve is thus:

$$\hat{p}=\kappa_{pw}\{\hat{w}-[\kappa_{wz}\hat{z}+(1-\kappa_{wz})g_z]\}\;+\;(1-\kappa_{pw})\pi^c\;+f_p(y,v) \tag{10.5}$$
$$f_p(y,v)=\beta_{py}\,(y-1)\;+\;\beta_{pv}\,(v-v^o)/v^o.$$

The positive influence of the wage share in the equation can be explained by a target markup rate $\mu$ that firms may wish to realize.[5] Besides the other arguments in (10.5), firms raise prices if labor costs are currently so high that $pY<(1+\mu)\,wL$, which is equivalent to $(1+\mu)\,wL/pY-1=(1+\mu)\,v-1>0$. If the target markup is consistent with equilibrium income distribution, $1+\mu=1/v^o$ and we obtain the wage share deviations specified in (10.5).

The contemporaneous cross rates of inflation in WPC and PPC reflect the idea of myopic perfect foresight in the nominal variables. The wage and price Phillips curves have to take the role of $\kappa_{wp}$, $\kappa_{w\pi}$, $\kappa_{wz}$ and $\kappa_{pw}$, $\kappa_{p\pi}$, $\kappa_{pz}$ as weights into account, whereas the weights on current inflation ($\kappa_{wp}$) and the inflation climate ($\kappa_{wp\pi}$) should add up to one.

Since the rates of wage and price inflation appear on both sides of (10.4) and (10.5), the equations still have to be solved for the reduced-form expressions of the two inflation rates. They are computed as:

$$\hat{w}=\kappa_{wz}\hat{z}+(1-\kappa_{wz})g_z\;+\;\pi^c\;+\;\kappa\,[f_w(e,v)+\kappa_{wp}f_p(y,v)] \tag{10.6}$$
$$\hat{p}=\pi^c\;+\;\kappa\,[f_p(y,v)+\kappa_{pw}f_w(e,v)]\,, \tag{10.7}$$

with $\kappa:=1/(1-\kappa_{wp}\kappa_{pw})$. With (10.6) and (10.7) we can begin to derive the law of motion for the wage share. Logarithmic differentiation of $v$ now yields $\hat{v}=\hat{w}-\hat{p}-\hat{z}=\kappa\,[(1-\kappa_{pw})f_w-(1-\kappa_{wp})f_p]-(1-\kappa_{wz})(\hat{z}-g_z)$. The difference between actual and trend productivity growth, in turn, is given by Equation (10.3), $\hat{z}-g_z=\hat{y}-\hat{e}$. Using (10.2) for $\hat{e}$, we provisionally obtain:

$$\begin{aligned}\hat{v}=\;&\kappa[(1-\kappa_{pw})f_w(e,v)-(1-\kappa_{wp})f_p(y,v)]\\&-(1-\kappa_{wz})[(1-\beta_{ey})\hat{y}+\beta_{ev}(v-v^o)/v^o]\end{aligned} \tag{10.8}$$

It remains to substitute (10.1) for $\hat{y}$ in the last square bracket. Before, however, we have to introduce our re-specification of the interest rate, which also enters this equation.

It is noteworthy that in the core expression governing the motions of the wage share, the first square bracket in (10.8), the inflation climate cancels out. $\pi^c$ nevertheless takes effect on the economy through Equation (10.7) for the rate of price inflation, which enters the dynamic IS equation that determines $\hat{y}$ in (10.1). Hence, with $\kappa_{wz}<1$, the climate variable has also a direct impact on the wage share in (10.8).

More specifically we assume that the dynamic behavior of the inflation climate is described by:[6]

$$\dot{\pi}^c=\beta_\pi[\kappa_\pi(\hat{p}-\pi^c)+(1-\kappa_\pi)(\pi^\star-\pi^c)], \tag{10.9}$$

where $\beta_\pi$ is an adjustment speed parameter and $\kappa_\pi$ a weight parameter between 0 and 1, and $\pi^\star$ is to be thought of as the target rate of inflation of the central bank. It is publicly known and agents have some faith that monetary policy will succeed in bringing inflation back to this target. The degree of their confidence *vis-à-vis* the trend-chasing adaptive expectations component is measured by $(1-\kappa_\pi)$, which can also be referred to as the central bank's credibility. In the analysis of the next sections, we assume for starting the zero credibility case, where $\kappa_\pi = 1$, and will afterwards study the effects from increasing the weight of the regressive expectations, when $\kappa_\pi < 1$.

## *The monetary policy rule*

The last variable to consider is the rate of interest set by the central bank. Estimations of Taylor rules with interest rate smoothing terms typically produce a good fit on the basis of a high persistence parameter: In line with Clarida *et al.*(1998), Gerdesmeier and Roffia (2003) and others, Proaño *et al.* (2006) for example estimate an interest rate smoothing coefficient of 0.92 per quarter. These inertia were often taken as support for the point of view that the central bank adopts an interest rate smoothing device. Recent research, however, casts doubts on this interpretation, due to the following reasons.

- At the time when the central bank sets the interest rate, it has only preliminary information about the data, in particular, about the output gap ($y-1$ in our model). The deviations from the final, revised data used in the econometric studies are non-negligible, and especially for the output gap these measurement errors are strongly autocorrelated.
- The natural rate of interest entering the Taylor rule will not be a constant, but the assumptions of the central bank about it will, likewise, move in an autocorrelated manner.
- Actual monetary policy follows a rule only as a guide. Thus, deviations from the rule during episodes are an appropriate response to special circumstances, not evidence of partial adjustment (for example, the credit crunch shock 1992–1993; the worldwide financial crisis 1998–99; or commodity price scares 1988–1989 and 1994–1995).[7]

In this perspective, the lagged interest rate in the estimations may just be a proxy for these serially correlated shocks, so that policy rule estimations with their typically high inertia are not a proven description of actual CB behavior. Conversely, it may even be said that any estimation of a relatively straightforward formulation of a rule *should* exhibit a considerable degree of autocorrelation in the residuals, reflected by a Durbin–Watson statistic below 1.5.

On these grounds we choose to return to the original Taylor rule without a partial adjustments mechanism, for whose policy coefficients we can draw on evidence from the literature. Specifically, we borrow a result from Rudebusch (2002, section 6). With a maximum likelihood estimation of the federal funds rate 1987–1999, he establishes for the demeaned quarterly data,

$$i_t = 1.24\hat{p}_t^{(4)} + 0.33y_t + \xi_t\,, \qquad \xi_t = 0.92\,\xi_{t-1} + \omega_t \qquad (10.10)$$
$$(\sigma_\omega = 0.35\%,\ \bar{R}^2 = 0.96)$$

($\hat{p}_t^{(4)}$ is the average of the last four quarter-to-quarter inflation rates). By combining (10.10) with the other equations, we do not need to worry about the latter's numerical coefficients. Indeed, eliminating the interest rate equation from resulting 5D system has been found to have only a minimal bearing on the coefficients in the remaining equations.

Furthermore, one can one step further and invoke the information contained in the term structure of the interest rates. Rudebusch (2002) demonstrates that a slow partial adjustment of the short rate to new information by the Federal Reserve should imply the existence of predictable future variation in the short rate that is not present with serially correlated shocks. In his study he reveals a general lack of predictive information in the yield curve about changes in the short rate, which suggests the absence of policy inertia. Rudebusch and Wu (2004) rigorously analyze this issue in a combined model that includes the macro variables as well as a no-arbitrage term structure and also allows for both types of policy rule dynamics—partial adjustment and persistent shocks. Letting "the data judge between these interpretations", they find there is little term structure evidence suggesting interest rate smoothing in the Federal Reserve's policy actions.

We conclude from these arguments that even a simple rule like (10.10) is to be preferred to a Taylor rule with an interest rate smoothing parameter. Therefore, using the same nominal equilibrium rate of interest $i^o$ as in (10.1) and the same target rate of inflation $\pi^\star = \hat{p}^o$ as in (10.9), we employ the interest rate reaction function,

$$i = i^o + \beta_{ip}(\hat{p} - \pi^\star) + \beta_{iy}(y-1) \tag{10.11}$$

where the numerical order of magnitude of the policy coefficients derives from (10.10). A side-effect of using an original Taylor rule instead of one with interest rate smoothing is that we save one dynamic variable when setting up the differential equations system. For an analytical treatment of its Jacobian matrix to study stability this is, however, of no great help since, of course, the influence of the rule is still present, and several of the other entries in the matrix are already complicated enough.

## *The 4D differential equations system*

The laws of motion set up in the previous sections can be summarized in a system of four differential equations, where the state variables are the wage share $v$, capacity utilization $y$, the employment rate $e$, and the inflation climate $\pi^c$. For a compact representation which nevertheless makes the variables involved explicit, we define the functional expressions $h_p$ for the rate of price inflation $\hat{p}$ in (10.7) and $h_r$ for the real rate of interest $r := i - \hat{p}$ from (10.11) and (10.7),

$$\begin{aligned} h_p &= h_p(v,y,e,\pi^c) := \pi^c + \kappa[f_p(y,v) + \kappa_{pw} f_w(e,v)] \\ h_r &= h_r(v,y,e,\pi^c) := (\beta_{ip}-1)h_p(v,y,e,\pi^c) + \beta_{iy}(y-1) + i^o - \beta_{ip}\pi^\star \end{aligned}$$

Furthermore, refer to the right-hand side of (10.1) for the growth rate of utilization $\hat{y}$ as:

$$\begin{aligned} h_y &= h_y(v,y,e,\pi^c) \\ &:= -\beta_{yy}(y-1) - \beta_{yi}h_r(v,y,e,\pi^c) + \gamma_{yv}(v-v^o)/v^o + \beta_{yi}(i^o - \pi^\star) \end{aligned}$$

and abbreviate the first square bracket (including $\kappa$) in (10.8) for the changes in the wage share $\hat{v}$ as:

$$h_v = h_v(v,y,e) := \kappa[(1-\kappa_{pw})f_w(e,v) - (1-\kappa_{wp})f_p(y,v)]$$

On this basis, the autonomous system to be investigated in continuous time reads:

$$\dot{v} = v[h_v - (1-\kappa_{wz})(1-\beta_{ey})h_y - (1-\kappa_{wz})\beta_{ev}(v-v^o)/v^o] \tag{10.12}$$

$$\dot{y} = y\,h_y \tag{10.13}$$

$$\dot{e} = e\,\beta_{ey}\,h_y - e\,\beta_{ev}(v-v^o)/v^o \tag{10.14}$$

$$\dot{\pi}^c = \beta_\pi[\kappa_\pi h_p + (1-\kappa_\pi)\pi^\star - \pi^c] \tag{10.15}$$

Since the adjustment principles were directly specified in deviation form, it is obvious that $v = v^o$, $y = 1$, $e = e^o$, $\pi^c = \pi^\star$ constitute a stationary point of (10.12)–(10.15). Equating the right-hand sides of these equations to zero and dividing by $v$, $y$ and $e$, respectively, we have a system of four linear equations which, except for a fluke, are linear independent. This establishes the (generic) uniqueness of the economy's steady state position. Referring to the introduction of Equation (10.2), which modified the original specification of Okun's law, it has to be stressed that linear independence relies on a nonzero coefficient $\beta_{ev}$ in (10.14); otherwise (10.13) and (10.14) provide the same information and a continuum of equilibria would be obtained. Because they imply values of, for example, $y$ and $\hat{p}$ different from 1 and $\pi^\star$, whereas the latter serve as benchmark or target values in the price Phillips curve and the Taylor rule, these stationary points would not be consistent states of equilibrium, so that stability of this set (rather than a specific point) of equilibria would not be a meaningful property, either.

## *The discrete-time formulation*

For the deterministic and stochastic simulations of the next sections, we use a discrete time version of the continuous time framework described above, consisting of the following equations:

$$\pi^c = \pi^c_{t-1} + 0.25 \cdot \beta_\pi \left[\kappa_\pi \hat{p}_{t-1} + (1-\kappa_\pi)\pi^\star - \pi^c_{t-1}\right] \tag{10.16}$$

$$\hat{p}_t = \kappa\left[\beta_{py}(y_{t-1}-1) + \kappa_{pw}\beta_{we}(e_{t-1}-e^o) + (\beta_{pv} - \kappa_{pw}\beta_{wv})(v_{t-1}-v^o)/v^o\right] + \kappa[\varepsilon_{p,t} + \kappa_{pw}\varepsilon_{w,t}] + \pi^c_t \tag{10.17}$$

$$y_t = 1 + \beta_{yy1}(y_{t-1}-1) + \beta_{yy2}(y_{t-2}-1) - \beta_{yi}[i_{t-1} - \hat{p}_t - (i^o - \pi^\star)] + \gamma_{yv}(v_{t-1}-v^o)/v^o + \epsilon_{y,t} \tag{10.18}$$

$$\hat{y}_t = 4(y_t - y_{t-1})/y_{t-1}. \tag{10.19}$$

$$\hat{e}_t = \beta_{ey1}\hat{y}_{t-1} + \beta_{ey2}\hat{y}_{t-2} + \beta_{ey3}\hat{y}_{t-3} - \beta_{ev}(v-v^o)/v^o + \epsilon_{e,t} \tag{10.20}$$

$$e_t = (1 + 0.25\hat{e}_t)e_{t-1}, \tag{10.21}$$

$$\hat{z}_t = g_z + \hat{y}_t - \hat{e}_t \tag{10.22}$$

$$\hat{w}_t = \kappa\left[\beta_{we}(e_{t-1}-e^o) + \kappa_{wp}\beta_{py}(y_{t-1}-1) + (\kappa_{wp}\beta_{pv} - \beta_{wv})(v_{t-1}-v^o)/v^o\right] + \kappa\left[\varepsilon_{w,t} + \kappa_{wp}\,\varepsilon_{p,t}\right] + \kappa_{wz}\hat{z}_t + (1-\kappa_{wz})g_z + \pi^c_t \tag{10.23}$$

$$\hat{v}_t = \hat{w}_t - \hat{p}_t - \hat{z}_t \tag{10.24}$$

$$v_t = (1 + 0.25\,\hat{v}_t)\, v_{t-1} \tag{10.25}$$

where the $\varepsilon_{x,t}$-terms $(x = p, y, e, w, i)$ are supposed to be i.i.d. serially uncorrelated random shocks and the discrete-time version of the differential equation (10.9) for the inflation climate is obtained by transforming the time derivative $\dot{\pi}^c$ to $(\pi^c_t - \pi^c_{t-1})/h$, with $h = 0.25$. For simplicity, the rates of change of productivity and the wage share use the continuous-time growth rate formulae.

The Taylor rule is taken over from (10.10). For the stochastic simulations, the inflation gap refers to the mean of the last four inflation rates (which almost coincides with the four-quarter rates of inflation); see Equation (10.26c). This smoothing effect is meaningful to protect against quarterly outliers, but it is not necessarily needed in the noiseless setting of the impulse-response exercises. Since under the special circumstances of just one shock to a tranquil steady state position we wish the central bank to react without delay to the impulse, the inflation gap is based on the contemporaneous quarter-to-quarter rate of inflation in this case; see (10.26a). We use the two specifications of the Taylor rule for the impulse-response and stochastic experiments, namely:

$$i_t = i^o + \alpha_p(\hat{p}_t - \pi^\star) + \alpha_y(y_t - 1) \tag{10.26a}$$

$$= i^o + \alpha_p(\hat{p}_t^{(4)} - \pi^\star) + \alpha_y(y_t - 1) + \eta_{i,t} \tag{10.26b}$$

$$(\hat{p}_t^{(4)} = 0.25 \cdot \textstyle\sum_{j=0}^{3} \hat{p}_{t-j})$$

$$\eta_{i,t} = \rho_i \eta_{i,t-1} + \varepsilon_{i,t}. \tag{10.26c}$$

As equations (10.16)–(10.26) are formulated, they constitute a system written in recursive form. Note that the contemporaneous dating of inflation in the utilization equation (10.18) together with the contemporaneous dating of productivity growth $\hat{z}_t$ in the wage Phillips curve require us to compute $\hat{p}_t$ before $y_t$, and $\hat{w}_t$ after $y_t$; the latter because of (10.22). Hence the wage and price inflation rates are no longer determined in two successive equations. In the stochastic version, the $\varepsilon_{x,t}$-terms ($x = p, y, e, w, i$) are supposed to be i.i.d. serially uncorrelated random shocks; or they specify the impulse shock at $t = 0$ and are zero otherwise. The system can be simply iterated forward once a history of utilization $y_{0-j}$ and inflation rates $\hat{p}_{0-j}$ ($j = 0, \ldots, 3$) is given, and initial values for the wage share $v_0$, the employment rate $e_0$, the inflation climate $\pi_0^c$, and the disturbance $\eta_0$ in the Taylor rule (10.26c).

Before proceeding with the model's stability properties, we first turn our attention to the empirical consistency of the theoretical model discussed in these sections.

## Econometric estimation and calibration of the model

In numerous previous studies such as Flaschel and Krolzig (2006), Chen and Flaschel (2006), and Proaño *et al.* (2006), wage and price Phillips curves similar to the ones described by Equations (10.4) and (10.5) have been estimated. Among other things, such studies have shown that they represent a significant improvement compared to single reduced-form price Phillips curve equations.

The main purpose of this section is to derive appropriate parameter coefficients of the model, and more specifically, to find adequate parameter values for the inflation climate equation formulated in Equation (10.9). To do this, we use as a starting point the econometric estimation results of a similar study by Proaño *et al.* (2006), who estimate with aggregate time series of the US and the euro area the following set of equations:

$$\hat{w}_t = \beta_{we} e_{t-1} - \beta_{wv} \ln(v_{t-1}) + \kappa_{wp} \hat{p}_t + \kappa_{w\pi} \pi_t^{12} + \kappa_{wz} \hat{z}_t + c_w + \varepsilon_{wt} \tag{10.27}$$

$$\hat{p}_t = \beta_{pu} u_{t-1} + \beta_{pv} \ln(v_{t-1}) + \kappa_{pw} \hat{w}_t + \kappa_{p\pi} \pi_t^{12} - \kappa_{pz} \hat{z}_t + c_p + \varepsilon_{pt} \tag{10.28}$$

$$u_t = \beta_{uu1} u_{t-1} + \beta_{uu2} u_{t-2} - \beta_{ui}(i_{t-1} - \hat{p}_t) + \gamma_{uv} v_{t-1} + c_u + \varepsilon_{ut} \tag{10.29}$$

$$\hat{e}_t = \beta_{eu1} \hat{u}_{t-1} + \beta_{eu2} \hat{u}_{t-2} + \beta_{eu3} \hat{u}_{t-3} + \varepsilon_{et} \tag{10.30}$$

$$i_t = \beta_{ii} i_{t-1} + \beta_{ip} \hat{p}_t + \beta_{ip} u_t + c_i + \varepsilon_{it}. \tag{10.31}$$

with $\hat{w}_t = \ln(w_t) - \ln w_{t-1}$ for example, and $\pi^{12}$ representing a moving average of price

*Table 10.1* Quarterly data used in the econometric estimations

| *Variable* | *Description* |
|---|---|
| $e$ | employment rate |
| $i$ | federal funds rate |
| $p$ | implicit GDP price deflator |
| $u$ | capacity utilization in the manufacturing sector |
| $v$ | wage share (real compensation per unit of output) |
| $w$ | compensation per hour |
| $z$ | output per hour |
| $\pi^{12}$ | moving average of price inflation over the past 12 quarters with linearly declining weights (serves to represent the inflation climate) |

*Note*: US economy; wages, output and hours refer to the non-farm business sector.

inflation over the past 12 quarters with linearly declining weights, which serves to represent the inflation climate.

Proaño *et al.*(2006) estimate the system of equations (10.27)–(10.31) by System-GMM.[8] In their estimation of the US economy, all coefficients are strongly significant and with the desired sign, or in the desired range. In addition $\kappa_{wp}$ and $\kappa_{w\pi}$ (nearly) add up to unity, as they should (see below). In detail, for the sample period 1961:4–2004:4 the following point estimates for the reaction coefficients were obtained:[9]

$$\begin{array}{llll} \beta_{we}=0.58 & \beta_{wv}=0.27 & \kappa_{wp}=0.48 & \kappa_{w\pi}=0.49 \\ \kappa_{wz}=0.23 & & & \\ \beta_{pu}=0.16 & \beta_{pv}=0.22 & \kappa_{pw}=0.55 & \kappa_{p\pi}=0.57 \\ \kappa_{pz}=- & & & \\ \beta_{uu1}=1.13 & \beta_{uu2}=-0.23 & \beta_{ui}=0.05 & \gamma_{uv}=-0.10 \\ \beta_{eu1}=0.17 & \beta_{eu2}=0.12 & \beta_{eu3}=0.05 & \\ \beta_{ii}=0.92 & \beta_{ip}=0.11 & \beta_{iu}=0.11 & \end{array} \tag{10.32}$$

Regarding the order of magnitude of the coefficients that connect levels and rates of change, it has to be noted that all growth rates are annualized, i.e. the first differences in logs in (10.27)–(10.31) are multiplied by four.

## *The role of the inflationary climate*

To highlight the importance of the values of the inflation climate parameters for the dynamics of the system, we perform a simple experiment. We assume that indeed $\pi^{12}$ can be used as a proxy for the outcome of an adaptive expectations formation process and set accordingly $\kappa_\pi$ equal to one and neglect the regressive expectations formulated in Equation (10.16), as done by Proaño *et al.* (2006). Regarding the adjustment speed of $\beta_\pi$, we simulate Equation (10.16) with historical data and select a value that minimizes the root mean square deviation between the endogenously determined climate $\pi_t^c$ and $\pi^{12}$. The minimization problem is solved by $\beta_\pi = 0.65$, at which the two series are indeed as close as 0.35 percentage points.

The implications of a such rigid inflation climate as it would be if $\pi^c = \pi^{12}$ can be observed by inserting the numerical parameter values from (10.32) (with $\kappa_{pw} = 0$ and $\kappa_{p\pi} = 1$, in addition) into the discrete-time system (10.16)–(10.26a), (10.26c) and performing a standard impulse-response experiment, which for a Keynesian demand-driven model should be ideally a demand shock. Correspondingly, we set the initial shock to the utilization

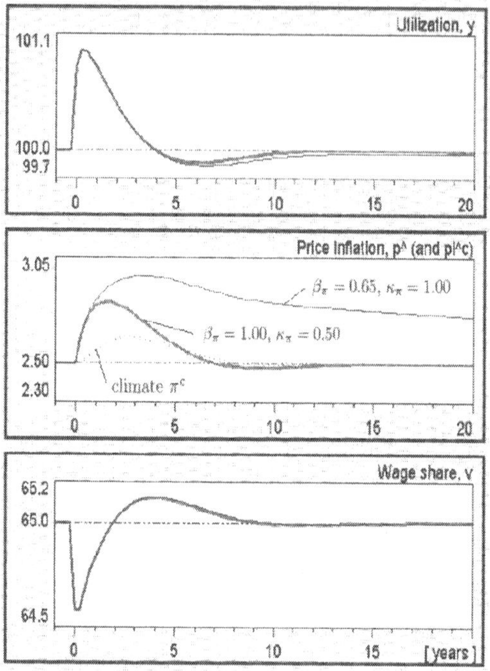


*Figure 10.1* Response of the discrete-time model to a demand shock

equation (10.18) equal to the standard error of the estimation equation (10.29), that is, $\varepsilon_{y,t} = 0.77\%$ in (10.18) for period $t = 0$, and zero again thereafter (as all the other $\varepsilon$-terms).

We make only four modifications: (*i*) symbol $u$ is replaced with $y$; (*ii*) the weight $\kappa_{pz}$ appearing in (10.28) becomes obsolete since the benchmark inflation term in the model's price Philips curve takes the weights of actual and trend productivity in the wage Phillips curve into account; (*iii*) as discussed in "The monetary policy rule" above, the interest rate smoothing approach to the Taylor rule in (10.31) is discarded in favor of the Rudebusch (2002) estimation of Equation (10.10) with the autocorrelated disturbances; (*iv*) following the discussion of Okun's law in "Output and emplyment adjustments", we choose a small value like 0.01 for the additional parameter $\beta_{ev}$ in Equation (10.20).

Since the disequilibrium reactions in both the continuous-time and discrete-time model versions refer to the deviations of the variables from their equilibrium values, the dynamics are independent of the numerical specification of the steady state position. For concreteness, we may choose the following values for the target rate of inflation, the nominal interest rate, the employment rate, the wage share, and trend productivity growth,

$$\pi^\star = 2.5\% \qquad i^o = 5.0\% \qquad e^o = 94\% \tag{10.33}$$

$$v^o = 65\% \qquad g_z = 2.0\%. \tag{10.34}$$

The steady state values of the other variables are easily derived from here.

The resulting adjustment paths of utilization, price inflation and the wage share back to their steady state values are depicted in Figure 10.1. The time paths of $y_t$ and $v_t$ almost coincide with the paths from another experiment, which will be discussed in a moment. The reactions of utilization are quite in line with what is well-known from a great variety of VAR responses to a demand shock: a return back to normal in a few years, with a weak subsequent overshooting. Adjustments of the wage share are far less often studied in the literature, but convergence of this variable occurs at the same time scale.

The behavior of the rate of inflation $\hat{p}_t$ is, however, completely different. As the upper thin line in the middle panel of Figure 10.1 demonstrates, the monotonic convergence of this time series after it has reached its peak at $t = 3.25$ is extremely slow. It actually takes 83 years until price inflation enters a corridor of $\pm$ 0.096 percent around the steady state value of 2.50 percent, which is 10 percent of the maximal deviation in the third year. Convergence of wage inflation, by the way, is not much faster: $\hat{w}_t$ reaches the corresponding corridor after 67 years. All the more remarkable is the balancing of these slow adjustments, which leads the wage share back to its equilibrium value within ten years.

Clearly, the sluggish convergence of $\hat{p}_t$ and $\hat{w}_t$ is not an acceptable property of a model that places strong emphasis on the wage–price dynamics. It is an immediate idea to put the blame on the inflation climate, which may be suspected to react much too hesitatingly. The improvement by employing a faster speed of adjustment $\beta_\pi$ is, however, rather limited. For example, even if $\beta_\pi$ is increased from 0.65 to 2.00, the convergence time of price inflation as it was just specified is still 26.75 years.

Because of their built-in mean reverting tendencies, it is certainly more promising to activate the regressive expectations in the climate's adjustment equation (10.16), that is, to reduce the weight parameter $\kappa_\pi$ below unity. A few explorations suffice to verify this intuition not only qualitatively but also quantitatively; convergence can indeed be decisively accelerated in this way. Concretely, we have a closer look at $\kappa_\pi = 0.50$ and $\beta_\pi = 1.00$. These values have already been extensively used in the numerical investigations of the structural models in Chiarella *et al.* (2005, Ch 5–7 and 9). There they have been introduced on an *a priori* basis, and possibly several of the other parameters of the model had to "adjust" to these values in the calibration studies. By contrast, here the other parameters are already given by the econometric estimation and we adjust $\kappa_\pi$ and $\beta_\pi$ to them, on the basis of an evaluation of the implied impulse-response properties.

The result of this modification of $\kappa_\pi$ and $\beta_\pi$ are the bold lines in Figure 10.1. While, as already said, the differences in the two time series of utilization and the wage share are hardly visible, convergence of the rate of price inflation now occurs at a reasonable speed. We add that apart from a short transitional stage of three quarters, wage inflation behaves in a like fashion.

The dotted line in the middle panel of Figure 10.1 illustrates the role of the inflation climate $\pi_t^c$ for the improved adjustment pattern. In comparison to the case of purely adaptive expectations ($\kappa_\pi = 1$), where right after the start $\pi_t^c$ follows $\hat{p}_t$ relatively closely (not shown in the diagram), the restrained reactions of $\pi_t^c$ under $\kappa_\pi = 0.50$ attenuate the effects of the initial shock in size as well as duration; the inflation rate peaks at a value of 2.82 percent, as opposed to the previous 2.96 percent, already at $t = 1.50$. Even more important is the feature that after the turning point the climate has a greater potential to pull inflation downward. Whereas under $\kappa_\pi = 1$ the climate seeks to keep track of inflation, under $\kappa_\pi = 0.50$ inflation could almost be said to follow the climate in this phase. This characterization is supported by the observation that the original adjustment speed of $\pi_t^c$ produces quite similar trajectories, when $\kappa_\pi = 0.50$ and $\beta_\pi = 0.65$. So it is really the weight parameter $\kappa_\pi$ that is responsible for the faster convergence of wage and price inflation.

As next we proceed to re-estimate the model parameters with the climate $\pi_t^c$ constructed from (10.16) instead of $\pi_t^{12}$, as in Proaño *et al.* (2006). For easier reference, this climate series may be called the endogenous inflation climate (although the parameters $\kappa_\pi$ and $\beta_\pi$ were exogenously chosen). Since in the GMM system estimations, Equations (10.29)–(10.31) for

*Table 10.2* Alternative econometric estimations of wage and price Phillips curves

| Dep.Var. | Regressors | | | | | | | | | |
|---|---|---|---|---|---|---|---|---|---|---|
| | $\pi^{12}$ | $\pi^c$ | $\hat{p}$ | $\hat{w}$ | $e_{-1}$ | $y_{-1}$ | $\ln v_{-1}$ | $\hat{z}$ | $R^2$ | DW |
| $\hat{w}$: (*a*) | 0.49 | — | 0.48 | — | 0.58 | — | −0.26 | 0.23 | 0.49 | 1.99 |
| (*b*) | — | 0.77 | 0.35 | — | 0.58 | — | −0.24 | 0.24 | 0.51 | 2.02 |
| (*c*) | — | 0.58 | 0.42 | — | 0.51 | — | −0.23 | 0.24 | 0.51 | 2.02 |
| (*d*) | — | 0.61 | 0.39 | — | 0.52 | — | −0.22 | 0.22 | 0.51 | 2.00 |
| $\hat{p}$:(*a*) | 0.57 | — | — | 0.55 | — | 0.16 | 0.21 | — | 0.63 | 1.65 |
| (*b*) | — | 0.75 | — | 0.46 | — | 0.08 | 0.23 | −0.15 | 0.76 | 1.75 |
| (*c*) | — | 0.45 | — | 0.55 | — | 0.00 | 0.27 | −0.21 | 0.70 | 1.79 |
| (*d*) | — | 0.88 | — | 0.12 | — | 0.14 | 0.26 | −0.12 | 0.82 | 1.32 |

*Note*: Rows (*a*) – (*c*) are from GMM system estimations of (10.27) – (10.31) with the same instrumental variables as listed in fn 8, (*d*) are nonlinear least squares; (*a*) are the results from PFES and in (*c*) the coefficients on $\pi^c$ and $\hat{p}$, or $\hat{w}$ respectively, are constrained to sum up to one. Constants are omitted. All nonzero estimates have highly significant *t*-statistics.

utilization, employment and the interest rate are just marginally affected by this revision, we concentrate on the two Phillips curves (10.27) and (10.28). The results are summarized in Table 10.2, where rows (*a*)–(*c*) report the GMM estimations and row (*d*) is based on nonlinear least squares.[10]

Row (*a*) shows the estimation results when we constrain the coefficient $\kappa_{pw}$ equal to zero and $\kappa_{p\pi}$ equal to unity. The only alteration in row (*b*) is the substitution of the endogenous climate for $\pi^{12}$. In particular, the coefficients on $\pi^c$ and $\hat{p}$ in the wage Phillips curve, and $\pi^c$ and $\hat{w}$ in the price Phillips curve, are still unconstrained. Comparing (*a*) and (*b*), the changes in the wage Phillips curve are seen to be limited, only the coefficient on $\hat{p}$ decreases somewhat. The latter is partly undone in row (*c*) when the coefficients on the inflation rates $\pi^c$ and $\hat{p}$ are required to sum up to one. In this case the responsiveness of wage inflation to variations in the employment rate shows a moderate decline. Interestingly, these results are quite independent of the system approach; the ordinary single equations least squares approach yields practically the same numerical values and summary statistics.[11]

As already in the wage Phillips curve, a remarkable feature is the role of the wage share. Its coefficients ($\beta_{wv}$ and $\beta_{pv}$) always come out significant and with the correct sign, and they are even scarcely affected by the specification of the inflation climate in the estimations. This consistency is strong support for the theoretical approach (10.4) and (10.5) to the Phillips curves. These Phillips curves are additionally corroborated in another, less obvious detail, namely, the compatibility of the coefficients on the productivity growth rates in the two curves. If the coefficient on $\hat{z}$ in the price Phillips curve is designated $\beta_{pz}$ then, according to (10.5), it is given by $\beta_{pz} = -\kappa_{pw}\kappa_{wz}$. From row (*c*), the latter are estimated as $\kappa_{pw} = 0.55$ and $\kappa_{wz} = 0.24$. Their signed product, $-\kappa_{pw}\kappa_{wz} = -0.13$, is close to the estimate of $\beta_{pz} = -0.15$ in row (*b*) in the second part of Table 10.2. It differs more from $\beta_{pz} = -0.21$ in (*c*), but the specification of the influence of the growth rate of labor productivity in (10.5) can still be considered to be acceptable.

Concerning the price Phillips Curve, the incorporation of our endogenous inflation climate considerably enhances the properties of the estimation, increasing the $R^2$ as well as the DW statistic.

### *Model calibration*

On the basis of Table 10.2 and the results of previous empirical and numerical studies of Chiarella *et al.* (2005) and Asada *et al.* (2006), we use the following parameter values for the next deterministic and stochastic simulations:

$$\begin{array}{llll}
\text{Climate}: & \beta_\pi = 1.00 & \kappa_\pi = 0.50 & \\
\text{WPC}: & \kappa_{wp} = 0.42 & \beta_{we} = 0.51 & \\
 & \beta_{wv} = 0.23 & \kappa_{wz} = 0.24 & \\
\text{PPC}: & \kappa_{pw} = 0.55 & \beta_{py} = 0.00 & \beta_{pv} = 0.27 \\
\text{IS}: & \beta_{yy1} = 1.13 & \beta_{yy2} = -0.23 & \\
 & \beta_{yi} = 0.05 & \gamma_{yv} = -0.10 & \\
\text{Okun}: & \beta_{ey1} = 0.17 & \beta_{ey2} = 0.12 & \\
 & \beta_{ey3} = 0.05 & \beta_{ev} = 0.01 & \\
\text{Taylor}: & \beta_{ip} = 1.24 & \beta_{iy} = 0.33 & \rho_i = 0.92
\end{array} \tag{10.35}$$

Though the econometric estimation with the improvements in Table 10.2 appears rather reliable, one may feel uneasy about a price Phillips curve without economic activity playing an active role.[12] The uneasiness would be justified if $\beta_{py} = 0$ would give rise to some unfamiliar dynamic phenomena. To check this, let us re-examine the demand shock impulse-response function from above with the new parameters from (10.35). To begin with, consider the impact reactions in the same quarter $t = 0$ in which the shock $\varepsilon_{y,t}$ in (10.18) occurs. The main effect is a lower wage share, which is brought about by the change in labor productivity. The argument is that the (strong) increase in the growth rate $\hat{y}_0$ (strongly) raises the productivity growth rate, which immediately, with factor $\kappa_{wz}$, translates into higher wage inflation $\hat{w}_0$ in (10.23). Since $\kappa_{wz} < 1$, the change in $\hat{z}_0$ dominates the change in $\hat{w}_0$ in (10.24) for $\hat{v}_0$, so that the wage share $v_0$ falls.

In the next quarter, $t = 1$, the inflation climate in (10.16) is not yet affected, but the lower wage share has a negative effect on the subsequent equation, which determines price inflation. This is due to the fact that the composed coefficient on $v_{t-1}$ in (10.17) results to be positive, $\beta_{pv} - \kappa_{pw}\beta_{wv} = 0.27 - 0.55 \cdot 0.23 > 0$. Owing to $\beta_{py} = 0$, this is the only change in (10.17). As a consequence, the positive demand shock in $t = 0$ causes a *fall* in the rate of inflation one quarter later. This stands in contrast to what we have obtained in Figure 10.1, and may seem counterintuitive.

In fact, the reaction is reminiscent of what is known in the literature as the "price puzzle". There it refers to monetary policy where it has been observed that a contractionary innovation by the central bank tends to increase, rather than decrease, the rate of price inflation.[13] It is easily verified that a negative interest rate shock in our model produces the same result, a fall in $y$ and a rise in $\hat{p}$. Hence it can be said that our model with the estimated parameters from (10.35) does reproduce the price puzzle, and because of the (weak or even) vanishing influence of output in the price Phillips curve and the, as it turns out, positive influence of the wage share on price inflation, the model also provides a theoretical explanation for it.

Nevertheless, the rate of price inflation starts increasing in quarter $t = 2$. This is because $y$ increases further in $t = 1$ and now also raises the employment rate $e$. The strong shock to $\hat{z}$ was only transitory, and wage inflation $\hat{w}_1$ in (10.23) returns close to normal. Thus, $\hat{p}_1 < \hat{p}^o$ is the greatest deviation from the steady state values in the growth rate formula (10.24) for the wage share. The resulting increase in $v$ together with the increase in $e$ then leads to $\hat{p}_2 > \hat{p}_1$ in the subsequent quarter. The adjustment process has now gathered momentum and, with respect to six selected variables, Figure 10.2 shows how it unfolds in the following periods.

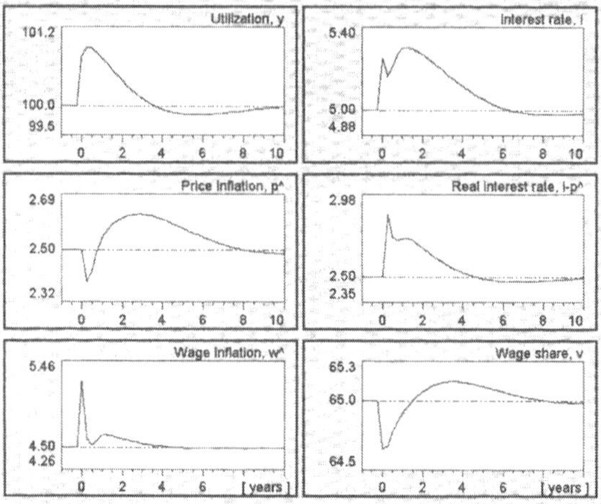


*Figure 10.2* Response of the model to a demand shock, with parameters from (10.35)
*Note*: Dotted lines are based on $\gamma_{yv} = +0.10$, as opposed to the estimated coefficient $\gamma_{yv} = -0.10$ for the bold lines.

The speed of convergence is the same as in Figure 10.1, which is the first litmus test that the numerical coefficients have to pass. Another and more ambitious criterion to evaluate the adjustment paths of the variables is a comparison with the impulse-response functions that one obtains from an atheoretical vector autoregression. Since we are here interested in the trajectories of $y$, $\hat{p}$, $\hat{w}$, $v$ and $i$ (with a slight delay, the employment rate $e$ moves quite in line with $y$), we estimated a VAR with four lags in the six variables $y$, $e$, $\hat{p}$, $\hat{w}$, $v$ as well as $i$ and computed the response of the variables to a one standard deviation innovation to $y$. The outcome over the first ten years is shown in Figure 10.3. Because the shock to $y$ is of the same size as our demand shock in Figure 10.2, the two figures can be directly compared.

The overall impression of this comparison is a fine qualitative match of the responses in the model and from the VAR. The initial reaction of the variables are in the same direction and the adjustment patterns regarding turning points, overshooting and speed of convergence are quite the same.[14] In particular, the VAR displays the same kind of price puzzle in the middle-left panel and the wage share falls at the beginning, where even the size of the initial reactions of the two variables is the same.[15] The main quantitative differences of Figure 10.3 from Figure 10.2 are the higher amplitude of the upper turning points of $\hat{p}$, $\hat{w}$ and $i$ (but not $v$) after nine, eight and seven quarters, respectively, and the moderate impact reaction of wage inflation when we compare it to the fierce reaction in our model, which we have seen originates with the sudden change in the productivity growth rate. The positive aspects of the match are nonetheless predominant, so that the qualitative and to some extent even quantitative properties of the model's impulse-response functions in Figure 10.2 can be taken as strong support for the model and its parameters in (10.35).

After having derived from econometric estimations adequate parameter values and calibrated the remaining parameters from the impulse-response analysis just discussed, we turn now to the characterization of the local stability properties of the model.

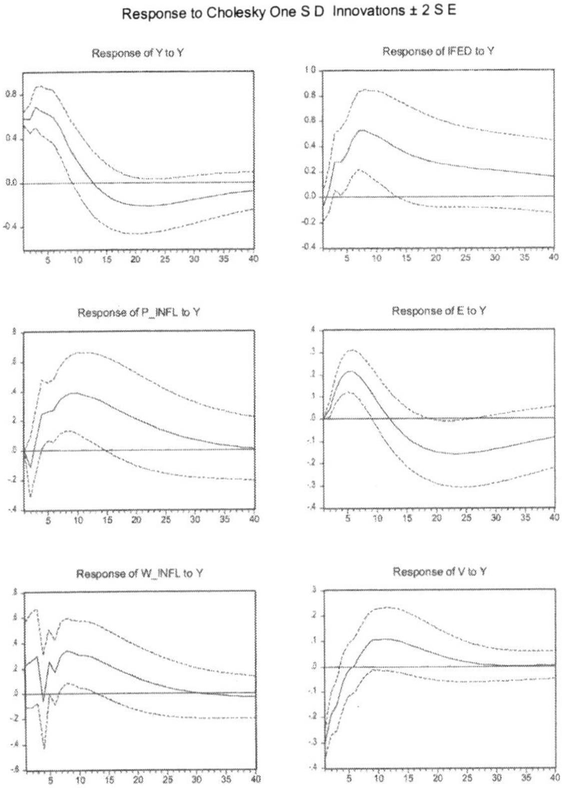


*Figure 10.3* VAR impulse-response functions to a demand shock

## Wage and price flexibility: eigen-value analysis

As already stated by Rose (1967), the real wage channel is likely to possess ambiguous stability properties, which are likely to depend on the one hand on the relative flexibilities with which prices and wages respond to the utilization measures on the goods and labor markets, respectively, and on the other hand, by the way in which output responds to changes in the wage share, or real wages for that matter, which concerns the distinction of profit-led and wage-led economies. Thus, as also discussed by Proaño *et al.* (2006), the real wage rate can act in a stabilizing or destabilizing manner, where each case itself can be brought about by two completely different sets of conditions.

Let us concentrate on the destabilizing real wage channel and let it be understood that the following statements on rising or falling levels of the variables mean that they rise or fall relative to a trend. Consider an increase of the real wage rate $w/p$, which raises consumption $C$ of workers and depresses investment $I$ (and perhaps also consumption out of rentiers' income). If $\gamma_{yv} < 0$, the economy is profit-led (PL) and the latter effect is dominant. Capacity utilization $y$ as well as the employment rate $e$ decrease, and so do prices and wages. In a situation that may be called goods market led (GML), when prices react more vigorously to $y$ than wages to $e$, real wages will nevertheless increase. On the whole, as sketched in the upper part of Figure 10.4, a positive feedback loop comes into being, which has a destabilizing influence on the economy.

$$w/p\uparrow \overset{\text{PL}}{\Longrightarrow} C\uparrow, I\downarrow\downarrow \Longrightarrow y\downarrow, e\downarrow \overset{\text{GML}}{\Longrightarrow} p\downarrow\downarrow, w\downarrow \Longrightarrow w/p\uparrow$$

$$w/p\uparrow \overset{\text{WL}}{\Longrightarrow} C\uparrow\uparrow, I\downarrow \Longrightarrow y\uparrow, e\uparrow \overset{\text{LML}}{\Longrightarrow} p\uparrow, w\uparrow\uparrow \Longrightarrow w/p\uparrow$$

*Figure 10.4* Adverse real wage effects.

If these forces together are sufficiently strong, they may even succeed in destabilizing the economy as a whole. By this expression we presently mean that the steady state of the differential equations system (10.12)–(10.15), would no longer be attractive anymore. The positive feedback loop can be made arbitrarily strong by sufficiently increasing the coefficient $\beta_{py}$ in the price Phillips curve relative to $\beta_{we}$ in the wage Phillips curve (the responsiveness of prices to utilization relative to the responsiveness of wages to the employment rate), and by sufficiently decreasing the (negative) parameter $\gamma_{yv}$ in the IS curve. In a profit-led economy, it can thus be said that $\beta_{py}$ tends to be destabilizing (i.e. rising values of this coefficient), while $\beta_{we}$ and $\gamma_{yv}$ tend to be stabilizing since increasing them may sufficiently weaken this mechanism in relation to other feedbacks in the economy with a stabilizing potential.

In contrast, assume the economy is wage-led (WL, by $\gamma_{yv} > 0$) and wage and price adjustments are labor market led (LML), such that now wages are markedly more flexible than prices. After an initial increase of real wages, the signs of the reactions of $y$, $e$ and then $p$, $w$ are reversed in this scenario; all of these variables are increasing and the lower part of Figure 10.4 makes clear that the real wage rate increases, too. As a consequence, the parameters change their role: higher values of $\beta_{py}$ are stabilizing, and $\beta_{we}$, $\gamma_{yv}$ tend to be destabilizing.

As elementary as this feedback argument is, it provides us with the insight that higher price or wage flexibility cannot be generally characterized, or recommended, as stabilizing. A crucial factor that has to be taken into account for that are the reactions of output, whether they constitute a profit-led or wage-led regime, and how strong such a regime is.

It is easily verified that normal real wage effects, where $w/p\downarrow$ at the end of the chains sketched in Figure 10.4, are obtained if in a profit-led regime the nominal adjustments are labor market led, or if in a wage-led regime they are goods market led.

While this discussion is fairly general, it can be made more specific by investigating the stability properties of our numerical economy. To save us dealing with the technical effort caused by the distributed lags in the discrete-time system, we use the convenient differential equations (10.12)–(10.15) for this kind of analysis.[16] That is, we set up the Jacobian matrix of this four-dimensional system, which is straightforward, and compute the eigen-values, which must all have negative real parts for the steady state to be (locally asymptotically) stable.

We cannot take over all of the parameters from (10.35); some of them have to be adjusted to the continuous-time setting, which are the coefficients in the determination of output and the employment rate. According to the remarks on Equation (10.1) for the growth rate of utilization, the adjustment speed $\beta_{yy}$ is given by $\beta_{yy} = (1 - \beta_{yy1} - \beta_{yy2})/0.25$, and $\beta_{yi}$ and $\gamma_{yv}$ are obtained from dividing their discrete-time counterpart in (10.35) by 0.25, or multiplying it by $v^o/0.25$, respectively. As remarked on Equation (10.2) for the growth rate of the employment rate, $\beta_{ey}$ in this equation is given by the sum of $\beta_{ey1}$, $\beta_{ey2}$, $\beta_{ey3}$ from (10.35). Underlying the eigen-value analysis of (10.12)–(10.15) are, therefore, the following numerical coefficients,

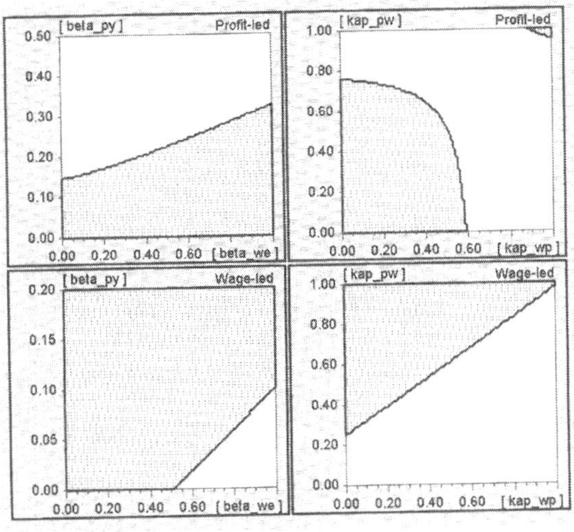


*Figure 10.5* Parameter diagrams under profit-led and wage-led conditions.

*Note*: Parameter combinations in the dotted area induce stability of the steady state position. Profit-led and wage-led scenarios are here given by $\gamma_{yv} = -1.5$ and $\gamma_{yv} = +2.0$, respectively.

$$\begin{array}{llll} \text{Climate, WPC, PPC, Taylor as in (10.35)} & & & \\ \text{IS:} & \beta_{yy} = 0.40 & \beta_{yi} = 0.20 & \gamma_{yv} = -0.26 \\ \text{Okun:} & \beta_{ey} = 0.30 & \beta_{ev} = \ \ 0.01 & \end{array} \tag{10.36}$$

We first of all make sure that the steady state position of this continuous-time system continues to be stable. From the discussion of Okun's law and the role of the coefficient $\beta_{ev}$ in its specification, we already know that the leading eigen-value $\lambda$ (the one with maximum real part), which turns out to be real, is not much smaller than zero ($\lambda = -0.0070$, to be exact).

*Ceteris paribus* variations of the central parameter $\gamma_{yv}$ confirm the intuition from above that both too strongly profit-led and too strongly wage-led regimes are destabilizing, though an unstable economy itself requires fairly extreme values of the parameter; the steady state is stable if $-1.513 < \gamma_{yv} < 2.008$, and unstable outside this interval. This is a noteworthy observation for model builders in a Kalecki-Steindl tradition, for whom the distinction between profit-led and wage-led regimes plays an important role and who tend to view wage-led regimes as being more favorable for stability. Nevertheless, we have more to say on this in the next section.

The result that, within the feedback loops considered in Figure 10.4, the wage and price flexibilities $\beta_{we}$ and $\beta_{py}$ have opposite effects in profit-led and wage-led regimes carries over to the total economy. The left part of Figure 10.5 illustrates this by means of parameter diagrams for these coefficients, which indicate that all pairs $(\beta_{we}, \beta_{py})$ in the dotted area give rise to a stable equilibrium, and all pairs outside to an unstable equilibrium. To make the effects stand out, the diagrams assume that the profit-led and wage-led regimes are constituted by the switching values just mentioned, i.e. by $\gamma_{yv} = -1.5$ and $\gamma_{yv} = +2.0$, respectively. The upper-left panel shows that in such a profit-led economy more wage flexibility (higher values of $\beta_{we}$) can make an unstable equilibrium stable, and more price flexibility (higher values of $\beta_{py}$) can destabilize it. By contrast, in the wage-led economy more wage flexibility is destabilizing, and more price flexibility is stabilizing.

*Table 10.3* Characterization of parameters as stabilizing and destabilizing the steady state position

| | $\beta_{we}$ | $\beta_{py}$ | $\beta_{wv}$ | $\beta_{pv}$ | $\kappa_{wp}$ | $\kappa_{pw}$ | $\kappa_{wz}$ | $\beta_{\pi}$ | $\kappa_{\pi}$ |
|---|---|---|---|---|---|---|---|---|---|
| profit-led: | S | D | S | S | D | D | S | NE | NE |
| wage-led: | D | S | S | S | D | S | NE | NE | NE |

*Note*: S and D mean that a *ceteris paribus* increase of the parameter tends to stabilize or destabilize the equilibrium, respectively; NE that it has largely negligible effects.

The influence of the wage share in the wage as well as the price Phillips curve is conducive to stability, a property that holds in profit-led and wage-led economies alike. Computing the same type of diagrams (not shown) for the corresponding coefficients, pairs $(\beta_{wv}, \beta_{pv})$ in a neighborhood of the origin are found to render the steady state unstable, while sufficiently large values of them render it stable. In fact, the $(\beta_{wv}, \beta_{pv})$-parameter diagrams do not look very different for $\gamma_{yv} = -1.5$ and $\gamma_{yv} = 2.0$.[17]

The right part of Figure 10.5 is concerned with effects from $\kappa_{wp}$ and $\kappa_{pw}$. These parameters may be easily forgotten in a discussion on stability, since they 'only' serve to obtain an expression for benchmark inflation and weight current inflation rates against the inflation climate for that purpose. The two diagrams on the right part of the figure point out that this neglect would be unwarranted: both parameters have an impact on stability just as much as the familiar wage and price flexibilities $\beta_{we}$ and $\beta_{py}$. Moreover, their role is not as symmetric as the role of $\beta_{we}$ and $\beta_{py}$. In the profit-led economy, $\kappa_{wp}$ and $\kappa_{pw}$ are both destabilizing, whereas in the wage-led economy $\kappa_{wp}$ maintains its destabilizing potential and $\kappa_{pw}$ becomes stabilizing. Interesting is also the small stability region in the top-right corner of the upper diagram, from which it is seen that, under the given circumstances, not only sufficiently low but also sufficiently strong (common) weights may stabilize the steady state.

Table 10.3 succinctly summarizes the effects just described. It also contains information about the remaining three parameters $\kappa_{wz}$, $\beta_{\pi}$, $\kappa_{\pi}$ in the two Phillips curves, which was obtained by similar parameter diagrams. The negligible effects from variations of $\beta_{\pi}$ and $\kappa_{\pi}$ are perhaps a bit surprising. From the discussion of the slow convergence of the economy under $\kappa_{\pi} = 1$, increases of this parameter toward unity might have been expected to have some destabilizing potential; and in many low-dimensional models with purely adaptive expectations, a faster adjustment speed usually turned out to be destabilizing, too.

Given that the stability results here presented are based on values of $\gamma_{yv}$ that are far lower or higher than the estimated $\gamma_{yv} = -0.10$, the relevance of the analysis may be questioned. We think it is nevertheless useful. First, a side result which so far we have failed to emphasize is that the stability region around our set of numerical parameters is quite large. Stability of the steady state is thus not sensitive to larger changes of the parameters that might result from other estimations, which in more less sophisticated ways could try to incorporate the inflation climate coefficients $\kappa_{\pi}$ and $\beta_{\pi}$.

Second, the identification of positive or negative feedback loops such as in Figure 10.4 is an important possibility to explain why certain parameters are stabilizing or destabilizing. These arguments ultimately refer to the stability properties of a state of equilibrium, and the eigen-value analysis can verify or falsify conjectures deriving from those feedback mechanisms. A third point is that the extreme values of $\gamma_{yv}$ underlying Figure 10.5 served to obtain clear-cut pictures of the parameters' stabilizing or destabilizing potential. The idea is that, under more reliable values of $\gamma_{yv}$, these effects still find some reflection when the stability investigation is extended and a less rigorous notion is used of what is considered to be (de)stabilizing. This brings us back to the stochastic economy.

## Variabilities in the stochastic economy

So far, the discussion of stabilizing and destabilizing parameters referred to the deterministic part of the model, where variations of them may turn an unstable equilibrium into a stable one and *vice versa*. In mainstream macroeconomics, however, stability of the equilibrium point is usually presupposed,[18] or, especially in (quasi-) linear models, it is a direct consequence of an econometric estimation method. These models are shock-driven, and obviously our model together with its estimation belongs to the same category. In this perspective, an expression like stabilization refers to the stochastic economy and the variabilities of certain state variables, meaning that a parameter variation reduces the standard deviation of the time series of that variable.

We can thus make our analysis on the consequences of wage and price stability more specific by investigating the stability properties of our numerical economy when it is subject to stochastic shocks. This approach, standard in the present mainstream literature, see e.g. Smets and Wouters (2003), is shock-driven, and obviously our model together with its estimation belongs to the same category.[19] In this perspective, an expression like stabilization refers to the stochastic economy and the variabilities of certain state variables, meaning that a parameter variation reduces the standard deviation of the time series of that variables.

As stated before, the discrete-time formulation of our system described by Equations (10.16)–(10.26) can be simply iterated forward once a history of utilization $y_{0-j}$ and inflation rates $\hat{p}_{0-j}$ $(j = 0, \ldots, 3)$ is given, and initial values for the wage share $v_0$, the employment rate $e_0$, the inflation climate $\pi_0^c$, and the disturbance $\eta_0$ in the Taylor rule (10.26c). The dating $t = 0, 1, 2, \ldots$ of the variables refers to the quarters $t = 0, 1, 2, \ldots$, but all rates of change continue to be annualized. As in the continuous-time formulations above, each variable on the right-had side of the equations is specified as a deviation from its steady state value, thus absorbing the constant in the estimation equations.

Regarding the stochastic terms $\varepsilon_{x,t}$ in the system, we adopt the standard deviations $\sigma = \sigma(\varepsilon_{x,t})$ of the estimated GMM residuals of Franke *et al.* (2006):

$$\begin{array}{lll} \sigma(\varepsilon_{p,t}) = 1.32\% & \sigma(\varepsilon_{w,t}) = 2.08\% & \sigma(\varepsilon_{y,t}) = 0.77\% \\ \sigma(\varepsilon_{e,t}) = 0.00\% & \sigma(\varepsilon_{\imath,t}) = 0.35\% & \end{array} \tag{10.37}$$

The outcome of a model simulation over 4000 quarters is compared with the empirical benchmarks of the analyzed variables in Table 10.4. Five out of the six standard deviations are of the same order of magnitude as their benchmark values. The only exception is the variability of the employment rate, which is certainly too low. This is another hint that the modeling of the employment dynamics needs to be improved. Nevertheless, this shortcoming does not impair the ordering of wage and price inflation, according to which the rate of wage inflation should turn out be more variable than the rate of price inflation. On the whole, the model-generated variabilities shown in Table 10.4 are encouraging and can be taken as further corroboration of the model.

Instead of the extreme values of $\gamma_{yv}$ in the previous section, let a profit-led and wage-led regime be constituted by the estimated value $\gamma_{yv} = -0.10$ and, respectively, by $\gamma_{yv} = 0.10$.[20] The bold face figures in the upper part of Table 10 reproduce the standard deviations from Table 10.4 (where the employment rate is now omitted). The outcome of a *ceteris paribus* change of $\gamma_{yv}$ from $-0.10$ to 0.10 in the baseline case is given by the bold face figures in

*Table 10.4* Standard deviations of the time series

| | Standard deviations of | | | | | |
|---|---|---|---|---|---|---|
| | $y$ | $e$ | $\hat{w}$ | $\hat{p}$ | $v$ | $i$ |
| Stochastic economy: | 2.37 | 0.79 | 1.68 | 1.50 | 1.12 | 2.13 |
| Empirical benchmarks: | 2.15 | 1.47 | 1.50 | 1.42 | 0.95 | 2.17 |

the lower part of the table. This modification is stabilizing in the sense that it reduces the standard deviations of utilization and the wage share, but these effects are not universal. The standard deviations of the two rates of inflation slightly rise, though this may not be reckoned significant, and that of the interest rate increases more distinctly.[21] Nevertheless, contrasting the profit-led with the wage-led baseline case, the latter can be said to bring about a stabilization in utilization $y$ and the wage share $v$, at the price of, if at all, a weak destabilization in $\hat{p}$, $\hat{w}$ and $i$.

Knowing from the eigen-value analysis that too low as well as too high values of $\gamma_{yv}$ destabilize the steady state position, we may also examine other values of this parameter. In fact, we find destabilization (in the present sense) in both directions, where significant effects are already observed at far less extreme variations. For example, $\gamma_{yv} = -0.20$ increases the standard deviation of utilization to $\text{sd}(y_t) = 3.90$ and $\gamma_{yv} = 0.30$ increases it to $\text{sd}(y_t) = 3.35$, while the standard deviations of the other variables increase, too.

Concentrating on the two regimes $\gamma_{yv} = -0.10$ and $\gamma_{yv} = 0.10$, Table 10 presents the variabilities resulting from *ceteris paribus* variations of all of the parameters in the Phillips curves. We have explored several values for each coefficient, for positive and negative deviations from the estimated value alike. Within the range considered, the effects on the standard deviations are usually monotonic and they have the opposite sign if the coefficient is decreased instead of increased. So the reported coefficients are sufficiently representative.

A general feature of the experiments is that (by and large) the changes in the standard deviations of utilization and the wage share on the one hand, and of wage inflation, price inflation and the interest rate on the other hand, go in the same direction. There are indeed parameters where the variabilities of the two groups of variables go in opposite directions; most notably this is the case for $\beta_{pv}$ in both regimes and for $\beta_{py}$ in the wage-led regime. Hence, in contrast to the eigen-value approach, the notion of (de)stabilization is here multi-faceted.

The distinction between the two groups of variables helps to organize the information in Table 10. It is also used in the qualitative summary of Table 10.6, which will therefore be more convenient for a brief overview. This classification of the parameters as stabilizing, destabilizing and ambiguous, in the profit-led case as possibly opposed to the wage-led case, is the upshot of our investigation of the properties of the stochastic model.

Besides the sometimes different effects on $(y, v)$ and $(\hat{p}, \hat{w}, i)$, it is interesting to compare Table 10.6 with Table 10.3, where the characterization of (de)stabilization was based on the eigen-value analysis. In particular, the evaluation of wage and price flexibilities is now revised. According to Table 10.6, higher wage flexibility is destabilizing, for all variables and not only in the wage-led but also the profit-led regime. Higher price flexibility continues to be stabilizing in the wage-led case, but this only applies to $y$ and $v$, whereas the nominal magnitudes become more volatile in both regimes.[22] These findings are worth emphasizing as they are ground for caution against inexpensive recommendations of more wage (and perhaps also price) flexibility.

*Table 10.5* Variabilities in the stochastic model under *ceteris paribus* variations of the wage–price parameters.

| | Standard deviations of | | | | | | | | | |
|---|---|---|---|---|---|---|---|---|---|---|
| | $y$ | $\hat{p}$ | $\hat{w}$ | $v$ | $\imath$ | $y$ | $\hat{p}$ | $\hat{w}$ | $v$ | $i$ |
| | *Profit-led* ($\gamma_{yv} = -0▷10$) | | | | | *Wage-led* ($\gamma_{yv} = +0▷10$) | | | | |
| baseline: | **2.37** | **1.50** | **1.68** | **1.12** | **2.13** | **1.90** | **1.53** | **1.70** | **0.90** | **2.29** |
| $\beta_{we}$ = 1.00: | 2.41 | 1.70 | 1.91 | 1.26 | 2.38 | 2.03 | 1.84 | 1.98 | 1.07 | 2.76 |
| $\beta_{py}$ = 0.38: | 2.79 | 2.72 | 2.77 | 1.31 | 3.98 | 1.69 | 2.02 | 2.04 | 0.78 | 2.85 |
| $\beta_{wv}$ = 0.50: | 2.25 | 1.45 | 1.78 | 0.98 | 2.18 | 1.86 | 1.44 | 1.66 | 0.78 | 2.13 |
| $\beta_{pv}$ = 0.50: | 2.24 | 1.73 | 1.70 | 0.96 | 2.27 | 1.84 | 1.70 | 1.77 | 0.76 | 2.44 |
| $\kappa_{wp}$ = 0.80: | 2.56 | 2.18 | 2.48 | 1.33 | 2.84 | 2.01 | 2.30 | 2.64 | 1.10 | 3.27 |
| $\kappa_{pw}$ = 0.80: | 2.40 | 2.09 | 2.14 | 1.04 | 2.91 | 1.83 | 2.07 | 2.07 | 0.80 | 2.87 |
| $\kappa_{wz}$ = 0.50: | 2.20 | 1.48 | 1.76 | 0.90 | 2.12 | 1.98 | 1.55 | 1.81 | 0.83 | 2.32 |
| $\beta_{\pi}$ = 1.50: | 2.36 | 1.35 | 1.57 | 1.12 | 1.98 | 1.90 | 1.65 | 1.80 | 0.90 | 2.41 |
| $\kappa_{\pi}$ = 0.80: | 2.39 | 2.09 | 2.12 | 1.13 | 2.72 | 1.91 | 2.32 | 2.35 | 0.90 | 3.20 |

*Note*: Estimated values in parentheses.

*Table 10.6* Characterization of parameters as stabilizing and destabilizing in the stochastic economy

| | $\beta_{we}$ | $\beta_{py}$ | $\beta_{wv}$ | $\beta_{pv}$ | $\kappa_{wp}$ | $\kappa_{pw}$ | $\kappa_{wz}$ | $\beta_{\pi}$ | $\kappa_{\pi}$ |
|---|---|---|---|---|---|---|---|---|---|
| *Effects on* $(y, v)$ | | | | | | | | | |
| profit-led : | D | D | S | S | D | A | S | NE | NE |
| wage-led : | D | S | S | S | D | S | A | NE | NE |
| *Effects on* $(\hat{p}, \hat{w}, i)$ | | | | | | | | | |
| profit-led : | D | DD | A | D | D | D | NE | S | D |
| wage-led : | D | D | S | D | DD | D | NE | D | DD |

*Note*: D (DD), S, A, NE means that a *ceteris paribus* increase of the parameter is (strongly) destabilizing, stabilizing, ambiguous, or has largely negligible effects; that is, it increases (D, DD) or decreases (S) the variabilities of the corresponding group of variables.

## Wage–price dynamics and income distribution

In many industrialized countries the position of workers has come under severe pressure in the last one or two decades. In this section we design an experiment that allows us to study, in a stylized vacuum, the consequences of such a shift in the general economic climate.

The experiment is again of an impulse-response type in an otherwise deterministic setting. Suppose the economy smoothly grows on its steady state path and then, all of a sudden, the benchmark wage share $v^o$ unanimously drops in all components of the model, from 66 percent to 65 percent, say. The other equilibrium values, in particular the natural rate of employment $e^o$, are assumed to be unaffected by this change.

The wage share $v^o$ as a benchmark plays a role in three parts of the model. First, in the wage bargaining processes, where the fall of $v^o$ directly reflects the weaker position of workers since $v$ enters the structural wage Phillips curve with a negative coefficient. Hence wage increases initially decelerate. Second, in the price Phillips curve the reduction of $v^o$ can be interpreted as a higher markup firms are striving for, the immediate effect being a faster rise of prices. To be exact, these tendencies of lower wage inflation and higher price inflation are maintained in the reduced-form expressions (10.6) and (10.7) for the two rates of inflation.

In the IS curve (10.1), which is the third point, two aspects are to be distinguished. On the one hand, shareholders and managers demand higher profit margins and if they cannot be currently realized, firms cut back on their investment expenditures. On the other hand, also in their consumption demand workers are aware of the general deterioration of their position. To make the scenario not overly pessimistic, let us leave aside the possibility of precautionary saving and assume that, as long the present wage share still exceeds the new $v^o$, they consume proportionately more.[23] Nevertheless, in our profit-led economy with $\gamma_{yv} = -0.10 < 0$ the 'investment strike' of firms dominates. Hence the fall of $v^o$ has a contractionary effect on output.

The adjustment process that has thus been set in motion is depicted by the bold lines in Figure 10.6. The decline of the wage share to its new and lower equilibrium value is achieved by lower rates of wage inflation and higher rates of price inflation. Their deviations from the steady state values are, however, quite limited, so that the reduction of the wage share is gradual and it takes about four years until it has completed its adjustment. The initial decline in economic activity (relative to potential output) continues for two years, when utilization has fallen to 99.1 percent. As the subsequent recovery is quite slow, we can summarize that on the whole the adjustments to the new equilibrium position take five or six years, at the

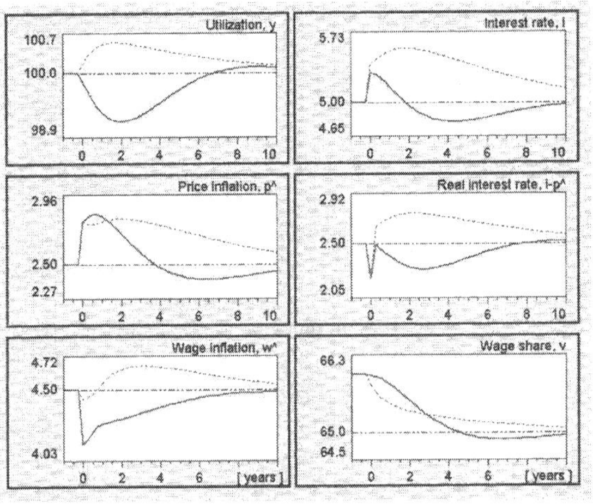


*Figure 10.6* Response of the model to a sudden decrease of $v^o$ from 66% to 65%

*Note*: Dotted lines are based on $\gamma_{yv} = +0.10$, as opposed to the estimated coefficient $\gamma_{yv} = -0.10$ for the bold lines.

cost of a mild recession and only weak nominal disturbances.

By changing the sign of the coefficient $\gamma_{yv}$ from negative to positive in the IS curve, Figure 10.6 also considers what happens if the economy were wage-led (see the dotted lines). Maintaining the hypothesis that the gap $(v - v^o)$, which at $t = 0$ has become positive, induces workers to raise their consumption, this time the output effect is positive. The expansion is, however, less pronounced than the contraction in the previous scenario. This is due to the fact that although the rise in price inflation is similarly moderate, the return of $\hat{p}$ to the target rate of inflation takes more time than before. This feature together with the initial positive output response implies a higher, and longer lasting, increase in the interest rate, such that also the real rate of interest is above its equilibrium value, which is a negative counter-effect on output.

It may also be noted that apart from a negligible intermezzo at the beginning, the rate of wage inflation does not decrease in this experiment, but it rises. The wage share can nevertheless adjust in a downward direction since prices are rising faster than wages. The first reactions in $v$ are even stronger than in the profit-led economy, but convergence slows down afterwards.

Of course, the kind of experiment reflects the present change in economy and society in a very simplistic manner. It might, however, be a starting point for richer stories to tell which, in particular, may include some of the agents' long-term expectations and the overall consumer sentiment. Because of the crucial role it assigns to income distribution, our model can here serve as a workhorse to explore important feedback effects beyond the standard supply-side arguments.

## Concluding remarks

This chapter has started out with the specification of a theoretical framework in the tradition of Keynes and Goodwin, where the adjustment of wages and prices is sluggish, aggregate demand drives output and income distribution, in form of the wage share, affects the dynamical system through a variety of channels. We obtained a closed dynamic system, which thus constitutes a semi-structural Keynes–Goodwin model. Within this theoretical framework, we studied the consequences of high wage and price flexibility for the local stability properties of the system. As a main result of this analysis, we found that both high wage and price flexibility might lead to instability in the system, depending on whether the system is profit- or wage-led.

Even if its semi-structural nature is accepted, the model has one weak point that in any case urges for improvement. This is the specification of Okun's law that basically links the change of the employment rate $e$ to the changes of utilization $y$. As convenient as it is, the specification implies that if for some reason $y$ and $e$ move too much out of line, the latter will exhibit (near) random walk behavior. In addition, the variability of $e$ is too low in relation to that of $y$. Another feature that should be mentioned in this context is our problematic identification of the number of jobs (in the concept of the employment rate) and the number of hours worked (in the concept of labor productivity). Instead of a slight modification in an equation for the composed variable $e$ = labor employed / labor supplied, one may think about two separate adjustment equations for jobs and hours.[24] In this way a further utilization variable generally varying over the business cycle would enter the stage: actual hours per worker employed. We intend to take this issue up next in future research.

## Notes

1 Software to compute the stability regions in the parameter diagrams and run the dynamic simulations under alternative numerical coffiecients is available on request.

2 For each of the topics sketched in the first paragraph many small-scale macrodynamic models have been put forward in the literature. Besides Chiarella *et al.* (2005), however, we do not know of other disequilibrium modeling approaches that address these themes simultaneously, with a similar degree of complexity, and (two of the present authors may say) with similarly meticulous care.

3 Just for the continuous-time model it would be possible to circumvent this problem by integrating the growth rate equation $\hat{e} = \beta_{ey}\hat{y}$ as $e/e^o = y^{\beta_{ey}}$, where $e^o$ is the given 'natural' rate of employment. In the discrete-time model, however, we wish to maintain the three lags of the changes in utilization on the right-hand side of (10.30), whereby the uniqueness problem crops up again.

4 From a neoclassical point of view, the evolution of labor supply is an autonomous process and, given the rate of technical progress, establishes the growth potential of the economy, to which firms adjust in long-run equilibrium. Thus, $g^o = g_\ell + g_z$. A more Keynesian perspective is that $g^o$, in the end, derives from the (long-term) animal spirits of the firms, and it is the labor force (through migration or discouraged and encouraged workers, for example) that in the long-run adjusts to it, yielding $g_\ell = g^o - g_z$. Both interpretations are possible here.

5 See Chiarella *et al.* (2005: 111ff.), where also an empirical study by Brayton *el al.* (1999) is discussed. In fact, the wage share expression in (10.5) can be related to a significant influence of an actual markup variable in the latter work.

6 For comparison Proaño *et al.* (2006) use in a similar theoretical framework solely an adaptive expectations mechanism which, when estimated, is proxied by a 12-quarter moving average.

7 We may refer to Rudebusch's (2002: 19ff.) quotation of Chairman Alan Greenspan's testimony to Congress on June 22, 1994: "Households and businesses became much more reluctant to borrow and spend and lenders to extend credit—a phenomenon often referred to as the 'credit crunch.' In an endeavor to defuse these financial strains, we moved short-term rates lower in a long series of steps that ended in the late summer

of 1992, and we held them at unusually low levels through the end of 1993—both absolutely and, importantly, relative to inflation." Thus, as Rudebusch emphasizes, this episode appears better described as a persistent 'credit crunch' shock than as a sluggish partial adjustment to a known desired rate.

8 Besides the strictly exogenous variables, the following instruments were used: the contemporaneous and lagged first differences of an 'employment rate' constructed from hours, the real interest rate, the lagged nominal interest rate, lagged productivity growth, and four lags of the employment rate, the first differences in utilization, and the wage share (detrended by the Hodrick-Prescott filter).

9 The constants can be omitted since Proaño *et al.* (2006) do not discuss their implications for a steady state solution, i.e. a stationary point of system (10.27)–(10.31).

10 Nonlinear only in the respect that the sums of the coefficients on $\pi^c$ and the corresponding inflation variable are constrained to one.

11 Incidentally, estimation by two-stage least squares leads to results similar to those in Table 10.2. The lower Durbin–Watson in the least squares estimation in (*d*), although it produces the highest $R^2$, underlines the necessity of including the instrumental variables.

12 At least if the curve is not thought to be derived from an infinite horizon optimization as in the new-Keynesian models, where price inflation responds to marginal cost, which in turn are often proxied by a wage share variable. Then, however, also future values of the wage share would have to show up on the right-hand side of the Phillips curve.

13 For a documentation of this feature see, e.g., Christiano *et al.* (2005).

14 Except that the VAR implies slower convergence for the interest rate, which not the least is due to the rate's high coefficient of 0.91 on the first lag of itself. This is a general problem of all VARs including a rate of interest.

15 The feature that in Figure 10.3 the three variables $v$, $\hat{w}$ and $i$ react immediately at $t=0$, while $\hat{p}$ only changes at $t=1$, is a consequence of the chosen ordering of the variables in the VAR, which is made explicit in the note to Figure 10.3. Thus all variables ranked after $y$ are affected by the impulse to $y$ still in the same quarter, where sign and size of the reaction is given by their covariance with $y$.

16 Besides, transforming (10.16)–(10.26a) into a well-defined difference equations system analogous to (10.12)–(10.15) would not be a trivial task, either.

17 This nice result should, however, not be overrated. Within a richer structural framework these parameter diagrams may loose their unambiguity; see Chiarella *et al.* (2005, Figure 7.8 on p. 316). For a real wage feedback diagram similar to Figure 10.4 above, which also includes effects from $\beta_{we}$ and $\beta_{py}$ (some of which are destabilizing!), see ibid. 310ff.

18 In the rational expectations models, it is the reduced-form representation of the motions of the predetermined variables that is stable.

19 In mainstream macroeconomics, however, stability of the equilibrium point is usually presupposed (in rational expectations models, it is the reduced-form representation of the motions of the predetermined variables that is stable) or, especially in (quasi-) linear models, it is a direct consequence of an econometric estimation method.

20 Since for each set of parameters the same sequences of random shocks are used, it suffices to run a single experiment over 4,000 quarters.

21 The latter may appear somewhat surprising given that the interest rate is determined by the Taylor rule and the variability of $y$ decreases more than the variability of $\hat{p}$ increases. The phenomenon must have something to do with the serial correlation of the disturbances in the rule and the interest rate inertia it causes. Perhaps a certain phase shift of $\hat{p}$ versus $y$ affects persistence in such a way that, under $\gamma_{yv} = 0.10$, the more extreme values of the interest rate are favored. An even more astonishing case is the increase of $\beta_{wv}$ in the profit-led regime in Table 10, where the variabilities of both $y$ and $\hat{p}$ decrease but that of $i$ increases.

22 Similar differences from Table 10.3 can be observed for the weight parameter $\kappa_{pw}$.

23 This is certainly another place where a more structural modeling is desirable that explicitly distinguishes between the disposable incomes of workers and (interest and) profit earners.

24 An explicit distinction between the two variables and econometric estimations of gradual adjustments of each of them can be found in Franke (2006, Section 6).

## References

Asada, T., Chen, P., Chiarella, C. and Flaschel, P. (2006). Keynesian dynamics and the wage-price spiral. a baseline disequilibrium model, *Journal of Macroeconomics* **28**: 90–130.

Blanchard, O. J. and Katz, L. (1999). Wage dynamics: Reconciling theory and evidence, *The American Economic Review* **89**: 69–74. Papers and Proceedings of the One Hundred Eleventh Annual Meeting of the American Economic Association (May, 1999).

Brayton, F., Roberts, J. and Williams, J. (1999). What's happened to the Phillips curve?, *Finance and Economics Discussion Series 1999-49*, Board of Governors of the Federal Reserve Bank System.

Calvo, G. A. (1983). Staggered prices in a utility maximizing framework, *Journal of Monetary Economics* **12**: 383–398.

Chen, P. and Flaschel, P. (2006). Measuring the interaction of wage and price Phillips curves for the U.S. economy, *Studies in Nonlinear Dynamics and Econometrics* **10**: 1–35.

Chiarella, C., Flaschel, P. and Franke, R. (2005). *Foundations for a Disequilibrium Theory of the Business Cycle. Qualitative Analysis and Quantitative Assesment*, Cambridge University Press, Cambridge, UK.

Christiano, L., Eichenbaum, M. and Evans, C. (2005). Nominal rigidities and the dynamic effects of a shock to monetary policy, *Journal of Political Economy* **113**: 1–45.

Clarida, R., Galí, J. and Gertler, M. (1998). Monetary policy rules in practice: Some international evidence, *European Economic Review* **42**: 1033–67.

Erceg, C. J., Henderson, D. W. and Levin, A. T. (2000). Optimal monetary policy with staggered wages and prices, *Journal of Monetary Economics* **46**: 281–313.

Flaschel, P. and Krolzip, H.-M. (2006). Wage-price Phillips curves and macroeconomic stability: basic structural form, estimation and analysis. In: C. Chiarella, P. Flaschel, R. Franke and W. Semmler (eds) *Quantitative and Empirical Analysis of Non Linear Dynamic Macromodels*. Amsterdam: Elsevier.

Franke, R. (2006). Themes on Okun's Law and beyond, *Schwartz CEPA technical report*, New School University.

Franke, R., Flaschel, P. and Proaño, C. R. (2006). Wage-price dynamics and income distribution in a semi-structural Keynes–Goodwin model, *Structural Change and Macroeconomic Dynamics* **17**(4): 452–465.

Gerdesmeier, D. and Roffia, B. (2003). Empirical estimates of reaction functions for the euro area, *Working Paper 206*, European Central Bank.

Proaño, C. R., Flaschel, P., Ernst, E. and Semmler, W. (2006). Disequilibrium macroeconomics dynamics, income distribution and wage-price Phillips curves: evidence from the US and the euro area, *Macroeconomic Policy Institute (IMK) Working Paper 04/2006 paper*.

Rose, H. (1967). On the non-linear theory of employment, *Review of Economic Studies* **34**: 153–173.

Rudebusch, G. D. (2002). Term structure evidence on interest rate smoothing and monetary policy inertia, *Journal of Monetary Economics* **49**: 1161–87.

Rudebusch, G. D. and Wu, T. (2004). *A Macro-finance Model of the Term Structure, Monetary Policy, and the Economy*, mimeo, San Francisco: Federal Bank of San Francisco.

Smets, F. and Wouters, R. (2003). An estimated dynamic stochastic general equilibrium model for the euro area, *Journal of the European Economic Association* **1**(5): 1123–1175.

# Part III
# Multisectoral and microfounded approaches

# 11 Decomposition methods for analyzing intra-regional and inter-regional income distribution

*Srinivas Raghavendra*

## Motivation

The decade of the nineties witnessed the revival of empirical growth literature, which brought with it a renewed interest in question of the world distribution of income. Treating the world economy as a closed unit, there are number of methods proposed in the literature to estimate the distribution of world income – ranging from calculating per capita GDP of individual countries (Quah, 1996), Jones (1997), or calculating population-weighted GDP per capita taking into account the within-country income disparities (Bourguigon and Morrisson, 2002) to integrating individual country density functions to construct the world income distribution (Sala-i-Martin, 2002). In another interesting study, an attempt has been made to decompose the total inequality between the individuals in the world, by continents and regions (Milanovic, 2002).

In this chapter, we propose an alternative framework to study the world income distribution based on the method proposed by Richard Stone and Richard Goodwin (Goodwin, 1949 and 1980; Stone's foreword to Pyatt *et al.*, 1977). The underlying idea in these methods is the emphasis placed on the intertwining of the question of income distribution with the existing structure of production, where income distribution affects final demand, and hence the structure of production and the structure of production, in turn, influences factor demands and hence the structure of income distribution.

Given that the world economy is a closed unit and the constituent economies are inextricably interwoven through the process of globalization, it is then obvious that the issue of income distribution of the world economy as a whole is interrelated to questions of structural interdependencies through trade among its members. This question of linkages between economic systems and the spillover and possible feedback effects is not new in the literature and it dates back to Machlup (1943), Goodwin (1949) and Metzler (1950).

Richard Goodwin, in his pioneering work, formalized the structural interdependencies in an economy by computing the compound-matrix multiplier using the Leontieff input-output table. Metzler's proposition was to understand 'the mechanism by which an expansion or contraction of income in one region or country is transmitted to other regions or countries . . . the conclusions apply without modification to the regions within a single country, or, indeed to any regional classification of the world economy, such as the economies comprising Eastern Europe, Western Europe, Latin America, and similar regions.'[1] These important results coincided with the international efforts to systematically organize a system of social accounts going beyond the simple Keynesian income categories.[2]

These two developments served as the initial condition for Richard Stone's proposal for reclassifying the social accounting matrix and decomposing the compound-matrix multiplier to separate out the intra ('own') and inter ('indirect') components. Pyatt *et al.* (1977) conducted the first empirical exercise along these lines for the Sri Lankan economy to understand the interrelation between the structure of production and income distribution. Subsequently, Richard Goodwin (1983) used this decomposition technique to develop a world trade multiplier to analyze the interrelation between unemployment and world trade.

Given this history of analyzing the income distribution in an accounting framework, it seems reasonable to use this method for analyzing the world income distribution instead of relying on probabilistic approaches. This decomposition is pertinent from the point of view of understanding whether the inter-regional income disparities are mainly mediated through the intra-regional income disparities implied by their structure of production and thereby assessing the impact of various growth policies on the macro structure of the economies.

In this chapter we discuss how this technique could be harnessed to study the question of world income distribution. In the following section, we briefly discuss the aggregate SAM framework in a regional perspective. In 'Extension: the case of relative income distribution' we show how this decomposition method could be used in the case of two regions and discuss the economic implications of different multipliers. In 'Conclusion: a framework for empirical estimation' we generalize the this procedure for three regions and discuss various limitations of such an exercise in extending it to higher order geographical dimensions. We conclude by some general remarks on applying this method to India, including those of data requirement and its consistency.

## Analytical framework

The principle of a Social Accounting Matrix (henceforth SAM) is really nothing more than that of double entry bookkeeping in accounting. A SAM is a series of accounts in each of which incomings and outgoings must balance and what is 'incoming' into one account must be 'outgoing' from another account. In this respect, a SAM resembles traditional national accounts. For want of space, we shall keep the discussion on the framework of a SAM at the most aggregated level, which will bring out the essential point underlying this analysis. The SAM for any region would have some principal accounts pertinent to the region and two accounts relating to current and capital transactions with the rest of the world. For each region, considered as part of an integrated system, each of the own-region 'domestic' accounts records incomes and outlays wholly within the region as well as the origin of receipts and destination of payments externally.[3] The external transactions are recorded in some detail between the region and other regions, and the rest of the world.

Essentially embracing the concepts developed by Stone (1961), a distinction has been drawn between functional flows (transactions) and geographical (inter-regional) flows.[4] Thus, all transactions between different functional accounts are represented as taking place within each region. Inter-regional flows in the accounting system therefore represent transfers, which simply augment the receipts of an account in one region and simultaneously deplete the same (functional) account in the other region. In sum, therefore, this way of representing regional accounts allows the functional and geographical elements of transactions to be clearly distinguished. The idea here is to collate the social accounting matrices for different regions according to these broad principles and analyze the linkages between economic systems and the spillover and possible feedback effects one system may have on another by decomposing the transactions matrix, in a common unit of account, to delineate effects of intra ('direct effects') country income disparity from inter ('cross effects') group income disparities.

In the multiplier decomposition studies the objective is to delineate the effects and linkages that may take place between the designated endogenous accounts and the accounts exogenous to the system. In a study that covers a broader geographical dimension, say, a country or a region, say the EU etc., these designated categories and their disaggregations must be carefully done to avoid inconsistencies so that the final, reclassified transaction matrix be of a good representation of the production structure of the economy or a group of economies in question. In this section, first we shall consider a simplified two-region system and then generalize to a three-region system to show how the decomposition technique results in different multipliers and in that process, we shall also discuss some of the limitations of this exercise for higher-order systems.

In the case of two-region systems, by endogenizing households as well as factors of production, the impact multiplier $M$ of exogenous outlays $x$ on endogenous income y, represented as:

$$y = Mx \tag{11.1}$$

captures the reciprocal relationship between income distribution and the structure of production. It can further be shown that $M$can be multiplicatively decomposed to yield:

$$y = M_3 M_2 M_1 x \tag{11.2}$$

where the components of $M$can be ascribed to the separate effects of multipliers wholly within a group of accounts ($M_1$); the effect of an exogenous injection which feeds back upon itself but via other parts of the system ($M_2$); or simply the effect of an increase in income in one group of accounts has upon another ($M_3$). The separation of these effects gives a useful picture of structural independence within the endogenous accounts of the system. The derivation of the compound multiplier from the transaction matrix is as follows.[5] Defining $U$ as the matrix of endogenous account transactions, bordered by the vector x, a row vector $w'$ of payments by endogenous accounts to the consolidated exogenous account, and a scalar $\psi$ representing the consolidated payment between exogenous accounts; then the complete social accounting matrix S where:

$$S = \begin{bmatrix} U & x \\ w' & \psi \end{bmatrix} \tag{11.3}$$

has the property that:

$$Si = S'i = \begin{bmatrix} y \\ \theta \end{bmatrix} \tag{11.4}$$

where $y$ is the vector of endogenous account totals and a scalar of total receipts and payments by the exogenous account. Thus defining:

$$U = A\hat{y} \tag{11.5}$$

where $A$ is a matrix of average propensities with respect to income across the broad group of endogenous transactions. From these definitions, it follows that:

$$y = (I - A)^{-1} x = Mx \tag{11.6}$$

where $M$ is the compound accounting multiplier showing the effect of exogenous injections $x$ on endogenous income $y$ at given prices. Extending the basic SAM and decomposing multipliers further according to regional dimension means that attention will be focused on the patterns of inter-regional trade and transfers and their impact on income distribution.

The decomposition technique proposed by Richard Stone can be derived for a two-region system, by reorganizing and reclassifying the transaction matrix as outlined above. This can be expressed analytically as follows:

$$S = \begin{bmatrix} U_{11} & \hat{u}_{12} & x_1 \\ \hat{u}_{21} & U_{22} & x_2 \\ w'_1 & w'_2 & \psi \end{bmatrix} \tag{11.7}$$

where the account totals are:

$$Si = S'i = \begin{bmatrix} y_1 \\ y_2 \\ \theta \end{bmatrix} \tag{11.8}$$

The analytical structure of $S$ would be maintained even if the endogenous accounts were disaggregated further into say, separate factor, household or commodity accounts. This is the advantage of this method – one can do this analysis for different levels of disaggregation to study the impact of exogenous injections on various accounts. Expressing the proportion of inter-regional transfers from region $i$ to $j$ as a proportion of total outlays in region i as $\hat{c}_{ij}$, where:

$$\hat{u}_{ij} = \hat{c}_{ij} y_i \tag{11.9}$$

and $U_{ii}$ as the product of average propensities $C_{ii}$ and total outlays $y_i$,

$$U_{ii} = C_{ii} \hat{y}_i \tag{11.10}$$

gives a final two-equation system in $y$ and $x$:

$$\begin{aligned} y_1 &= C_{11} y_1 + \hat{c}_{12} y_2 + x_1 \\ y_2 &= \hat{c}_{21} y_2 + C_{22} y_2 + x_2 \end{aligned} \tag{11.11}$$

The commodity trade element of $\hat{c}_{ij}$, shows the proportion of imports to the total supply (domestic plus imports) in region i. This may be written as:

$$\begin{bmatrix} y_1 \\ y_2 \end{bmatrix} = \begin{bmatrix} C_{11} & \hat{c}_{12} \\ \hat{c}_{21} & C_{22} \end{bmatrix} \begin{bmatrix} y_1 \\ y_2 \end{bmatrix} + \begin{bmatrix} x_1 \\ x_2 \end{bmatrix} \tag{11.12}$$

and solved as:

$$\begin{bmatrix} y_1 \\ y_2 \end{bmatrix} = \begin{bmatrix} (I - C_{11})^{-1} & 0 \\ 0 & (I - C_{22})^{-1} \end{bmatrix} \left\{ \begin{bmatrix} 0 & \hat{c}_{12} \\ \hat{c}_{21} & 0 \end{bmatrix} \begin{bmatrix} y_1 \\ y_2 \end{bmatrix} + \begin{bmatrix} x_1 \\ x_2 \end{bmatrix} \right\} \tag{11.13}$$

This becomes:

$$\begin{bmatrix} y_1 \\ y_2 \end{bmatrix} = \begin{bmatrix} 0 & B_{12} \\ B_{21} & 0 \end{bmatrix} \begin{bmatrix} y_1 \\ y_2 \end{bmatrix} + \begin{bmatrix} (I - C_{11})^{-1} & 0 \\ 0 & (I - C_{22})^{-1} \end{bmatrix} \begin{bmatrix} x_1 \\ x_2 \end{bmatrix} \tag{11.14}$$

where $B_{12} = (I - C_{11})^{-1} \hat{c}_{12}$ and $B_{21} = (I - C_{22})^{-1} \hat{c}_{21}$ so that:

$$\begin{bmatrix} y_1 \\ y_2 \end{bmatrix} = \begin{bmatrix} I & -B_{12} \\ -B_{21} & I \end{bmatrix}^{-1} \begin{bmatrix} (I - C_{11})^{-1} & 0 \\ 0 & (I - C_{22})^{-1} \end{bmatrix} \begin{bmatrix} x_1 \\ x_2 \end{bmatrix} \tag{11.15}$$

or:

$$y = M\, M_1 x \tag{11.16}$$

where $y$ and $x$ are stacked vectors of endogenous account incomes and exogenous outlays, respectively; and $M$ and $M_1$ are multiplier matrices since $M \geq I$ *and* $M_1 \geq I$. Together, they capture the total repercussions within and between endogenous accounts in the inter-regional systems.

$M_1$ is the intra-regional multiplier matrix. It shows the multiplier effects that results from linkages wholly within each of the regions taken separately. Thus, an exogenous outlay of $x_1$ in region 1 may create multiplier repercussions within that region via $(I - C_{11})^{-1}$, but the zero off-diagonal sub-matrices indicate that the multiplier matrix as a whole capture no inter-regional repercussions; and similarly for region 2.

The second component of the overall multiplier matrix, which premultiplies the intra-regional multiplier matrix in equation (11.16), is $M$and this may referred to as the 'inter-regional' multiplier matrix. It captures all of the (spatial) repercussions between the accounts of one region and those of the other, but it excludes all of the 'within region' effects since these have already been accounted for by $M_1$. Note that the inter-regional multiplier essentially depends upon the linkages represented by $\hat{c}_{12}$ and $\hat{c}_{21}$, and the degree of departure of $M$from the identity matrix depends on the strength of bilateral trade linkages and other endogenous inter-regional transfers. This can be seen by multiplicatively decomposing the inter-regional multiplier matrix $M$further.

$$\begin{aligned} M &= \begin{bmatrix} I & -B_{12} \\ -B_{21} & I \end{bmatrix}^{-1} \\ &= \begin{bmatrix} (I - B_{12}B_{21})^{-1} & (I - B_{12}B_{21})^{-1} B_{12} \\ (I - B_{21}B_{12})^{-1} B_{21} & (I - B_{21}B_{12})^{-1} \end{bmatrix} \\ &= \begin{bmatrix} (I - B_{12}B_{21})^{-1} & 0 \\ 0 & (I - B_{21}B_{12})^{-1} \end{bmatrix} \begin{bmatrix} I & B_{12} \\ B_{21} & I \end{bmatrix} \\ &= M_3 M_2 \end{aligned} \tag{11.17}$$

where $M_3$ and $M_2$ represent the matrices in equation (11.17). Like $M_1$,$M_3$ is block diagonal and hence shows the extent to which outlays in one region affect the incomes of endogenous accounts in the same region. But $M_3$ shows the component multipliers accounting for inter-regional feedback effects and may therefore be referred to as an inter-regional 'closed-loop' multiplier matrix. The matrix $M_2$, is also a multiplier matrix (since$M_2 \geq I$) and has identity matrices in its diagonal. Analogous to the decomposition in equation (11.2), $M_2$ is an inter-regional 'open loop' multiplier matrix. It captures the effect that one region has upon the other, after accounting for all 'own-region' effects and hence the block diagonal matrices are identity matrices. The total inter-regional multiplier effect for 'own-region' is obtained as the product of corresponding diagonal blocks of $M_3$ and $M_1$; while the equivalent multiplier effect of one region upon the other is the product of the appropriate inter-regional 'open loop' effect and the total 'own-region' effect for the former region. Hence the total multiplier relationship for the two-region system can be expressed as:

$$y = M_3 M_2 M_1 x \tag{11.18}$$

This clarifies the nature of the separate effects involved in the regional system and the decomposition technique would be great help in delineating the different effects of exogenous injections on the endogenous accounts.[6] Considering the above technique for a three-region system to trace out the effects of a multilateral trade on endogenous accounts, the analogue of equation (11.13) is:

$$\begin{bmatrix} y_1 \\ y_2 \\ y_3 \end{bmatrix} = \begin{bmatrix} C_{11} & \hat{c}_{12} & \hat{c}_{13} \\ \hat{c}_{21} & C_{22} & \hat{c}_{23} \\ \hat{c}_{31} & \hat{c}_{32} & C_{33} \end{bmatrix} \begin{bmatrix} y_1 \\ y_2 \\ y_3 \end{bmatrix} + \begin{bmatrix} x_1 \\ x_2 \\ x_3 \end{bmatrix} \tag{11.19}$$

and solution for the system is:

$$y = (I - B)^{-1}(I - C)^{-1}x \tag{11.20}$$

where:

$$(I - C)^{-1} = \begin{bmatrix} (I - C_{11})^{-1} & 0 & 0 \\ 0 & (I - C_{22})^{-1} & 0 \\ 0 & 0 & (I - C_{33})^{-1} \end{bmatrix}$$

and:

$$(I - B)^{-1} = \begin{bmatrix} I & -B_{12} & -B_{13} \\ -B_{21} & I & -B_{23} \\ -B_{31} & -B_{32} & I \end{bmatrix}^{-1}$$

As in the two-region case, equation (11.20) may be viewed as the product of an inter-regional multiplier $M$and intra-regional multiplier $M_1$, where:

$$M_1 = (I - C)^{-1} \text{ and } M = (I - B)^{-1}.$$

However, unlike the two-region case $M$ does not exhibit the same simple structure for immediate further decomposition to inter-regional open and closed loop effects.[7] For example, consider the way in which exogenous outlays in one region may leak into other regions and feedback on to itself. In this three-region system there are four routes. For any region say region 1, there are two finds of bilateral feedbacks (via region 2 and region 3) and two kinds of trilateral feedbacks (via region 2 first and then region 3, or region 3 first and then region 2). These direct and indirect effects can be calculated and decomposed from the inter-regional multiplier in equation (11.20). In sum, as in the case of two-region system, the overall impact multiplier for the three-region system may be expressed as:

$$y = M_4 M_3 M_2 M_1 x \tag{11.21}$$

Thus the impact multiplier may be decomposed into four separate multiplier components, each capturing inter- and intra-effects of an exogenous injection on the endogenous accounts.

## Extension: the case of relative income distribution

So far, we have discussed how a SAM could be used to measure the changes in the level of income of the endogenous accounts caused by exogenous and unitary shocks. In this section we will discuss how this framework can also be articulated into a setting of income distribution to calculate the relative income distribution using the above analysis. We use the measurement proposed by Roland-Holst and Sancho (1992) to calculate the relative income distribution and propose a simple, straightforward extension of their method to further decompose to delineate the changes in the relative income distribution due to the exogenous shocks.

The multiplier analysis starts by dividing the total accounts of a SAM into two separate categories: endogenous accounts and exogenous accounts. If we consider a social accounting matrix with k endogenous institutions and l exogenous institutions, the total accounts T are the sum of the two types: T=k+l. The SAM can then be written as,

$$\begin{bmatrix} y_k \\ y_l \end{bmatrix} = \begin{bmatrix} A_{kk} & A_{kl} \\ A_{lk} & A_{ll} \end{bmatrix} \begin{bmatrix} y_k \\ y_l \end{bmatrix} \tag{11.22}$$

where $A_{ij}$ , as discussed in 'Analytical framework' above, are sub-matrices that contain the expenditure share coefficients. Then the multiplier effect of the exogenous injections can be obtained as:

$$y_k = A_{kk}y_k + A_{kl}y_l = (I - A_{kk})^{-1}A_{kl}y_l = Mx \tag{11.23}$$

where $M = (I - A_{kk})^{-1}$ is the matrix of multipliers and $x = A_{kl}y_l$ is the vector of exogenous injections. The multiplier matrix $M$ shows the overall effect of a unitary increase in the exogenous components on the endogenous accounts. Therefore, the element $m_{ij}$ of $M$ quantifies the changes in the income of the institution i as a consequence of a unitary and exogenous injection received from the institution j.

From equation (11.23), it is clear that the multipliers corresponding to endogenous institutions illustrate the changes in the absolute level of income. To study the changes in the relative income of the endogenous institution due to the exogenous shocks, Roland-Holst and Sancho (1992) proposed a measure to calculate the distributive incidence. We summarize their result, by normalizing equation (11.23) such that,

$$y_k^* = \frac{y_k}{e'y_k} = (e'Mx)^{-1}Mx \tag{11.24}$$

where $e'$ is a unitary row vector. From the above definition, the changes in the relative income of the endogenous components generated by an increase in the exogenous injections are equal to:

$$\begin{aligned} dy_k &= (e'Mx)^{-1}[I - (e'Mx)^{-1}(Mx)e']Mdx \\ &= \frac{1}{e'y_k}\left[I - \frac{y_k}{e'y_k}e'\right]Mdx \\ &= R\,dx \end{aligned} \tag{11.25}$$

In the above expression, $R$ is the *redistribution matrix* and shows the change in the relative income of the endogenous accounts caused by a change in the exogenous injections. Every individual element of the matrix, $r_{ij}$, determines the magnitude and direction of the change in the relative income of the institution i as a result of an inflow from the institution j. It is interesting that, irrespective of which endogenous components are chosen in the model, the sum of the columns in the matrix of redistribution is zero.[8]

Now in equation (11.25), instead of the compound multiplier if we use its decomposed parts of inter and intra, we may get corresponding decomposed redistribution matrices. This would be interesting because these redistribution matrices would capture the origin of the change in the relative income of the institutions due to an exogenous shock. In other words, we would be able to delineate the total change in the relative income of institutions due to an exogenous shock into 'intra' and 'inter' categories corresponding to the respective multiplier component. In a sense, we would be able to quantify and decompose the total change in the relative income of institutions into the change that is mediated through 'own' (intra) accounts and the change that is mediated through 'other' (inter) accounts. We can see this straightaway if we substitute the decomposed compound multiplier in additive form in equation (11.25).

First let $D = \frac{1}{e'y}\left[I - \frac{y}{e'y}e'\right]$ and substituting:

$$M = M_1 + [M_2M_1 - M_1] + [M_3M_2M_1 - M_2M_1] \tag{11.26}$$

we get:

$$dy = \{DM_1 + D[M_2M_1 - M_1] + D[M_3M_2M_1 - M_2M_1]\}\,dx$$

which can be written as:

$$dy = [R_1(x) + R_2(x) + R_3(x)]\,dx \tag{11.27}$$

The first term $R_1$ would capture the change in the relative income distribution that results from linkages wholly within each of the accounts and the other two terms would capture the change in the relative income distribution due to inter-regional linkages in the accounting structure. By decomposing the redistribution matrix we would be able to delineate the intra-income disparity and inter-income disparity between a region or between different geographical regions.

We could do this decomposition exercise to understand the change in relative income distribution due to an exogenous injection at various level of disaggregation. First, we could analyze this at the level of productive sectors, by taking different sectors into consideration when classifying the endogenous accounts and do this exercise to calculate the relative income distribution in various sectors. Second, we could use this decomposition technique to analyze the functional income distribution. By considering factors of production say labor and capital, as two separate accounts, and study the impact of exogenous demand affect the relative income distribution of the factors of production. Third, from an institutional point of view, we could analyze the relative position of households by disaggregating the household sector in a meaningful way and study the relative position of various institutions that are in this sector. For instance, we could study the change in relative income distribution of different consumer groups and analyze the personal income distribution. By disaggregating the macro economy at different levels or viewing the macro economy at various levels of resolution would unravel the structural constraints that inhibit the process of income distribution.

## Conclusion: a framework for empirical estimation

In the recent empirical growth literature, the issue of world income distribution has taken the center stage. Treating the world economy as a closed unit, there are number of methods proposed in the literature to estimate the distribution of world income – ranging from calculating per capita GDP of individual countries or calculating population-weighted GDP per capita taking into account the within-country income disparities to integrating individual country density functions to construct the world income distribution. In another interesting study, an attempt has been made to decompose the total inequality between the individuals in the world, by continents and regions.

Here we proposed an alternative framework to study the world income distribution based on the method proposed by Richard Stone and Richard Goodwin. The underlying idea in these methods is that the question of income distribution is intertwined with the existing structure of production, where income distribution affects final demand, and the structure of production and the structure of production influences factor demands and hence the structure of income distribution. We discussed how the decomposition methods, using the accounting framework of the social accounting matrix, proposed in the literature could be harnessed to measure the changes in the level of income of the endogenous accounts caused by exogenous and unitary shocks.

We also discussed how this decomposition method could be used to the problem of income distribution, by calculating the redistribution matrix for different accounts. We proposed a simple, straightforward extension in calculating the redistribution matrix to delineate the total change in the relative income distribution into 'direct' and 'indirect' effects. This is important from the policy perspective, because the decomposition of the redistribution matrix reveals the structural constraints that limit the process of income distribution or redistribution.

Even though empirical estimates are crucial in order to assess the advantages of the proposed method over the existing methods, it is, however, pertinent as a crucial prerequisite to provide a framework for constructing an inter-regional SAM and such an attempt is made here in the context of Indian economy. In India, given the data constraint, construction of SAM has proved to be very difficult, particularly, in the context of the distribution of income.[9] The original national SAM for India was assembled by Pradhan *et al.* (1999) contains 60 productive sectors, two factors of production, and 12 household occupational categories. This is an updated and expanded version of the 1989–1990 IO table prepared by the Indian Central Statistical Organization. The data used to construct the national India SAM has been drawn from various sources including input-output tables, national accounts, government budgets, household survey, industrial surveys and agriculture production statistics. There is the issue of consistency here because different bodies of statistics are collected by a variety of agencies, which do not work on an agreed set of definitions and classifications. This can be adjusted and updated using well-known numerical techniques like conjugate gradient algorithm or quasi-newton methods.[10] The

*Table 11.1* Structure of the inter-regional social accounting matrix (SAM)

| *Expenditure* <br> *Income* | | *Production sectors* <br> *NWSE* | *Factors of production* <br> *NWSE* | *Institutions* <br> *NWSE* | *Capital* <br> *NWSE* | *ROW* | *Total income* |
|---|---|---|---|---|---|---|---|
| Production | N | | | | | $C_{RW}^{N}$ | $T_N^Q$ |
| sectors | W | BLOCK | | BLOCK | | $C_{RW}^{W}$ | $T_W^Q$ |
| | S | I | | II | | $C_{RW}^{S}$ | $T_S^Q$ |
| | E | | | | | $C_{RW}^{E}$ | $T_E^Q$ |
| Factors of | N | | | | | | $T_N^F$ |
| production | W | BLOCK | | | | | $T_W^F$ |
| | S | III | | | | | $T_S^F$ |
| | E | | | | | | $T_E^F$ |
| Institutions | N | | | | | | $T_N^I$ |
| | W | BLOCK | BLOCK | BLOCK | BLOCK | | $T_W^I$ |
| | S | IV | V | VI | VII | | $T_S^I$ |
| | E | | | | | | $T_E^I$ |
| Capital | N | | | | | | $T_N^K$ |
| | W | | | BLOCK | | | $T_W^K$ |
| | S | | | VIII | | | $T_S^K$ |
| | E | | | | | | $T_E^K$ |
| ROW | | $X_N^{RW} \ldots X_E^{RW}$ | | | | | $T^{RW}$ |
| Total expenditure | | $T_N^Q \ldots T_E^Q$ | $T_N^F \ldots T_E^F$ | $T_N^I \ldots T_E^I$ | $T_N^K \ldots T_E^K$ | $T^{RW}$ | |

national SAM could serve as a benchmark for the estimation of its regional components to study the repercussions of exogenous injections on the endogenous accounts.

As our objective is to construct an inter-regional social accounting matrix using these regional components, which has been estimated for Northern, Southern, Western and Eastern regions.[11] The schematic structure of the inter-regional SAM and various matrices, referred here as Blocks, involved in the construction is given in Table 11.1.

As schematized in Table 11.1, it is pertinent from the point of view of income distribution that we reconstruct a national SAM to incorporate the inter-regional transfers between productive sectors, institutions, factors of production and capital in each of the sub-regions of an economy. Each of these can be further disaggregated depending on the data availability and comparability. Such a construction, we believe, would be useful to study the repercussions of exogenous shocks on the relative income distribution and at a broader level, for an analysis of the structural interlinkages between the regions and their influence on the process of income distribution.

## Acknowledgements

This chapter was presented in Richard Goodwin Workshop at the 17th Annual Conference of EAEPE in Bremen, Germany. I would like to thank Professor Vela Velupillai for his inspiration and guidance. The usual disclaimer applies.

## Notes

1 Metzler (1950: 329).
2 The initial versions came from the Organization for European Economic Co-operation (OEEC) in 1950 and the United Nations, which drew up the first edition of the System of National Accounts published as UNSO in 1953. See Stone (1977) for an historical account of the evolution of 'social accounting' around the world.
3 For a detailed account of the social accounting framework and the decomposition technique, see Pyatt *et al.* (1977) or Pyatt and Round (1979)
4 Or one could use the terminology of 'endogenous' and 'exogenous' accounts for 'functional' and 'inter-regional' flows.
5 The detailed derivation of the compound multiplier and its decomposition is found in Pyatt *et al.* (1977), Pyatt and Round (1979) and Round (1985).
6 The matrix $M_1$ has some interesting features, especially insofar as it related to the phenomenon of 'cross-hauling' of commodities between regions, although it more general and related to all inter-regional transfers. For two-region systems, the cross-hauling phenomenon is especially simple (two-way trade between two regions). However, for third and higher-order systems, the nature of the cross hauls is more complex. See Round (1985) for a detailed exposition on this issue.
7 See Round (1985) for a detailed formalization and discussion on this point.
8 See Roland-Holst and Sancho (1992).
9 See Pradhan *et al.*(1999) for a brief history on various attempts to build a Social Accounting Matrix for India.
10 See Stone *et al.* (1942) and Byron (1978).
11 See Bussolo *et al.* (2003).

## References

Bourguignon, F. and Morrisson, C. (1998) "Inequality and development: the role of dualism", *Journal of Development Economics*, 57(2): 233–57.

Bourguignon, F. and Morrisson, C. (2002) "Inequality among world citizens: 1820–1992", *American Economic Review* 92(4): 727–44.

Bussolo, M., Chemingui, M. and O'Connor, D. (2003) "A multi-region social accounting matrix (1995) and Regional Environmental General Equilibrium Model for India (REGEMI)", Working Paper No. 213. OECD Development Centre.

Byron, R.P. (1978) "The estimation of large social accounting matrices", *Journal of the Royal Statistical Society, Series A (General)*, 141: 359–67.

Goodwin, R.M. (1949) "The multiplier as matrix", *Economic Journal*, 59(236): 537–55.

Goodwin, R.M. (1980) "World trade multipliers", *Journal of Post Keynesian Economics*, 2(3): 319–44.

Goodwin, R.M. (1983) "The world matrix multiplier", in *Essays in Linear Economic Structure*, London: Macmillan .

Jones, C.I. (1997) "On the evolution of the world income distribution", *Journal of Economic Perspectives*, 11(3): 19–36.

Machlup, F. (1943) *International Trade and National Income Multiplier*, Philadelphia: The Blakiston Company.

Metzler, L.A. (1950) "A multiple-region theory of income and trade", *Econometrica*, 18: 329–54.

Milanovic, B. (2002) "True world income distribution, 1988 and 1993: first calculation based on household surveys alone", *Economic Journal*, 112(476): 51–92.

Milanovic, B. and Yitzhaki, S. (2002) "Decomposing world income distribution: does the world have a middle class?" *Review of Income and Wealth*, 48(2): 155–78.

Pradhan, B.K, Sahoo, A. and Saluja, M.R. (1999) "A social accounting matrix for India, 1994–95", *Economic and Political Weekly*, 34(8) (Special Issue).

Pyatt, G., Roe, A. *et al.* (1977) *Social Accounting for Development Planning with Special Reference to Sri Lanka*, Cambridge: Cambridge University Press.

Pyatt, G. and Round, J.I. (1979) "Accounting and fixed price multipliers in a social accounting matrix framework", *Economic Journal*, 89: 850–73.

Quah, D. (1996) "Twin peaks: growth and convergence in models of distribution dynamics", *Economic Journal*, 106: 1045–55.

Roland-Holst, D.W. and Sancho, F. (1992) "Relative income determination in the United states: a social accounting perspective", *Review of Income and Wealth,* 38(3): 311–27.

Round, J.I. (1985) "Decomposing multipliers for economic systems involving regional and world trade", *Economic Journal*, 95(378): 383–99.

Sala-i-Martin, Xavier (2002) "The World Income Distribution", unpublished manuscript. Barcelona: Universitat Pompeu Fabra.

Stone, J.R.N. (1961) "Social accounts at the regional level: a survey", in W. Isard and J. Cumberland (eds) *Regional Economic Planning: Techniques of Analysis for Less Developed Areas* , Paris: OECD.

Stone, R. (1977). "Foreword", in Pyatt, G., Roe, A. *et al.* (eds) *Social Accounting for Development Planning with Special Reference to Sri Lanka*, Cambridge: Cambridge University Press.

Stone, R., Champernowne, D.G. and Meade, J.E. (1942), "The precision of national income estimates", *Review of Economic Studies*, IX(2): 111–25.

# 12 Computational explorations of vertically coupled markets

*Nicolás Garrido*

## Introduction

> To go from two identical markets to *n* nonidentical ones will require the prolonged services of yet unborn calculating machines.
>
> Richard Goodwin (1947: 204)

Inter-industry economic analysis has been in economists' thoughts since the very beginning of economics. Neumann[1] (1945), Leontief (1951) and Sraffa (1960) build up the bases of the modern studies of inter-industrial economics. Topics such as production as a circular flow, joint production and fixed capital can not be revisited without explicit reference to these seminal works. There are different approaches to deal with the complexity of multisectoral dynamics. Some references for the interested reader are, Goodwin (1949), Solow (1959), Morishima (1965), Pasinetti (1973), Takayama (1985), Pasinetti (1990) and Kurz and Salvadori (1995).

In a pioneer paper, Goodwin (1947) shows how two interrelated markets affect each other's dynamics. In Goodwin's paper each market has a cobweb dynamic, while the interrelation, i.e. the coupling between the markets, is ". . . a term in the supply or demand curve proportional to the price in the other markets".

In this chapter, we explore the vertical coupling between markets. Two markets are vertically coupled when the primary factor for one is provided by the other. We are interested in describing how two or more vertically interrelated markets affect each other's dynamics. The interrelationship between two vertically coupled markets is given by a flow of four items: orders from one market to the other, commodities trying to satisfy the orders, a price of the commodity and the payments of the orders.

In autarky, every market has an independent price and quantity adjustment mechanism. However, when the markets are vertically coupled the independence is broken and any constraint in a market is diffused through its vertical links.

In our economy, every market adjusts price and quantity taking into account only the local information. Moreover, markets do not clear throughout price adjustment in every period. Instead, there is quantity rationing, which is combined with a price adjustment mechanism. The quantity rationing in our economy emerges because the effective demand and supply in each market depends on what is happening in the other markets.

Our basic building block to model price and quantity dynamics of a single market is Ezekiel's cobweb model where the price does not clear the market. We extend the cobweb model through the introduction of an inventory system and a money balance in every market. Moreover, the changes to those inventories depend on the flow of information, commodities and money between the markets. When the flow of orders, i.e. the demand, exceeds the availability in a market, i.e. the supply, there is an excess of demand. This means that the demand is partially satisfied. Therefore the demand will obtain in every period the minimum between what is available and its demand. This type of problem between vertically coupled markets is common, and we have to use non-linearities to specify them. The non-linearities in this chapter are ceilings and floors to the variables, representing quantity rationing and budget constraints. For instance, in the previous case the demand obtained the floor between demand and availability, i.e. $\min\{d, a\}$. The introduction of these non-linearities makes the model difficult to study analytically.

Day and Tinney (1969) explore a case of two markets vertically coupled. They show how the presence of constraints in a two coupled cobweb model, leads to the existence of a set of different dynamic regimes. Indeed, every time that a ceiling or a floor is reached, there is a new regime with different dynamic behavior. Muellbauer and Portes (1978) analyze the behavior of a macroeconomic model with rationing, emphasizing the interaction between goods and labor markets.

In almost a century of existence, the basic cobweb dynamic has been the starting point for the study of different economic behaviors. Thus, the model has been used to study how expectations might change the results of the model, Jensen and Urban (1984), Hommes (1991), or how non-linearities produce a rich set of dynamics, Chiarella (1988), or how risk adverse behavior can increase the stability of the model, Hooton (1950), or how rich is the combinations of the previous features, like in Hommes (1994), Brock and Hommes (1997), Goere and Hommes (2000) and Chiarella *et al.* (2006).

The importance of studying vertically coupled interaction between markets or firms has been recently shown by Nakano and White (2006). The authors show, using data from the Ohat industrial district in Tokyo, that the supplier prime buyer relationships are strictly hierarchical and constitute a directed acyclic graph.

In our network of vertically coupled markets there are three type of markets: final good markets, intermediary markets and markets of natural resources. They differ because they have different demand and inventory of input specifications. The demand in the final good market is given exogenously, while in the intermediary and natural resource markets the demand is the result of the requirement of other markets. All the three type of markets have inventory of output. However, as we assume that the natural resource is an infinite source of input, the markets differ in the inventory of inputs. The final good and intermediary markets have inventory of inputs, whereas the natural resource markets do not[2]. Thus, production decisions on natural resource markets are a function of prices and budget, whereas in final good and intermediary markets production decisions depend on input availability and price. In final good and intermediary markets, the budget will constrain the availability of inputs for the next period.

The specification of the network of markets grows in complexity through the sections. We start with the basic building block introducing inventory of output production and budget constraint. Next, we make the simplest vertical coupling specification using two markets and we explore its aggregated results. Next we describe the three type of markets: final good market, intermediary markets, and natural resource markets. In this section we explore all the different topologies of vertical integration that may occur within four markets. We decide to work with four markets because this is the lowest number of markets that allows us to study the network having two markets of the same type. With four markets, we can have topologies where there are two final good markets, or two intermediaries or two natural resource markets and one of each of the other markets. Finally, the main conclusions about the computational exercise are reported in the last section.

## The basic building block

In this section we study a single market. We depart from the cobweb theorem as presented in Ezekiel (1938) introducing three modifications: first, the market does not clear in every period, second, we make explicit the inventories of outputs and input and, third, we introduce budget constraints.

Assume an industry comprising a set of similar firms. Each firm produces an homogeneous good. Firms are ignorant about the demand, however they base each period's decision on an implicit maximizing calculation, which is subject to inventories and financial constraints.[3]

Neither firms nor consumers solve intertemporal problems to make their decisions. Instead, they make their best decision using the current information and constraints. Firms set the price according to the results obtained from the previous period and this new price is the main source of information for the production plan during the current period.

When there is only one market, the firms' production decision is represented by a linear aggregate supply, and the demand at time $t$ is linear in the current price.

In the next two sub-sections we introduce output inventory and the budget constraint in the basic cobweb model.

### *Inventory of output*

The inventory of output has been implicitly present since the very beginning in Ezekiel's theorem through the concept of reserve demand. The reserve demand is the amount of inventory that the producer wishes to have for precautionary motives. In Ezekiel's model the reserve demand is embedded into the demand function. However, there is no inventory dynamic, because the author assumes that it has no influence into neither the price equilibrium nor the transition of the dynamical system.

Once we introduce the inventory explicitly, the system of equation that represents the market dynamic is given by,

$$z_t = s_{t-1} - d_{t-1} \tag{12.1}$$

$$p_t = p_{t-1} + \alpha((1+\rho)d_{t-1} - s_{t-1}) \tag{12.2}$$

$$s_t = f(p_t) + \delta z_t \tag{12.3}$$

$$d_t = a + bp_t \tag{12.4}$$

At the beginning of the period $t$, suppliers compute the remaining inventory of the previous period, $z_t$ and the price for the current period. The inventory, as specified in Equation (12.1) is the difference between the supply and the demand of the previous period.

We assume that firms have a proportion $0 \leq \rho \leq 1$ of the demand as inventory for precautionary motives. Moreover, firms use price to adjust the desire level of inventory. Thus, at the beginning of the period, they adjust the price according to the previous excess of demand including the inventory as specified in Equation (12.2). If firms want to increase (decrease) their inventories they raise (reduce) prices.

The production is developed during the current period. The availability of period $t$ is given by the production according to the price established at the beginning of the period, and the inventory remaining from the previous period $z_t$. The inventory of output might suffer a depreciation $0 \leq \delta \leq 1$ as consequence of being stored from one period to the next.[4]

We assume in Equation (12.3) that the supply function is linear in the price, therefore the supply of the current period is given by $f(p_t) = c + dp_t$.

We simplify even further our specification assuming that the demand is linear, and it depends on the price of the current period, Equation (12.4). The sensitivity of the demand to the price is given by $b < 0$.

In this building block, a market does not clear in every period through price. The markets are connected through the network of production, and any quantity rationing in a market influences the production and stability of the network. The quantity rationing introduces a difference between a notional and the effective demand (see Muellbauer and Portes 1978), which make impossible the price clearing based on the notional demand at the end of every period.[5]. Although the model does not converge in every period to a market clearing price, using appropriate parameters for the stability of the model specified by Equations 12.1 to 12.4, eventually the adaptive process will converge to a market clearing price.

Thus, the introduction of inventory leads us to represent the dynamical system by the following system of difference equations,

$$
\begin{aligned}
p_t &= m_{1,0} + m_{1,1}p_{t-1} + m_{1,2}z_{t-1} \\
z_t &= m_{2,0} + m_{2,1}p_{t-1} + m_{2,2}z_{t-1}
\end{aligned} \tag{12.5}
$$

Where $m_{1,0} = \alpha(a - c + a\rho)$, $m_{1,1} = 1 + \alpha(b - d + b\rho)$, $m_{1,2} = -\delta\alpha$, $m_{2,0} = c - a$, $m_{2,1} = d - b$, $m_{2,2} = \delta$.

Notice that the slope of the demand is negative, $b < 0$; the slope of the supply is always positive, $d > 0$; the autonomous demand $a$ is positive; the autonomous supply $c$ is positive and lower than the autonomous demand, $a > c$; the speed of adjustment is positive and lower than one, $0 < \alpha < 1$, the entrepreneurs wish to have an inventory which is a proportion of the demand lower than one, $0 < \rho < 1$ and finally, the inventory depreciation $\delta$ vary in the range $[0, 1]$.

We can express the system of equation as a difference of the steady as follows:

$$
\begin{pmatrix} p_t^d \\ z_t^d \end{pmatrix} = \begin{pmatrix} m_{1,1} & m_{1,2} \\ m_{2,1} & m_{2,2} \end{pmatrix} \begin{pmatrix} p_{t-1}^d \\ z_{t-1}^d \end{pmatrix} \tag{12.6}
$$

Where $z_t^d = z_t - z^\star$ and $p_t^d = p_t - p^\star$. The equilibrium of the system is given by:

$$
p^\star = \frac{a - c + a\rho(1-\delta)}{d - b + b\rho(\delta - 1)} \tag{12.7}
$$

$$
z^\star = \frac{\rho(ad - cb)}{d - b + b\rho(\delta - 1)} \tag{12.8}
$$

Notice that without depreciation, i.e. $\delta = 1$, the steady state price is the same as the one obtained in the standard Ezekiel's Cobweb model. Moreover, the inventory $z^\star$ is the proportion $\rho$ of the demand in equilibrium.

The stability of the system now is given by the roots of the characteristic equation of (12.5). In other words,

$$
\begin{aligned}
\lambda_{1,2} = \frac{1}{2}\Big(&1 + \delta + \alpha(b - d + b\rho) \\
&\pm \sqrt{(d\alpha - 1 - b\alpha - b\alpha\rho - \delta)^2 - 4(\delta + b\alpha\delta\rho)}\Big)
\end{aligned}
$$

Without depreciation the equilibrium price of our building block model with inventory is the same as in the standard cobweb model. However, there is a modification in the transitional dynamics, i.e. in the path to the equilibrium. Although we do not make a complete characterization of the model stability exploring the roots $\lambda_{1,2}$, it is straightforward to see

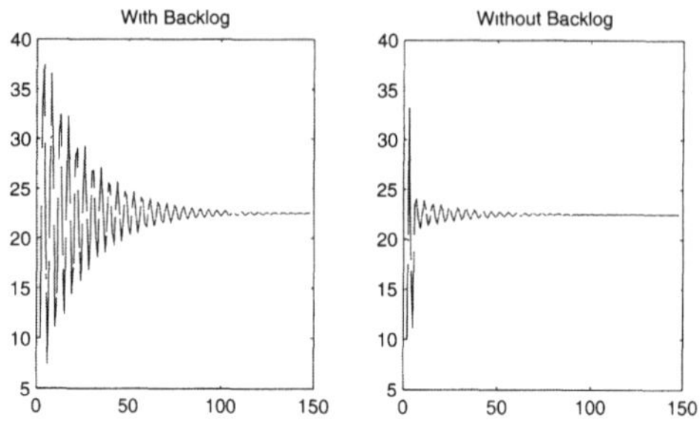


*Figure 12.1* Transition with and without backlog

that in this case the standard condition of the cobweb model $0 < |\frac{d}{b}| < 1$ does not guarantee the convergence to the equilibrium price.[6]

## *The effect of backlog*

In our specification, if the inventory is negative, i.e. excess of demand during the previous period, the availability (or the supply) for the current period is reduced. This variation on the availability is due to the satisfaction of the backlog from the previous period. If firms are concerned with satisfying the backlog, this means that there is a commitment with the previous period excess of demand.

However, if firms do not worry about the backlog, the excess of demand from the previous period does not affect the supply but only the price. In this case, the availability for the current period is given by $s_t = f(p_t) + \max(\delta z_t, 0)$.

The introduction of backlogs does not change the steady state of the model. However, it does effect the transitional phase of the price dynamic.

Notice that the backlogs are introduced in our model as a non-linearity. This non-linearity divides the dynamic of the model in two regimes: first, when the inventory is positive, and a second, when the inventory is negative. When the model has oscillations in its transitional phase to the steady state, there is an interaction between both regimes. This interaction reduces the amplitude of the oscillations; in another words, it makes the transition to the equilibria smoother.

In order to show the role of the backlogs during the transitional phase we run simulations, setting arbitrary values to the set of seven parameters $\theta = \{a, b, c, d, \alpha, \rho, \delta\}$ that characterize a market.

We select the parameters so that we have damped oscillations. Thus, we set $a = 100$, $b = -2$, $c = 10$, $d = 2$, $\alpha = 0.5$, $\rho = 0.1$ and $\delta = 1$.

With these parameters, the equilibrium values of the system are given by $p^\star = 22.5$ and the inventory is $z^\star = 5.5$.[7]

In order to explore the differences between having or not having a backlog, we use our set of parameters to set the initial value problem with the initial conditions given by $p(0) = 1$ and the demand and supply for the initial period equal to zero.

As shown in Figure 12.1, in both cases the price equilibrium is the same: $p^\star = 22.4$. However, they have different transitional dynamics.

In order to understand why there is a difference in the transition of the system with and without backlog, notice that any excess of demand is eliminated through an increase on the availability and the reduction of the demand. Both increase availability and reduction of the demand is obtained through price increasing.

In the standard specification, when there is backlog, the excess of demand has two effects on the increase of supply running in opposite direction: first, it increases the price and, second, it reduces the availability for the current period. While the rise of price increases the supply, the backlog produces a reduction of supply. The interaction of these two forces reduces the effect of increasing the price on the excess of demand. Firms, as consequence, set even higher prices to reduce the excess of demand. When the price is high enough so that the backlog is satisfied, it will reveal a big excess of supply, because the high price has depressed the demand. Thus, a cycle of price reduction will began until a new excess of demand is obtained.

If we eliminate the backlogs, the excess of demand has a clear effect: it increases the price to reduce the excess of demand during the current period, through a reduction of the demand and an increase of the supply. As a consequence, the system without backlog converges faster than the system with it.

## Money balance

In this section we introduce the effect of the budget constraints in a cobweb model.

The firms' budget grows with sales and it is reduced with the payments for production factors. Assuming that every unit of output requires a unit of input to be produced, this means that the money balance grows if the price is greater than the unitary cost factor, i.e. $p_t > c_t$.

As a consequence of introducing the budget dynamic, the dynamical system is represented by,

$$
\begin{aligned}
z_t &= s_{t-1} - d_{t-1} \\
p_t &= p_{t-1} + \alpha((1+\rho)d_{t-1} - s_{t-1}) \\
m_t^e &= m_{t-1} && (12.9) \\
s_t &= f(p_t, m_t^e, m_{t-1}) + \delta z_t && (12.10) \\
d_t &= a + bp_t \\
m_t &= m_{t-1} + min(s_t, d_t)p_t - g(f(p_t, m_t^e, m_{t-1}))c_t && (12.11)
\end{aligned}
$$

We assume that producers have to pay the primary factors order, placed at the end of period $t-1$, when they arrive at the beginning of the period $t$. Thus, when producers send their orders for the primary factor market, they have to have an expectation about the available cash at the beginning of the next period. In the simplest case we assume that their expectation about their available cash for the next period is static. This means that the expected budget for the next period is equal to the budget available at the beginning of the current period. This is represented by Equation (12.9).

The availability for the current period, represented by Equation (12.10), is given by the inventory $z_t$ and the production. The production this time is made according to the price and budget constrained available at the beginning of the period $t$, $m_{t-1}$. Recall that a producer has to pay the primary factor at the beginning of the period $t$. If the budget does not cover the size of an order, the suppliers of the producer will deliver only what can be afforded by the budget of the producer.

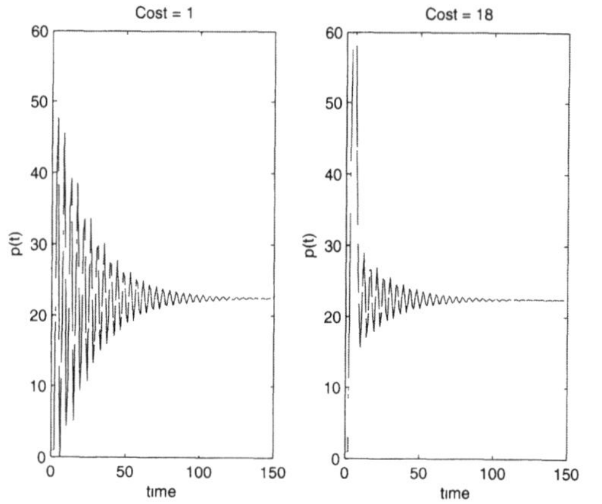


*Figure 12.2* Simulation with budget constraints evolution and different costs

At the end of a period $t$, the producer knows the excess of demand (or supply) of the market. Therefore, he is able to compute the price and production requirement for the next period. Using this information and the expected budget $m^e_t$, the producer sets the size of the order for the next period.

Equation (12.11) represents the cash flow at time $t$. Thus, $m_t$ increases with the sales $min(s_t, d_t)p_t$ and it is reduced with the payment to the primary factor $g(f(p_t, m^e_t, m_{t-1}))c_t$, where $g(\cdot)$ represents the amount of primary factor required to produce $f(\cdot)$, and $c_t$ is the unitary cost of the primary factor at time $t$. If markets are not coupled, the unitary cost is constant.

Using this new specification we run two simulations using the same set of parameters $\theta$ and initial conditions than before. We add the initial amount of cash available: $m_0 = 1000$. The two simulations have different primary factor prices $c_t$. We present the evolution of the price series for both simulations in Figure 12.2. In the left panel, we show that when the unitary cost is low enough, for instance $c_t = 1$, the dynamic behavior and equilibrium values do not change as compared to the previous dynamic shown when we introduce inventories with backlog.

In the right panel it is shown that as the price of the primary factor rises, the amplitude and the number of oscillations during the transitional phase are reduced. The reduction of the amplitude and in the number of oscillations is due to the budget constraint. When the cost of production is high, the market does not have big excesses of supply as a response to big excess of demand, because producers are not able to afford big orders. As a consequence, the oscillations are reduced and the transition to equilibria is smoother than the case where the cost of production is low.

When the cost of production is above the price equilibrium of the model, the system adjusts its price to the unitary cost of production. The main reason for this is that the market reduces its supply and this produces an excess of demand, leading to a price increase.

We obtain a different specification if producers can pay the primary factors received at the beginning of period $t$ at the end of that period. In this case, as shown in Equation (12.9), producers include in their budget expectation the sales that they expect to obtain during the current period. We assume that producers have static expectations about their sales. This means that they expect to have the same sales as the previous period. This modification

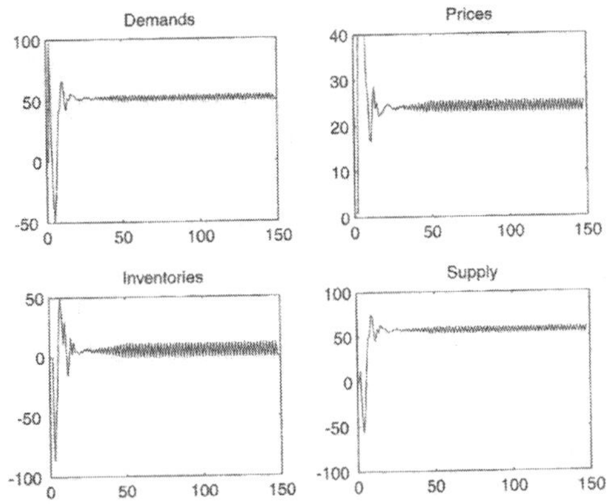


*Figure 12.3* Dynamics of the simulation with one period credit and unitary costs higher than equilibrium price

is equivalent to claiming that the suppliers of primary factors give to the firms in the final good market a credit on the basis of the expected sales.

This one period credit modifies the availability specified in Equation (12.10) as well. This time, as it is represented in Equation (12.14), the cash available at the beginning of the period $t$, $m_{t-1}$ does not constrain the production of the supply side.

$$z_t = s_{t-1} - d_{t-1} \tag{12.12}$$

$$p_t = p_{t-1} + \alpha((1+\rho)d_{t-1} - s_{t-1}) \tag{12.13}$$

$$m_t^e = m_{t-1} + \max(\min(s_{t-1}, d_{t-1}), 0)p_t \tag{12.14}$$

$$s_t = f(p_t, m_t^e) + \delta z_t \tag{12.15}$$

$$d_t = a + bp_t \tag{12.16}$$

$$m_t = m_{t-1} + min(s_t, d_t)p_t - g(f(p_t, m_t^e))c_t \tag{12.17}$$

When we consider the introduction of this one period credit, there are two interesting cases to be described: when the cost of the input factor is below and above the equilibrium price of the model $p^\star$. When the price of the primary factor is below the equilibrium price, the model behaves as the original specification of our building block of equations one to four. There are no changes, according to neither the transitional dynamics nor the equilibrium results.

However, when the primary factor price, i.e. unitary cost $c_t$, is above the final good equilibrium price, a new dynamic effect occurs as a consequence of the interaction between the budget and the production dynamic. There are two cases: first, when the unitary cost is above the price where there is a null demand, i.e. $c_t > -\frac{a}{b}$. In this case the market does not work. The second case is when the unitary cost is above the equilibrium price and below the price where the demand becomes null, $p^\star < c_t < -\frac{a}{b}$.

In this second case, as it is shown in the simulation represented in Figure (12.3), the interaction of the budget and the cobweb dynamic introduces permanent oscillations.

The sequence of events leading to the permanent oscillations of the model is a consequence of the following: first, when the budget is big enough so that it does not constrain, the standard cobweb dynamic drives the price toward the equilibrium price $p^{\star}$ below the high unitary cost. As the firm is paying a unitary cost higher than the equilibrium price, this produces a contraction of the budget. Due to the credit system, producers are able to operate with a negative budget. However, the one period credit obtained by the firm is not big enough to ask the size of the order that the firm would like to order. The immediate effect of this is that firms' production is reduced. As a consequence, there is an excess of demand making the price rise above the unitary cost of production. In turn, this expands the budget until it becomes positive. Once the budget becomes positive, the standard adjustment mechanism of the cobweb model starts to work leading the price toward its long-run equilibrium, beginning the whole process again.

## Vertically coupled markets

In this section we specify the model of vertical coupling between markets. First, we present the vertical coupling between two markets without considering the budget dynamics. We present this model to describe the dependence between two vertically coupled markets. For this simple case, we present analytical results, therefore we do not introduce non-linearities. Later, we introduce into the coupled system monetary balance, and the non-linearities that will be used in all the simulations.

### *The simplest coupling*

In the simplest case, there are two markets, a final good and a natural resource market. The natural resource market produces inputs or primary factors for the final good market. In this market the final good is sold to the final consumers. We assume that there is an exogenous final demand curve, which is unknown for the agents in the final good market.

Production in our economy is a linear flow from the services of primary factors to final goods; in other words, there is no production as a circular flow. In order to produce a unit of the final good, a unit of primary factor is required. Producers in both markets set prices during the current period to be the same as during the previous one, i.e. static expectations. Producers in the downstream market believe that the amount of primary factor needed for the period is given by the demand received during the previous period. Therefore, the requirements for the period are equal to the demand of the previous one. With this assumption, the vertical coupling can be represented as,

$$z_{t,f} = s_{t-1,f} - d_{t-1,f} \tag{12.18}$$
$$p_{t,f} = p_{t-1,f} + \alpha((1+\rho)d_{t-1,f} - s_{t-1,f}) \tag{12.19}$$
$$d_{t,f} = a_f + b_f p_{t,f} \tag{12.20}$$
$$s_{t,f} = c_f + d_f p_{t,f} + \delta z_{t,f} \tag{12.21}$$
$$z_{t,n} = s_{t-1,n} - d_{t-1,n} \tag{12.22}$$
$$p_{t,n} = p_{t-1,n} + \alpha((1+\rho)d_{t-1,n} - s_{t-1,n}) \tag{12.23}$$
$$d_{t,n} = d_{t-1,f} \tag{12.24}$$
$$s_{t,n} = c_n + d_n p_{t,n} + \delta z_{t,n} \tag{12.25}$$

Where $f$ and $n$ indicate final good and natural resource market respectively.

We assume that producers in the final good market expect that the demand for the next period will be the same as the current one. The producers wish to have for the next period the inputs that allow them to satisfy the demand. Thus, they order to the natural resource market the size order accordingly to the demand of the previous period. Thus, in this preliminary specification Equation (12.24) captures the link between both markets.

The equilibria values for the prices and inventories of both markets are given by,

$$p_f^\star = \frac{a_f - c_f + \rho a_f(1-\delta)}{d_f - b_f + \rho b_f(\delta - 1)} \tag{12.26}$$

$$z_f^\star = \frac{\rho(a_f d_f - b_f c_f)}{d_f - b_f + \rho b_f(\delta - 1)} \tag{12.27}$$

$$p_n^\star = \frac{(1+\rho-\rho\delta)z_f^\star}{\rho d_n} - \frac{c_n}{d_n} \tag{12.28}$$

$$z_n^\star = \frac{\rho(a_f d_f - b_f c_f)}{d_f - b_f + \rho b_f(\delta - 1)} \tag{12.29}$$

Notice that the equilibrium of the final good market in Equation (12.26) and (12.27) are the same as (12.7) and (12.8).

On the other hand, given the coupling between the two markets specified in Equation (12.24), in equilibrium the inventory of both markets are the same, $z_f^\star = z_n^\star$. The inventory in equilibrium is the proportion $\rho$ of the demand in the final good market in equilibrium, i.e. $z_f^\star = \rho\left(a_f + b_f p_f^\star\right)$.

The price equilibrium in the natural resource market, Equation (12.28) is a function of the inventory in steady state. This means that the price in the natural resource market depends on the price of the final good market.

The dependency of the primary factor price on the final good price persists even if the producers in the final good market, instead of using the demand, use the production during the current period to specify their requirement to the natural resource market. In other words, if Equation (12.24) is given by $d_{t,n} = s_{t-1,f} = c_f + d_f p_{t-1,f}$.

For this simple case, we conclude that when there is a vertical coupling between two markets, and the demand is exogenously given in the final good market, the natural resource market follows the final good market.

## *Inventories and budget in coupled markets*

When markets are vertically coupled there are two inventories: the final good (output) inventories and the input (or factors) inventories. Modelling both inventories is unnecessary when we deal with the simple case of two vertically coupled markets. However, when an industry requires two primary factors coming from different markets, both inventories are fundamental components of the inter-sectoral dynamic. For instance, assume an economy with three markets, where two of them provide a different primary factor for the third one. In this case, a delay in the supply of one of the primary factors accumulates inventories of the other primary factor in the final good firms. In turn, this changes the excess of demand or supply in all the other markets, triggering changes in prices and inventories through the whole network.

In this section, we increase the complexity of the previous specification introducing inventory of inputs and money balance for every market. Moreover, we introduce two non-linearities; the first is to verify when there is quantity rationing and the second is to prevent a market selling its production at a price lower than its cost.

Thus, our vertically coupled markets are represented by,

$$z_{t,f} = s_{t-1,f} - d_{t-1,f} \tag{12.30}$$
$$v_{t,f} = v_{t-1,f} + \min(s_{t-1,n}; d_{t-1,n}) - g(f(p_{t-1,f}, v_{t-1,f})) \tag{12.31}$$
$$c_{t,f} = C(\mathbf{h}, p_{t-1,n}) \tag{12.32}$$
$$p_{t,f} = \max(c_{t,f}; p_{t-1,f} + \alpha((1+\rho)d_{t-1,f} - s_{t-1,f})) \tag{12.33}$$
$$m^e_{t,f} = m_{t-1,f} \tag{12.34}$$
$$s_{t,f} = f(p_{t,f}, v_{t,f}) + \max(\delta z_{t,f}, 0) \tag{12.35}$$
$$m_{t,f} = m_{t-1,f} + \min(s_{t,f}, d_{t,f})p_{t,f} - \min(s_{t-1,n}; d_{t-1,n})p_{t-1,n} \tag{12.36}$$
$$d_{t,f} = \max(a + bp_{t,f}, 0) \tag{12.37}$$
$$z_{t,n} = s_{t-1,n} - d_{t-1,n} \tag{12.38}$$
$$m^e_{t,n} = m_{t-1,n} \tag{12.39}$$
$$p_{t,n} = \max(\bar{c}; p_{t-1,n} + \alpha((1+\rho)d_{t-1,n} - s_{t-1,n})) \tag{12.40}$$
$$s_{t,n} = f(p_{t,n}, m^e_{t,n}) + \max(\delta z_{t,n}, 0) \tag{12.41}$$
$$m_{t,n} = m_{t-1,n} + \min(s_{t,n}, d_{t,n})p_{t,n} - g(f(p_{t,n}, m^e_{t,n}))\bar{c} \tag{12.42}$$
$$d_{t,n} = \max\left(\min(d_{t,f}, m^e_{t,f}/p_{t-1,n}), 0\right) \tag{12.43}$$

At the beginning of a period $t$, firms compute their final good inventories for the current period $z_{t,f}$ and $z_{t,n}$ represented by Equations (12.30) and (12.38).

Equation (12.31) explains the evolution of the inventory of the primary factor held by the final good market at time $t$, $v_{t,f}$. The inventory of the primary factor increases according to the shortest side of the natural resource market in the previous period, $\min(s_{t-1,n}; d_{t-1,n})$. On the other hand, the inventory decreases according to the factors used during the production of the previous period, $g(f(p_{t-1,f}, v_{t,f}))$. The function $g(\cdot)$ computes the amount of inputs needed to produce $f(p_{t-1,f}, v_{t,f})$.

Equation (12.32) computes the unitary cost of production for the final good market. The vector $\mathbf{h}$ represents the technology of production and $p_{t-1,n}$ is the price of the natural resource market during the previous period. For instance, for the Leontief production functions, $h_1$ is the amount of factors from provider 1 required to produce a unit of the final good. The reader should note that in the case of two vertically coupled markets there is only one supplier. However, in further specifications the number of suppliers may change. We assume that the unitary cost of production for a primary factor or natural resource market is constant and equal to $\bar{c}$.

We assume that the firms expect their prices to remain above, or at least equal to, the unitary cost of production. Thus, there exists a floor in the expected prices, which is given by the prices of the primary factors and the production technology. This is represented in Equations (12.33) and (12.40).

We retain here the assumption that the expected budget for the current period is the available cash at the end of the previous period. This is explicitly stated in Equations (12.34) and (12.39) for the downstream and upstream markets. In another words, primary factor firms do not give any credit to final good firms.

The supply of the current period, Equation (12.35), is a function of the current price but constrained by the inventory of primary factors. Notice that the supply of the upstream market, Equation (12.41), is not constrained by the input inventory. We assume that the natural resource market does not need to have input inventories. Natural resources are always ready to be used for production. However, primary factor markets have budget

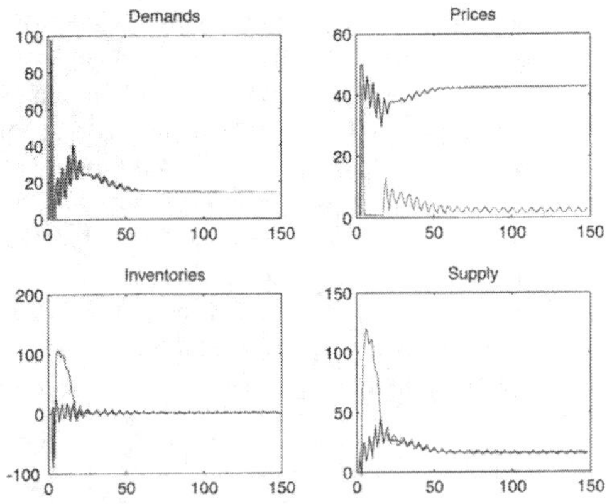


*Figure 12.4* Simulation of coupling market

constraints. That is to say, the suppliers in the natural resource market can produce the amount of inventories that they can afford for this period.

The current availability of goods for the market is equal to the current production plus the inventory of final goods coming from the last period without taking into account backlogs. As in the previous section, the inventory does not suffer any depreciation, i.e. $\delta = 1$.

The monetary balance is computed at the end of the period $t$. Equations (12.36) and (12.42) show that the budget grows with the sales of the current period and it decreases with the payments to the input market. Notice that the firms pay for the primary factors received at the beginning of the period. Therefore, these factors are paid according to the price of the previous period.

Equation (12.37) represents the exogenously given demand for final goods and it depends on the price during the current period.

Finally, Equation (12.43) captures the coupling between both markets. Firms in the final good market use their last received demand as the forecast of the immediate future. They place an order to the primary factor market according to the expected demand. The size of the order is constrained by the expected budget $m^e_{t,f}$ and the price of the primary factor $p_{t-1,n}$. Notice that using this time line, an order placed by the downstream market in period $t$, might be fulfilled in period $t+2$.

In Figure 12.4 we show the result of a simulation using the previous specification. The market parameters are the same than the specified previously. The initial conditions for both markets are $p(0) = 1$, $v(0) = 10$, $m(0) = 1.000$ and all the initial demands and supplies are zero.

The equilibria obtained from the simulation of both coupled markets is not the same as the one computed analytically in (12.26) to (12.29). The difference between the two results is the consequence of the quantity rationing and the adaptive mechanism of prices with minimum price. The interaction of these two mechanisms between the two markets produces a vicious circle that increases the price in the final good market and reduces the price in the natural resource market.

The vicious circle starts when the natural resource market has an excess of supply. This reduces the price in the natural resource market to adjust the demand and its production.

This reduction in the production produces a rationing of inputs to the final good market. As a consequence, the final good market has an excess of demand. This is translated into a price increase in the final good market, with a reduction of the final good demand. This reduction produces smaller size orders to the natural resource market, increasing the excess of supply of the natural resource market. Thus, the cycle starts again. This cycle is stopped when the price in the natural resource market reaches the individual cost of production $\bar{c}$. The price in the natural resource market does not go below $\bar{c}$, therefore the two markets stabilize their prices.

Finally, the analytical equilibria described in (12.26) to (12.29) are now unstable. If the initial conditions of the simulations are the equilibria $p^{\star}_{f,n}$ and $z^{\star}_{f,n}$ the simulations remain there. However, any perturbations move the system toward the simulated equilibrium described before.

## Exploring topologies

In this section, we explore all the possible topologies of network of markets vertically coupled that exist, using up to four markets. An economy is characterized by the network topology that specifies how the four markets are connected.

Notice that there are three types of commodity markets: final good markets, intermediary markets and natural resource markets. Using all the permutations of four markets it is possible to study multiple cases. This includes cases where all the four markets are in autarky or cases where there are two markets of one type and one of each of the others markets, all interconnected.

An economy, or its topology, can be specified by an adjacency matrix $A$[8]. Every element of the adjacency matrix $a_{i,j}$ indicates whether or not the market $i$ provides goods for market $j$.

We assume that a market is not coupled with itself, therefore, there are no self-loops in the network. This means that the main diagonal of the adjacency matrix $A$ is null. If all the elements of the matrix are null, the economy is composed of four independent markets.

Moreover, we assume that production in our economies is a linear flow which leads from the services of the primary factors of production to final goods. In another words, a downstream market can never be a provider of an upstream one. Thus, the adjacency matrix is triangular inferior or $a_{i,j} = 0$ if $i < j$.[9]

When two different markets have the same input supplier, there is potential for a *rationing* problem between the two downstream markets. If the input market is short of supply, it has to use a mechanism of rationing to distribute its production among its demand. We assume that the factor market distributes its available goods in proportion to the demand of each downstream market. For example, suppose two downstream markets, 1 and 2, have the same upstream market 3. Markets 1 and 2 order from market 3 the amounts $d_1$ and $d_2$ respectively. If the availability of the factor market is lower than this demand, i.e. $s_3 < d_1 + d_2$, the factor market rations according to: $s_3 \frac{d_1}{d_1+d_2}$ for market 1 and $s_3 \frac{d_2}{d_1+d_2}$ for market 2.

Using these assumptions, it is possible to represent every economy with $M = 4$ markets by an integer. An example will help to present the counting mechanism. Let us assume an economy represented by the following adjacency matrix,

$$A = \begin{bmatrix} 0\,0\,0\,0 \\ 1\,0\,0\,0 \\ 0\,1\,0\,0 \\ 0\,1\,1\,0 \end{bmatrix} \tag{12.44}$$

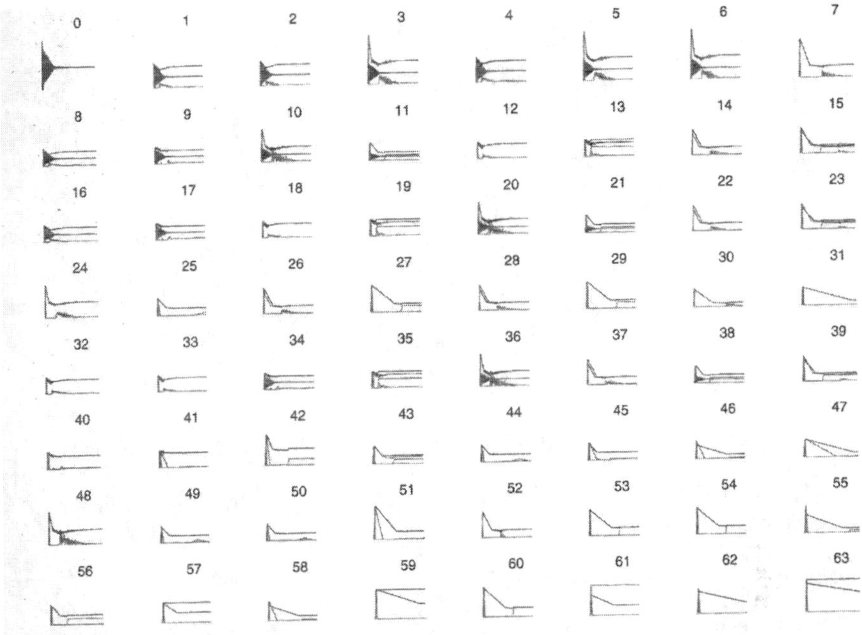


*Figure 12.5* Price evolution for the 64 economies

Notice that only the six digits in the triangular inferior matrix are useful for identifying the economy. Thus, the topology can be identified by an string of six binary digits, $k = 101011$. Every digit $k_i$ with $i = 1..6$ is distributed in the adjacency matrix according to,

$$A = \begin{bmatrix} 0 & 0 & 0 & 0 \\ k_1 & 0 & 0 & 0 \\ k_2 & k_3 & 0 & 0 \\ k_4 & k_5 & k_6 & 0 \end{bmatrix} \tag{12.45}$$

Using this representation, there are $2^6 = 64$ topologies or economies having $M = 4$ markets. The binary string of our example, i.e. 101011, is identified with the economy number 43.[10] We denote the set of 64 economies by $E$.

We explore, using simulations, each of the 64 economies. In every simulation the markets use the same set of parameters $\theta$, and they start from the same initial conditions $\iota$. In another words:

1 $\theta_1 = \{a = 100, b = -2, c = 10, d = 2, \alpha = 0.5, \rho = 0.1, \delta = 1\}$ and $\theta_1 = \theta_2 = \theta_3 = \theta_4$
2 $\iota_1 = \{p(0) = 10, m(0) = 1000, v(0) = 10 d(0) = 0, s(0) = 0\}$ and $\iota_1 = \iota_2 = \iota_3 = \iota_4$

In Figure 12.5 we show all the price series generated by all the economies in $E$.

According to the price series generated by the simulations, it is possible to define a relation of equivalence to produce a partition on $E$.

All the economies $e \in E$ but one, have a topology linking at least two of the four markets. The economy 0, is the exception because it has four independent markets. We define $I_k$ as the index set of the coupled markets in $e_k$.[11]. For instance, $I_0 = \{\emptyset\}$ and $I_{32} = \{1, 2\}$[12] Note that the cardinality of an index set is $\sharp I_i \geq 2$ for any economy $e_i$ different from $e_0$.

After running a simulation every economy $e_j$ produces a set of price series $\mathbf{p}_j(t) =$

*Table 12.1* Partition of $E$ according to $\mathbf{p}_i = \mathbf{p}_j$

| *Cardinality* | *Economies' subsets* |
|---|---|
| 6 | $g_1$= {1 , 2 , 4 , 8 , 16 , 32} |
| 5 | $g_2$={14, 22, 26, 28, 37} |
| 4 | $g_3$={11, 21, 38, 56}, $g_4$={9, 17, 34, 40}, $g_5$={3, 5, 6, 24} and $g_6$={10, 20, 36, 48} |
| 3 | $g_7$={15, 23, 39}, $g_8$={49, 50, 44}, $g_9$={13, 19, 35}, $g_{10}$={53, 54, 60} and $g_{11}$={12, 18, 33} |
| 2 | $g_{12}$={27, 29} and $g_{13}$={46, 58} |
| 1 | 7, 52, 30, 43, 45, 47, 59, 31, 63, 61, 42, 41, 25, 55, 62, 51 and 57 |

$\{p_{j,k}(t) : k \in I_j\}$. For instance, the economy $e_0$ has an empty price set, $\mathbf{p}_0(t) = \{\emptyset\}$ and $e_{32}$ has $\mathbf{p}_{32}(t) = \{p_{32,1}(t), p_{32,2}(t)\}$.

The set of prices of two economies, $k$ and $s$ are equal, i.e. $\mathbf{p}_k(t) = \mathbf{p}_s(t)$, if the following two conditions are satisfied,

1 $\sharp I_k = \sharp I_s$
2 The relation $p_{k,i}(t) = p_{s,j}(t) \forall t$ with $i \in I_k$ and $j \in I_s$ is bijective.

The first condition indicates that the number of coupled markets are the same in both economies, and the second specifies that both economies produce the same price series.

We say that two economies $e_i$ and $e_j$ are related, $e_i \Re e_j$, if and only if $\mathbf{p}_i(t) = \mathbf{p}_j(t) \forall t$. Is easy to prove that $\Re$ is a relation of equivalence,[13] therefore it does produce a partition on $E$.

Thus, the set $E$ is partitioned in 30 subsets. The sub-sets have different cardinalities. When the sub-sets have cardinalities greater than 1 we name the subsets with $g$. When the cardinalities of the subset is of size 1, we will denote the economy with the number of the economy. In Table 12.1 we present the full partition produced by the relation of equivalence.

Every economy in a class has the same topology. For instance, in Figure 12.6, we plot the topologies of two classes having three economies each. The first row, from left to right, has the class with the economies $\{15, 23, 39\}$. Every economy in this class has the node label 4 as the primary factor market of the other three markets. There are two final good markets, and one of the final good markets receives a good from an intermediary market. The second row has a common topology as well.

Both equivalence classes in Figure 12.6 have the same composition of commodity markets. Both set of economies, in the first and in the second row have two final good, one intermediary and one natural resource market. The difference between both equivalence classes is given by the links between the markets that compose the economies. This difference, produces unalike dynamics. There are some composition of commodity markets, which accept a great variety of links, producing multiple dynamics.

In Table 12.2 we show how many economies it is possible to generate with different compositions of commodity markets. The first, second and third columns indicate the number of final good, intermediary and natural resource markets respectively. The fourth column counts the number of economies and the fifth column the number of equivalence classes. Thus, the first row indicates that there are 10 economies, in 10 classes with one final good, two intermediary and one natural resource market.

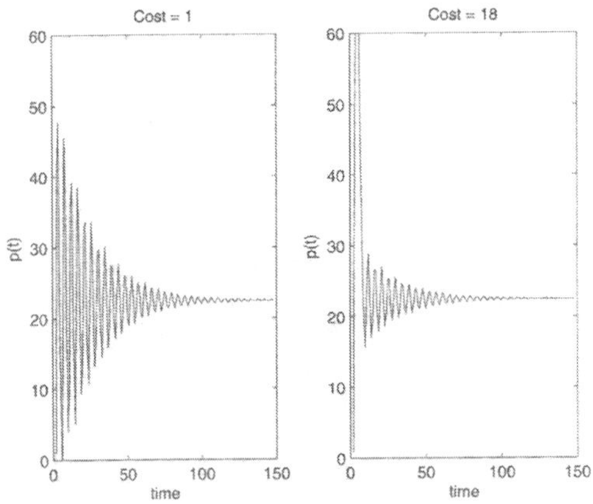


*Figure 12.6* First row $g_9 = \{13, 19, 35\}$ and second row $g_7 = \{15, 23, 39\}$

*Table 12.2* Number of economies with the same composition of commodity markets

| *Composition*⋆ *f* | *i* | *n* | *Number of economies* | *Classes of equivalences* |
|---|---|---|---|---|
| 1 | 2 | 1 | 10 | $\{e_{43}, e_{45}, e_{47}, e_{59}, e_{63}, e_{61}, e_{41}, e_{55}, e_{51}, e_{57}\}$ |
| 2 | 1 | 1 | 10 | $\{g_7, g_9, g_{12}, e_{25}, e_{31}\}$ |
| 1 | 1 | 2 | 10 | $\{g_8, g_{10}, g_{13}, e_{42}, e_{62}\}$ |
| 2 | 0 | 2 | 9 | $\{g_{11}, g_2, e_{30}\}$ |
| 1 | 1 | 1 | 9 | $\{g_3, g_4\}$ |
| 1 | 0 | 1 | 6 | $\{g_1\}$ |
| 2 | 0 | 1 | 4 | $\{g_5\}$ |
| 1 | 0 | 2 | 4 | $\{g_6\}$ |
| 3 | 0 | 1 | 1 | $\{e_7\}$ |
| 1 | 0 | 3 | 1 | $\{e_{52}\}$ |

⋆ number of final demand (f), intermediary (i), and natural resource market (n).

## Analyzing topologies

Formally, every class of equivalence in Table 12.1 represents a different dynamical system. However, given our specification, there are some classes that when they are interpreted from the economic point of view, produce similar behaviors.

In order to describe the links between the markets in an economy, we will describe the topologies of an economy using the standard Graph Theory notation.[14] For instance, the simplest economy with two markets is $T_1 = \{M, L\}$, with the set of markets $M = \{f_1, n_1\}$, describing that there are two markets, a final good and a natural resource market. The link between the markets is described as $L = \{\{n_1, f_1\}\}$, which indicates that there is only one link from the natural resource market, $n_1$, to the final good market $f_1$. The topology $T_1$ describe all the economies on the class $g_1$. The topology of $g_6$ is $T = \{M, L\}$ with markets $M = \{f_1, n_1, n_2\}$ and links $L = \{\{n_1, f_1\}, \{n_2, f_1\}\}$.

All the economies, without intermediaries, have the same vicious circle that we explained at the end of the previous section. Therefore, in all these economies, the final good markets set a high price and the natural resource establish prices which are very close to their unitary production cost. For the simplest case with one final good and a natural resource market, the simulations with the set of parameters $\theta$ gives a mean price[15] of $p_f^\star = 42.72$ and $p_n^\star = 2.27$ for the final good and the natural resource market respectively.

When a new final good market is introduced into the simplest $g_1$ class, we obtain the economy $T = \{\{n_1, f_2, f_1\}, \{\{n_1, f_1\}, \{n_1, f_2\}\}\}$ representing the class $g_5$. In this case, the mean prices are $p_{f_{1,2}}^\star = 46.58$ and $p_{n_1}^\star = 1.81$. The price in the final good markets increases because the quantity rationing is higher when there are two markets buying to the unique natural resource market. If there are three final good markets, as in the case of economy $e_7$, the price in the final good markets are increased further to $p_{f_{1,2,3}}^\star = 47.21$. However, there is an increase in the natural resource market price, to $p_{n_1} = 3.33$. There are two effects contributing to change the price of the natural resource price. First, there is a reduction of the demand as a consequence of the increases of the price on the final good market. Second, there is an increase of the demand as a consequence of the new final good market. The second effect dominates the first one, therefore the natural resource market increases its price to adjust the excess of demand produced by the new market.

The topologies $g_5$ and $g_6$ are identified by Nakanao and White (2006) as the most repeated triad, or dynamics engines, of the supplier/prime buyer relationships in the Ohta Industrial District in Japan.

### *Heterogeneity*

The classes of equivalence constructed in Table 12.1 assume that all the markets are homogeneous. Indeed, every market uses the same set of parameter $\theta$.

If markets are heterogeneous in their parameters, i.e. $\theta_1 \neq \theta_2 \neq \theta_3 \neq \theta_4$, the classes of equivalences of the homogeneous case are broken. Indeed, using the same relation of equivalence than before, we obtain a partition of 64 sub-sets on $E$ when markets differ in their parameters.

However, if the difference among the parameters in the parameter sets is kept within a given limit, i.e. $\exists \epsilon_\alpha, \forall \alpha_\imath \in \theta_\imath$ and $\alpha_\jmath \in \theta_\jmath, |\alpha_\imath - \alpha_\jmath| < \epsilon_\alpha$, every class of equivalence from the homogeneous class leaves its fingerprints in the patterns produced by prices in the heterogeneous case.

In Figure 12.7 we plot the price series of simulations for the two classes of equivalences of Figure 12.6. The parameter set of each market and their initial conditions are given by,

1 $\theta_1 = \{a = 100, b = -1, c = 15, d = 2, \alpha = 0.5, \rho = 0.1, \delta = 1\}$
2 $\theta_2 = \{a = 50, b = -1.3, c = 10, d = 1, \alpha = 0.5, \rho = 0.1, \delta = 1\}$
3 $\theta_3 = \{a = 100, b = -1.6, c = 10, d = 2, \alpha = 0.5, \rho = 0.1, \delta = 1\}$
4 $\theta_4 = \{a = 100, b = -2, c = 10, d = 0.9, \alpha = 0.5, \rho = 0.1, \delta = 1\}$
5 $\iota_1 = \{p(0) = 10, m(0) = 1000, v(0) = 10 d(0) = 0, s(0) = 0\}$ and $\iota_1 = \iota_2 = \iota_3 = \iota_4$

Although the price series are not equal and the price equilibrium differs among them, there is a common behavior throughout the classes. The common behavior within a class is characterized by two "stylized patterns" on the price series. First, the transition from the initial conditions to the equilibrium are similar and, second, the equilibrium values have the same order within a class. The last pattern means that if the equilibrium prices of an economy have this order: $p_1 > p_2 > p_4 > p_3$, any other economy in the same class of equivalence has the same equilibrium market price order.

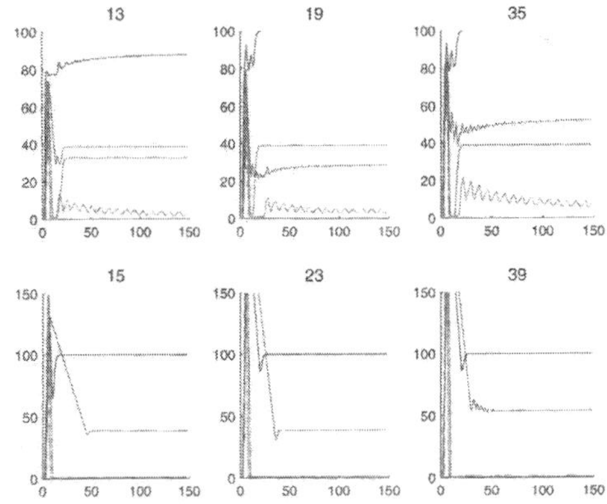


*Figure 12.7* First row $\{13, 19, 35\}$ and second row $\{15, 23, 39\}$

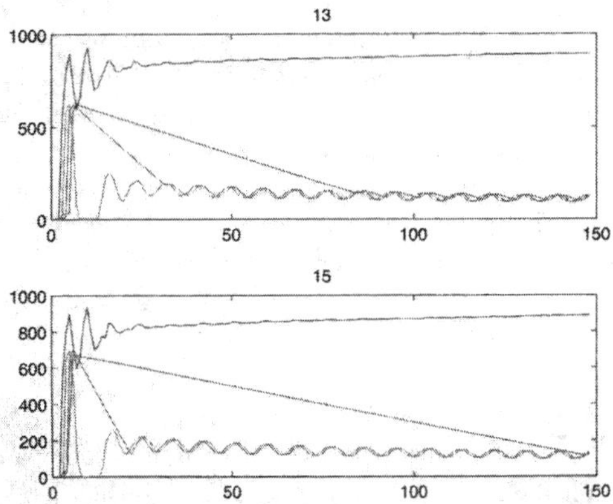


*Figure 12.8* Economies $e_{13}$ and $e_{15}$ with dominance of market 1

When a market has, relative to the other markets in the economy, a high volume of transactions, the operation of the big market constrains all the other markets in the economy. Thus, the dominant market may subject the economy to its volume of operation. In Figure 12.8 we show the price series of economies 13 and 15 when we introduce a dominant market. In the simulations we use the same parameter sets used in the heterogeneous case. The dominant market is introduced through a modification in the demand of market 1. Thus, $\theta_1 = \{a = 1000, b = -1, c = 15, d = 2, \alpha = 0.5, \rho = 0.1, \delta = 1\}$.

When all the markets have the same parameters, economies $e_{13}$ and $e_{15}$ belong to different classes of equivalence. However, when we introduce the dominant market both economies produce quite similar price series. Indeed, the dominance of market 1 makes irrelevant the coupling between markets 4 and 2 in economy $e_{15}$.

## Conclusion

The aim of this chapter was to explore the effects of vertical couplings between markets in the price dynamics of the markets. There is a vertical coupling between two markets when the good produced by one of them is the primary factor for the other one. We explore, through simulations, all the vertical coupling that may exist using up to four markets.

The production in our economies is a linear flow from the services of primary factors to final goods. Indeed, all the network topologies of our models are a directed acyclic graph. If we start a path from any market and follow the direction of the links, there is no way to return to the node of origin. According to Nakano and White (2006) the directed acyclic graph is the general property of the supplier/prime buyer network in large-scale industrial districts. The network that we explore in this chapter is small, up to four markets, and has to be considered as the drivers or dynamical engines of bigger networks.

In the first part of this chapter we present analytical results, using simplified specifications. When more constraints are introduced to the models, simulations were used to explore the results of different specifications.

We observed that using up to four markets there are 30 different topologies. Each topology, assuming that the parameters of the markets are homogeneous, produces a different price time series. Exploring economies having only final good and natural resource markets, without intermediaries, we identified that quantity rationing with the adaptive price adjustment mechanism specified, produces a big difference between the price on the final good and the natural resource market. While natural resource market sets prices very close to their unitary cost, final good markets set very high prices.

We also show that if, in a vertical network, there is a market having a high volume of transactions, relative to the other markets in the network, the behavior of the market with high volume constrains the behavior of all the other markets.

## Acknowledgements

I am much indebted to Vela Velupillai for introducing me to Richard Goodwin's work. I thank to two anonymous referees and the contributions of the participants at the Goodwin workshop held in Bremen, November 2005.

## Notes

1 The first version of this paper written in 1937 is in German.
2 However, there is a fix unitary cost of extraction of the natural resources. Thus, the extraction is constrained by the available budget. In a sense, the budget is a measure of the inventory of inputs.
3 The interested reader may obtain an explicit maximizing calculation, for the case with two goods in Day and Tinney (1969).
4 If the depreciation is complete, that is to say $\delta = 0$, the model is equivalent to the Goodwin (1949) cobweb model, where the price expectation is adjusted according to the excess of demand.
5 This independence between the price setting and the instantaneous market clearing resembles the Marshallian fish market as explained in Leijonhufvud (2006)
6 See Shone (2002: Ch. 8) for details about the convergence conditions of the standard cobweb model
7 The complex root of the system is $\lambda_{1,2} = 0.05 \pm 0.9473i$. The system oscillates as $z_{1,2}(t) = R^t[cos(t\phi) \pm sin(t\phi)]$ with $R = \sqrt{\alpha^2 + \beta^2}$ and $tan\phi = \frac{\alpha}{\beta}$. In our case $R =$

0.948 and $\phi = 1.518$ radians, which means that our system has oscillations of periods 4.13. As $R < 1$ the system will eventually converge to the equilibrium values.

8 See Grimaldi (1998).

9 This is not equivalent to say that the topologies of our economies can be described by *trees* having four nodes. In our case, there are some leaves that are linked between them. see Grimaldi (1998) for more details on the Graph Theory.

10 The rule to transform a binary number $101011_2$ into its decimal representation $43_{10}$ is: $1 \times 2^5 + 0 \times 2^4 + 1 \times 2^3 + 0 \times 2^2 + 1 \times 2^1 + 1 \times 2^0$.

11 Given that A is the adjacency matrix of $e_k$, the index set is defined as $I_k = \bigcup_{a_{i,j}=1} \{i,j\}$. The union of all the indexes i and j where $a_{i,j} = 1$.

12 The number 32 in decimal is equal to 100000 in base 2.

13 Reflexive: $e_i \Re e_i$ for i=1..64. This means $\mathbf{p}_i(t) = \mathbf{p}_i(t) \forall$ t.
Symmetric: $e_i \Re e_j$ implies $e_j \Re e_i$. This means $\mathbf{p}_i(t) = \mathbf{p}_j(t)$ and $\mathbf{p}_j(t) = \mathbf{p}_i(t) \forall$ t.
Transitive: $e_i \Re e_j$ and $e_j \Re e_k$ implies $e_i \Re e_k$. This means $\mathbf{p}_i(t) = \mathbf{p}_j(t)$ and $\mathbf{p}_j(t) = \mathbf{p}_k(t) \forall$ t implies $\mathbf{p}_i(t) = \mathbf{p}_k(t) \forall$ t.

14 See Grimaldi (1998).

15 We run the simulations for 300 periods. The values presented here are the mean of the last 100 periods, where the time series of prices is stable around the mean.

## References

Brock, W.A and Hommes C.H. (1997) 'Rational routes to randomness', SSRI working paper 9506, University of Wisconsin, (1997).

Day, Richard and Herbert Tinney (1969) 'Cycles, Phases and Growth in the Generalised Cobweb Theory', *The Economic Journal*, 79(313): 90–108.

Chiarella, Carl (1988) 'The cobweb model. Its instability and the onset of chaos', *Economic Modelling*, October, 5(4): 377–84.

Chiarella, Carl, Xue-Zhon He, Hing Hung and Peiyuan Zhu (2006) 'An analysis of the cobweb model with boundedly rational heterogeneous producers', *Journal of Economic Behavior & Organization*, 61(4): 750–68.

Ezekiel, Mordecai (1938) 'The Cobweb Theorem'. *The Quarterly Journal of Economics*, 52(2): 255–80.

Goodwin, Richard (1946) 'Innovations and the Irregularity of Economic Cycles'. *Review of Economic Statistics*, 28: 104.

Goodwin, Richard (1947) 'Dynamical Coupling with Especial Reference to Markets Having Production Lags'. *Econometrica* 15(3): 181–204.

Goodwin, Richard (1949) 'The Multiplier as Matrix'. *Economic Journal* 59: 537–55.

Goere, J. and Carl Hommes (2000), 'Heterogeneous beliefs and the non-linear cobweb model', *Journal of Economic Dynamics and Control* 24: 761–98

Grimaldi, Ralph (1998). *Discrete and Combinatorial Mathematics. An applied introduction*. Boston, MA: Addison-Wesley Publishing Company, Inc.

Hommes, Cars (1991) 'Adaptive learning and roads to chaos: the case of the cobweb', *Economic Letters* 36: 127–32.

Hommes, Cars (1994) 'Dynamics of the cobweb model with adaptive expectations and nonlinear supply and demand', *Journal of Economic Behavior and Organization* 24: 315–35.

Hooton F. G. (1950) 'Risk and the Cobweb Theorem', *The Economic Journal*, 60(237): 69–80.

Jensen, Roderick and Robin Urban (1984) 'Chaotic price behaviour in a non-linear cobweb model' *Economic Letters* 15: 235–40.

Kurz, Heinz and Neri Salvadori (1995) *Theory of Production: A Long-Period Analysis*. Cambridge: Cambridge University Press 1995.

Leijonhufvud, Axel (2006). 'Agent-Based Macro' in L. Tesfatsion and K. Judd (eds) *Handbook of Computational Economics*, 2nd edn. Amsterdam: North-Holland.

Leontief, W. (1951) *Studies in the Structure of the American Economy*. New York: Oxford University Press.

Muellbauer John and Richard Portes (1978) 'Macroeconomics Models with Quantity Rationing', *The Economic Journal*, 88(352): 788–821.

Morishima, Michio (1965) *Equilibrium, Stability and Growth: A Multi-Sectorial Analysis*. Oxford: Clarendon Press.

Nakano, Tsutomu and Douglas R. White (2006) 'The Visible Hand in a Production-Chain Market: A Market Equilibrium from Network Analytical Perspective' SFI Working Paper 06-05-015.

Neumann, John von (1945) 'A Model of General Economic Equilibrum'. *Review of Economic Studies*, 13: 1–9.

Pasinetti, Luigi (1973). 'The Notion of Vertical Integration in Economic Analysis'. *Metroeconomica*, XXV: 1–29.

Pasinetti, Luigi (1990) 'Normalised General Coordinates and Vertically Integrated Sectors in a Simple Case' in K. Velupillai (ed.) *Nonlinear and Multisectoral Macrodynamics*. London: Macmillan.

Shone, Ronald (2002) *Economic Dynamics. Phase Diagrams and their Economic Application*, 2nd edn. Cambridge, Cambridge University Press.

Solow, Robert (1959) 'Competitive Valuation in a Dynamic Input-Output System', *Econometrica* 27: 1–24.

Sraffa, Piero (1960) *Production of Commodities by Means of Commodities - Prelude to a Critique of Economic Theory*. Cambridge: Cambridge Unviersity Press.

Takayama, Akira (1985) *Mathematical Economics*, 2nd edn, Cambridge: Cambridge University Press.

# 13 Microfounded animal spirits and Goodwinian income distribution dynamics

*Reiner Franke*

## Introduction

While rational expectations are the ruling paradigm in macroeconomic theory, expectations in the real world are far more diffuse and do not only concern just one variable such as typically the rate of inflation. Apart from that, expectations are not homogeneous as they are in these models where everything boils down to the representative agent. Insofar as expectations enter the agents' economic decisions, a more appropriate concept appears to be that of an aggregate climate index, which still allows the individual agents to have different attitudes and make different decisions. If here the microeconomic basis is made explicit and a procedure is given of how to derive a macroeconomic adjustment equation for the climate variable, then from the viewpoint of heterodox theory this would be a more satisfactory approach to the microfoundations of macroeconomics and the treatment of expectations than the optimizing framework where all agents are blessed with the same rational expectations.

A route in this direction was contrived more than 20 years ago in a stimulating book in the social sciences by Weidlich and Haag (1983). Unfortunately, their approach has not found its way into contemporary macroeconomic theory. As we see it, two reasons are responsible for this neglect. First, the formulation of the model did not only refer to a probabilistic framework, its analysis also utilized concepts from the theory of statistical mechanics like the Master equation and the Fokker-Planck equation, which are largely unknown to many economists. In their work they usually study trajectories of definite aggregate variables, whereas these equations are concerned with the evolution of an entire probability distribution or at least, in the mean field approximations, with the time path of expected values. Even the latter concept, however, can be hard to assess, namely, if the stochastic equilibrium of the system is – most interestingly – characterized by a bimodal (or multi-modal) probability density function, in which case expected values would become meaningless in predicting the likely value of a variable.

A second aspect is insufficient marketing. Although the approach was employed in a number of macroeconomic papers, the topics they dealt with were somewhat detached or "exotic" (Kraft *et al.*, 1986; Haag *et al.*, 1987; Weise and Kraft, 1988), or the ordinary reader probably soon drowned in a sea of specification details so that he or she could no longer appreciate the essence of the approach (Weidlich and Braun, 1992; despite the promising title of this chapter). Nevertheless, macroeconomists with a wider area of interest could have also learned from several related articles in highly reputable journals, in particular by Kirman (1993), Orléan (1995), or Lux (1995, 1997, 1998). In sum, the approach by Weidlich and Haag (1983) or similar formulations in the 1990s offered macroeconomists a good chance to introduce microfounded expectation formation into their models in a very convenient, even standardized way, but this chance was largely missed.[1]

Referring to the fields of macroeconomics, the present chapter can be seen as providing a better marketing for the basic idea developed by Weidlich and Haag. The main innovation in this respect is the derivation of an ordinary adjustment equation for the *realized* values of an aggregate climate index, which moreover can be done without any recourse to the statistical mechanics apparatus.[2] This macroeconomic equation is based on the concept of state-dependent transition probabilities that govern the switches of the individual agents between optimism and pessimism, for which we postulate an element of hetero-reference and self-reference. It may here be emphasized that the latter can also be described as giving rise to herding. The resulting design is in fact well compatible with Keynes' discussion of "The state of long-term expectation" in Chapter 12 of the *General Theory*, so that the often quoted "animal spirits" and their endogenous evolution over time are given a more precise meaning.[3]

After delineating the way from the micro to the macro level, we present an elementary (and non-exotic) macroeconomic application. Interpreting the climate variable as a business climate determining fixed investment of firms and combining it with a simple multiplier theory and a wage Phillips curve, a two-dimensional differential equations system is obtained that can be characterized as a Goodwin growth cycle model (in the sense of Goodwin, 1967). The following features should make our contribution attractive to (at least) the Goodwin community and establish its *raison d'être* in the great stock of models in a Goodwinian tradition: while its reduced form is of a similarly clear structure, our model has a richer theoretical basis than Goodwin's prototype model; the model is structurally stable, where the condition on the dynamic stability of the steady state growth path depends on the responsiveness of the animal spirits, or the herding effect; in the unstable case caused by strong herding the economy exhibits persistent and bounded cyclical behavior in economic activity and income distribution, which prevails without the need to invoke an extrinsic nonlinearity of more or less flexible ceilings or floors.

The remainder of this chapter is organized as follows. The next section puts forward the agents' transition probabilities and derives the adjustment equation for the macroeconomic business climate from them. Specified in a so-called feedback index that determines the level of the transition probabilities, subsequently the concepts of self-reference and hetero-reference are introduced. "Goodwinian prototype model" completes the model with a simple multiplier theory and a wage Phillips curve. It formulates the two differential equations, provides the local stability condition and then, which is the most interesting part, studies the global dynamics by means of phase diagrams and the Poincaré-Bendixson Theorem. To get a first feeling for the robustness of the dynamic properties, "Respecifications of the model" examines two modifications. First a delay between desired and realized investment is discussed, which will add a third dimension to the system. The second modification concerns the specification of the herding mechanism, where in the feedback index the influence of the level of the business climate is replaced with its rate of change. After all, a verbal characterization of the model would hardly be affected by this alternative formulation. The final section concludes.

## Dynamic adjustments of a general business climate

### *From microscopic transition probabilities to a macroscopic differential equation*

Let the business sector consist of $2N$ firms, whose number remains fixed over time. In each point in time a single firm can be characterized as being either optimistic or pessimistic about the future prospects of the economy. Designating an optimistic and pessimistic attitude by $(+)$ and $(-)$, respectively, let $n_t^+$, $n_t^-$ be the number of optimistic and pessimistic firms at time $t$ ($n_t^+ + n_t^- = 2N$). Next, put $n_t = (n_t^+ - n_t^-)/2$ and define $x_t = n_t/N$. Supposing that there is no systematic relationship between attitudes and the size of the firms, $x_t$ is the average attitude of firms or, as we will call it, the general *business climate*. Clearly, $-1 \leq x_t \leq 1$; optimism and pessimism balance in a state $x_t = 0$; and at $x_t > 0$ ($x_t < 0$) optimistic (pessimistic) firms form a majority.

Firms may well change their attitude over time. For the time being, we consider this process in discrete time with adjustment periods of length $\Delta t > 0$. The changes will depend on a great variety of macroscopic aspects and idiosyncratic circumstances, which one will not want to specify in all of their details. It rather seems suitable to introduce random elements in this respect, in order to keep the modeling simple and to avoid arbitrary assumptions. Therefore, the basic concept to describe the changes in the business climate are the transition probabilities of the individual firms: at time $t$, let $\pi_t^{-+}$ be the probability *per unit of time* that a firm changes from pessimistic to optimistic, and $\pi_t^{+-}$ the probability for an opposite change. More exactly, $\Delta t\, \pi_t^{-+}$ is the probability that a firm who is pessimistic at $t$ will have become optimistic at the end of the period at $t+\Delta t$; and likewise $\Delta t\, \pi_t^{+-}$ for an optimistic firm. These probabilities are uniform across the population. They are, however, not fixed but vary with certain other macro variables in the economy (which will be discussed further below).

Let us beforehand examine how, given $\pi_t^{+-}$ and $\pi_t^{-+}$, the climate changes from $t$ to $t+\Delta t$.[4] If we consider the 'excess' number of optimistic firms $n_t$, it rises by 1 if a pessimistic firm becomes optimistic (when $n_t^+$ increases and $n_t^-$ decreases by 1). Symmetrically, $n_t$ declines by 1 if an optimistic firm turns pessimistic. Denoting by $k_t^+$ and $k_t^-$ the number of converts of the first and second type, respectively, we have:

$$n_{t+\Delta t} = n_t + k_t^+ - k_t^- \tag{13.1}$$

As the number of pessimistic firms at time $t$ can be written as $n_t^- = N - n_t$, the number $k_t^+$ of firms turning optimistic can be viewed as arising from $N - n_t$ random draws of the type success/failure, each of which has probability $\Delta t\, \pi_t^{-+}$ for the event 'success', i.e. switch (and the complement for the no-switching event). The number of these events are then added up. Hence, the random variable $k_t^+$ has a binomial distribution $B(N - n_t, \Delta t\, \pi_t^{-+})$.[5] Analogously, $n_t^+ = N + n_t$ being the number of optimistic firms in $t$, the random variable $k_t^-$ is distributed as $B(N + n_t, \Delta t\, \pi_t^{+-})$.

The expected values of these variables are $E(k_t^+) = (N - n_t)\, \Delta t\, \pi_t^{-+}$ and $E(k_t^-) = (N + n_t)\, \Delta t\, \pi^{+-}$, their variances amount to $\mathrm{Var}(k_t^+) = (N - n_t)\, \Delta t\, \pi_t^{-+}\, (1 - \Delta t\, \pi_t^{-+})$ and $\mathrm{Var}(k_t^-) = (N + n_t)\, \Delta t\, \pi_t^{+-}\, (1 - \Delta t\, \pi_t^{+-})$. If the expected values are large enough (exceeding 5 or 10), the two binomial distributions are (very) well approximated by the Gaussian distributions with the same first and second moments. Taking for granted that the population is large and $n_t$ not too close to the boundaries $\pm N$, we get:

$$k_t^+ = E(k_t^+) + \sqrt{\mathrm{Var}(k_t^+)}\,\xi_t^+ ,\; k_t^- = E(k_t^-) + \sqrt{\mathrm{Var}(k_t^-)}\,\xi_t^- \tag{13.2}$$

where $\xi_t^+$ and $\xi_t^-$ are two independent random draws from the standard normal distribution $N(0,1)$ (with mean zero and variance equal to one). Furthermore, the difference between two normal distributions yields a normal distribution again. Its mean is the difference between the two single means, its variance the sum of the two single variances. For the random variable $k_t = k_t^+ - k_t^-$, we thus have $E(k_t) = \Delta t \cdot [(N - n_t)\,\pi_t^{-+} - (N + n_t)\,\pi_t^{+-}] = \Delta t \cdot [(1 - x_t)\,\pi_t^{-+} - (1 + x_t)\,\pi_t^{+-}] \cdot N$ and $\mathrm{Var}(k_t) = \Delta t \cdot [(1 - x_t)\,\pi_t^{-+}\,(1 - \Delta t\,\pi_t^{-+}) + (1 + x_t)\,\pi_t^{+-}\,(1 - \Delta t\,\pi_t^{+-})] \cdot N$. It remains to divide (13.1) and (13.2) by $N$ and we obtain,

$$
\begin{aligned}
x_{t+\Delta t} &= x_t + \Delta t[(1 - x_t)\pi_t^{-+} - (1 + x_t)\pi_t^{+-}] \\
&\quad + [(\sqrt{\Delta t D_t}/\sqrt{N})]\xi_t \qquad (13.3) \\
D_t &:= (1 - x_t)\pi_t^{-+}(1 - \Delta t \pi_t^{-+}) + (1 + x_t)\pi_t^{+-}(1 - \Delta t \pi_t^{+-}) \qquad (13.4) \\
\xi_t &\sim N(0,1)
\end{aligned}
$$

Equation (13.4) abstracts from the many individual and accidental switches in the firms' attitudes and summarizes them in a macroscopic stochastic equation that governs the changes in the climate. In statistical mechanics this type of equation is known as the Langevin equation. The equation is there usually derived by first setting up the entire probability distribution $P = P(x, z, t)$ of $x$ and a possible set of additional variables $z$, and then analyzing its change over time. For this purpose the powerful tool of the Fokker-Planck equation (FPE) is employed, which is itself a second-order approximation. There is indeed an intimate connection between FPE and the Langevin equation. Regarding (13.4) it is shown by the fact that the term in the first square brackets is the drift coefficient in FPE, and $D_t$ corresponds to its fluctuation or diffusion term.[6]

For our present purpose we can stick with (13.4). It suffices to note that the noise level in the equation decreases with the size of the population. Then, for the rest of this chapter, let $N$ be so large that this intrinsic stochastic component can be safely ignored. For the theoretical analysis it is furthermore convenient to let the adjustment period shrink to zero, $\Delta t \to 0$. Equation (13.4) remains well-defined and, dropping the time index, the business climate is seen to be governed by a differential equation,

$$
\dot{x} = (1 - x)\,\pi^{-+} \; - \; (1 + x)\,\pi^{+-} \qquad (13.5)
$$

Clearly, this equation can be taken on its own and treated like any other ordinary differential equation. The focus therefore shifts to the specification of the transition probabilities $\pi^{-+}$ and $\pi^{+-}$.

## Feedbacks in the individual transition probabilities

The transition probabilities will change in response to the variations of a set of several variables that the firms observe. These effects can generally be summarized in a single feedback index $f$, which attains positive and negative values in different stages the economy goes through. Let positive and negative be related to the probability $\pi^{-+}$ of switching from pessimistic to optimistic, that is, an increase in the feedback index increases $\pi^{-+}$ and decreases the complementary probability $\pi^{+-}$.

It is an obvious concept, which Weidlich and Haag (1983) have also found very helpful in their formal analysis, to assume that the changes of the transition probabilities depend on the changes of the index $f$ in a linear way. More precisely, on the *relative* changes, so that we have $d\pi^{-+}/\pi^{-+} = \alpha\, df$ for some constant $\alpha$. As it is only a matter of scale of the feedback index, $\alpha$ can be taken to be unity without loss of generality. Symmetry is another natural assumption to make, which gives us $d\pi^{+-}/\pi^{+-} = -df$. Introducing $\nu > 0$ as an 'integration constant', the specification of the transition probabilities reads ('exp' being the exponential function),

$$\pi^{-+} = \pi^{-+}(f) = \nu \exp(f), \qquad \pi^{+-} = \pi^{+-}(f) = \nu \exp(-f) \tag{13.6}$$

Certainly, (13.6) ensures positive values of the probabilities. The complementary condition that the feedback index is bounded, such that the probabilities are less than unity, should be a property of the model into which (13.6) is incorporated (or the outcome of an empirical estimation). The adjustment equation (13.5) of the business climate $x$ itself becomes:

$$\dot{x} = \nu\,[(1-x)\exp(f) \;-\; (1+x)\exp(-f)] \tag{13.7}$$

An individual firm may well have its specific reasons to maintain or switch to one of the attitudes. With more information on such a firm its behavior could then be described in terms of conditional probabilities, or each firm could be equipped with transition probabilities of its own. Intuition says that these firm-specific probabilities (or rather feedback indices) would average out across the whole population.[7] In any case, from our macroscopic point of view we only need to refer to the unconditional probabilities, which are uniformly, or representatively, given by (13.6).

A special feature of the specification of the transition probabilities is $\pi^{-+} = \pi^{+-} = \nu > 0$ when $f = 0$. Hence even in the absence of active feedback forces or when the different feedback variables neutralize each other, the individual firms will still change their attitude with a positive probability. While these reversals, which can occur in either direction, are to be ascribed to idiosyncratic circumstances, from our bird's-eye view they appear as purely random and, given that the population is large, will cancel out if we consider them in the aggregate, implying $\dot{x} = 0$ in (13.7). Since $\nu$ in (13.6) measures the general responsiveness (per unit of time) of the transition probabilities to the arrival of new information, it is not just a technical integration coefficient but can be characterized as a *flexibility parameter* (Weidlich and Haag, 1983: 41).

As indicated in the Introduction, in specifying the feedback two concepts are considered. The first is the concept of self-reference, which grasps the idea that waves of optimistic and pessimistic sentiment are generated by means of a self-exciting mechanism. Accordingly, the probability of switching from pessimistic to optimistic is larger than in the opposite direction if the prevailing disposition in the population of firms is already optimistic (and *vice versa*). Setting up the index $f$ in an additive way, the first term in $f$ is therefore given by the current business climate $x$, multiplied by a constant coefficient $\phi_x$ that measures how strongly firms tend to join the current majority. Borrowing the expression from the financial markets literature, $\phi_x$ can be referred to as the model's *herding parameter*.[8]

While the first concept essentially constitutes a process of herding, as it has just been called, we additionally introduce a hetero-referential mechanism. It takes account of the more "objective" factors that may induce firms to change their attitude. These factors may reinforce or put a curb on the herding dynamics, or they may even reverse it. In a Goodwinian spirit and regarding the prospects of their investment, we assume that higher profits in the economy increase the probability of a pessimistic firm to become optimistic or, if it is already optimistic, to maintain this attitude. This overall profitability is measured by the share of aggregate profits in national income. Thus the profit share can feature as the second term in the feedback index: entering it in a positive way, the transition probability $\pi^{-+}$ increases when the profit share increases.

Instead of the profit share, it will be more convenient in the presentation of the model to refer to its complement, the wage share, which we denote by $v$. This macro variable is included as a negative entry in the feedback index, such that *ceteris paribus* a value of $v$ below (above) a benchmark $v^o$ induces a higher (lower) probability $\pi^{-+}$. The strength of this objective feedback factor in relation to the business climate is represented by a positive coefficient $\phi_v$. In sum, the feedback index $f$ in (13.7) is specified as:

$$f = \phi_x x \; - \; \phi_v \, (v - v^o) \tag{13.8}$$

Equations (13.7) and (13.8) show that the macroeconomic business climate is driven by itself (the auto-feedback) and by the macroeconomic wage share (the hetero-feedback). Note that in a state of balanced income distribution and balanced optimism and pessimism, when $v = v^o$ and $x = 0$, the auto-feedback is positive and thus destabilizing if $\phi_x > 1$, and it is negative and thus stabilizing if $\phi_x < 1$. This follows easily from partially differentiating $\dot{x}$ with respect to $x$, which evaluated at $x = 0$ yields $\partial \dot{x} / \partial x = 2\nu\,(\phi_x - 1)$. The herding parameter $\phi_x$ will also be of central importance in the full macro model that we are going to formulate in the next section.

Before, however, we should return to Equation (13.7) and make an important observation whose economic significance goes far beyond the present modeling framework. Independently of the way in which the feedback index may be specified, if $f$ remains bounded in a model, the boundaries $\pm 1$ of the climate $x$ are repelling. Clearly, as $x$ gets close to 1 in (13.7), the first term in square brackets tends to vanish. Since the second term is positive and bounded away from zero, the time derivative $\dot{x}$ will eventually turn negative and the climate will decrease. Conversely, if $x$ gets sufficiently close to $-1$, the derivative will be positive and $x$ will rise again. We emphasize that apart from the exponential function in the specification (13.6) of the transition probabilities, which there quite innocently was only introduced to make the relative changes of $\pi^{-+}$ and $\pi^{+-}$ linearly dependent on the changes in $f$ and, as a consequence, to prevent the probabilities from falling down to zero, no further nonlinearity is required for this global self-stabilization mechanism to work out. As far as the adjustments of the aggregate climate variable is concerned, modeling could be done without designing any extrinsic ceiling or floor.

## A Goodwinian prototype model

### *Utilization and changes in income distribution*

To build up a small macrodynamic model on the basis of the herding dynamics specified above, we only have to combine the differential equation (13.7) for the business climate with an equation that determines the motions of the external norm $v$ in the feedback index (13.8), which is here the wage share. Two elements are sufficient for that. First, as in many other models of Goodwinian type to discuss income distribution dynamics, the motions of the wage share can be easily derived from a wage Phillips curve with economic activity as the driving force. Second, following the Keynesian tradition and viewing economic activity as basically demand-driven, it is convenient to postulate a direct influence of the business climate on investment and thus, *via* the multiplier, on aggregate demand and finally output. We are now going to formulate these ideas in a simple way.

To begin with the demand side, we concentrate on fixed investment as the only active component of demand and conceive it as an increasing function of the business climate. Considering the micro level, each individual firm has two investment options, which are given by a minimal growth rate $g_{min}$ if the firm is pessimistic, and a maximal growth rate $g_{max}$ if the firm is optimistic. Let $g^o$ be the growth rate of the aggregate capital stock which will prevail in a balanced state of the business climate, when $x = 0$. Since the aggregate capital growth rate $g$ equals $g_{min}$ if $x = -1$, and $g_{max}$ if $x = 1$, the equilibrium growth rate is:

$$g^o = (g_{min} + g_{max})/2 \tag{13.9}$$

Generally, a climate $x$ gives rise to the capital growth rate:

$$g = g(x) = g^o + \beta_{gx} x \qquad (\beta_{gx} := (g_{max} - g_{min})/2) \tag{13.10}$$

The other components of demand are assumed to be proportional either to the capital stock $K$, which may serve as a trend indicator, or to disposable income, which itself is supposed to be a linear function of total income $Y$ and of $K$. We furthermore assume a closed economy and continuous temporary equilibrium on the goods markets, so $Y$ is also total output. With suitable constants $c_1, \ldots, c_4$ and $s$ the economy's (constant) propensity to save out of disposable income, the market clearing condition gives $Y =$ net investment + capital depreciation + consumption + government spending $= gK + c_1 K + (1-s) \cdot$ disposable income $+ c_2 K = gK + (c_1 + c_2) K + (1-s)(Y + c_3 K) = gK + c_4 K + (1-s) Y$. Put $\beta_u = c_4/s$ and let $u = Y/K$ denote the output–capital ratio, which indicates the utilization of the capital stock. Dividing the market clearing condition by $K$ and solving it for $u$, a simple multiplier relationship is obtained,[9]

$$u = g(x)/s + \beta_u = (g^o + \beta_{gx} x)/s + \beta_u \tag{13.11}$$

Obviously, the variations of capital utilization, which represent the stages of the business cycle, can be directly identified with the variations of the business climate.

To model the variations of the wage share, let $w$ be the nominal wage rate, $z$ labor productivity, $p$ the price level, and $u^o$ a 'normal' rate of capital utilization. The Phillips curve mentioned above can then be set up as a money wage Phillips curve, which reads,

$$\hat{w} = \hat{z} + \hat{p} + \beta_w (1-v)(u - u^o) \tag{13.12}$$

The structural coefficients behind $\beta_u$ in (13.11) are assumed to be consistent with $u^o$, that is, $u^o = g(0)/s + \beta_u = g^o/s + \beta_u$.[10] The term $1-v$ is a convenient device that below will prevent wages from totally exhausting the national product. The responsiveness of money wages to the changes in economic activity are thus measured by the product $\beta_w(1-v)$, whose variations will be negligible if the amplitude of the wage share is small.

The sum of productivity growth $\hat{z}$ and price inflation $\hat{p}$ in (13.12) constitutes a reference level for wage inflation, in the sense that in a state of normal utilization $u = u^o$, the wage share $v = wL/pY = (w/p)/z$ remains invariant ($L$ being employment), which it does by virtue of $\hat{v} = \hat{w} - \hat{p} - \hat{z} = 0$. Current wage inflation exceeds reference wage inflation if the capital stock is overutilized, $u > u^o$, a situation for which one may assume that it goes along with an unemployment rate below its 'natural' level; conversely, wage inflation falls short of $\hat{z} + \hat{p}$ in a state of under-utilization.

A differential equation for the wage share is now readily obtained. Logarithmic differentiation of $v$ yields $\hat{v} = \hat{w} - \hat{p} - \hat{z} = \beta_w (u - u^o)(1-v)$. Plugging in utilization from (13.11), taking the consistency condition on $\beta_u$ into account, and putting $\beta_{gs} = \beta_{gx}/s$, we have:

$$\dot{v} = \beta_w \beta_{gs} v (1-v) x \tag{13.13}$$

To sum up, equations (13.7) and (13.13), where (13.8) has to be substituted for $f$ in (13.7), constitute a system of two differential equations in the state of confidence, $x$, and the wage share, $v$.

### Local and global analysis of the complete model

For a mathematical analysis of the global dynamics it is useful to work with hyperbolic functions in the climate adjustments. The definitions for the hyperbolic sine and cosine (sinh and cosh) allow us to reformulate (13.7) as $\dot{x} = 2\nu\{[\exp(f) - \exp(-f)]/2 - x[\exp(f) + \exp(-f)]/2\} = 2\nu[\sinh(f) - x\cosh(f)]$. With $\tanh = \sinh/\cosh$ for the hyperbolic tangent and writing out the feedback index in full, this equation becomes:

$$\dot{x} = 2\nu\{\tanh[\phi_x x - \phi_v(v - v^o)] - x\}\cosh[\phi_x x - \phi_v(v - v^o)] \qquad (13.14)$$

The system to be investigated is thus given by (13.13) and (13.14).[11] Clearly, $v = v^o$ and $x = 0$ constitute a point of rest. Since $\dot{v} = 0$ implies $x = 0$ (if we disregard the meaningless cases $v = 0$ and $v = 1$), cosh is everywhere positive, and tanh is a strictly increasing function, this equilibrium is unique. It goes without saying that aggregate output and capital grow in line in this situation, at the rate $g^o$. The individual firms are, however, heterogeneous in this respect: half of them have their capital stock growing at the rate $g_{min}$, and the other half at the rate $g_{max}$. In addition, there is some change going on under the macroeconomic surface, since, as observed before, individual firms will still randomly switch from one attitude, or growth rate, to the other.

Regarding a local stability analysis of (13.13) and (13.14), the Jacobian matrix $J$ that is associated with its equilibrium point is easily computed as:

$$J = \begin{bmatrix} 0 & \beta_w \beta_{gs} v^o(1 - v^o) \\ -2\nu\phi_v & 2\nu(\phi_x - 1) \end{bmatrix} \qquad (13.15)$$

The determinant is unambiguously positive, and the sign of trace $J = 2\nu(\phi_x - 1)$ depends on the coefficient $\phi_x$ alone. The equilibrium is therefore established to be locally asymptotically stable if the herding parameter $\phi_x$ is less than unity, whereas it is locally repelling if $\phi_x$ is greater than one.

The global properties of (13.13) and (13.14) can be studied by means of phase diagrams. The isocline $\dot{v} = 0$ is trivially given by the straight line $x = 0$, and fortunately also the isocline of the business climate, $\dot{x} = 0$, can be explicitly computed. To this end note that $\dot{x} = 0$ if (and only if) the term in curly brackets in (13.14) vanishes. Applying the inverse function $\text{arctanh}(\cdot)$ to both sides of the equation $\tanh[\phi_x x - \phi_v(v - v^o)] = x$, using the identity $\text{arctanh}(x) = (1/2) \cdot \ln[(1+x)/(1-x)]$, and solving the resulting equation for $v$, we have that $\dot{x} = 0$ is equivalent to:

$$v = v^{iso}(x) := v^o + \frac{1}{\phi_v}\left[\phi_x x - \frac{1}{2}\ln\left(\frac{1+x}{1-x}\right)\right] \qquad (13.16)$$

$v^{iso}(x)$ tends to $-\infty$ as $x$ approaches 1, and to $+\infty$ as the climate approaches $-1$ from the right. The derivative of the function is:

$$dv^{iso}(x)/dx = \left[\phi_x - \frac{1}{1 - x^2}\right] / \phi_v \qquad (13.17)$$

Since the fraction in (13.17) is always equal to or greater than one, it follows that in the stable case, when $\phi_x < 1$, the isocline is everywhere downward sloping. Figure 13.1a shows the phase diagram thus resulting. As it drawn, the diagram suggests that the equilibrium is approached in a cyclical manner. This is ensured if $\phi_x$ is sufficiently close to 1. The reason is that with the positive determinant and trace $J = 2\nu(\phi_x - 1)$, the Jacobian has two purely imaginary eigen-values if $\phi_x = 1$, and the non-degenerate imaginary parts of

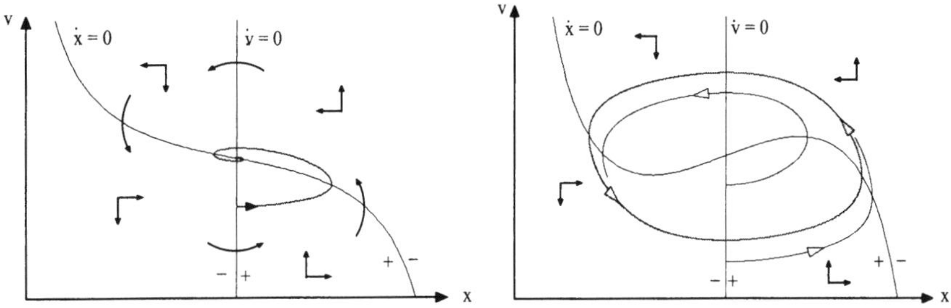


*Figure 13.1* Phase diagrams of system (13.13) and (13.14)

the eigen-values are maintained if $\phi_x$ does not depart too much from unity. However, as $\phi_x$ decreases further, the slope of $v^{iso}(\cdot)$ becomes steeper and so convergence toward the equilibrium may eventually occur in a monotonic way, from the north-west and south-east, respectively.

Figure 13.1a furthermore suggests that stability is not only local but also global, which was confirmed in all our numerical explorations. Nevertheless, it cannot generally be ruled out that trajectories starting in a far distance from the equilibrium do not converge to it any longer. Should this happen, the arguments of the unstable case apply and these trajectories converge toward a closed orbit, quite similar to what is shown in the outer regions of Figure 13.1b.

If the parameter $\phi_x$ exceeds unity, the slope (13.17) is positive at $x=0$. Since it is negative for $x$ close to $\pm 1$, there must be at least one local minimum between $-1$ and 0, and one local maximum between 0 and 1. By equating (13.17) to zero it is easily found that these are the only ones, the two solutions being $x_{1,2} = \pm\sqrt{(\phi_x - 1)/\phi_x}$. Thus, the phase diagram in Figure 13.1b is obtained.

It has already been noted that $\pm 1$ are reflecting boundaries for the climate $x$. As can be seen from (13.13), the wage $v$ cannot reach its lower and upper boundaries 0 and 1, either. Hence, all meaningful motions of $v$ and $x$ are contained within in a compact set, which is the basic condition for the Poincaré-Bendixson Theorem to apply. Given that the equilibrium is unique and locally repelling, each trajectory must accordingly converge toward a closed orbit.

It might be felt that, as illustrated in Figure 13.1b, there is only one such periodic motion. We know that the trajectories are spiralling outward when being close to the equilibrium, and they are spiralling inward in the outer regions of the phase plane. If one had an index that measures the force at which the system spirals inward at positive values, and the force at which it spirals outward at negative values, then, according to intuition, this index should steadily increase as one goes from within to the outside. If the index changes continuously, such that it is zero on a closed orbit, the existence of just one periodic orbit would be established; it would then be a unique limit cycle indeed. On the other hand, the monotonicity property is plausible. After all, the model exhibits only one essential nonlinearity, in the exponential functions in Equations (13.7) or (13.14), respectively, and owing to their convexity, this nonlinearity might be said to be monotonic. Generally, however, it seems hard to find a rigorous mathematical proof for a unique limit cycle.

Since the climate index is directly connected to the rate of utilization in (13.11), the motions of $x$ can also be identified with the motions of the macroeconomic employment rate. The cyclical trajectories in Figure 13.1 are therefore in close correspondence to the closed orbits of the wage share and the employment rate in the prototype Goodwin model (supposing that employment and output move quite in line). The present model, however, has a richer theoretical basis and even a microeconomic underpinning. In addition, it is structurally stable. This means, first, that the steady state position can be asymptotically stable or unstable, where the condition determining this property has a clear economic message: strong herding tends to be destabilizing. A second point is that there does not exist a continuum of closed orbits; our periodic trajectories are at least locally unique.

## Respecifications of the model

The task of a prototype model is to cast ideas about a few elementary feedback mechanisms into a simple form that is easy to analyze and whose results make good economic sense. Having this achieved in the previous section, a next question is for the robustness of the properties of the model when some of its details are slightly modified (a study of their generalizations would then be a further step). In this respect, we are here concerned with two topics. First, we will introduce a lag into the channel from the business climate to aggregate demand. Second, we maintain the idea of the auto-feedback in the climate adjustments, but introduce an accelerationist element into the specification of the feedback index.

### *Delays in investment demand*

In the basic model it has been assumed that a change in the climate index instantaneously translates into investment demand. In this section we account for the fact that it will typically take some time until the change in a manager's attitude will find its way into an approved decision within the firm, an order to one or several other firms, the production of the corresponding goods and, at the end, the delivery of the final product. Especially the third lag will be considerable for many items of fixed investment, the so-called gestation period.

A convenient way to model the delays just sketched is the distinction between a desired and an actual capital growth rate, $g^d$ and $g$, respectively, and the assumption that $g$ partially adjusts toward $g^d$. If $\beta_{gg} > 0$ denotes a constant speed of adjustment, this gives us $\dot{g} = \beta_{gg}\,(g^d - g)$. Desired capital growth continues to be given by Equation (13.10), now written as $g^d = g^d(x) = g^o + \beta_{gx}x$. Taken together, the differential equation for $g$ as a third dynamic state variable reads,

$$\dot{g} = \beta_{gg}\,(g^o + \beta_{gx}x - g) \tag{13.18}$$

Instead of (13.11), capital utilization is now given by $u = g/s + \beta_u$. Normal utilization being $u^o = g^o/s + \beta_u$, the "output gap" in the Phillips curve becomes $u - u^o = (g - g^o)/s$, so that the climate variable in (13.13) for the changes of the wage share is replaced with this gap in the capital growth rates. The adjustments of the climate index are not directly affected by the delays in effective demand. Thus (13.18) is combined with the two differential equations,

$$\dot{v} = (\beta_w/s)\,v\,(1-v)\,(g - g^o) \tag{13.19}$$

$$\dot{x} = 2\nu\,\{\tanh[\phi_x x - \phi_v(v - v^o)] - x\}\,\cosh[\phi_x x - \phi_v(v - v^o)] \tag{13.20}$$

The three-dimensional system (13.18)–(13.20) has a unique equilibrium, $(g, v, x) =$

$(g^o, v^o, 0)$. The Jacobian evaluated at this point is:

$$J = \begin{bmatrix} -\beta_{gg} & 0 & \beta_{gg}\beta_{gx} \\ (\beta_w/s)\,v^o(1-v^o) & 0 & 0 \\ 0 & -2\nu\,\phi_v & 2\nu\,(\phi_x - 1) \end{bmatrix}$$

The many zero entries allow an easy computation of the Routh-Hurwitz stability conditions. The necessary and sufficient conditions for local asymptotic stability, i.e. that all eigen-values have negative real parts, are $A_1 > 0$, $A_2 > 0$, $A_3 > 0$, $B > 0$, where:

$$\begin{aligned} A_1 &= -\operatorname{trace} J = \beta_{gg} + 2\nu\,(1 - \phi_x) \\ A_2 &= J_1 + J_2 + J_3 = 2\nu\,\beta_{gg}\,(1 - \phi_x) \\ A_3 &= -\det J = 2\nu\,\phi_v\,\beta_{gg}\,\beta_{gx}\,\beta_w\,/\,s \\ B &= A_1 A_2 - A_3 \\ &= 2\nu\,\beta_{gg}\,\{(1 - \phi_x)[\beta_{gg} + 2\nu\,(1 - \phi_x)] - \phi_v\,\beta_{gx}\,\beta_w\,/\,s\} \end{aligned}$$

($J_i$ are the three principal minors, the determinants of the $2\times2$ submatrices obtained after deleting the $i$-th row and column of $J$). The equilibrium of this economy continues to be unstable if the herding parameter exceeds one, $\phi_x > 1$. However, unity constitutes no longer the unequivocal benchmark for stability, *via* the mixed term $B$ the other parameters take some effect, too. At small values of $\beta_{gg}$ and moderate values of $\phi_v$, $\beta_{gx}$, $\beta_w/s$, the coefficient $\phi_x$ must be sufficiently below one for $B$ to be positive; that is, herding must be sufficiently weak. In particular, it is perhaps a bit surprising that strong feedback reactions $\phi_v$ of the firms to reductions of their profitability tend to be destabilizing. Note also the destabilizing influence of wage flexibility, i.e. the slope parameter $\beta_w$ in the Phillips curve. On the other hand, in the presence of $\phi_x < 1$ high enough adjustment speeds $\beta_{gg}$ in (13.18) could always stabilize the equilibrium. This is as it should be, since in the limit, $\beta_{gg} \to \infty$, the prototype model would be re-established.

Of course, a global analysis of (13.18)–(13.20) with the nice and clear-cut results of the prototype model is here not possible. We can nevertheless make two observations. First, since the determinant of $J$ is always negative, loss of stability as one of the parameters varies occurs by way of a Hopf bifurcation, which at least in a vicinity of the critical parameter set gives rise to a pair of complex eigen-values and thus oscillatory motions. Second, all trajectories remain within a compact set. This has already been noted for the wage share and the climate index. In addition, it is easily seen in (13.18) that the capital growth rate $g$ cannot leave the interval $[g^o - \beta_{gx}, g^o + \beta_{gx}]$ (since $\pm1$ are the lower and upper bounds of $x$, which it actually will never hit). It follows from this boundedness (and the uniqueness of the equilibrium) that monotonic divergent movements of the trajectories cannot be sustained; sooner or later they must bend around and display some kind of cyclical behavior. Generally, however, we cannot make similarly elementary statements about the regularity of these fluctuating motions; in particular, whether for all three variables the upper and lower turning points of the times series will be above and below the equilibrium values. On the basis of the experience with the prototype model and the fact that the present version of the model is not so much different, this is a credible working hypothesis – which would then have to be checked in a careful numerical analysis.

### *The moving-flock effect*

Even without economic theory, financial markets know the notion of herding and in this connection occasionally indulge in allusions to market sheep. If we take up the metaphor of a flock always in search for a greener grass, then the individual sheep may not wait until the majority has gathered on a better spot and bleats invitingly, it rather follows the other sheep in its neighborhood as soon as they begin moving. In terms of our feedback index $f$, this means that firms may not only be influenced by the level of the current majority of optimism or pessimism, but they may also respond to the motions of this crowd, i.e. to the recent changes in the general climate. Accordingly, in addition to $x$ the feedback index may also include the rate of change of $x$. For easy reference, let us call the impact of the level of $x$ on the feedback index the *majority effect*, and the influence of the changes in $x$ the *moving-flock effect*.

Both concepts are well described as herding. *A priori* it is not obvious why one specification should be rejected in favor of the other. In principle, this should be an empirical question. In another study (Franke, 2007) we have tested the present approach to model a general business climate and its changes over time with two leading sentiment indicators for the German economy (the ZEW and ifo indices for six-months ahead expectations of the general business situation), where instead of the wage share the hetero-referential variable in the feedback index was a measure of economic activity. The estimations were quite successful, and for both indices the moving-flock effect turned out highly significant. It was even justifiable, and for reasons of parsimony preferable, to discard the majority effect altogether. Against this background it should be examined what it means for our small macro model if the majority effect is replaced with the moving-flock effect.

While the empirical estimations were carried out in discrete time and the rates of change were of the form $(x_t - x_{t-\tau})/\tau$ (where the exact lags $\tau$ are important for the goodness-of-fit), we have to work with time derivatives if, for better comparability, we want to remain in the previous continuous-time setting. Introducing a positive coefficient $\phi_{dx}$ on $\dot{x}$, the feedback index $f$ in (13.8) changes to $f = \phi_{dx}\dot{x} - \phi_v(v - v^o)$. Conceptually, $\dot{x}$ is here a backward-derivative, $\dot{x}(t) = \lim[x(t) - x(t-\Delta t)]/\Delta t$ for $\Delta t \to 0$, whereas in the differential equation for $x$ the expression on the left-hand side is a forward-derivative, $\dot{x}(t) = \lim[x(t+\Delta t) - x(t)]/\Delta t$. In the mathematical treatment, however, there is no longer any role for these distinctions. Returning to the direct impact of the climate on investment and capital utilization in "A Goodwinian prototype model"(or $\beta_{gg} = \infty$ when we refer to "Delays in investment demand"), we again use (13.13) for the motions of the wage share and so get the following dynamic system

$$\dot{v} = \beta_w \beta_{gs} v(1 - v)x \tag{13.21}$$

$$\begin{aligned} \dot{x} &= h(v, x, \dot{x}) \\ &:= 2\nu\{\tanh[\phi_{dx}\dot{x} - \phi_v(v - v^o)] - x\}\cosh[\phi_{dx}\dot{x} - \phi_v(v - v^o)] \end{aligned} \tag{13.22}$$

Technically, the adjustments of the climate are now described by an implicit differential equation for $\dot{x}$. For numerical simulations it would, of course, be appropriate to discretize (13.22) along the lines sketched above, so that we get a recursive system and no problems arise. For a mathematical analysis, Equation (13.22) has to be solved for the derivative $\dot{x}$. An explicit solution will (probably) not be possible, but the Implicit Function Theorem ensures the existence of such a solution, which we write as:

$$\dot{x} = H(v, x) \tag{13.23}$$

The properties of the (continuously differentiable) function $H(\cdot, \cdot)$ can be studied by computing its partial derivatives.

More precisely, a unique function $H(\cdot, \cdot)$ exists (with finite values) in a neighborhood of the equilibrium $(v, x) = (v^o, 0)$. There might be points $(\tilde{v}, \tilde{x})$ for which the partial derivative

$\partial h[v,x,H(v,x)]/\partial\dot{x}$ converges to 1 as $(v,x) \to (\tilde{v},\tilde{x})$. Here $H(\tilde{v},\tilde{x})$ could exist and would not be differentiable at this point, or $H(v,x)$ tends to plus or minus infinity as $(v,x)$ tends to $(\tilde{v},\tilde{x})$. A solution path of the climate, $x = x(t)$, as a continuous function of time will, however, still exist, only that it will have a kink at the time $t_k$ when $x(t_k) = \tilde{x}$. As concerns the derivatives of the function $H(\cdot,\cdot)$, they are easily obtained by applying the Implicit Function Theorem to the identity $h(v,x,\dot{x}) - \dot{x} = 0$. This yields:

$$\frac{\partial H(v,x)}{\partial z} = \frac{-\partial h[v,x,H(v,x)]\,/\,\partial z}{\partial h[v,x,H(v,x)]\,/\,\partial \dot{x}\; - \;1} \qquad (z = v,x) \qquad (13.24)$$

The derivatives are less cumbersome than they might look at first sight, and they are particularly simple when they are evaluated at the equilibrium point. The Jacobian of (13.21) and (13.23) then reads,

$$J = \begin{bmatrix} 0 & \beta_w \beta_{gs} v^o (1 - v^o) \\ \dfrac{2\nu\,\phi_v}{2\nu\,\phi_{dx} - 1} & \dfrac{2\nu}{2\nu\,\phi_{dx} - 1} \end{bmatrix} \qquad (13.25)$$

With respect to stability it will be expected that the herding coefficient $\phi_{dx}$ takes the role of $\phi_x$ in "A Goodwinian prototype model". In contrast to the Jacobian (13.15), however, where $\phi_x$ only enters in one of the diagonal elements, $\phi_{dx}$ in (13.25) also shows up in the corresponding off-diagonal element. This implies that the sign of the determinant of $J$ is no longer unique, as $\det J = -2\nu\,\phi_v\,\beta_w\beta_{gs}\,v^o(1-v^o)/(2\nu\,\phi_{dx} - 1)$. Since the sign of the trace of $J$ equals the sign of $(2\nu\,\phi_{dx} - 1)$, it can be concluded that the equilibrium of system (13.21), (13.22) is locally asymptotically stable if $\phi_{dx} < 1/2\nu$. The stability condition can thus be expressed in the same words as in "Local and global analysis of the complete market": local asymptotic stability prevails if the herding effect is sufficiently weak.

Conversely, a strong herding effect ($\phi_{dx} > 1/2\nu$) will destabilize the equilibrium. The difference from "Local and global analysis of the complete market" is that here instability tends to be more pronounced since, owing to $\det J < 0$ in this case, the equilibrium is of the saddle-point type. As a consequence, local divergence occurs in a monotonic way.

Nevertheless, although there is locally no scope for cyclical motions, the monotonic behavior cannot be sustained in the outer regions of the state space. The global self-stabilizing mechanism in the adjustments of the business climate that has been pointed out in the discussion of Equation (13.14) is equally at work in (13.22). Hence system (13.21), (13.22), too, exhibits persistent fluctuations in the wage share $v$ and the climate index $x$.

It may be noted that for a more rigorous mathematical analysis the Poincaré-Bendixson Theorem is no longer available, simply because the function $H(\cdot,\cdot)$ in (13.23) might not be continuously differentiable. Owing to the possible discontinuities or even poles of $H(\cdot,\cdot)$, it may also be problematic to derive a phase diagram. These problems should not be too surprising if we go back to the discrete time foundations of the climate adjustment equation with a finite (though arbitrarily small) period $\Delta t$. In this setting the above mentioned distinction between forward and backward time derivatives would be regained and we obtain a three-dimensional discrete time system (with state variable $v_t$, $x_t$, $x_{t-\Delta t}$). Locally there may be a perfect correspondence between a 2D continuous-time and a 3D discrete time system, but one cannot count on this to hold also globally on the entire $(v,x)$-plane.

While we have emphasized the self-stabilizing forces in eqs (13.14) and (13.22) if the equilibrium is unstable, it should be added that, in the present moving-flock variant of our model, they are relatively weak. A few exploratory simulations with the discrete time system are sufficient to show that even with an extremely short adjustment period $\Delta t$, the climate comes very close to its boundaries $\pm 1$. These motions are moreover so fast that in comparison the oscillations in the wage share are of secondary importance. That is, the accelerationist element in the climate adjustments is so strong that the dynamics is essentially reduced to extreme up and downs of the climate variable itself. If one adheres to the paradigm of an unstable equilibrium and self-sustaining cyclical behavior around it, then system (13.21), (13.22) or its discrete time counterpart does not seem to be a very attractive model.

Despite the model's unpleasant properties, the moving-flock specification of herding should not be dismissed too early. First, one cannot simply ignore empirical evidence of this mechanism, as it was worked out by Franke (2007) for German survey expectations. Second, the influence of the (backward) time derivative in the feedback index is probably too drastic a specification. The strong accelerationist tendencies should weaken if the moving-flock element is based on longer lags in the rates of change of $x$ (in a stochastic framework such longer lags would be mandatory, anyway). Third, generally herding may be represented by a combination of the moving-flock effect and the majority effect. Fourth, the accelerationist tendencies may also be less dominating if the rest of the model has a richer feedback structure and the business climate acts on it in a less direct and less absolute way.

## Conclusion

This chapter has advanced a convenient modeling strategy to build up macroeconomic adjustments from the micro level of individual firms or agents having two modes of behavior. As a very attractive feature it was, in particular, pointed out that the resulting dynamic macro equation contains a mechanism of global self-stabilization with reflecting boundaries for the aggregate index variable. It is obvious that this approach can be applied to a great variety of decision problems in economics. Here we focused on an interpretation of the index variable as a general business climate determining fixed investment, which can give the Keynesian notion of animal spirits a more precise and tractable meaning.

It was, moreover, shown that the climate and its adjustments can be easily combined with other elements from the (heterodox) macroeconomic literature. Invoking a simple multiplier and an ordinary wage Phillips curve, we actually obtained a parsimonious version of an enriched demand-driven Goodwin growth cycle model. In contrast to Goodwin's design, however, it admits asymptotic stability as well as instability of the steady state, responsible for which is exclusively the intensity of herding in the formation of the business climate. Most nicely, if herding is strong such that the equilibrium is repelling, the economy will necessarily converge toward a trajectory with persistent and periodic oscillations in the two Goodwin variables economic activity and income distribution. To check the robustness of the results, we also briefly checked two modifications and demonstrated that they qualitatively survive.

Future research may be concerned with integrating the business climate adjustments into other and more encompassing macro models, which also have a role for monetary (and perhaps other) policy. A second topic is an extension of the microeconomic framework to three states, so that agents do not only have the choice between two extremes like optimism and pessimism but are also allowed to switch to an intermediate option. First explorations indicate that even with strong herding two regimes may prevail: one exhibiting persistent and bounded fluctuations similar to those in this chapter, and one with a second long-run equilibrium position that proves to be attractive. The greatest task, however, will be an econometric estimation of the unobserved animal spirits, either in a model building block or an entire macro model. This problem could, for example, be addressed by using the Kalman filter or the method of simulated moments, respectively.

## Notes

1 Taylor and O'Connell (1985), Franke and Asada (1994), and Flaschel *et al.* (1997: Ch. 12) are three of the few macrodynamic contributions whose central expectational variable is an economy-wide business climate, which is there called a state of confidence. The dynamic adjustments of the latter, however, were formalized in an ad-hoc manner. Without essentially affecting the final results, this part of the models could be easily, and conceptually more satisfactorily, reformulated along the lines propounded in the present chapter. Hence, the implicit criticism of not having been sufficiently alert to a fruitful and innovative idea in the past also falls back on the author of this chapter, especially since he knew of the articles by Weise and Kraft (1988) and Lux (1995) already quite early.

2 However, this chapter cannot claim the copyright on this procedure. The main arguments have been put forward in a recent article by Alfarano and Lux (2007) on an agent-based stochastic volatility model for financial markets, where the authors use them to discuss some simulation details (in Appendices A1 and A2).

3 Regarding the expression of "animal spirits" in the macroeconomic literature a note of caution is in order. In the dynamic stochastic general equilibrium models of mainstream theory, animal spirits are synonymous to sunspot equilibria (which most of these macroeconomists view as a theoretical curiosity). This is a situation where equilibrium is indeterminate and endogenous persistent fluctuations are generated by "coordinated" (and thus self-fulling) revisions of expectations (since, technically, agents can be conceived of as observing a random variable that follows a finite Markov process; Woodford, 1990). Two examples are Galí (1994) and Farmer and Guo (1994).

4 The following argument draws on Alfarano and Lux (2007: Appendices A1 and A2).

5 A binomial distribution $B(m,\pi)$ is the probability distribution for the number of successes ($k$) in a sequence of $m$ independent sucess/failure experiments, each of which yields success with probability $\pi$. The probability of getting exactly $k$ successes is given by $\binom{m}{k}\,\pi^k\,(1-\pi)^{m-k}$, the mean is $m\pi$, and the variance $m\pi(1-\pi)$.

6 See Weidlich and Haag (1983: 22–6) for a succinct presentation of the relationship between FPE and the Langevin equation in continuous time. An example of this treatment in discrete time is Alfarano *et al.* (2005: 23ff, 46ff).

7 Under some mild conditions it should be possible to employ the Central Limit Theorem and prove this mathematically. Simone Alfarano made some exercises in a related framework to spell out the details (private communication).

8 The firms might also have a general predisposition towards optimism or pessimism, which could be easily captured by including a positive or negative constant in the feedback index $f$. The mechanisms of the model would not be affected in any way by this non-neutrality, only the steady state growth rate would be somewhat "distorted".

9 After solving for $u$, the structure of Equation (13.11) would be preserved if utilization is added as another determinant of investment in (13.10), such that $g = g^o + \beta_{gx}x + \text{const}\cdot(u-u^o)$, where $u^o$ is the level of normal utilization introduced in a moment.

10 On the basis of the steady state calibration in Chiarella *et al.* (2005: 85ff), we could set $s = 0.069$ and $\beta_u = 0.266$. In this way an annualized steady state growth rate $g^o = 3\%$ yields an equilibrium output–capital ratio $u^o = 0.70$ (for likewise annualized production flows), which it is argued at the same place is a reasonable order of magnitude. However, even if relatively wide variations of $u$ were permitted, the associated deviations of the capital growth rates from $g^o$ would still be unrealistically low. Or one accepts that a higher savings propensity to mitigate this problem implies unrealistic macroeconomic proportions elsewhere in the model. This is the price one

has to pay for the simple specification of the demand side with its fixed proportions, as well as for the convenience of temporary equilibrium on the goods market.

11 Besides the few remarks in the text, only the following properties of the hyperbolic functions will be used in the analysis of (13.14): $\tanh(0) = 0$; $\cosh(0) = 1$; $\tanh'(0) = 1/[\cosh(0)]^2$.

## References


Alfarano, S. and Lux, T. (2007), "A noise trader model as a generator of apparent power laws and long memory", *Macroeconomic Dynamics*, 11 (Supplement 1), 80–101.

Alfarano, S., Lux, T. and Wagner, F. (2005), Estimation of agent-based models: The case of an asymmetric herding model", *Computational Economics*, 26, 19–49.

Chiarella, C., Flaschel, P. and Franke, R. (2005), *Foundations for a Disequilibrium Theory of the Business Cycle*. Cambridge: Cambridge University Press.

Farmer, R. and Guo, J.T. (1994), "Real business cycles and the animal spirit hypothesis", *Journal of Economic Theory*, 63, 42–72.

Flaschel, P., Franke, R. and Stemmer, W. (1997), *Dynamic Macroeconomics. Instability, Fluctuations, and Growth in Monetary Economies*. Cambridge, MA: MIT Press.

Franke, R. and Asada, T. (1994), "Expectations dynamics in a Keynes–Goodwin model of the business cycle", *Journal of Economic Behavior and Organization*, 24, 273–95.

Franke R. (2007), "Estimation of a microfounded herding model of German survey expectations", Working Paper, Department of Economics, University of Kiel.

Galí, J. (1994), "Monopolistic competition, business cycles, and the composition of aggregate demand", *Journal of Economic Theory*, 63, 73–96.

Goodwin, R.M. (1967), "A growth cycle model", in C.H. Feinstein (ed.), *Socialism, Capitalism and Growth*. Cambridge: Cambridge University Press.

Haag, G., Weidlich, W. and Mensch, G. (1987), "The Schumpeter clock", in D. Batten *et al.* (eds), *Economic Evolution and Structural Adjustment*. Berlin: Springer.

Kirman, A. (1993), "Ants, rationality, and recruitment", *Quarterly Journal of Economics*, 108, 137–56.

Kraft, P., Landes, T. and Weise, P. (1986), "Dynamic aspects of a stochastic business cycle model", *Methods of Operations Research*, 53, 445–53.

Lux, T. (1995), "Herd behaviour, bubbles and crashes", *Economic Journal*, 105, 881–96.

Lux, T. (1997), "Time variation of second moments from a noise trader/infection model", *Journal of Economic Dynamics and Control*, 22, 1–38.

Lux, T. (1998), "The socio-economic dynamics of speculative markets: Interacting agents, chaos, and the fat tails of return distributions", *Journal of Economic Behavior and Organization*, 33, 143–65.

Orléan, A. (1995), "Bayesian interactions and collective dynamics of opinion: Herd behavior and mimetic contagion", *Journal of Economic Behavior and Organization*, 28, 257–74.

Taylor, L. and O'Connell, S. (1985), "A Minsky crisis", *Quarterly Journal of Economics*, 100, 871–86.

Weidlich, W. and Braun, M. (1992), "The master equation approach to nonlinear economics", *Journal of Evolutionary Economics*, 2, 233–65.

Weidlich, W. and Haag, G. (1983), *Concepts and Models of a Quantitative Sociology. The Dynamics of Interacting Populations*. Berlin: Springer.

Weise, P. and Kraft, M. (1988), "Cumulative processes, disproportionalities, and Spiethoff's theory of the business cycle", in P.Flaschel and M. Krüger (eds), *Recent Approaches to Economic Dynamics*, Frankfurt a.M.: P. Lang.

Woodford, M. (1990), "Learning to believe in sunspots", *Econometrica*, 58, 277–307.

# 14 Goodwin's structural economic dynamics in the context of globalization

*Michael Landesmann and Robert Stehrer*

## Introduction

In this chapter we explore a model which had its origins in joint work with Richard Goodwin during the 1990s (see Landesmann and Goodwin (1994) and Landesmann *et al.* (1997)) and which has developed further in a number of contributions by the authors of this chapter (see Landesmann and Stehrer (2000), Stehrer (2002a, 2002b), Landesmann and Stehrer (2002, 2004a, 2004b, 2007a, 2007b).

The specific feature of the model is that it brings together two of the central concerns of Richard Goodwin's interest in modeling the dynamics of capitalist dynamics: one, that there is an important macroeconomic link between the dynamics of income distribution and that of (fluctuating) economic growth. Two, that the dynamics of capitalist economies is characterized by features of structural change which requires disaggregated economic modeling.

We shall first outline the directions in which income distributional issues have been extended from Goodwin's original classical concern with the distribution between profits and wages to one which allows the consideration also of rents and of wage structures across different groups of employees. Second, we shall discuss the issues linked to international economic integration ("globalization") which can be addressed by means of the model introduced below.

### *Income distribution and the dynamics of capitalist economies*

The classical Goodwin concern with income distribution was that of fluctuating income shares of capitalists and of workers (the profit and the wage shares respectively) and how such fluctuating income shares in turn affect expenditure structures (between consumption and investment) and hence the accumulation dynamic of a capitalist economy. In his later writings (see e.g. Goodwin and Punzo (1987)) Goodwin extended his concern with income distribution to include Schumpeterian (or Marshallian) features in that he was interested how technical change might affect income distribution and here he introduced Schumpeter's notion of non-equilibrium profits (or Marshall's "quasi-rents"). Such non-equilibrium profits arise because an economy is not in a perfectly competitive steady-state position when the "impulse" (or "shock") of technological change hits an economic system; typically, such a "shock" leads to a heterogeneity of businesses in terms of the speeds by which they introduce new techniques of production and hence reap differential rates of return (or "quasi-rents"). Goodwin (following Schumpeter) attempted to track the evolving "profit" (or, as we shall name them, “rent”) dynamic which follows such a technological impulse and which is shaped by changing imperfectly competitive market structures (these show up in the size of mark-up rates on costs) and the changing bargaining positions of workers in different sectors of the economy. We shall follow this line of modeling the “transitory dynamics” of the wage-profit-rent dynamic in the context of the model below.

Furthermore, there was an interest by Goodwin not to forget the Keynesian issue of potential effective demand failures which might affect the dynamics of capitalist economies. He attempted to show, especially in the context of rapid technological change which moves the economy away from steady-state income distributional shares, that there could be an increase in the potential for effective demand failures, i.e. of a difference between growth potential and actual growth. We show how these issues get integrated into the model tracking the structural dynamic of capitalist economies below.

### *Structural economic dynamics in the context of globalization*

The second set of features which we want to incorporate into the model are the issues arising for the growth dynamic in the specific context in which the international economy finds itself at the moment, namely that of much intensified international interdependencies (i.e. of “globalization”). There are many characteristics of globalization which our model is able to track and we shall demonstrate this when exploring the general formal structure of the model. In the specific application which we choose to explore in the simulation part of this chapter, we shall focus on “outsourcing”. In other papers we have explored other venues through which globalization might impinge upon the income distributional and effective demand features of global economic growth: such venues include international direct investment flows, the differentiation between international financial and direct investment flows, global macroeconomic imbalances, etc.

## Modeling the dynamics of integrated economies

We shall now present in non-formal terms the basic structure of the model and to which uses the model can be put.

The model has a price and a quantity side: the price dynamics is determined by productivity and wage dynamics and, in disequilibrium, by changing market structures (reflected in rents). The quantity dynamics is determined by techniques adopted in different industries, by expenditure patterns and resulting output and employment structures. There are important links between the price and the quantity side: for example, the wage-rent dynamic is affected by the bargaining strengths of workers (of different skill groups) and this is dependent upon (un)employment rates and hence upon output levels and the choice of techniques. On the other hand, expenditure patterns (across products and industries) and hence output structures are, in turn, dependent upon income distribution (between profits/rents and wages, on the one hand, and the wage rates of different income – or skill – groups).

In the context of internationally integrated economies (the focus of this chapter) a number of specific issues can be addressed by means of the following Goodwinian model of structural economic dynamics.

### *Dynamics of international trade specialization*

This is a core aspect of international economic integration. We adopt basically a Ricardian approach (with some Schumpeterian features) to the determination of international trade specialization. Trade specialization is determined through comparative advantage positions of different economies: hence the ratios of relative (cost plus profit/rent) prices determine the pattern of trade specialization. The specific issue which we shall concentrate on in this chapter is the changing pattern of "North"-"South" integration and the resulting changes in international trade specialization which emerge from a process of productivity catching-up. It is clear from what has been said above, that the distributional bargaining over rents also features prominently in the determination of the dynamics of comparative advantage.

### *International foreign direct investment flows*

The model allows a consideration of international direct investment flows by making such flows dependent upon the relative profitability of such investments in different international locations (countries and sectors). The basic determinants are similar to those of comparative advantage in trade specialization, i.e. productivity and wage/rent dynamics, but in this case it is not the determination through relative prices which matters but through relative per-unit rents.

### *Labor market effects of international economic integration*

This was the focus of a number of papers by the authors (see Landesmann and Stehrer (2000, 2007b) as it was in the large and expanding literature on "globalization" (see e.g. Slaughter (1998), Feenstra and Hanson (1997, 2001), Choi and Greenaway (2000), ILO (2007)). The way we deal with the issue of labor market effects of international economic integration is to understand how the dynamics of productivity development (neutral or skill biased) as well as wage developments (skill specific bargaining) affects specialization and output dynamics and through that the demand for different skill types of workers. Of particular interest to us are results which are in line with empirical observations, but not necessarily in line with the predictions of the classical Heckscher–Ohlin–Samuelson (HOS) model which is often adopted in this context (see also Slaughter (1999) for a critical evaluation of the HOS model in this context). An example is the increasing demand pressure for skilled workers (as reflected in rising skill premia) in both Northern as well as catching-up Southern economies.

### *Income distributional determinants of expenditure patterns*

The model allows for real income effects on the expenditure structures across commodities (non-linear Engel curves) and this affects national and global expenditure patterns in two ways: Different patterns of income distributions (e.g. wage structures between skilled and unskilled workers) will affect expenditure patterns and these can have important implications for overall development paths (see Landesmann and Stehrer (2007b) where the qualitative differences between a "Latin American" and a "South East Asian" development scenario is explored). Second, global expenditure (and trade) patterns will be affected by real income developments across countries.

### *Effective demand issues linked to globalization*

Just as in earlier joint contributions with Goodwin (Landesmann and Goodwin 1994, Landesmann *et al.* 1997) we emphasize potential trade-offs between the speed of structural change and the potential for effective demand problems to arise. In the international context, the evolution of the relationship between supply potential and effective demand is particularly affected by the increasing need to hedge against increased risks involved in investing abroad (or, more generally, into more risky investment opportunities) through a counterbalancing investment into liquid assets. Furthermore, the increased openness to international trade means a stronger pressure to compete in cost terms with less reliance on domestic components of demand, which poses a "public goods" problem in relation to global effective demand.

### *Development strategies of the "South"*

International patterns of specialization and the international allocation of foreign direct investment depends – see above – upon the relative productivity and wage-rent dynamics in different economies. The productivity dynamics might in turn depend upon technology development (in the North) and technology adoption (in the South) which in turn depends on factors such as the availability of skilled labor, foreign direct investment as a carrier of knowledge, etc. There are a number of mechanisms through which technology development and adoption can be endogenized in our model. Furthermore, the wage structures and the wage-rent-price dynamics depend upon bargaining structures, labor supply policies, the degree of competition on markets, etc. all of which can be parameterized in our model and can thus represent policy strategies.

### *Regionalism, home market bias and the welfare costs of protection*

The formation of preferential regional trading blocs and remnants of protectionist barriers remain features of the current global economy. We explore the impact of such characteristics for developmental and growth dynamics of different economies. In particular, we can show how the size of economies or of regional blocs (as well as their internal structure of complementarity) has real income and welfare implications.

### *The non-tradable sector, Balassa–Samuelson and exchange rate dynamics*

Part of the macroeconomic dynamic of a global economy is to deal with global imbalances and with exchange rate dynamics as an equilibrating device. Apart from the fact that the uneven productivity (and relative price) dynamic underlying the well-known Balassa-Samuelson effect can be well replicated in our model, we also introduce the effects of monetary policy choices in determining international relative price and exchange rate dynamics.

### *"Outsourcing" and "off-shoring"*

The current chapter will focus on the particular application of the more general model upon the effects of outsourcing upon international patterns of specialization and its effects on labor markets in the North and the South. We introduce outsourcing in the form of a change in the possibilities for vertical differentiation of production stages which allows a deepening of the international division of labor. "Off-shoring" is often used to name the possibility of relocating service activities (which also serve as important inputs) abroad which were formally considered as non-tradable. It will be interesting to examine whether the "fragmentation" (i.e. relocation of production stages) in goods production (which were always tradable) and of services (an important share of which remains non-tradable) makes a difference with regard to patterns of international global macroeconomic dynamics (e.g. through different exchange rate effects).

## The model

The specific model set-up in this chapter is for a set of three goods which are produced by use of intermediate inputs and heterogeneous labor. Production in sector 1 can be broken down into two stages. Sectors 1 and 2 produce tradeable goods where trade between two economies ("North" and "South") is determined by price competitiveness and consumer preferences (or a parameter reflecting trade barriers). We assume however that trade of goods in sector 2 is only possible for final consumption goods (i.e. there is no trade in demand for intermediate inputs in this sector). For sector 1 we assume that stage 1 produces an intermediate input solely used in stage 2 which produces the final good; that good can then also be traded across countries. Outsourcing will take place when the output of stage 1 can also be traded as intermediate input good. Sector 3 produces non-tradeable goods. Structural change and macroeconomic distributional shifts arise from exogenous shocks in sectoral labor productivity with a sluggish price-to-cost adjustment process and responses of the wage rates which reflect the bargaining power of workers as well as macroeconomic factors like the level of unemployment.

We start the exposition of the model with assumptions on technology, then introduce price and wage dynamics and, finally, discuss the modeling of the output levels and structure.

### *Technology*

#### *Intermediate inputs*

The matrix for intermediate input coefficients (commodity input per unit of output) for a particular country $c$ generally takes the form:

$$A^c = \begin{pmatrix} a^c_{1_1 1_1} & a^c_{1_1 1_2} & 0 & 0 \\ 0 & a^c_{1_2 1_2} & a^c_{1_2 2} & a^c_{1_2 3} \\ a^c_{2 1_1} & a^c_{2 1_2} & a^c_{22} & a^c_{23} \\ a^c_{3 1_1} & a^c_{3 1_2} & a^c_{32} & a^c_{33} \end{pmatrix}$$

where $a_{i_k j_l}$ denotes input of sector $i$'s production stage $k$ in sector $j$ and production stage $l$.[1] Specifically we assume that stage 2 in sector 1 is a specific input only in this sector but also needs inputs from sectors 2 and 3. With two countries the intercountry table (see Isard, 1951) is then given by

$$A = \left( \begin{array}{cccc|cccc} a^{NN}_{1_1 1_1} & a^{NN}_{1_1 1_2} & 0 & 0 & a^{NS}_{1_1 1_1} & a^{NS}_{1_1 1_2} & 0 & 0 \\ 0 & a^{NN}_{1_2 1_2} & a^{NN}_{1_2 2} & a^{NN}_{1_2 3} & 0 & 0 & 0 & 0 \\ a^{NN}_{21_1} & a^{NN}_{21_2} & a^{NN}_{22} & a^{NN}_{23} & 0 & 0 & 0 & 0 \\ a^{NN}_{31_1} & a^{NN}_{31_2} & a^{NN}_{32} & a^{NN}_{33} & 0 & 0 & 0 & 0 \\ \hline a^{SN}_{1_1 1_1} & a^{SN}_{1_1 1_2} & 0 & 0 & a^{SS}_{1_1 1_1} & a^{SS}_{1_1 1_2} & 0 & 0 \\ 0 & 0 & 0 & 0 & 0 & a^{SS}_{1_2 1_2} & a^{SS}_{1_2 2} & a^{SS}_{1_2 3} \\ 0 & 0 & 0 & 0 & a^{SS}_{21_1} & a^{SS}_{21_2} & a^{SS}_{22} & a^{SS}_{23} \\ 0 & 0 & 0 & 0 & a^{SS}_{31_1} & a^{SS}_{31_2} & a^{SS}_{32} & a^{SS}_{33} \end{array} \right) = \begin{pmatrix} A^{NN} & A^{NS} \\ A^{SN} & A^{SS} \end{pmatrix}$$

which reflects the assumption of the non-tradability of sector 3, and the further assumption that trade in sector 2 is only possible in consumer goods (but not in intermediate inputs). We also have restricted the matrix in a way that intermediate inputs trade is only possible for stage 2 of sector 1. Additionally, we shall assume that $a^{rr}_{1_k 1_1} + a^{cr}_{1_k 1_1} = a^{r}_{1_k 1_1}$. This implies that the (physical) input per unit of output does not depend upon whether it is purchased at home or abroad. The determination of the input coefficients off the block-diagonal are discussed below.

## *Total factor productivity and input of labor*

We assume that there are two types of labor – skilled and unskilled – which are needed as inputs for production. At this stage we do not allow for substitution of intermediate inputs and labor (Morishima 1964, 1992) but we do allow for substitution of the two types of labor by specifying a CES production function:[2]

$$q^c_{\iota_k} = T^c_{\iota_k} \left( \sum_{z=L,S} \alpha^c_{z,\iota_k} (\tilde{a}^c_{z,\iota_k} l^c_{z,\iota_k})^{\rho^c_{\iota_k}} \right)^{1/\rho^c_{\iota_k}}$$

with elasticity of substitution equal to $\sigma^c_{\iota_k} = 1/(1-\rho^c_{\iota_k})$ and total factor productivity denoted by $T^c_{\iota_k}$. We refer to parameters $\tilde{a}^c_{z,\iota_k}$ as "factor augmenting" parameters and to parameters $\alpha^c_{z,\iota_k}$ as "share" parameters; the latter are restricted according to $\sum_{z=L,S} \alpha^c_{z,\iota_k} = 1$.[3] At a specific point in time labor productivity is determined by technology. This specification further assumes constant returns to scale. Given the wage rates for both types of labor, one can determine the labor input (of a particular type) per unit of output and the skill intensity in a particular sector which is given by:

$$\frac{a^c_{l,S,\iota_k}}{a^c_{l,L,\iota_k}} = \left( \frac{w^c_{S,\iota_k}}{w^c_{L,\iota_k}} \right)^{-\sigma^c_{\iota_k}} \left( \frac{\alpha^c_{S,\iota_k}}{\alpha^c_{L,\iota_k}} \right)^{\sigma^c_{\iota_k}} \left( \frac{\tilde{a}^c_{S,\iota_k}}{\tilde{a}^c_{L,\iota_k}} \right)^{\sigma^c_{\iota_k}-1}.$$

Technical progress can take the form of a reduction in $T^c_{\iota_k}$ which may take place exogenously or be the outcome of R&D activities. Furthermore, countries lagging behind the technological frontier can also exploit the "advantage of backwardness" (see Gerschenkron 1962) to catch-up to the technological frontier through technology transfer. There is, furthermore, some evidence that technological diffusion but also more generally catching-up processes in productivity levels may follow an S-shaped pattern (see e.g. Karshenas and Stoneman (1995) on this). Our functional specification of the development of the technological potential $\mathcal{T}^c_{i_k}$ is:

$$\dot{\mathcal{T}}^c_{i_k} = \gamma^c_{\mathcal{T},i_k} \mathcal{T}^c_{i_k}(1 - \mathcal{T}^c_{i_k})$$

which thus follows a logistic pattern. This can be seen as the time path of exploiting the technological potential of a new "general purpose technology" (GPT) (see e.g. Helpman (1998) for an overview) or the gradual diffusion of new process technology across a mature or catching-up economy. Related to such a potential is a level of total factor productivity $\bar{T}^c_{i_k}$ which represents a type of "ceiling" of technological possibilities associated with a particular GPT or with the diffusion processes linked to a particular process technology. The actual level of total factor productivity is then linked to this potential via

$$\dot{T}^c_{i_k} = \gamma^c_{T,i_k}(\bar{T}^c_{i_k} \mathcal{T}^c_{i_k} - T^c_{i_k})$$

where $\gamma^c_{T,i_k}$ refers to the speed by which actual labor productivity tracks the development of the technological potential, i.e. the degree to which it utilizes technological possibilities. In a catching-up context this also allows the modeling of a "conditional" convergence pattern. Finally, it is important to note that this form of technological change is Hicks neutral, i.e. the factor intensity remains constant for fixed relative wages.

## *Costs and prices*

The costs of production are determined by labor input per unit of output by type of labor, the sector and skill specific nominal wage rate $w^c_{z,i_k}$ as well as the costs of intermediate inputs,

$$c^c_{i_k} = \sum_{j,r} \sum_{l,k} p^r_{j_l} a^{rc}_{j_l i_k} + \sum_{z=L,S} w^c_{z,i_k} a^c_{l,z,i_k}.$$

where $p^r_{i_k}$ denotes prices in sector *i* and stage *k* in country *c* expressed in currency of country *c*.[4]

In the (long-run) competitive equilibrium prices equal average costs. However, if costs are changing as labor productivity is increasing, or the nominal wage rate changes, etc. prices may not adjust immediately to unit costs. There may be a sluggish price-to-cost adjustment due to time lags, strategic pricing behavior of firms, etc. We model this in the following differential equation:

$$\dot{p}^c_{i_k} = -\delta^c_{p,i_k}(p^c_{i_k} - (1 + \pi^c_{i_k})c^c_{i_k}) \tag{14.1}$$

where $0 < \delta^c_{p,i_l} < 1$ denotes an adjustment parameter and $\pi^c_i \geq 0$ denotes a long-run mark-up rate on costs. If prices deviate from costs plus mark-up, rents emerge which we shall denote by $r^c_{i_k} = p^c_{i_k} - (1 + \pi^c_{i_k})c^c_{i_k}$. Note that these rents might even become negative which means that firms face losses. Further, we define mark-up profits as $m^c_{i_k} = \pi^c_{i_k} c^c_{i_k}$ and total surplus (per unit) as $s^c_{i_k} = m^c_{i_k} + (1 - \kappa^c_{r,i_k})r^c_{i_k}$ where $\kappa^c_{r,i_k}$ denotes a bargaining parameter over rents in the wage equation discussed below.

## *Wages and labor market*

Another component which determines unit costs are nominal wages which may grow or fall for three reasons: first, transitory rents are partly distributed to workers; second, excess supply (demand) of workers in the labor market drives wages down (up); and third, we assume wage equalization across sectors in the long run. These three factors are formalized as follows:

$$\dot{w}^c_{z,\imath_k} = \kappa^c_{r,\imath_k} \frac{r^c_{\imath_k}}{a^c_{l,z,\imath_k}} + \kappa^c_{u,z} u^c_z w^c_{z,\imath_k} + \kappa^c_{w,z} \frac{w^c_{z,\imath_k} - \bar{w}^c_z}{w^c_{z,\imath_k}} \tag{14.2}$$

$0 \leq \kappa^c_{r,\imath_k} \leq 1$ is the proportion of per unit (transitory) rents $r^c_{\imath_k}$ paid to workers; this reflects the bargaining strength of workers (bargaining coefficient). Although this parameter may change over time we assume it to be constant. This parameter is multiplied by the rents per worker $r^c_{\imath_k} q^c_{\imath_k} / a^c_{l,\imath_k} q^c_{\imath_k}$. This particular specification implies that there is sector-specific bargaining over rents. If there is only economy-wide bargaining the first term has to be replaced by $\kappa^c_r \frac{\sum_{\imath_k} r^c_{\imath_k} q^c_{\imath_k}}{\sum_{\imath_k} a^c_{l,\imath_k} q^c_{\imath_k}}$. The second term on the rhs of the wage dynamics equation reflects the impact of unemployment on the dynamics of the wage rates ($\kappa^c_{u,z} \leq 0$). The unemployment rate is defined as $u^c_z = (h^c_z - \sum_{\imath_k} l^c_{z,\imath_k})/h^c_z$ where $h^c_z$ and $l^c_{z,\imath_k}$ denote labor supply and demand of a particular skill type $z$, respectively. This represents a simple linear Phillips curve effect. Third, there is an impact on the wage dynamics if wage rates differ across sectors. This reflects the common assumption that wage rates become equalized across sectors because of inter-sectoral labor mobility and corresponding pressures on nominal wage rates. The weighted average wage rate (across sectors) is defined as $\bar{w}^c_z = \sum_\imath l^c_{z,\imath_k} w^c_{z,\imath_k} / \sum_{\imath_k} l^c_{z,\imath_k}$. In the case that the average wage $\bar{w}^c_z$ is higher than the sectoral wage $w^c_{z,\imath_k}$ the wage in sector $i$ will rise, in the other case fall. This term works across all sectors. Thus in the formulation used in the simulations, there are two sector-specific terms and one economy-wide term having an influence on wage rates in each sector.

Sectoral labor demand is determined by labor input per unit of output $a^c_{z,l,\imath_k}$ and the levels of output, i.e. $l^c_{z,\imath_k} = a^c_{l,z,\imath_k} q_{\imath_k}$ and overall labor demand is $l^c_z = \sum_{\imath_k} a^c_{l,z,\imath_k} q_{\imath_k}$. Labor supply $h^c_z$ is assumed to be exogenously given and set to one for all countries and skill-types, thus $h^c_z = 1$. This in particular implies that we assume equal country sizes and endowment structures with respect to employment. Of course, this may be generalized as population growth rates differ across countries or participation rates may change. However, as we are in this chapter mainly interested in the effects of technological changes and catching-up processes, we stick to this simplifying assumption.

## *Quantity system*

Following on from the discussion of the price system, the quantity system must be specified. Demand for goods consists of demand for intermediates and two different components out of income, namely demand out of workers' incomes (consumption) and demand out of "retained earnings" (investment to increase production capacities).

### *Demand for intermediate inputs*

As already mentioned above intermediate input per unit of output is fixed over the simulation period which also determines demand as $\sum_{j,l} a_{\imath_k J_l} q_{J_l}$. However, outsourcing allows to purchase intermediate inputs not only domestically but also abroad. The decision on how much to spend abroad is modeled using a CES specification. The expenditure share of sector $j_l$ in country $r$ spent on intermediate inputs of sector $i_k$ in country $c$ is determined as:

$$\mu^{cr}_{A,\imath_k J_l} = (p^c_{\imath_k})^{1-\varsigma^r_{A,\imath_k J_l}} (b^{cr}_{A,\imath_k J_l})^{1-\varsigma^r_{A,\imath_k J_l}} (\beta^{cr}_{A,\imath_k J_l})^{\varsigma^r_{A,\imath_k J_l}}$$

$$\cdot \left[ \sum_c (p^c_{\imath_k})^{1-\varsigma^r_{A,\imath_k J l}} (b^{cr}_{A,\imath_k J l})^{1-\varsigma^r_{A,\imath_k J l}} (\beta^{cr}_{A,\imath_k J l})^{\varsigma^r_{A,\imath_k J l}} \right]^{-1}$$

where we assume that the parameter $\sum_c \beta^{cr}_{A,\imath_k J l} = 1$ for reasons outlined above. This parameter together with $b^{cr}_{A,\imath_k J l}$ indicates country preferences, trade barriers, etc. Further, the parameter $\varsigma^r_{A,\imath_k J l}$ denotes the elasticity of substitution between the intermediate inputs across different supplying countries. As we assume that the intermediate inputs are substitutes (across countries) we restrict this elasticity to $\varsigma^r_{A,\imath_k J l} > 1$ for all $i_k$ and $j_l$ and all countries $r$. These assumptions assure that $\sum_c \mu^{cr}_{A,\imath_k J l} = 1$ for all countries $r$. The quantity of intermediate input in sector $j_l$ of country $r$ is then:

$$\underbrace{\sum_c E^r_{A,J l} \mu^{cr}_{A,\imath_k J l} \frac{1}{p^c_{\imath_k}}}_{\cdot = a^{cr}_{\imath_k J l} q^r_{J l}} = q^r_{J l} \sum_c a^{cr}_{\imath_k J l} = a^r_{\imath_k J l} q^r_{J l}$$

where $E^r_{A,J l}$ denotes nominal expenditures of sector $j_l$ in country $r$ on intermediate inputs. The remaining part has to be spent on labor input. Thus:

$$\begin{aligned} a^{cr}_{\imath_k J l} &= \frac{1}{q^r_{J l}} \mu^{cr}_{A,\imath_k J l} \frac{E^r_{A,J l}}{p^c_{\imath_k}} = \frac{\sum_c p^c_{\imath_k} a^{cr}_{\imath_k J l} q^r_{J l}}{q^r_{J l}} \mu^{cr}_{A,\imath_k J l} \frac{1}{p^c_{\imath_k}} \\ &= \frac{P^r_{A,J l} a^r_{\imath_k J l} q^r_{J l}}{q^r_{J l}} \mu^{cr}_{A,\imath_k J l} \frac{1}{p^c_{\imath_k}} = \frac{P^r_{A,J l} a^r_{\imath_k J l}}{p^c_{\imath_k}} \mu^{cr}_{A,\imath_k J l} \end{aligned}$$

where $P$ denotes an appropriate price index. Using:

$$\sum_c a^{cr}_{\imath_k J l} = P^r_{A,J l} a^r_{\imath_k J l} \sum_c \frac{1}{p^c_{\imath_k}} \mu^{cr}_{A,\imath_k J l} = a^r_{\imath_k J l}$$

this price index becomes:

$$P^r_{A,J l} = \left( \sum_c \frac{1}{p^c_{\imath_k}} \mu^{cr}_{A,\imath_k J l} \right)^{-1}.$$

Thus, finally we get:

$$a^{cr}_{\imath_k J l} = \frac{\left( \sum_c \frac{1}{p^c_{\imath_k}} \mu^{cr}_{A,\imath_k J l} \right)^{-1} a^r_{\imath_k J l}}{p^c_{\imath_k}} \mu^{cr}_{A,\imath_k J l}.$$

This formulation differs somewhat from other models (see the endogenous growth literature) where the availability of a higher number of varieties of intermediate inputs (sometimes modeled as further inputs from additional countries) has a positive effect on productivity. This is not the case here as we stick to the assumption of a fixed ratio of input to output (i.e. the input coefficients $a^r_{\imath_k J l}$ are constant). In particular, outsourcing to another country does not show up as a productivity effect. However, outsourcing allows the allocation of expenditures more efficiently which reduces costs of production.

### *Consumption demand*

Consumption patterns are determined by relative prices as well as real income levels. A typical worker of skill type $z$ in industry $j_k$ in country $r$ receives nominal income given by his wage rate $y^r_{z,J k} = w^r_{z,J k} + \kappa^r_{r,J k} r^r_{J k} / a^r_{l,z,J k}$ where the second term results from bargaining of workers over rents. Expenditures are allocated across consumer goods $i_k = 1_2, 2, 3$ and for these goods across countries $c$ in a two-stage budgeting process. For the second stage (expenditures for a particular good $i_k$ over country brands) we assume that expenditure shares $\gamma_{i_k}^{cr}$ are given by the CES specification:

$$\gamma_{i_k}^{cr} = (p_{i_k}^c)^{1-\varsigma_{i_k}^r} (\beta_{i_k}^{cr})^{\varsigma_{i_k}^r} \left[ \sum_c (p_{i_k}^c)^{1-\varsigma_{i_k}^r} (\beta_{i_k}^{cr})^{\varsigma_{i_k}^r} \right]^{-1}$$

where $\varsigma_{i_k}^r$ denotes the elasticity of substitution across countries and $\beta_{i_k}^{cr}$ are preference parameters (which could also reflect trade barriers, etc.). The term in brackets can be interpreted as the price of good $i_k$ in country $r$. In the first stage expenditures have to be allocated across goods. We assume that individuals have the same preferences. The nominal shares then depend on real income levels and relative prices. For the specification we use a (simplified) formulation derived from an Almost Ideal Demand System see (Deaton and Muellbauer1980):

$$\gamma_{i_k,(z,j_l)}^r = \alpha_{AIM,i_k} + \beta_{AIM,i_k} \left( \ln y_{z,j_l}^r - \ln \tilde{P}^r \right) + \sum_{m,n} \gamma_{AIM,i_k m_n} \ln \tilde{p}_{m_n}^r$$

with:

$$\ln \tilde{P}^r = \alpha_{AIM,0} + \sum_{i,j} \alpha_{AIM,i_j} \ln \tilde{p}_{i_j}^r + \tfrac{1}{2} \sum_{i,k} \sum_{j,l} \gamma_{AIM,i_k j_l} \ln \tilde{p}_{i_j}^r \ln \tilde{p}_{j_l}^r$$

where $\tilde{p}_{i_k}^r = \left[ \sum_c (p_{i_k}^c)^{1-\varsigma_{i_k}^r} (\beta_{i_k}^{cr})^{\varsigma_{i_k}^r} \right]$ denotes the price index from the CES specification. We assume that the parameters satisfy the constraints:

$$\sum_{i,k} \alpha_{AIM,i_k} = 1, \quad \sum_{i_k} \beta_{AIM,i_k} = 0$$

and $\gamma_{AIM,i_k j_l} = \gamma_{AIM,j_l i_k}$.

The nominal expenditure share of a typical worker $(z,j_l)$ in country $r$ on goods $i_k$ in country $c$ is then $\mu_{i_k(z,j_l)}^{cr} = \gamma_{i_k}^{cr} \gamma_{i_k,(z,j_l)}^r$. As $\sum_c \gamma_{i_k}^{cr} = 1$ and $\sum_{i,k} \gamma_{i_k,(z,j_l)}^r = 1$ we also have $\sum_{i,c} \mu_{i_k(z,j_l)}^{cr} = 1$. Summing up over worker types and industries in a particular country $r$ yields consumption demand for good $i_k$ in country $c$, i.e.:

$$f_{i_k}^c = \frac{1}{p_{i_k}^c} \sum_{r,j,z,l} \mu_{i_k(z,j_l)}^{cr} y_{z,j_l}^r a_{l,z,j_l}^r q_{j_l}^r.$$

The term $a_{l,z,j_l}^r q_{j_l}^r$ is demand for labor, this is multiplied by nominal income $y_{z,j_l}^r$. This sum is allocated across goods (by industries and countries) via nominal expenditure shares $\mu_{i_k(z,j_l)}^{cr}$. Summing up over industries $j_l$, skill types $z$ and countries $r$ determines demand for goods $i_k$ in country $c$.

For later use we define the consumer demand matrix as:

$$D_f = \left[ \sum_z \frac{1}{p_{i_k}^c} \left( \mu_{i_k(z,j_l)}^{cr} y_{z,j_l}^r a_{l,z,j_l}^r \right) \right]_{i,k,j,l,c,r}.$$

### *Investment behavior*

Demand out of retained earnings will be invested. Investment takes the form of hiring new workers and intermediate inputs. The decision in which country and sector investment takes place is determined by relative rents. Investments will determine the capacity growth rates (but not demand) of the particular sectors. Increasing capacities basically means hiring workers and purchasing intermediate inputs to increase production capacities. The peculiarity here is that investors have to decide in which sector and countries capacities should be increased. We shall assume throughout that when investing abroad the sourcing structure of the foreign economy is applied. As should be clear now we also assume that per unit profits and rents which are not distributed to workers, i.e. $s_{\iota_k}^s = m_{\iota_k}^s + (1 - \kappa_{r,\iota_k}^s) r_{\iota_k}^s$, are entirely used for investment.[5] Total rents plus profits in nominal terms in the economy $s$ and sector $i$ are then given by $s_{\iota_k}^s q_{\iota_k}^s$. In an integrated global economy investors may decide in which country and sector to invest. This decision may depend on several factors, e.g. (expected) per unit rents, sectoral growth rates, relative unit costs, degrees of excess capacity, etc.

### *Balanced growth*

Before discussing the modeling of such an investment behavior it is interesting to look at the hypothetical investment which would guarantee a (worldwide) balanced growth path. Assume that a sector attracts the share $\xi_{Jl}^s = c_{Jl}^s q_{Jl}^s / \sum_{\iota,k,r} c_{\iota_k}^r q_{\iota_k}^r$ of the total value of surplus $\sum_{\iota,k,r} s_{\iota_k}^r q_{\iota_k}^r$. At time $t$ the input coefficients for intermediates and labor are given. The amount to be invested has to be allocated across all inputs. As in the short run substitution is not possible[6] this can be modeled as a Leontief production function. Standard derivation of cost-minimizing inputs of factors yields the nominal value to hire additional workers of skill type $z$:

$$\xi_{Jl}^s \sum_{\iota,r} s_{\iota_k}^r q_{\iota_k}^r \frac{w_{zJl}^s a_{l,zJl}^s q_{Jl}^s}{c_{Jl}^s q_{Jl}^s} / w_{zJl}^s = \left[ \sum_{\iota,r} s_{\iota_k}^r q_{\iota_k}^r \right] \xi_{Jl}^s \frac{a_{l,zJl}^s q_{Jl}^s}{c_{Jl}^s q_{Jl}^s}$$

Inserting for $\xi_{Jl}^s$ yields:

$$\left[ \sum_{\iota,r} s_{\iota_k}^r q_{\iota_k}^r \right] \frac{c_{Jl}^s q_{Jl}^s}{\sum_{\iota,k,r} c_{\iota_k}^r q_{\iota_k}^r} \frac{a_{l,zJl}^s q_{Jl}^s}{c_{Jl}^s q_{Jl}^s} = \frac{\sum_{\iota,r} s_{\iota_k}^r q_{\iota_k}^r}{\sum_{\iota,k,r} c_{\iota_k}^r q_{\iota_k}^r} a_{l,zJl}^s q_{Jl}^s$$

The first term on the rhs represents the ratio of the total value of retained earnings to the value of costs. The whole expression denotes the change of this input (as these expressions can be derived analogously for all other, i.e. worker and intermediate, inputs). Dividing the expression by the actual level of factor employment ($a_{l,zJl}^s q_{Jl}^s$) gives the growth rate $g_{Jl}^s = \frac{\sum_{\iota,k,r} s_{\iota_k}^r q_{\iota_k}^r}{\sum_{\iota,k,r} c_{\iota_k}^r q_{\iota_k}^r}$. As this holds for all sectors in all countries one may write $g^* = g_{Jl}^s$. In equilibrium no extra rents arise and under the further assumption of equal mark-up rates across countries and industries, i.e. $\pi_{\iota_k}^c = \pi$ for all $i, k, c$ this expression can be rearranged to:

$$g^* = \frac{\sum_{i,k,r} \pi c_{\iota_k}^r q_{\iota_k}^r}{\sum_{i,k,r} c_{\iota_k}^r q_{\iota_k}^r} = \pi$$

and thus the classical relationship between growth rates and mark-up rate holds.[7] It has to be assumed that the (skilled and unskilled) labor force is growing at the same rate (i.e. holding the relative factor endowment constant).

*Actual investment behavior*

In the simulations below we apply a CES-formulation to model investment spending out of the part $\tilde{r}^c_{i_k} = (1-\kappa^c_{r,i_k})r^c_{i_k}$ of retained earnings. (Focussing on investment behavior outside the steady-state, we assume that steady-state mark-up profits $m^c_{i_k}$ are invested only in the particular sector where these are arising.) Retained earnings arising in sector $j_l$ of country $r$ are invested in sector $i_k$ of country $c$ according to:

$$\nu^{cr}_{i_kj_l} = \left(\exp(-\tilde{r}^c_{i_k})\right)^{1-\sigma^r_{i_k}} (\eta^{cr}_{i_kj_l})^{\sigma^r_{i_k}} \left[\sum_c \left(\exp(-\tilde{r}^c_{i_k})\right)^{1-\sigma^r_{i_k}} (\eta^{cr}_{i_kj_l})^{\sigma^r_{i_k}}\right]^{-1}$$

where $\sigma^r_{i_k}$ denotes the elasticity of substitution and $\eta^{cr}_{i_kj_l}$ is a parameter determining a home and/or sector bias (e.g. when setting $\eta^{cr}_{i_kj_l} = 0$ for all $r \neq c$ no international investment flows would take place or in the case $\eta^{cr}_{i_kj_l} = 0$ for all $i_k \neq j_l$ only sector specific international flows would occur). Applying the same logic as above, the capacity growth rate of sector $j_l$ is then given by:

$$g^r_{j_l} = \frac{\sum_{i,k,c} \nu^{rc}_{j_li_k} \tilde{r}^c_{i_k} q^c_{i_k} + m^r_{j_l} q^r_{j_l}}{c^r_{j_l} q^r_{j_l}}.$$

Note that in the special case $\tilde{r}^c_{i_k} = 0$ and $m^r_{j_l} = \pi c^r_{j_l}$ we again get $g^r_{j_l} = g^* = \pi$.

*Demand-driven growth dynamics*

So far we have discussed the expansion of capacities which may or may not coincide with the changes in demand. Demand is given by:

$$q^d = [I - A(I+G]^{-1} D_f (I+G) q^d$$

where $q^d$ denotes total demand, $I$ is the identity matrix, and $G$ is a matrix with the growth rates on the diagonal; $[I - A(I+G)]^{-1}$ thus denotes a dynamic Leontief inverse.[8] The demand-driven dynamics of the economy is modeled as:

$$\dot{q} = \Delta_q (q^d - q^s) = \Delta_q ([I - A(I+G)]^{-1} D_f (I+G) q - q) \tag{14.3}$$

where $\Delta_q$ denotes a matrix with supply-to-demand adjustment parameters on the diagonal. On the balanced growth path demand equals supply and the economy is growing at rate $g^* = \pi$.

## External disequlibria and effective demand issues

In the following we want to point to two issues: first, that the way the model has been specified allows for substantial external disequilibria which can (and in the general case, would) characterise a process of international catching-up. Second, a readjustment of international patterns of specialisation and relocation of international production through foreign direct investment flows can also generate effective demand problems alongside with increasing the growth potential of the global economy.

On the subject of external disequilibria, we first define the trade and the income and expenditure balances in our model:

Imports of country $c$:

$$\sum_{i,k,j,l,r \neq c} \left(p^r_{i_k} a^{rc}_{i_kj_l} (1+g^c_{j_l}) q^c_{j_l}\right) + \sum_{i,k,j,l,r \neq c} \left(p^r_{i_k} (\sum_z d^{rc}_{f,i_k(z,j_l)})(1+g^c_{j_l}) q^c_{j_l}\right)$$

Exports of country $c$:

$$\sum_{\imath,k,\jmath,l,r\neq c}\left(p^{c}_{\imath k}a^{cr}_{\imath k\jmath l}(1+g^{r}_{\jmath l})q^{r}_{\jmath l}\right)+\sum_{\imath,k,\jmath,l,r\neq c}\left(p^{c}_{\imath k}(\sum_{z}d^{cr}_{f,\imath k(z\jmath l)})(1+g^{r}_{\jmath l})q^{r}_{\jmath l}\right)$$

Nominal income (value added) generated in country $c$:

$$\sum_{\imath,k}\left(\sum_{z}y^{c}_{z,\imath k}a^{c}_{l_z,\imath k}(1+g^{c}_{\imath k})q^{c}_{\imath k}\right)+s^{c}_{\imath k}q^{c}_{\imath k})$$

Nominal output (gross output) generated in country $c$:

$$\sum_{\imath,k,\jmath,l,r}p^{c}_{\imath k}a^{cr}_{\imath k\jmath l}(1+g^{r}_{\jmath l})q^{r}_{\jmath l}+\sum_{\imath,k}\left(\sum_{z}y^{c}_{z,\imath k}a^{c}_{l,z\imath k}(1+g^{c}_{\imath k})q^{c}_{\imath k}\right)+s^{c}_{\imath k}q^{c}_{\imath k})$$

Value of demand country $c$ attracts:

$$\sum_{\imath,k,\jmath,l,r}\left(p^{c}_{\imath k}a^{cr}_{\imath k\jmath l}(1+g^{r}_{\jmath l})q^{r}_{\jmath l}\right)+\sum_{\imath,k,\jmath,l,r}\left(p^{c}_{\imath k}(\sum_{z}d^{cr}_{f,\imath k(z\jmath l)})(1+g^{r}_{\jmath l})q^{r}_{\jmath l}\right)$$

Second, on the issue of effective demand problems, which may arise in the context of intensified structural change, internationalization and catching-up processes, we allow for a certain portfolio behavior in relation to international foreign direct investment and investment into "secure" liquid assets. Formally, a leakage of expenditures may be modeled as a fraction $0\leq\lambda^{rc}\leq 1$ for $c,r=1,\ldots,C$ of $s^{r}_{k}$ which is spent on a non-interest bearing financial asset. The capacity growth rate of a particular sector then becomes

$$g^{r}_{\jmath l}=\frac{\sum_{\imath,k,c}\nu^{rc}_{\jmath l\imath k}[(1-\lambda^{rc})\tilde{r}^{c}_{\imath k}]q^{c}_{\imath k}+m^{r}_{\jmath l}q^{r}_{\jmath l}}{c^{r}_{\jmath l}q^{r}_{\jmath l}}.$$

This implies that the growth rate is lower – *ceteris paribus* (with given real wage rates) – the higher the share of rents in total profits and the more internationally mobile expenditures out of rents are (the higher international capital market integration is).[9] This can be seen by setting $\nu^{rc}_{jk}=0$, i.e. the extreme case when there are no international flows, and $\lambda^{rc}=0$; in this case there would be no leakage at all. The specification thus implies that a shift away from the long-run macro-distribution between wage income and profit income (which would lead to a rise in the capacity growth rate in the absence of any leakage effect) would be reduced in the presence of such a leakage. On the other hand, internationally mobile capital reallocates capital to sectors/economies with greater productivity growth (and thus higher rents) and thus contributes to the higher global potential output. The model thus reveals an interesting trade-off: international economic integration (through strong trade linkages and foreign direct investment flows) leads to a potential growth dividend with respect to exploiting the benefits of comparative advantage and also the reallocation of investible funds towards those economies and sectors which undergo strong productivity/catching-up growth (and these get reflected in their rent dynamic). Both these two factors lead to a boost in the global productivity potential (inputs are produced in the cheapest cost locations). At the same time, international economic integration and the dynamic of fast productivity and catching-up growth can lead to a higher likelihood of effective demand problems. First, uneven productivity growth or catching-up patterns across sectors leads to a redistribution of income towards rents and these – in the context of our model specification – allow a leakage in spending which would not happen with wage income. Second, a relocation of production abroad through increased foreign investment flows can induce a compensating hedging behavior in the form of investment into liquid assets (see footnote above). Both these two factors can lead to a higher "leakage" effect causing an effective demand problem, i.e. a deviation of actual output from potential output.

### *The outsourcing story*

The issue which we shall concentrate on the following are the effects of trade integration and catching-up with and without outsourcing. There has been a large literature on this issue (see e.g Arndt and Kierzkowski (2001) for an overview) emphasizing that outsourcing in its various forms can increase many-fold the tradability of goods and services. As production processes get vertically differentiated ("fragmented") it becomes possible to establish an international division of labor at a more differentiated level. In our model we capture the scope for further international integration by subdividing one sector into two stages. Without outsourcing, comparative advantages can only be exploited at the level of fully vertically integrated sectors. Once outsourcing occurs, the different stages of production within such a sector can benefit from international specialization and this has implications for the international division of labor and hence for efficiency gains, growth potential and labor market developments. We shall analyze these issues in the context of our model.

## Simulation studies

### *Structural change and international economic integration*

The two regions ("North", "South"), three sectors simulations discussed in the following are designed to examine the following issues: we shall introduce, first, the pattern of productivity catching-up and show the implications (together with the specified wage behavior) for the dynamics of international trade specialization. Next, we shall show the implications for the relative demand for skills, the resulting wage dynamics (i.e. including the skill premium) and the dynamics in unit rents. The latter allows us to make conjectures about the structure of foreign direct investment flows. Third, we shall analyze the scenarios for external disequilibria and effective demand problems which might be generated by such a process of catching-up and the structural adjustments which accompany such a process. Fourth, the model includes real income effects on expenditure patterns and this is another dimension of structural change tracked by the model simulations. Finally, the comparison of simulation runs with and without "outsourcing" possibilities show the additional impact which the deepening of the division of labor through outsourcing can have upon all the four issues mentioned above.

### *Simulation strategy*

The model above was introduced in a general manner. In the simulation studies presented in this section we focus on a model with $C = 2$ countries, denoted by $N$ and $S$ (for North and South) and $N = 3$ sectors. To start with, the first sector is vertically integrated as already discussed above. The size of the countries with respect to population (equal to labor force) is the same and set to $h^c = 2$. We assume that $h^c_S = 0.8$ and $h^c_U = 1.2$, i.e. we also assume an equal structure of endowments with respect to skill types. This set-up allows us to concentrate on the Ricardian dimension of international trade specialization (based on relative productivity and cost differences across sectors) in the context of catching-up. The Heckscher-Ohlin dimension, based on differences in countries' factor endowment structures, can be brought in at a later stage. Empirically, this matches the case of a number of catching-up economies (such as Eastern Europe as well as countries in South East Asia) which have either rather advanced skill endowments or have made major efforts in this direction.[10] Country $N$ is the advanced economy (the "North") in terms of productivity levels. The "Southern" economy $S$ is characterized by lower (total factor) productivity levels; the initial gaps differ across sectors with more skill intensive sectors showing higher gaps. As the "South" catches up with the "North" the gap in total factor productivity becomes equal across sectors (in the limit the gap might become zero). Assuming equal catching-up parameters this implies that country $S$ will experience higher rates of change in productivity in those industries which start off with a larger initial gap relative to the leader (this amounts to an application of Gerschenkron's famous hypothesis of the "advantage of backwardness" to the industrial level (Gerschenkron 1952, 1962; see also Landesmann and Stehrer (2001) for a theoretical discussion and empirical analysis of this use of the Gerschenkron hypothesis). One may also differentiate between a "weak" and a "strong" Gerschenkron effect. We define a *"weak"* Gerschenkron effect when catching-up of the industries follows the same logistic. This does not imply that productivity growth is equal as the "gap" from the frontier matters at each point of time. A *"strong"* Gerschenkron effect takes place when the convergence parameter is higher in industries with the larger initial gap. This may even imply a 'switch-over in comparative (productivity) advantage' that can take place in the course of catching-up. Empirically, we found evidence for both "weak" and "strong" Gerschenkron patterns at the industrial level (see Landesmann and Stehrer (2001)). In this chapter we shall only apply the "weak" Gerschenkron scenario.

There are three sectors of which two are producing tradable goods; we shall refer to them as "skill intensive" and "labor intensive" respectively. As already noted above, the initial gap is larger in the skill intensive sector. By assuming the Gerschenkron dynamics, productivity growth rates in the successful catching-up economy are therefore higher in this sector. The third sector produces non-tradeable goods. With respect to income elasticities the labor intensive goods sector (sector 2) is characterized by income elasticities below one, i.e. expenditure shares are decreasing with rising (real) income and the services sector shows income elasticities above one. The remaining skill intensive tradable goods sector is assumed to have income elasticities equal to one (note that from this sector only stage 2 is considered to be a consumer good).

## Setting up the simulations

### The initial equilibrium

Let us shortly discuss the most important parameter values used in the subsequent scenarios. As in the theoretical section we start with the input matrix which we keep quite simple. The values in this matrix are set to:

$$A^c = \begin{pmatrix} 0.40 & 0.20 & 0.00 & 0.00 \\ 0.00 & 0.40 & 0.00 & 0.00 \\ 0.00 & 0.00 & 0.30 & 0.00 \\ 0.00 & 0.00 & 0.00 & 0.20 \end{pmatrix} \qquad \text{for } c = N, S.$$

This matrix shows that sectors 2 and 3 need inputs only from own sectoral outputs. Sector 1 is vertically integrated where stage 1 requires inputs from stage 2 but not vice versa. This

*Table 14.1* Technology parameters

| | *Sector* | *North* | *South* |
|---|---|---|---|
| Productivity $T^c_{i_k}$ | $1_1$ | 0.750 | 0.525 |
| | $1_2$ | 1.000 | 0.500 |
| | 2 | 0.600 | 0.480 |
| | 3 | 0.500 | 0.300 |
| Share parameters $\alpha^c_{S,i_k}$ | $1_1$ | 0.300 | 0.300 |
| | $1_2$ | 0.700 | 0.500 |
| | 2 | 0.450 | 0.450 |
| | 3 | 0.500 | 0.500 |
| Factor augmenting parameters $\tilde{a}^c_{z,i_k}$ | $1_1, 1_2, 2, 3$ | 1.000 | 1.000 |
| Elasticity of substitution $\sigma^c_{i_k}$ | $1_1, 1_2, 2, 3$ | 0.500 | 0.500 |

particular structure is chosen to keep the inter-industry flows as simple as possible when it comes to study the effects of outsourcing. The modeling of outsourcing is outlined below.

The initial technological situation is further characterized by given productivity levels, share parameters, factor augmenting parameters and elasticity parameters in the production function which are reported in Table 14.1.

As can be seen, we assume that there are cross-country differences only with respect to total factor productivity. The share parameters which determine the skill intensity of the sectors to a large extent are assumed to be equal across the two countries. In terms of isoquants this means that the isoquant for the South is the same as that for the North only shifted outward. The skill intensity of the sectors are mainly determined by the share parameters. As can be seen, production stage 2 of the first sector is most skill-intensive, followed by the non-tradable goods sector 3. The least skill intensive is stage 1 of good 1. The factor augmenting parameters are all set to one and the elasticity of substitution is 0.5. The actual skill intensity of the sectors is also determined by the relative wages; these are discussed in more detail below. However, incorporating this does not change the skill intensity ranking of the sectors.

Labor supply is fixed at $h^c_s = 0.8$, $h^c_u = 1.2$ and thus $h^c = 2$ which in particular implies equal (relative) factor endowments. The parameters of the CES demand system (determining demand for a particular good across countries) and the Almost Ideal Demand system are listed in Table 14.2.

The elasticity of substitution for the particular goods across countries $\varsigma^r_{i_k}$ for final goods trade is assumed to be equal for all countries and set to 2.5. This implies that the goods are seen as substitutes across countries. Furthermore, the industry specific country preference parameters $\beta^{cr}_{i_k}$ are equal across countries which in particular implies no home-bias effect and no exogenously specified regional preference pattern of trade. Thus all differences are determined by price structures. The exception to this are the non-tradable sectors (initially – i.e. before outsourcing – production stage 1 of sector 1 and sector 3) which – by definition – can only be demanded in the home country, see below). With respect to the Almost Ideal Demand System we assumed in particular that the traditional tradable sector (sector 2) shows income elasticities lower than one, i.e. the nominal expenditure shares decrease with income at constant relative prices) and the other two sectors have income elasticities equal to or larger than one (i.e. nominal expenditures shares increase with income at constant relative

*Table 14.2* Parameters for consumption behavior

| | *Sector* | *North and South* |
|---|---|---|
| EoS across countries $\varsigma^{r}_{\imath_k}$ | $1_1$ | . |
| | $1_2$ | 2.500 |
| | 2 | 2.500 |
| | 3 | . |
| Country preference parameter $\beta^{cr}_{\imath_k}$ | $1_1$ | 0.000 |
| | $1_2$ | 1.000 |
| | 2 | 1.000 |
| | 3 | 0.000 |
| $\alpha_{AIM,0}$ | | 0.000 |
| $\alpha_{AIM,i_k}$ | $1_1$ | 0.000 |
| | $1_2$ | 0.333 |
| | 2 | 0.333 |
| | 3 | 0.334 |
| $\beta_{AIM,\imath_k}$ | $1_1$ | . |
| | $1_2$ | 0.000 |
| | 2 | -0.100 |
| | 3 | 0.100 |
| $\gamma_{AIM,\imath_k J_l}$ | $1_1, 1_2, 2, 3$ | 0.000 |

prices); these properties are imposed by the parameter $\beta^{c}_{AIM,\imath_k}$. The exogenous expenditure shares are more or less equal for the three consumer goods.

Endowments, technology and preferences together determine equilibrium values for prices, wage rates and quantities under the full employment assumption. For this we further assume that $\sum_{\imath_k} p^{N}_{\imath_k} q^{N}_{\imath_k} = 1$ and $\sum_{\imath_k} p^{S}_{\imath_k} q^{S}_{\imath_k} = 0.6$ which is modeled as a normalization of the price levels. This assumption guarantees that the price level in the South is not much higher compared to the North due to lower productivity. Differences in price levels between countries can persist in this model without driving trade shares to zero because of the CES framework adopted which implicitly allows for product differentiation (Armington assumption) of products produced in different economies in the same sectors.[11] This can also be interpreted in the way that price levels are determined by money supply. The equilibrium values are derived by an iterative procedure; the most important of these values are listed in Table 14.3.[12]

Nominal wage rates of both skilled and unskilled labor are lower in the less developed countries mainly reflecting the lower sectoral productivity levels. Note that not the levels per se are important but the way they determine the structure of the economy (specialization in sectors with different labor inputs per unit of output). The skill premium is higher in the North which reflects the higher share of skill intensive sectors. The ranking of the skill intensity of the particular sectors was already discussed above and is not disturbed by relative wage rates (see above). Note that the skill intensity is lower in the North as the skill premium is higher. The driving factors behind this result are the assumption of the same factor share and factor augmenting parameters and the same endowment structure together with the specialization of the North towards higher skill intensive sectors. As we have assumed differences only with respect to total factor productivity levels the skill

*Table 14.3* Equilibrium values

| | *Sector* | *North* | *South* | *North/South* |
|---|---|---|---|---|
| Wage rate of unskilled $w^c_{L,i_k}$ | $1_1, 1_2, 2, 3$ | 0.177 | 0.152 | 1.164 |
| Wage rate of skill $w^c_{S,i_k}$ | $1_1, 1_2, 2, 3$ | 0.404 | 0.354 | 1.141 |
| Skill premium | $1_1, 1_2, 2, 3$ | 2.282 | 2.329 | 0.980 |
| Skill intensity $a^c_{S,i_k}/a^c_{L,i_k}$ | $1_1$ | 0.433 | 0.428 | 1.011 |
| | $1_2$ | 1.011 | 1.000 | 1.011 |
| | 2 | 0.599 | 0.592 | 1.011 |
| | 3 | 0.662 | 0.655 | 1.011 |
| Price levels $p^c_i$ | $1_1$ | 1.577 | 1.362 | 0.849 |
| | $1_2$ | 1.422 | 2.050 | 0.693 |
| | 2 | 1.356 | 1.332 | 1.018 |
| | 3 | 1.446 | 1.952 | 0.741 |
| Output $q^c_i$ | $1_1$ | 0.079 | 0.038 | 2.094 |
| | $1_2$ | 0.224 | 0.119 | 1.886 |
| | 2 | 0.283 | 0.252 | 1.210 |
| | 3 | 0.087 | 0.039 | 2.211 |

intensity ratio between North and South is equal across sectors. Price levels reflect the gaps in total factor productivity. Comparing $1_2$ and 2 one can see that the Northern economy has a comparative advantage in $1_2$ (which is more skill intensive). Comparing the two stages of production in sector 1 also shows a comparative advantage of North in the relatively more skill intensive stage $1_2$. Note that in our case this structure of comparative advantages is driven by the structure of total factor productivity and not – as usually worked out in the literature – by factor endowment structures. Thus our model – although showing features with respect to factor endowments and differences in skill intensities across sectors as e.g. in the Heckscher-Ohlin model – is in line with the Ricardian tradition where comparative advantages are determined by technology.

Finally, output levels are higher in the North in all sectors mainly driven by higher total factor productivity. The North is specialized in the skill intensive sectors for two reasons: first, higher real income shifts consumption towards these sectors and away from sector 2 and, second, international competition (so far only in consumer goods $1_2$ and 2) works toward specialization of the South in the labor intensive sector 2.

### *The dynamics*

For the transitory dynamics we have to specify the parameters determining the speeds of adjustment of prices, the response of nominal wage rates to disequilibria in the labor market and the effect of bargaining over rents as well as the dynamics of productivity. These parameter values are shown in Table 14.4.

As can be seen we assume the same parameter values for both countries and all sectors. This simplifies the interpretation of the simulation results. In this scenario we assume a rather sluggish price-to-cost adjustment and also have set bargaining over rents equal to zero. There is however a relatively strong Phillips curve effect and again a very small

*Table 14.4* Parameter values for adjustment dynamics

| | Sectors | North | South |
|---|---|---|---|
| Price adjustment parameter $\delta_{p,\iota}$ | $1_1, 1_2, 2, 3$ | 0.100 | 0.100 |
| Wage bargaining coefficients $\kappa^c_{s,i}$ | $1_1, 1_2, 2, 3$ | 0.000 | 0.000 |
| Phillips curve parameters $\kappa^c_u$ | $1_1, 1_2, 2, 3$ | 0.250 | 0.100 |
| Wage equalisation coefficient $\kappa^c_w$ | $1_1, 1_2, 2, 3$ | 0.010 | 0.010 |
| Logistic parameters $\gamma^c_{T,\iota_k}, \gamma^c_{\underline{T},\iota_k}$ | $1_1, 1_2, 2, 3$ | 0.050 | 0.050 |
| Final productivity level $\bar{T}^c_{\iota_k}$ | $1_1$ | 0.600 | 0.600 |
| | $1_2$ | 1.000 | 1.000 |
| | 2 | 0.750 | 0.750 |
| | 3 | 0.500 | 0.500 |

wage equalization effect. The parameter determining the logistic is set in a way that the catching-up potential is exploited within 15 to 20 years. The final total factor productivity levels for both economies are the same as the initial values for the North. This, in particular, implies that there is no technical change in the North and the South is fully catching-up to the Northern productivity level.[13] Finally, investment behavior is characterized by an "elasticity of substitution" of 2.5 and all the preference parameters are set equal to one (i.e. there is no country or sector specific bias of investment.) As we assume a fixed exchange rate this would distort equilibrium when keeping the "money supply" fixed. We thus allow for an ad-hoc adjustment of the money supply in the South which gradually adjusts following the same logistics as productivity. Outsourcing is modeled as a gradual change in the preference parameter $\beta^{rc}_{A,1_1 1_l}$ for $r \neq c$ and $l = 1, 2$ from 0 to 1, again following the same logistic as total factor productivity.

## Simulation results

### *Catching-up and final goods trade*

The point of the simulations is to illustrate some of the features of the model when applied to studying the impact of aspects of global economic integration. In particular, we shall look at the impact of catching-up processes of a (significant) group of "Southern" economies relative to more advanced economies of the "North". We assume that this catching-up process follows a "Gerschenkron pattern" (see above): this implies that in industries in which the initial technology gap to the more advanced Northern economy is particularly high, there will also be the strongest potential for technology transfer and hence productivity catching-up will be the strongest. This can be seen from Figure 14.1 in which the sectoral labor input coefficients for skilled and un-skilled labor can be seen for the South and the North respectively. Figure 14.1 shows that productivity catching-up is faster in sector 3 (the non-tradable sector) and sector 1 (which we shall call the "higher-tech" tradable sector) and, also, that the skill mix in stage 2 of sector 1 shows that it has a higher ratio of skilled to unskilled workers (and is therefore the "skill-intensive" stage of production). The relative fall in labor input coefficients combined with wage rate developments and price-to-cost adjustments determines the evolution of relative prices (see Figure 14.2). There are also indirect effects, as prices of inputs (other than labor) depend upon cost and price-to-cost

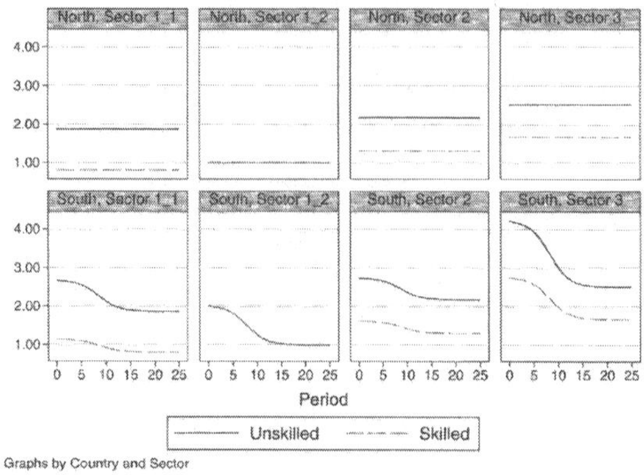


*Figure 14.1* Inputs per unit of output by sectors and countries

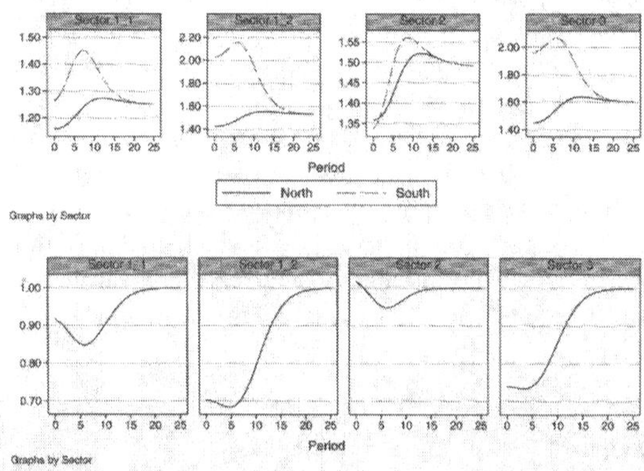


*Figure 14.2* Price levels and relative prices

adjustments in the sectors which produce these inputs and, in a situation in which substitution in the "sourcing" of these inputs across countries is allowed, relative price developments also reflect changing input sourcing behavior. Furthermore, the price levels shown in Figure 14.2 refer to "producer" prices which are in general not identical to the prices consumers are faced with when they purchase their goods, as the latter may substitute across countries which would require to calculate the price of a "basket" of imported and domestically produced goods. The initial equilibrium was designed in such a way that the services are relatively more expensive in the North; furthermore, the North has an absolute comparative advantage in the two trading sectors and a comparative advantage in the more skill-intensive sector $1_2$. Given the productivity, wage and price-to-cost adjustment dynamic we can see changes in price levels as well as in relative price structures. With respect to both levels and relative prices let us first mention that there is full convergence across countries; the levels at the end of the simulation period are the same for the North and the South. The relative price falls most strongly in the "high-tech" sector in all countries as this sector experiences

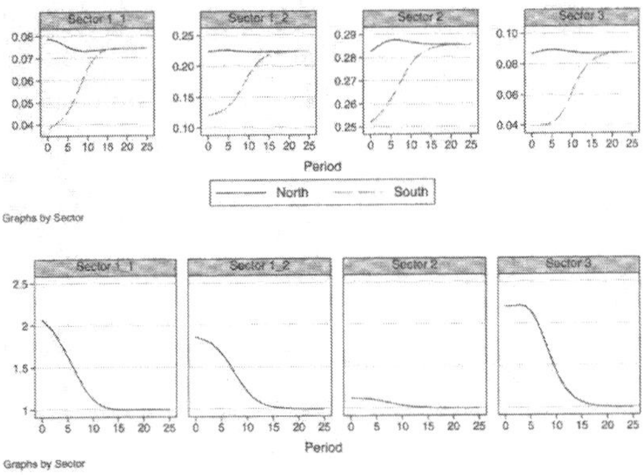


*Figure 14.3* Output levels and relative output

the strongest increases in productivity. This pattern is of course more pronounced in the South because of the higher initial gap. In terms of comparative advantage one can see that the North keeps the comparative advantage in this sector. The lower panels of Figure 14.2 present the relative price of the North relative to the South by sector type. The relative price dynamics is the basis for judging both absolute and relative competitive (and comparative) advantages of the North and South respectively. If we focus on the tradable sectors $1_2$ and 2, we can see that the North is losing absolute competitive advantage in sector $1_2$ (i.e. in the high-tech sector particularly in stage 2 which is the more skill-intensive stage). The reason for this is the Gerschenkron pattern of catching-up in productivity levels as the gaps are higher in the "higher-tech" sector 1, combined with the formulation of the wage equation (only partial rent-sharing and wage drift across sectors). The competitive situation in the "lower-tech" sector shows a slight improvement of the North and hence the North's comparative advantage position in the high-tech sector is declining as a result of the Gerschenkron pattern of catching-up.

The changes in the structure of relative prices as well as in real income levels imply changes in the output structure in each country for two reasons: first, the structure of demand changes due to substitution effects as well as real income effects (non-linear Engel curves) and, second, due to changing specialization patterns following the dynamics of absolute and comparative advantage. Figure 14.3 presents the dynamics of output quantities. Output in quantity terms in the traditional ("lower tech") tradable sector is rising much less in all countries due to negative substitution effects and the negative Engel-curve effects; the decline is less strong in the South as it gains in absolute cost terms against the North. The other two sectors show strong increases in output: in the modern sector this is due to substitution effects and in particular in the South due to specialization effects; in the services sectors the Engel curve effects compensate the substitution effects and this accounts for the increase in output levels.

Figures 14.4 to 14.7 present graphs with respect to labor market and income variables. Unemployment rates show quite a different pattern in the South and the North. The South experiences initially a fast drop in unemployment rates and later on the rates rise back to their initial levels (the Phillips curve dynamic leads to "equilibrium" positions in the labor markets). Hence, the South which experiences a fast rise in productivity levels

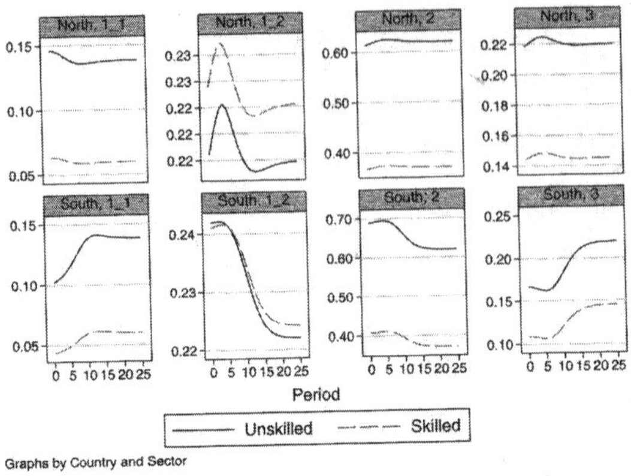


*Figure 14.4* Labour demand levels

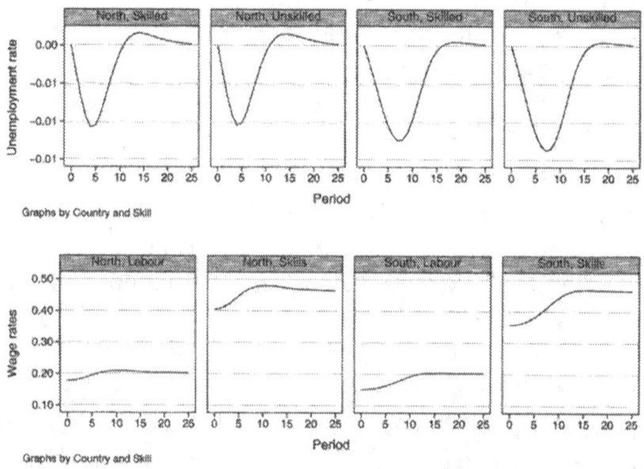


*Figure 14.5* Unemployment rate (in percent) and wage rate (lower panel)

reduces initially unemployment rates as it is able to attract demand through international specialization (demand shifts to the country which shows the fastest relative decline in price levels) and it is able to attract foreign investment which keeps up growth rates. Over time, however, the South loses the competitive position in the tradable sector as the Phillips curve term and the bargaining over rents leads to a rise in price levels. Nominal wage rates in the North are on the other hand falling mainly because of the Phillips curve effect and also because of a different rent dynamic (see below). Importantly, however, real wages are rising in all countries. As regards the development of the "skill premium" (i.e. the ratio of the wage rate of skilled vs unskilled workers) we can see in Figure 14.6 that there is a pretty sharp fall in the skill premium in the South followed by a recovery. The opposite takes place in the North. This – additionally to uneven productivity and thus wage dynamics – reflects the nature of trade specialization (the North keeps comparative advantage in the skill-intensive sector) but – over time – the South loses the relative price disadvantage in the skill-intensive sectors and, furthermore, there are demand shifts (given Engel coefficients)

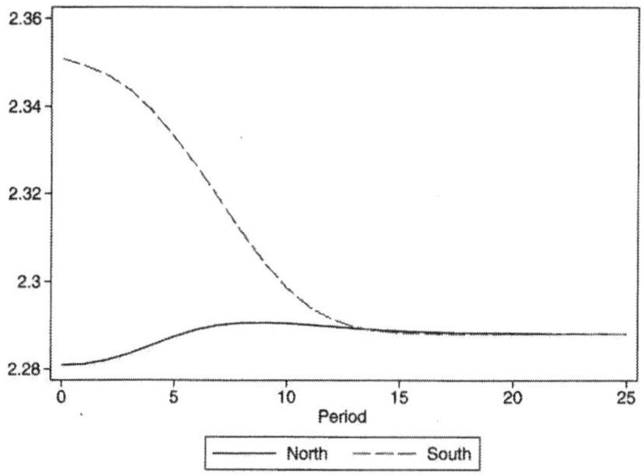


*Figure 14.6* Skill premium

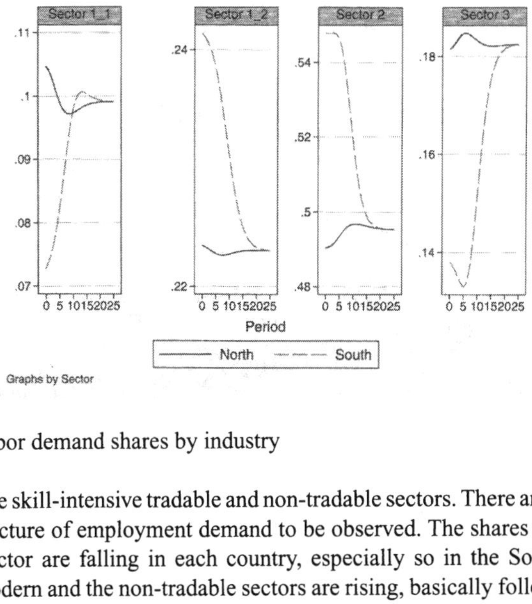


*Figure 14.7* Labor demand shares by industry

towards the more skill-intensive tradable and non-tradable sectors. There are also changes in the sectoral structure of employment demand to be observed. The shares of the traditional ("low tech") sector are falling in each country, especially so in the South, whereas the shares of the modern and the non-tradable sectors are rising, basically following the pattern of output dynamics.

Finally, let us look at the distributional effects of the productivity-wage and price-cost dynamics. Figure 14.8 presents the retained earnings in all countries and sectors. These are important as they determine the structure of investment behavior discussed above. Here we can see a markedly different picture for the South and the North: In the South we see the emergence of very high unit-rents in the modern sector and particularly in the skill-intensive second stage of sector one. This is driven by the relative productivity dynamics of the different sectors and the feature of our wage equation which allows for a "wage drift" across sectors and hence a more even development of wage rates across sectors than of productivity. This rent dynamic has, of course, implications for international investment as

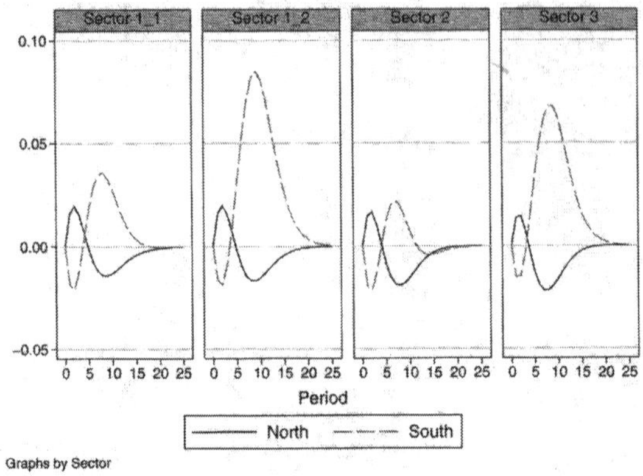


*Figure 14.8* Retained earnings

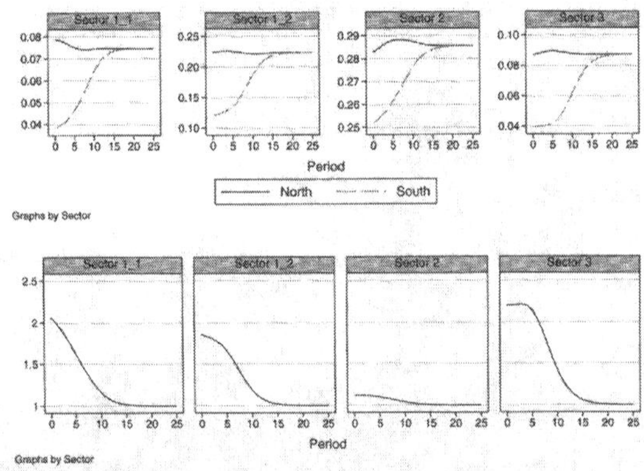


*Figure 14.9* Output levels and relative output

it makes investing into the sectors which experience the highest productivity (catching-up) dynamic very attractive. Given our Gerschenkron hypothesis these are the technologically more sophisticated (i.e. sectors with higher initial knowledge and productivity gap) and more skill intensive sectors.

## *The effects of outsourcing*

Let us now evaluate the effects of "fragmentation", i.e. the possibility of vertical segmentation of production stages in sector 1 and for international trade to take place in both its two production stages (formerly only the final output could be traded). We shall in the following only point to the differences with the "base run". Let us focus first on output and employment levels in the different sectors. As one would expect with the "outsourcing" possibility, there can be international trade and production specialization at a finer level. The South keeps a bit more employment in the less skill-intensive stage 1 (of sector 1) as it does

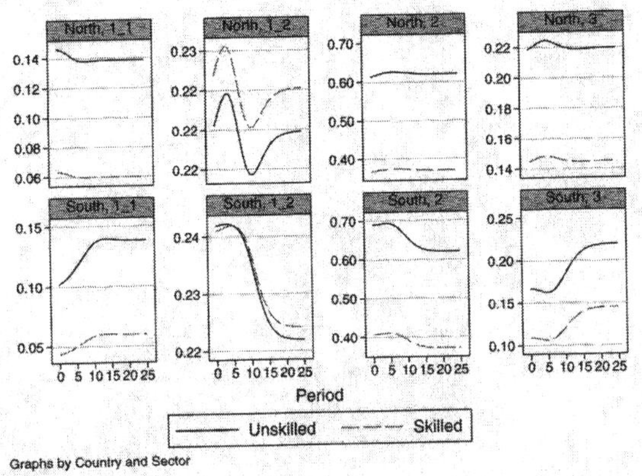


*Figure 14.10* Labour demand levels

have a comparative advantage in this sector. On the other hand, we also see an interesting dynamic in employment levels in the North in the skill-intensive stage: they first decline (as in the base run) but they then recover much more rapidly than without outsourcing. The reason for this is that the North benefits from the comparative advantage in this sector and the global efficiency effects which such finer specialization structure allows leading to faster real income catching-up of the South and hence to more demand in general and for skill-intensive traded goods in particular. In fact, given the Armington demand also for goods which are supplied by a country which does not have a comparative advantage in that commodity or stage, even production stage 1 (the input-supplying stage) has less of a fall in output levels in the North with outsourcing than without outsourcing because of the higher global demand for the final output of sector 1.

As regards distributional implications, we focus on the skill premium reflecting the relative demand for skilled vs unskilled labor and per-unit rents. As regards the skill premium one can see a smaller fall in the South in the outsourcing scenario than without outsourcing. Hence, in spite of the more detailed specialization pattern between North and South made possible through "fragmentation", the overall labor demand in the South has turned somewhat more towards skilled labor in the outsourcing than in the no-outsourcing run. The reason is that the shift in demand away from low-productivity, low-skill sectors has been stronger with outsourcing because of the higher real income, higher global growth scenario. This is also visible from the retained earnings graphs which show that the sectors with high income elasticities (sector 1 and the non- tradable sector 3) gain also in profitability in the outsourcing scenario relative to the no-outsourcing scenario; this has implications for the relative attractiveness of these sectors for foreign direct investment and is most likely due to cheaper relative input prices facilitated through outsourcing.

## Conclusions

This chapter has presented an extension of work started originally with Richard Goodwin. Goodwin's interests later on in his life were increasingly focused on integrating insights from macroeconomic and structural economic dynamics. In this chapter we have taken a global view of structural transformations: we have particularly focussed on issues of

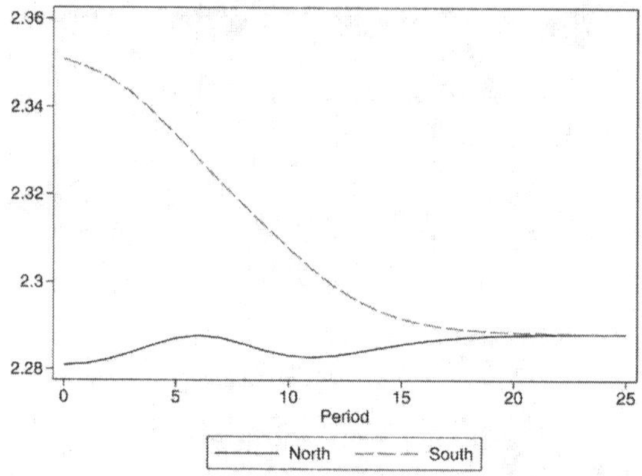


*Figure 14.11* Skill premium

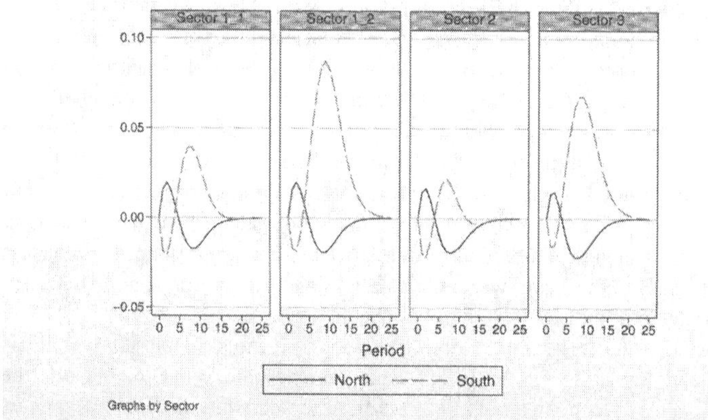


*Figure 14.12* Retained earnings

international catching-up and changes in international patterns of trade specialization. We have also allowed for other features of international economic integration, specifically through international investment flows. One of the specific features which characterizes today's global economy is the fast catching-up of a significant group of Southern economies and we have captured this catching-up process by means of a particular hypothesis – the Gerschenkron hypothesis which has been applied at the sectoral level. According to this hypothesis, the scope for technological and hence productivity catching-up is particularly high in areas in which the initial knowledge and productivity gaps are high. Very often the sectors in which this is true are also the more skill-intensive sectors (we have referred to literature which validates this hypothesis empirically). Given this background of exogenously driven patterns of catching-up, we have looked at the implications for the dynamics of trade specialization and looked in particular at the impact which a finer international division of labor has once we allow "fragmentation" i.e. the splitting of production stages and the sourcing of inputs from abroad. We also endogenized international direct investment decisions as a function of relative profitability. The model was a complex one which not only looked at supply-side issues (uneven productivity growth, cost dynamics, etc.) but also specified a relatively general expenditure structure with non-unitary Engel coefficients. Hence different real income paths lead to differences in expenditure patterns. In the analysis of the outsourcing phenomenon we showed that fragmentation does indeed lead to more scope for a finer specialization structure in international trade. This finer specialization structure might, however, lead to (initially) unexpected production and employment developments. For example, we showed that it is quite possible that international specialization gets deepened (the South specializing in less skill intensive sectors and production stages) and nonetheless the relative demand for skills increases and also output and employment developments do not develop to the detriment of more knowledge intensive sectors and stages of production. The reasons are the efficiency and real income gains which result from this finer pattern of specialization. In fact, knowledge- and skill-intensive sectors in Southern, catching-up economies become particularly attractive to foreign investors.[14]

## Notes

1 For simplicity, we sometimes skip the index for production stage if the production in a particular sector requires one stage only, e.g. $a^c_{33}$ means $a^c_{3_1 3_1}$. Further in this chapter we restrict the number of production stages to be one or two.

2 This is a slight abuse of notation as $q^c_{i_k}$ stands for total output which is produced with labor and intermediate inputs. However, as the intermediate input coefficients are constant, i.e. no substitution with labor inputs, we do not introduce a new symbol.

3 The rationale for this terminology stems from the fact that for $\rho^c_{i_k} \to 0$ the CES becomes a Cobb-Douglas production function with $q^c_{i_k} = T^c_{i_k} \prod_{z=L,S} (\tilde{a}^c_{z,i_k} l^c_{z,i_k})^{\alpha^c_{z,i_k}}$.

4 We assume throughout this chapter that the exchange rate between the two countries is equal to one and fixed over the entire period.

5 More elaborate versions of investment decisions can be introduced into the model, such as when some of the retained earnings get invested into financial assets which do not immediately increase productive capacity. We have analysed the implications of this in a number of papers which look at the effective demand problems which may result from this; see Landesmann and Stehrer, 2002 and 2007a.

6 Substitution mainly refers between the two types of labor.

7 The same result could be achieved by assuming that mark-up profits are only invested in the own sector.

8 For $g = \pi$ and a constant final demand vector $f$ this formulation collapses to the well-known equation $q^d = [I-(1+g)A]^{-1}(1+g)f$.

9 This particular formulation introduces a "liquidity bias" of internationally mobile capital. The idea here is that investment of rents abroad imply more risk and hence a certain amount is kept (in proportion to capital flows abroad) in liquid assets as a security. International mobility of capital hence allows reallocation of rents towards high rent/high productivity growth destinations, but it also increases the incidence of a "leakage" (into liquidity) into the system. Empirically, this fits the current observation where high FDI flows go together with a high volume of globally liquid assets.

10 When assuming different endowment structures the assumption of a fixed exchange rate would no longer hold when calculating equilibria. The same applies to endowment levels.

11 Similarly, one could also model this via a (fixed) exchange rate which would however impose a further notational burden.

12 Fixing the exchange rate to equal 1 leads to an equilibrium which in this specification has non-zero rents; however, the magnitudes are negligible.

13 As mentioned above, this is mainly for simplicity and allows an equilibrium even in the case of a fixed exchange rate.

14 Other papers have covered, in the context of this type of model, issues related to another of Goodwin's concerns: problems of effective demand which might get accentuated through processes of globalization such as the ones analyzed in this chapter (for this see Landesmann and Stehrer (2007a).

## References


Arndt, S. W. and H. Kierzkowski (2001). *Fragmentation: New Production and Trade Patterns in the World Economy*. Oxford: Oxford University Press.

Choi, E. and D. Greenaway (2000). *Globalisation and Labour Markets*. London: Blackwell.

Deaton, A. and J. Muellbauer (1980). *Economics and Consumer Behaviour*. Cambridge, UK: Cambridge University Press.

Feenstra, R. and G. Hanson (1997). Foreign direct investment and relative wages: Evidence from Mexico's maquiladoras'. *Journal of International Trade 42*(3-4), 371–393.

Feenstra, R. and G. Hanson (2001). Global production sharing and rising inequality: A survey of trade and wages. *NBER Working Paper 8372*.

Gerschenkron, A. (1952). Economic backwardness in historical perspective. In B. Hoselitz (Ed.), *The Progress of Underdeveloped Areas*. Chicago: University of Chicago Press.

Gerschenkron, A. (1962). *Economic Backwardness in Historical Perspective*. Cambridge (Mass.): Harvard University Press.

Goodwin, R. and L. Punzo (1987). *The Dynamics of a Capitalist Economy. A Multi-Sectoral Approach*. Oxford: Polity Press/Blackwell.

Helpman, E. (1998). *General Purpose Technologies and Economic Growth*. Cambridge/Massachusetts: MIT Press.

ILO (2007). *Trade and Employment. Challenges for Policy Research. A Joint Study of the International Labour Office and the Secretariat of the World Trade Organisation*. Geneva, Switzerland: ILO.

Isard, W. (1951). Interregional and regional input-output analysis: A model of a space-economy. *The Review of Economics and Statistics XXXIII*(4), 318–328.

Karshenas, M. and P. Stoneman (1995). Technological diffusion. In P. Stoneman (Ed.), *Handbook of the Economics of Innovation and Technological Change*, pp. 265–297. Oxford: Blackwell.

Landesmann, M. and R. Goodwin (1994). Productivity growth, structural change and macroeconomic stability. In L. Pasinetti and R. Solow (Eds.), *Economic Growth and the Structure of Long-Term Development*. London: Macmillan.

Landesmann, M., R. Goodwin, and R. Stehrer (1997). Structural economic dynamics: Catching-up and the global deflationary bias. In A. Simonovits and A. Steenge (Eds.), *Prices, Growth and Cycles. Essays in Honour of A. Bródy*. London: Macmillan.

Landesmann, M. and R. Stehrer (2000). Industrial specialisation, catching-up and labour market dynamics. *Metroeconomica/Review of International Economics 51*(1), 67–101.

Landesmann, M. and R. Stehrer (2001). Convergence patterns and switchovers in comparative advantage. *Structural Change and Economic Dynamics 12*, 399–423.

Landesmann, M. and R. Stehrer (2002). Technical change, effective demand and economic growth. In N. Salvadori (Ed.), *Old and New Growth Theories. An Assessment*. Cheltenham: Edward Elgar.

Landesmann, M. and R. Stehrer (2004a). Modelling international economic integration: Patterns of catching-up, foreign direct investment and migration flows. *wiiw Working Paper 27*.

Landesmann, M. and R. Stehrer (2004b). Technology diffusion, international competition and effective demand. *Revue d'Economie Industrielle 105*, 23–46.

Landesmann, M. and R. Stehrer (2007a). Goodwin's structural economic dynamics: Modelling schumpeterian and keynesian insights. *Structural Change and Economic Dynamics 17*(4), 501–524.

Landesmann, M. and R. Stehrer (2007b). Income distribution, technical change and the dynamics of international economic integration. *Metroeconomica/Review of International Economics 58*(1), 45–73.

Morishima, M. (1964). *Equilibrium, Stability and Growth: A Multi-Sectoral Analysis*. Oxford: Oxford University Press.

Morishima, M. (1992). *Capital and Credit: A New Formulation of General Equilibrium Theory*. Cambridge, UK: Cambridge University Press.

Slaughter, M. (1998). International trade and labour market outcomes: Results, questions and policy options. *The Economic Journal 108*(450), 1452–1462.

Slaughter, M. (1999). Globalisation and wages: A tale of two perspectives. *World Economy 22*, 609–630.

Stehrer, R. (2002a). Dynamics of trade integration and technological convergence. *Economic Systems Research 14*(3), 219–244.

Stehrer, R. (2002b). Technical progress in a dynamic input-output model with heterogenous labour. In R. Cowan and N. Jonard (Eds.), *Heterogenous Agents, Interactions and Economic Performance. Lecture Notes in Economics and Mathematical Systems*, pp. 323–339. Berlin: Springer Verlag.

# Index

9780415762014